Applied Linguistics and Language Study

General Editor: C. N. Candlin

Discourse and Learning

Papers in applied linguistics and language learning from the *Centre de Recherches et d'Applications Pédagogiques en Langues* (C.R.A.P.E.L.)

Edited by
Philip Riley

London and New York

Longman Group Limited
Longman House, Burnt Mill, Harlow,
Essex CM20 2JE, England
and Associated Companies throughout the world

Published in the United States of America by
Longman Inc., New York

First published 1985

ISBN 0 582 55374 1

BRITISH LIBRARY CATALOGUING IN PUBLICATION DATA
Discourse and learning. —
(Applied linguistics and language study)
1. Language and languages — study and teaching
2. Applied linguistics
I. Riley, Philip II. Series
407 P53

LIBRARY OF CONGRESS CATALOGING IN PUBLICATION DATA
Main entry under title:
Discourse and learning.
(Applied linguistics and language study)
Bibliography: p.
Includes index.
1. Language and languages — study and teaching.
I. Riley, Philip. II. Title. III. Series.
P51.D57 1984 418′.007 84-14357

Set in 10/12 pt Erhardt, Linotron 202

Produced by Longman Group (FE) Ltd
Printed in Hong Kong

To the memory of
Yves Châlon

1927–1972

Humani studium generis cui pectore fervet
O colat humanum te foveatque genus

Acknowledgements

Acknowledgements are made to the following publishers for permission to publish the papers mentioned below:

Oxford University Press, for 'You did say oral interactive discourse?' and 'When communication breaks down: levels of coherence in discourse', both of which appeared in *Applied Linguistics* **I**(3), a thematic issue on discourse analysis edited by John Sinclair; Hatier International for the chapter 'Mud and Stars: personal constructs, sensitization and learning' in *Description, Présentation et Enseignement des Langues* — R. Richterich, H. C. Widdowson collection LAL-CREDIF © Hatier, Paris 1981; Didier, 'On autonomy', published in French as 'A propos de l'autonomie; quelques éléments de réflexion' in *Etudes de Linguistique Appliquée* **41** 1981; the British Council, for 'Viewing comprehension: l'oeil écoute', in ELT Documents Special, *The teaching of listening comprehension* 1981; Pergamon Press, for the chapter 'Taking learners' needs into account in self-directed learning', in *Foreign Language Teaching: Meeting individual needs* edited by H. B. Altman and C. V. James 1980.

We are grateful to Sony (UK) Limited for permission to reproduce the artwork on page 29.

Contents

page

Preface xiii

Introduction: a note on the C.R.A.P.E.L. xix

Part One: Discourse 1

The structure of communicative interaction 12

1 You did say 'oral interactive discourse'? 21
H. Holec

2 Interactional structure: the role of role 35
M–J. Gremmo, H. Holec and P. Riley

3 When communication breaks down; levels of coherence in discourse 47
P. Riley

Reading and communicative competence 67

4 Learning a language — or learning to read? 74
M–J. Gremmo

5 From reading to writing acts 91
C. Henner–Stanchina

6 A comparative approach to the learning of specialized written discourse 105
O. Régent

Part Two: Learning 121

The psychology of learning versus learners' psychology 133

7 Foreign language acquisition processes in a secondary school setting: negation 135
A. Collin and H. Holec

8 Mud and stars: personal constructs, sensitization and learning 154
P. Riley

Autonomous learning schemes: principles and organization 170

9 On autonomy: some elementary concepts 173
H. Holec

10 Two years of autonomy: practice and outlook 191
C. Henner–Stanchina

11 Extending self-directed learning of English in an engineering college 206
H. Moulden

12 Teaching learning: redefining the teacher's role 233
M–J. Gremmo and D. Abé

13 Aspects of autonomous learning. Extracts from: 248
Learning oral expression autonomously
D. Abé, C. Henner–Stanchina and O. Régent
Evaluation in an autonomous learning scheme
C. Henner–Stanchina and H. Holec
Taking learners' needs into account in self-directed learning
H. Holec
An experiment in self-directed group learning
P. Riley and M. Sicre

The exploitation of authentic materials 283

14 The Sound and Video Library 286
P. Riley and C. Zoppis

15 A specialist? What specialist? 299
D. Abé, R. Duda and C. Henner–Stanchina

16 Using authentic documents for pedagogical purposes 321
D. Abé, F. Carton, M. Cembalo and O. Régent

17 Viewing comprehension: l'oeil écoute 332
P. Riley

The functional approach to the acquisition of spoken language 345

18 A beginners' course in spoken English based on the functional approach 346
H. Holec

19 Two experiments in communicative teaching 352
M–J. Gremmo and F. Carton

Epilogue 375

Bibliography 377

Index 387

Preface

Unusual books give unusual pleasure to introduce. This welcome collection, edited by Philip Riley from one of the most important centres of Applied Linguistics in Europe, is such an unusual book for the *Applied Linguistics and Language Study* series. For the first time we have a coherent collection of papers from one centre, representing in a sense a canon of research and development over a period of time, informed by a particular view of language, language learning and language teaching. Also, we have in the book an example of applied linguistics at its most characteristic, a demonstration of the interplay between theory and practice. In addition, we see how such an interplay, in the context of a working institution where language teaching is no mere appendage to research but its *raison d'être*, compels us to integrate two worlds, that of the classroom and the society which gives it support, and that of learning and communication. *Discourse and Learning* is thus an apt title for a collection of papers from the C.R.A.P.E.L (*Centre de Recherches et d'Applications Pédagogiques en Langues*); it captures well this sense of negotiation between learner and teacher, between social knowledge and cognitive knowledge, between institution and society which portrays, for those who were fortunate to have met him or who have read his writings, the spirit of Yves Châlon.

Philip Riley has taken great pains to organize the book so that it is no museum piece. It is a book with which he and I want the reader to be able to work as a manual for informed practice. To that end, he has provided a carefully assembled internal structure, including an informative introduction to each of the main parts, *Discourse* and *Learning*, and supplemented these with shorter explanations of the place and significance of each of the included papers, some of which have been combined and condensed for clearer understanding and easier use. One other objective is attained by this editing procedure; readers, as autonomous users, can access the book in different ways. There is more than a sense of chance which we hope will persuade the active reader to seek in Part One a rationale for the substance of the practical experimentation documented in the later chapters of Part Two. More than perhaps has been the case in earlier books in the *Applied Linguistics and Language Study* series, I hope that the organization of this book will stimulate the reader to create his or her own document, critiquing the ideas of the C.R.A.P.E.L. from personal experience and practice.

Let me, in this Preface, identify two areas of concern for applied linguistics, both of which are central to the topics in this book, and both of which are greatly sharpened by a reading of the papers collected within it.

The first concern involves the issue of *strategy*, in terms of both social and personal negotiation, and in terms of how these aspects may be defined and correlated. Now, although overcoming problems of communication is a major motivation for non-native speakers' strategic language use, what are significant for second language acquisition research are the inferences we can draw about language acquisition from these available data. Learners' language offers us 'windows' on their covert cognitive behaviour, giving us clues as to how they go about thinking and planning. Furthermore, as product, these data are the signals of successful acquisition. They are thus at once diagnostic and evaluative. Insofar as they provide evidence, albeit indirect, of how learners go about overcoming problems of communication, they also offer evidence of how learners create the conditions whereby this selectively perceived and addressed input can be transformed into intake. Now, if this is so, then it is clearly central that we describe this learner language in a manner which honours the way learners employ their resources in partnership, as it were, with their interlocutors. To accomplish such an account, as Philip Riley's collection amply shows, we shall need a dynamic model of discourse rather than one which sees input to the learner and output by the learner as unconnected phenomena, and sees each in static terms. Moreover, even in what has been said so far, it is clear that we shall need soon to examine more closely the connection between the strategies of communication and those of cognition and learning, and seek to resolve present confusions in the literature.

We shall have to set both parts of this book against each other and see what closer relationships can be established. In what ways are performance data indicative of cognitive problem-solving? To what extent do NS (native speakers) and NNS (non-native speakers) collaborate to assist NNS acquisition? (I return to this in my second area of concern below.) Are such performance data direct or indirect evidence? How do we evaluate the performance of advanced learners who may not betray any surface signs of communicative distress which would cause us, as observers, to detect instances of cognitive planning? If, for these and other reasons, mere observation of the data of social negotiation is inadequate for the estimation of personal and cognitive negotiation, then how do we elaborate and enrich our evidence? We seem to be in somewhat of an impasse. We do not yet have any clear way in which strategies of discourse and strategies of learning can be distinctively defined and shown to be related. We have no agreement among researchers as to where to look for data to support our views, no consensus on what is admissible evidence. What is to be done?

One way forward lies in a reading of the papers in this collection. Not that they provide an answer; they suggest some directions. We can, in the mode of the C.R.A.P.E.L., diversify the range of problem-solving tasks we invite L2 learners to tackle, and record their performances, particularly in contexts of authentic communicative use rather than in laboratory experiment; we can correlate studies of L2 reading and listening with those drawing on performance data; we can regard introspection and participant inferencing as central to our endeavour rather than relying on our external analysis of learner text. These are just some of the possible paths towards the goal of relating *Discourse* and *Learning* established by the title of Philip Riley's book: paths towards relating the cognitive strategies deriving from L1 knowledge, used initially to produce the 'unplanned' discourse of an early interlanguage stage, to the strategies of communication appropriate to L2 use employed to augment the learner's target language store for the purposes of 'planned' discourse. Central to such an endeavour, as this book makes plain, is the need to link a sociolinguistic theory of language use with a theory of second language development.

There is, however, a second area of concern, in some ways prior and more fundamental to applied linguistics than that which I have just been adumbrating. It is a concern which sits well with the social world of adult learners characterized by the work at the C.R.A.P.E.L. It has to do with *cooperation*. To what extent, in the input plus interaction data of second language research, are NNS cooperating with NS in a shared goal of creating the conditions for intake? It is hard enough in NS discourse to assess whether speakers are engaged in cooperation for real-world goals or merely for conversational goals. It is even more problematic in NNS discourse because of the violations of target language norms, not merely in terms of surface features but, presumably, in terms of discoursal conventions also. With such NNS are we dealing with motivated or non-motivated non-observance? Moreover, such questions do not exist only in some general situation of interaction. We may expect this question of norms to be activity-type specific, and insofar as NNS operate in a variety of such activity-types, even within a classroom, the problem of evaluating NNS speech is compounded.

Now such difficulties of evaluating cooperation between NS and NNS in respect of creating the conditions for acquisition are not restricted only to the classroom, they are pervasive in the world outside. Learners, after all, are thought either 'to know' or 'not to know' a language. Accordingly, inappropriate or unfamiliar use is regularly mistaken for deliberately different attitudes and behaviour. If we add to this observation the frequent assumption by NS that they are automatically equipped to judge how much of a language a NNS knows, simply by virtue of their being NS, we can hypothesize a negative cycle of socially created identity of incompetence, which in turn might be presumed to lead towards uncooperativeness in behaviour and attitude, in turn promotive of a defective communicative competence. Against this, especially for the kind of NNS in the workplace who form a mainstay of the C.R.A.P.E.L.'s learners, might be set such learners' greater instrumental needs to be able to communicate, if only in that workplace. Here, however, once again, it may be that the NNS's lack of power (both social and communicative) enhances the sense of distance between the NNS and the NS and reduces the opportunity for that NNS-led interaction deemed necessary if input is to be usefully negotiated for intake. Many adult L2 learners, despite the activities of the C.R.A.P.E.L., simply lack the environments for 'equal', unstressed peer-group interaction. Indeed, the pressures of society on immigrant workers to acquire language to achieve jobs, earn wages and avoid deportation, all act to instil a stress which militates against acquisition. It might be thought, though, that this scenario was one which classrooms were, in part at least, set up to obviate. It seems from the literature on classroom interaction, however, that classrooms often exacerbate the problem in that they convey a world in which it is unclear against whose values and principles the communications of NNS are being judged, and, indeed, against which social norms their performance is being evaluated. Frequently, learners in classrooms are locked into particular and restricted patterns of communication as a result of participating in an overly restrictive set of activity and task-types. A paucity of data — both of input and interaction — prevents them from acquiring those interactional behaviours held to be appropriate to distinct activity-types and they become locked in a no-learn situation. The same would be true presumably even if there were a variety of classroom activities, as long as the dimensions and contextual norms of these activity-types were not negotiated, not made plain.

The papers in this collection again provide no complete answer to this social and cognitive problem. They do, however, make the issue transparent; they offer a critique. In fact, they go further; they do so by acknowledging classroom communication to be a creation of all the participants, constitutive of a particular social and cultural milieu and demonstrative of the presence of constraints on the perception and evaluation of utterances by the participants. Moreover, in their pedagogic programmes, whether taught or autonomous, they consistently display a concern for the connection between classroom learning world and outside working world which many programmes and much second language acquisition research overlook.

Through these papers, then, we discern not only a consciousness of the link between *Discourse* and *Learning*, but also an awareness of the need to link this unity to the world of communication, viewed through a particular social theory. For me, this is perhaps the most important contribution of the C.R.A.P.E.L., and it shines through the papers in this admirable collection.

In an exploration of this communicative world we may cite Baudelaire:

La Nature est un temple ou de vivants piliers
Laissent parfois sortir de confuses paroles;
L'homme y passe à travers des forêts de symboles
Qui l'observent avec des regards familiers.

Christopher N. Candlin — *Lancaster*
General Editor — *1984*

Introduction: a note on the C.R.A.P.E.L.

. . . si l'on ne veut pas voir la pédagogie s'enliser dans le conformisme, il faut qu'à tout moment elle enseigne le refus de se conformer. Il n'est de pédagogie constructive que sauvage et la vraie pédagogie se moque de la pédagogie.

Si donc nous préférons substituer à la notion de formation pédagogique celle de réflexion sur l'expérience pédagogique concrètement vécue, nous déplaçons tout naturellement l'accent du pôle 'enseignant' au pôle 'enseigné' . . . Cette façon de voir exclut, d'entrée de jeu, tout enseignement dogmatique de la pédagogie, et récuse tout apprentissage fondé sur la notion de modèle universel également admirable et susceptible d'être imité.

Yves Châlon

The *Centre de Recherches et d'Applications Pédagogiques en Langues* (C.R.A.P.E.L.) was founded by Professor Yves Châlon in 1964 and its ethos and organization still bear the stamp of that remarkable man's personality. Although officially a *section* or department of the Faculty of Letters in the University of Nancy, the C.R.A.P.E.L. has also been described as 'an association,' 'a research workers' cooperative' or even 'a club'. It is a unique example of an approach to research based on collective enthusiasm: all of its members are practising language teachers who are interested in applied linguistics research for its own sake and who simply enjoy working together. The C.R.A.P.E.L., that is, employs no salaried researchers and its members are all part-time workers in the sense that they earn their livings in posts which have no direct relationship with the C.R.A.P.E.L.

Membership of the Centre is by informal co-option and at any one time there are usually about fifteen full members. In general, new candidates are recruited from among the teachers who work with the various courses (both within the University of Nancy and in adult education) for which the C.R.A.P.E.L. is responsible. A teacher might develop an interest in a particular project and start working with a research group; he or she may then move on elsewhere or may become more and more deeply involved in the work of the *Centre*, eventually becoming a member. It is all rather informal, rather unacademic and even rather un-French.

Research is carried out in sub-groups, usually consisting of three to five members. Each member, though, may belong to several such teams, so that at any given moment there may be as many as a dozen different research projects under way. The emphasis, with very few exceptions indeed, is on short-term practical pedagogical applications rather than on 'pure' linguistic research or on long-term studies. In fact, almost all the research projects are set up to deal with the specific problems posed by a particular course or group of learners.

In dealing with these problems, research groups are free to call on all disciplines for conceptual and methodological aid. At the C.R.A.P.E.L., applied linguistics is most definitely *not* regarded as being 'linguistics applied'. It is not, that is, a study of the implications of linguistic theory for language teaching. It is a conceptually eclectic investigation of all the factors — social, psychological, pedagogic and linguistic — which impinge on language learning and teaching.

This *specificity of response*, this concentration on the particular problems of actual groups, has two main results:

Firstly, it makes the members of the *Centre* wary about translating their ideas and experience directly into other learning situations. This is not to be taken as a lack of confidence or enthusiasm in our own work but simply as a recognition of the highly individual natures of learners and their situations. The right thing to do in our situation might be quite wrong in yours, and vice versa. We believe, therefore, that in any discussion about language teaching it is absolutely essential to make clear who the learners are and what the circumstances are in which the learning is to take place. This is why many of the articles which are included in this volume are reports on courses or descriptions of materials. We make no apologies, then, for going into such details. However, it is obvious that if matters were left there we would simply be suggesting 'recipes', which would run counter to the idea of the specific response. This in turn means that the level at which it is possible to compare two learning situations or to extrapolate from one to another is necessarily higher than that at which ingredients are simply listed. We know from experience that this lays us open to the charge that some of our work is too abstract. We can only reply that generalizations based on specific instances are not abstractions, not in the sense that they have no empirical basis or practical relevance; they are attempts to establish a rationale, to explain why we do what we do rather than something else, to identify a set of principles underlying the selection and implementation of those activities which, it is believed, will facilitate language acqui-

Part One
Discourse

A la question 'Des professeurs, pour quoi faire?, nous serions tentés de répondre, des professeurs pour écouter. Il ne suffit pas de descendre de sa chaire, ou disposer les chaises en circle, de séparer la barrière artificielle que représente le mobilier périmé hérité d'un âge pré-Gutenbergien, pour faire de la pédagogie rogérienne. Ce ne sont pas de simples ruses d'architecture ou de décoration qui résoudront les conflits inhérents à la relation pédagogique.

Yves Châlon

Introduction

Communication is a process whereby we create, negotiate and interpret personal meanings. In the two sections which make up Part One of this anthology, certain aspects of this process are taken for detailed examination and discussion. The first section deals with the structure of oral discourse produced in face-to-face interaction, while the second considers reading as a communicative activity.

Common to both sections, then, is an interest in the nature of meaning and in the different modalities by which it can be realized, transmitted and retrieved. These problems have been the subject of intense study and discussion during the last fifteen years or so: researchers in many domains, but in particular sociology and ethnology (Fishman 1971; Gumperz and Hymes 1972; see also p. 127) have found inadequate the type of linguistic analysis whose investigations are strictly limited to the internal functioning of the verbal code — phonology, morphology and syntax — independent of the circumstances in which the code is used. Consequently, there has been a widening of the field of research to include the external functioning of the verbal code as well, what people *do* with words. The emphasis in such an approach shifts from structure and grammar to function and communicative competence, from assembling sentences to doing things with utterances, from the sentence in isolation to the utterance in context.

This, then, is the domain of discourse analysis — as some investigators understand it at least — the description of the process whereby we create and relate, organize and realize meaning. Discourse analysis, that is, is an analysis of meaning, but meaning seen not in the traditional 'semantic' sense of isolated concepts. Rather, the discourse analyst studies meaning as a construct *either* of an individual collaborating with one or more other individuals in the creation of a unified discourse ('multi-source discourse') *or* of an individual interpreting a text produced by another individual and to which he does not or can not make any formal contribution ('single-source discourse').

These parameters of discourse, and in particular their relationship to the written and spoken forms — which is not a direct one — are the subject of the first paper by Henri Holec. However, before turning to the specific issues considered in the other papers in Part One it might be useful first to look at the more general topic of the creation of meaning. Simply for the sake of convenience, I will discuss face-to-face interaction and reading separately and each discussion will immediately precede the group of papers to which it refers. For the moment, then, I will be discussing oral interactive discourse. I will be returning to written discourse on p. 67. It is essential to remember, though, that this creative process is common to all discourse, indeed it is its defining characteristic, being what distinguishes discourse from text.

The creation of meaning in face-to-face interaction

Discourse analysts have quite abandoned the attempt to find one universal definition of meaning, *the* meaning of 'meaning'. There are two main reasons for this: the first, which has already been mentioned, is our growing awareness of discourse as a tool for the establishment and distribution of knowledge. From this point of view, communication is seen as a dialectic between social and personal knowledge, between what the language 'knows' and what individual speakers know. We shall return to this later.

Our second reason for rejecting a 'unitary' view of meaning is related to our increasing appreciation that meaning resides in and is conveyed by the combinations of and the inter-relationships between a number of semiotic systems, that it is not simply a property of words. These systems include 'all the means of communication capable of conventionally coded, short-term manipulation — language, tone of voice, gesture, posture, body movements, spatial orientation, physical proximity, eye contact and facial expression can be thought of as sition. It is this process we call 'research'. It begins every time a teacher steps into a classroom and extends into the furthest reaches of the cognitive and social sciences.

Secondly, since learners and their situations differ, there can be no question of research being directed at the discovery of the ideal language-teaching method. What is good for one learner will be bad for another. Any approach which, for theoretical or ideological reasons, limits the options available to learners is, to the extent that it does so, discriminatory. This is why we can say, hand on heart, that we do not believe in any of the 'ways' or '–ologies' or '–pedias' — and that we believe in all of them. In no sense is this a dereliction of our duty as a research centre to evaluate 'methods', to say that one way of teaching or learning a language is better than another: but we add the rider, better for whom? Approaches are not right or wrong in themselves or in some absolute sense (according to the latest developments in applied linguistics, say) but only in relationship to individual learners, their needs and their situations. To put it more concretely, if our learners choose to bury themselves in language laboratories for eight hours a day or to use the grammar-translation method, they are welcome to do so. Our responsibility as a research centre is to help make that choice a real one, an informed decision, by providing them with the necessary information and evaluation procedures. It is this process — helping learners to find the methodology which suits them best by making available the necessary conceptual and practical tools — which is the central focus of our research.

During recent years, the research topics which have been worked on have included applications of the following: communicative language teaching; discourse analysis and the study of interaction; speech act theory; argumentation; the use of authentic materials; non-verbal communication; listening and viewing comprehension; reading; sound libraries; autonomy and self-directed learning schemes; evaluation and self assessment; learning strategies; communication strategies; second-language acquisition; French as a second language; literacy schemes for immigrant workers; educational technology; video and computer applications.

The *Centre* publishes its own journal at the end of each year, the *Mélanges Pédagogiques*, from which all the papers in this collection are taken, with the exception of those listed under 'Acknowledgements'. The C.R.A.P.E.L. is partly self-financing through its publications and courses, but it also receives research equipment and maintenance grants from the University and the Ministry of Education as well as the salaries of the technical and secretarial staff of four.

Any anthology which tried to cover all the research topics which have been mentioned above would be both indigestible and unwieldy. Instead, two broad themes have been chosen which it is hoped will be of more general interest — the nature of discourse and the nature of learning — and which at the same time focus on those areas in which the C.R.A.P.E.L.'s influence is generally acknowledged, discourse analysis and the communicative approach to language teaching and learning, and self-directed ('autonomous') learning schemes.

That it was possible to make such a selection is an indication that even if the C.R.A.P.E.L.'s approach is highly eclectic, it is not just *ad hoc*. Nonetheless, the reader will certainly be aware of minor (we hope) inconsistencies, both pedagogical and linguistic, between the various papers published here. Partly this is due to the fact that the papers are by different hands — there is no C.R.A.P.E.L. 'party line' or ideology; partly it is due to the simple passage of time which allows experiments to be run, experience to be acquired, hypotheses to be proved and disproved — and minds to be changed.

It would probably have been possible to edit out most of these inconsistencies — or at least to paper over the cracks. But it would also have been a misrepresentation of the sort of continuing research done at the C.R.A.P.E.L. So editing has been kept to a minimum: in general, papers appear in their original form, except where passages have been deleted to avoid unnecessary repetition and where potentially confusing variations in terminology have been ironed out. No attempt has been made to benefit from hindsight, but of course preference has usually been given to the most recent paper on any particular topic.

I would like to thank Mme Mary Petit, secretary of the C.R.A.P.E.L., for the kindness, steadfastness and skill she has shown in the preparation of the manuscript.

Where papers were first published in French, the translations are by the editor.

Philip Riley — *Nancy*
C.R.A.P.E.L. — *1984*

being woven together to form the fabric of a conversation, and we can understand the communicative texture of an interaction best by seeing the relationship of the different strands' (Laver and Hutcheson 1972).

Basic to this approach is the concept of the *act of communication*. In face-to-face interaction an act of communication can be realized by a wide range of behaviours and conveyed along a number of different channels. From the purely communicative point of view, it makes no difference whether the realization is verbal or not. That is, a *speech act* is just one of the possible realizations of a communicative act: a shake of my head can communicate disagreement (to take just one aspect of the meaning of an act) as efficiently as the word 'No'.

Naturally enough, discourse analysts have tried to find ways of delimiting and defining 'acts' so that they can be usefully employed as units of descriptions. Attempts to base such definitions on the sentence or to identify supra-sentential structures on the basis of formal correspondences between sentences have only revealed the weaknesses and limitations inherent in such an approach (Harris 1952; Halliday and Hassan 1976). This is because, in very general terms, a sentence is the maximum unit of linguistic structure: the utterance is the minimal unit of language use. A sentence is defined in terms of the internal relationships which hold between its constituent parts, but an utterance is defined in terms of its external relations with non-linguistic items. A sentence is a unit of linguistic description: an utterance is a unit for the description of behaviour. The former is part of grammar, the latter part of an event.

In real life, we produce utterances, then, not sentences. Sentences are abstractions made by grammarians to account for certain types of regularity, structural likenesses, to be observed in linguistic forms. Of course, if we describe an utterance in terms of its grammatical structure alone, we *may* find that we are dealing with a sentence — though not all utterances are well-formed sentences, by any means. Let us take an example:

I met the baker's wife.

Only when it is used *on an instance*, in other words as part of a real communicative event, can we describe such an item as an utterance, since an utterance, by definition, enters into relationships with both its linguistic and non-linguistic context. Imagine that we were able to collect a dozen real-life occurrences of 'I met the baker's wife': if we described them grammatically we would have a dozen identical descriptions, such as 'Subject and Verb and Object'. But if we described them as utterances we would need a variety of descriptions corresponding to the variety of contexts in which they occurred.

One of the main sources of this variation would be differences in the common knowledge to which particular utterances made appeal. This is one reason why people who know one another well can communicate efficiently in a way which is often completely incomprehensible to an outsider, someone who does not belong to the group of people sharing a particular set of experiences or knowledge. Consider, for example:

A: Did you get the bus?
B: I met the baker's wife.

What are we to make of this exchange? Precious little, as long as we lack the knowledge or background information which, we assume, A and B share. This knowledge cannot be linguistic: if it were, we, as speakers of English, would be just as able to understand this exchange as A and B were, and in exactly the same way. To put it another way, there is no formal linguistic marker linking what B said with what A said, simply the fact that they were observed to say these things, in that order, and that they were apparently satisfied with their communication.

The knowledge, then, must be extra-linguistic. If I now tell you that the baker's wife is a notorious gossip, forever going on about her rheumatism, buttonholing people she meets for hours, you will immediately draw the same conclusion as A, namely that B missed the bus because he was delayed by the baker's wife. Such an inference, though, is totally dependent on A and B sharing that knowledge about the baker's wife, as we can see if the information is changed: if, for example, we say that the baker's wife is a good friend of B's and that she has a car, B will be 'heard as saying' that he did not take the bus, he was given a lift.

Another source of variation lies in the type of communicative act B intended to perform, in the illocutionary value of the utterance: it is quite easy to imagine it having the force of a complaint, say, or an apology. There would also be variations in its interactional function as well as in any longer-term plans of which this utterance might form a part, such as B persuading A that he needs his own car.

Participants collaborating together in interactive discourse learn one another's meaning from the information they exchange. In extremely general terms, we obtain this information from:

1. Our knowledge of the linguistic code — vocabulary and grammar;
2. Our knowledge of the world, including our knowledge of our

interlocutor and of his knowledge;

3. Our knowledge of the rules for relating 1 and 2 — procedural or interpretative rules.

When we use language, we use it for our own personal purposes and imbue it with our own personal meaning. That is, in interactive discourse the individual expresses and interprets *subjective* meaning and, to the extent that communication is successful, participants establish *intersubjective* meaning, the meaning which that discourse has for them. If we are to study this process, then, we obviously need to look at examples of individuals using language on instances, at authentic discourse, not at artificial or isolated examples or at grammatical structures. That is, to study meaning in interaction we need to look at utterances, not sentences, and we will need to consider separately the roles of speaker and addressee.

Now models based on the 'ideal speaker–hearer' or on *langue* do not take these distinctions into account: yet it is manifestly true that we do not simply have a mechanical, equal distribution of speaking turns amongst all the participants in an interaction, because we do not all have equal rights to the floor in all situations: our rights are directly related to our social and interactive roles in particular events (see Chapter 2). This is precisely why the last few years have seen the development of linguistic models which differ in important ways from those of mainstream linguistics: from de Saussure to Chomsky the focus of attention had remained linguistic structure, the sentence and the ideal speaker-hearer. Now, for some linguists at least, the focus is on language use, the utterance and the interactive pair. Instead of static models of *langue*, we are trying to develop dynamic models of *parole*, which means — among other things — trying to account for the ways in which we link utterances together, our own and those of other speakers, to create meaning in discourse.

In face-to-face interaction, in real time, any individual contribution may limit or influence subsequent contributions in a variety of ways: accounting for this process — for the nature of the individual contributions, for the operations by which they mesh and fuse into a single whole — accounting, that is, for multi-source discourse presents the linguist with an awesome list of problems. Ultimately, it would require a theory of human action and a theory of human knowing, implying as it does not only a description of all the constituents of communicative events, but also the full range of psychological, epistemological and socio-cultural factors involved in the perception of such events. Slowly, though, a number of conceptual landmarks are becoming discernible: for example, communicative competence, act, utterance, interaction, role, address and strategy. This last term is proving to be exceptionally rich in insights, providing as it does just the sort of epistemological bridge between acting and knowing whose necessity has already been mentioned. For the moment, though, I would just like to emphasize the point that, if we accept the view of interaction as collaboration (the existence of ideal speaker–hearer models makes this pleonasm necessary) then we are logically bound to accept the propositions that the meaning of an interaction is both a property of events and a collaborative construct. Of course, this is really only an extension of the definition of utterance put forward earlier: its meaning depends on use. Our definition of 'meaning', therefore, has the advantage of being *conversational* in two senses: it is the everyday use of the word and it is also a product of interactive collaboration. To the objection that sentences also have meaning of a sort, that, indeed, some philosophers distinguish between 'sentence meaning' and 'utterance use', the following replies can be made: firstly, the terminological disagreements are so complete that we are obliged to choose between competing and contradictory meanings of 'meaning', so that in general it seems best to keep it as a superordinate term — here, for example, one can talk about 'semantic meaning' and 'pragmatic meaning'; secondly, the distinguishing characteristic of pragmatic meaning and therefore of utterance is *reference*. Sentences do not refer, utterances do.

A number of approaches to the description of 'utterance linking' have been put forward in recent years. By 'utterance linking', I am referring to those aspects of discourse processing which enable speakers and hearers to relate *what is said* to *what is meant* in a given context of situation. (Useful general surveys include: Cole and Morgan 1975; Berrendonner 1977; Clark and Clark 1977; Candlin and Breen, forthcoming.) Since this problem has attracted the interest of philosophers, sociologists, ethnologists, anthropologists, psychologists and computer scientists as well as language teachers, there is a correspondingly rich profusion and confusion of terms: discourse processing, communicative strategies, interpretative strategies, inferencing, implicature, etc. This terminological variety is the reflection of wide variations of conceptual and methodological approach, but in very general terms all the researchers involved attempt to tackle either or both of the following questions: How do we attribute a 'real' meaning to indirect speech acts? How do we relate two utterances across turns?

One of the most copious and influential sources of attempts to tackle the first question is the work of a number of transformational–generative grammarians (Sadock 1970, 1975; Ross 1970, 1975). Briefly, they posit that the illocutionary force of an utterance is to be accounted for in the deep structure, the semantic component of their grammar. 'Ifids' (illocutionary force indicating devices) may be deleted in the surface structure, but native speakers are able to reconstruct the underlying structure by the application of various types of transformations. There are a number of powerful objections to this approach, but since I do not wish to trivialize their work, I shall not attempt what would necessarily be a superficial discussion here. For the moment, I will limit my comments to the following observation: questions of theory apart, their methodology — the formal analysis of decontextualized, often artificial sentences — prevents their saying anything relevant to the pragmatic values of utterances in context. Though such studies are often labelled 'Speech Act Theory', the term 'act' here is a complete misnomer: they are studies of the semantic cover of sentences — their *potential* use, if you like — generalizations about the meaning of linguistic items which have no reference. Moreover, they are based on the reduction of the ideal speaker–hearer which, as we have seen, disqualifies them from making interactive or social statements.

Other scholars have tried to establish sets of non-linguistic rules which speakers and hearers might apply in determining the meaning of utterances. These sets (which often describe very different aspects of discourse processing) include Grice's (1975) 'maxims', Searle's (1975) 'inferencing procedures', Gordon and Lakoff's (1971) 'conversational postulates' and Cicourel's (1973) 'interpretative procedures'. Common to all these models is the notion of the negotiation of meaning. The function of discourse is seen as the creation of a common meaning through the participants' sharing and comparing information. As Widdowson (1980) says:

> Communication is called for when the language user recognises a situation which requires the conveyance of information to establish a convergence of knowledge, so that this situation can be changed in some way. This transaction requires the negotiation of meaning through interaction. I refer to this negotiation as discourse. The term . . . therefore refers to the interaction that has to take place to establish the meaning value of utterances and to realise their effectiveness as indicators of illocutionary intent. This interactivity is a necessary condition for the enactment of any discourse.

There is a delightful scene in Peter Ustinov's film *Romanov and Juliet*, where Ustinov himself, playing the role of Head of a tiny Ruritanian state which is desperate to remain neutral, bustles to and fro between the American and Russian embassies in his country, informing them of the status of their intelligence relative to one another:

'They know!' he tells both ambassadors, who remain unperturbed. 'That's fine: we know they know', they reply calmly.

Off sets Ustinov again. 'They know you know', he reports back to both sides.

'Of course', comes the response — 'and we know they know we know'.

Fortified by alternate doses of bourbon and vodka, he teeters from one embassy to the other.

'They know you know they know you know!'

'No problem. We know they know we know they know we know . . .'

So it continues, until suddenly the point is reached where both ambassadors react in horror:

'What! They know we know they know we know they know we know they know we know! This is terrible! I must get on to Washington/Moscow at once . . .'

As always, much of the strength of this caricature is derived from its very close resemblance to the real thing. When people interact, it is essential for each of them to know just how much the others know if communication is to be efficient. The nature of this knowledge will vary according to the situation, but it is always there to some extent. If, every time we wished to say something, we had to say everything, we could say nothing: when we have something to say, we need first to know what does not need saying. That is, we have to decide what is irrelevant and what is already known to our interlocutor.

Here is a more serious, authentic example of meaning being negotiated: A is trying to explain to B where he lives:

A: 24, rue Marie-Odile. Got it?
B: That's Nancy?
A: Yeah.
B: I don't —
A: Look, you know Laxou?
B: Yeah.
A: You know the road to Toul, where it starts by the Renault garage one side?
B: Right. . .

A: and the Peugeot on the other?
B: Right . . . Yeah right.
A: So if you're coming from the middle of town, up the Avenue de Boufflers, it's off on the left. Just before you get there there's a big service station, you turn left just before.
B: Yeah, I know.

What we have here is a classic example of the formulation of place (as studied by Schegloff 1972). The aim of this piece of discourse, as clearly announced, is for A to share with B his knowledge concerning the whereabouts of the reference '24, rue Marie-Odile'. B indicates his ignorance, at the same time providing a starting-point for the negotiation: 'That's Nancy?'. He is in fact asking for confirmation of a hypothesis formed on the basis of A's failing to add the name of the town at the end of his address. This is not pure chance: A and B were in the same town, Nancy, which was therefore a shared piece of knowledge and which A did not need to negotiate.

Having established the general area of Nancy as their mutual field of reference, A now embarks on a process of progressive refinement. He does this by establishing a series of common points of reference ('You know . . . you know . . .') in relation to which he can introduce the new information in a way which would be meaningful to B. B signals that the points of reference are in fact, as A had presumed from his knowledge of B, common knowledge ('Right . . . Right . . . Yeah right.') Finally A, having pinpointed a landmark, uses it 'as the nearest thing' and switches to a description from B's perspective ('. . . if you're coming from the middle of town . . .') believing — rightly, as it turns out — that this accumulation of familiar knowledge will enable B to locate the unfamiliar ('Yeah, I know . . .').

It is this type of procedure which we refer to as the negotiation of personal knowledge. It is no use A giving B a map-reference, however objective and precise (unless B happens to have a copy of the same map, of course). A tries to select from his own store of information those items which are relevant and which he has good reason to believe will also be known to B. His own store of information will be the result of his experience, of course: this is why descriptions (for formulations of place are obviously just a sub-category of referential descriptions) vary according to speaker as well as hearer. If we stop passers-by for directions to the market place, one might say:

Go past the Pig and Whistle, keep going till you come to the King's Head, turn left, then when you get to the Mitre it's right opposite.

Another might say:

> Take the turning on the left of the Holy Redeemer, follow it all the way to St. Anne's Chapel and it's next to the Cathedral.

Speakers, then, vary their formulations according to their own knowledge and on the basis of their perception of their addressee's geographical (in this case) knowledge, which is itself an aspect of identity. (In France, where I have lived and worked for ten years, I am occasionally asked for directions by drivers on the main road which I walk along to get to the University. They are applying a very obvious 'deictic reasoning strategy': 'If he's walking to work, he lives near here, if he lives near here he will have the information I want', etc. However, as soon as I open my mouth, my accent contradicts their classification of me, and they often display an impatient disbelief, or even just drive off in the middle of my — absolutely correct! — instructions.) Our communicative behaviour towards people varies according to what we believe to be their degree and types of knowledge: we sort them into categories (good friend, colleague, foreigner, child, neighbour, etc.) and we select our descriptions on the basis of the information we believe members of such categories to possess — on what we know they know.

Pedagogical implications

These considerations help us formulate a question of immense interest to applied linguists, indeed to anyone investigating the learning process: what is the nature of the relationship between:

1. The negotiation of old and new knowledge between two or more participants engaged in an interaction, and;
2. The negotiation of old and new information within the individual, the extension of his cognitive categories?

These two topics correspond very approximately to two relatively new areas of applied linguistic research on second language acquisition — 'communication strategies' and 'interlanguage' (Corder 1980; Harding 1980; Faerch and Kasper 1983; Candlin and Breen, forthcoming). Unfortunately, though understandably enough, given the complexity of the issues involved, researchers have tended to concentrate on one or the other rather than on the relationships between them. As Breen and Candlin have pointed out:

> the possible relationships between communicative negotiation between people and negotiative interaction between the mind and the external world offer a rich area for psycho-sociolinguistic research (1980; see also Candlin's preface to Faerch and Kasper 1983).

Although linguists have been somewhat slow to appreciate the importance of this area, scholars in other disciplines have produced work which has considerable linguistic interest. One thinks, for example, of the British social anthropologists such as Evans-Pritchard, Malinowski and Radcliffe-Brown. Moreover, this topic has always been a traditional theme of philosophy and psychology: in the twentieth century, there is the work of Piaget (1953, 1969) on 'assimilation', Kelly (1969) on 'personal constructs' and Bruner (1973) on the extension of cognitive categories 'beyond the information given'. Another source of insights, and one which has yet to be tapped by applied linguists, is the work on environmental perception in general — 'mental maps' — carried out by geographers (Gould and White 1974; Pocock 1979; Spencer and Weetman 1981; Spencer and Darvizeh 1981; Goodey 1976).

All in all, it may well be that the processes we have been discussing here and which have been exemplified as mother-tongue communication strategies are system-constrained learning procedures. The negotiation of meaning is essentially a learning process and the ways in which it is carried out are, to some extent at least, the results of certain fundamental characteristics of language, in particular the nature of reference. The importance of this hypothesis for language-learning in general and for a communicative methodology in particular can hardly be exaggerated: if the communicative strategies used for the negotiation of meaning in the mother tongue are learning strategies (in some non-figurative sense) then they are obviously highly relevant to second-language learning. They may, in fact, be the only ways in which certain vital aspects of language use *can* be learnt.

In Chapters 1, 2 and 3, specific aspects of this approach to the functioning of spoken language will be taken for discussion. Chapters 4, 5 and 6 concentrate on written discourse and reading.

The structure of communicative interaction

Il est bien évident qu'une certaine rhétorique non seulement favorise indirectement les priviligiés de la naissance, mais qu'elle les dresse à se conformer beaucoup plus qu'à se former.

Yves Châlon

Numerous models already exist for the description of the syntax and morphology of natural languages. The course-planner, textbook writer or teacher who limits his syllabus to purely structural considerations has an embarrassingly rich choice of studies on which to base his programme. However, the advent of the 'communicative' or 'functional' approach to language acquisition has obliged applied linguists to search around for suitable descriptions for the structure of communicative behaviour and language use, based on pragmatic considerations.

The search has not been an easy one. Linguistic science has traditionally limited its scope to the study of the internal structures of the linguistic code, at the expense of the study of the external uses to which those structures may be put. For this reason, applied linguists (and indeed many other scholars who find that language impinges on their central object of interest; see pp. 126–7) have been obliged to cobble together or hammer out their own approach to the description of communicative behaviour. In very general terms, they have tried to clarify the ways in which illocutionary acts are realized and sequenced and in which information is ordered and negotiated, as well as specifying the different roles which participants may enact and identifying situational constraints which limit the options available. By any standards, many of the studies which have been produced are exceptionally rich and interesting, so much so that it would be quite invidious to select single items for reference here (but for general surveys and bibliographies see Brumfit and Johnson 1979; Coulthard 1977; Kramsch 1981; Maingenau 1976; Schmidt and Richards 1980; Riley 1980; Widdowson 1980; Edmondson 1981).

At the C.R.A.P.E.L., too, we have had a number of projects investigating different aspects of discourse analysis and communicative competence. The three papers in this section, for example, form a debate on the nature and meaning of *interaction*, an aspect of communicative behaviour which we found to be largely neglected by current models of discourse. As Henri Holec shows in Chapter 1, the term is a highly ambiguous one, usually because it is used in a vague and undefined way to refer to those features which distinguish *all* discourse from text. We have preferred to define interaction as the process by which discourse, as the collaborative construct of two or more participants, is produced.

The main questions which Henri Holec asks are: What do we mean by 'a discourse produced by more than one participant'? What is the relationship of this discourse type to the spoken and written forms? What is 'real time' as far as the encoding process is concerned? He shows that while there may be high statistical correspondences between, say, the written form and non-interactive discourse, only by regarding interaction as an independent variable can we account for a number of important discourse types.

As we saw earlier, among the important implications of this argument is the rejection of linguistic models based on 'the ideal speaker–hearer' as being inadequate for the description of interactive discourse. Not only do participants shift from speaker state to hearer state, but they clearly do not have equal rights to the floor in most situations. That is, this transition is not something insignificant and automatic: it is related to identity and role. It is the establishment of a relationship between 'role' and interaction — between who has the right to speak and when — which is the focus of Chapter 2. It is this explanatory power of our model which, we feel, justifies our regarding it as superior to the various 'systematics' for turn-taking, which remain, as it were, at an etic level. They describe *how* turns are taken but do not consider the problem of why they should be distributed in that way.

Chapter 3 presents our model of interaction in a more detailed way. By taking 'interaction' as a separate parameter of discourse and by distinguishing between speaker and hearer states, it is possible to describe the structure of discourse in a more delicate way than with models which conflate illocutionary acts and interactive acts. Crucial to the understanding of the distinction made between these two types of act is the notion of *address*. The notion of address was first investigated as one of a series of categories for the description of the communicative functions of non-verbal communication (see Riley 1976). Interactive acts can best be understood as manifestations of the distribution of address: the presence or absence of the right to take or give the floor, to reply, to close an interaction (or some part of it), to interrupt, these are all rights to perform certain categories of interactive acts.

Address is realized by a rule-governed set of behaviours which are usually, but not necessarily, non-verbal (see p. 15 and pp. 342–3) and by means of which a speaker selects and indicates his listener(s).

When we interact in a group we do not usually speak to all the group all the time; we speak to individuals and sub-groups. The mechanisms for this system of address are eye-contact, head-direction, gestures, orientation and posture. By observing this essentially very simple address behaviour we are able to state with a high degree of accuracy which participant(s) a speaker is speaking to for any given utterance.

Address is very important and interesting, because it provides us with an extremely powerful tool for the description of interaction. We now have a way of coding utterances that will apply equally well both to formal and informal types of interaction. By distinguishing for each successive utterance 1, 2, 3. . . which actor A, B, C. . . is the speaker (S), which the listener(s) (L) and which the hearer(s) (H) we are able to code each utterance in terms of participant states. Let us take as an example the following brief interchange. Three participants are engaged in completely informal conversation:

A: T'as vu *2001*?
B: Ben. . .non.
A: Toi?
C: Moi non plus.

This can be diagrammed and coded as in Table 1.

TABLE 1

	1	2	3	4
A	S	L	S	L
B	L	S	H	H
C	H	H	L	S

Legend: 1,2,3,4 – Utterances in serial order
A,B,C – Participants
S – Speaker
L – Listener(s): the participant(s) addressed by the speaker of a given utterance.
H – Hearer(s): the participant(s) not addressed by the speaker of a given utterance.

What this tells us is that between the second and third utterances there was a *change of address*. A spoke first to ('addressed') B, B replied. A then spoke to C, C replied. The address signals in this case were gaze and head-direction: as A spoke to B, he met her gaze, as he spoke to C he changed both gaze and head-direction, and C met his gaze. To put it another way, it was the address signals which enabled B and C to know whether or not A intended them to be the hearer or listener of his utterances. This is how they were able to distinguish between the 'Tu' of utterance 1, and the 'Toi' of utterance 3.

Patterns of consecutive codings, expressed in terms of codings, change of address and change of first speaker, will give us discourse units of varying types, in other words stretches of discourse corresponding to moves, exchanges, transactions, etc. . . In the example just given, the change of address could be said to mark the boundary between two exchanges. We are finding a close correlation between these participant states and several other very important aspects of discourse, such as topic, status, role and formality — this is exactly what one would expect, of course, but we have not been able to formalize these things before.

This concept of address also makes us face up to the problem of developing a model of discourse for groups above the dyad — groups with three or more participants. Up to now, discourse analysts have either shied away from groups of three or more participants or simply imposed a dyadic model willy-nilly on their data: they have treated group interactions as if they were a series of parallel dyads. It is significant that the one group situation where the dyadic model has been reasonably successful is the classroom. But there you have a close resemblance to the dyad: the teacher has rights which show in discourse, in particular he can choose the next speaker; the children have no choice of address, they talk to or through the teacher, not one another. Such an approach has a major disadvantage and one which has previously made analysts despair of ever handling, say, conversation; it assumes that whoever speaks next was the person spoken to, that he is 'in turn'. It cannot distinguish between:

A speaks to B — B replies.
A speaks to B — C replies.
A speaks to B and/or C — B and/or C replies.

Now a triadic (3 +) model *can* handle this: but — far more important — it does this not by the introduction of some purely abstract, algebraic dimension, but by integration of an observable system of behaviours, which in general, are non-verbal, such as the address system. Such behaviours fall into three main groups:

1. Those which are related to *content* (kinematopœia);
2. Those which are related to *illocutionary force*;

3. Those which are related to *structure of the interchange*, i.e. which are mechanisms for regulating the interaction.

Our contention, then, is that any description which omitted non-verbal communication would fail to represent or account for much which is essential. In particular, to omit Group 3 is to omit most of the interactive structure which it is the very aim of discourse analysis to make explicit. Not surprisingly, analyses which make use of the verbal component alone have proved extremely difficult, since by and large they impose on the verbal component functions which it does not have, or in which it has only a minor role: it is relatively rare to find much redundancy between Group 3 and the verbal component. Indeed sometimes there is none at all, and this is sufficient justification for setting up two separate 'levels' of linguistic organization (roughly corresponding to Groups 2 and 3), which we call Communicative Structure and Interactive Structure. Our model can be diagrammed as in Figure 1.

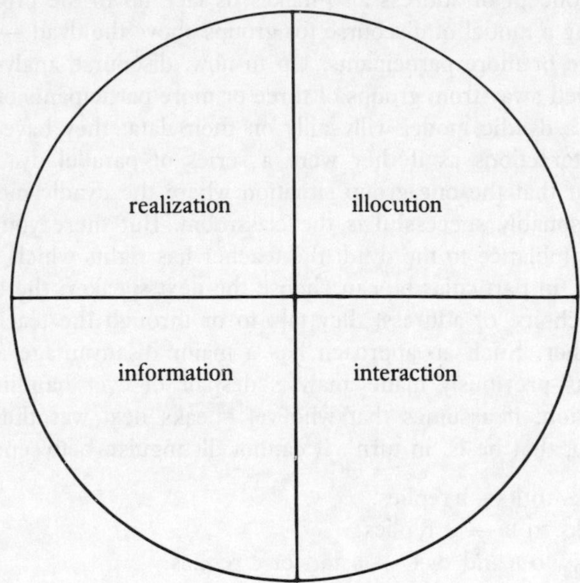

FIGURE 1

Realization: The set of message-bearing elements (verbal, para-linguistic, non-verbal) in a situation. These elements have substance and are realizations of various systems and structures whose organization can be described in terms such as class, units, structure and distribution. The textual function of such elements is described in terms of their internal relations (and without reference to the meaning they carry).

Illocution: Here we deal with the illocutionary forces of acts (whatever their realization); inviting, persuading, agreeing, etc. Sequences of these give us communicative structure. There is no one-to-one relationship between these acts and units of realization — they are *not* related at different levels of *delicacy*.

Information: This is the knowledge which is exchanged by participants in discourse to form their common ground and on which they base their formulations and interpretations of meaning.

Interaction: At this level we describe linguistic organization in terms of interactional tactics, turns, address, relative distribution of utterances; sequences of these give us discursive structure. Again, there is no one-to-one relationship between discourse acts and communicative acts, so that for example, the discursive act opening turn may be a greeting ('Hallo'), requesting information ('Been waiting long?'), apologizing ('Sorry I'm late'). This is why, we believe, attempts to define *illocutionary acts* in terms of *position in the structure of the discourse* are doomed to failure[1]. (There have been objections to the effect that this statement is over-categorical. Perhaps it is. But by providing a strong hypothesis on which to base our investigations, it formed the source of many of the insights into discourse structure discussed in this paper.) Even such a seemingly position-defined communication act as 'greeting' can in fact (and has been attested to) occur after a series of other acts.

This distinction between communicative and interactive acts, forced on us by the integration of non-verbal communication, throws light on a very thorny problem in the field — the problem of discur-

[1]It will be obvious that this approach to discourse structure differs radically from that of the team working at Birmingham University (cf. Sinclair and Coulthard 1975; Brazil, Coulthard and Johns 1980). However, their work still remains the most theoretically and methodologically complete in the field, and we would like to thank in particular David Brazil, Malcolm Coulthard and Tim Johns for the unfailing enthusiasm and generosity they have shown in so many discussions and for the practical and theoretical help they have given us on so many occasions.

sive embedding or interruptions. A simple example:

1: Would you like to come round for dinner tonight?
2: Yes I'd love to.

We can describe this in terms of inviting/accepting. But what about:

1: Would you like to come round for dinner tonight?
2: What time?
3: About eight.
4: Yes, I'd love to.

To the discourse analyst who does not distinguish between communicative acts and interactive acts, this causes considerable embarrassment. If he describes this as an 'interruption' or 'embedding', he is admitting his failure to describe discourse as a series of consecutive communicative acts, each of which imposes constraints on the next speaker, by imposing upon him a limited number of choices. Embedding or interruption is an admission of failure — it simply is not possible to predict what will come next. But the only other option is to define, say, requesting information, by position of occurrence — a near-impossibility because, semantic problems apart, it is going to force a different definition of 'requesting information' occurring after 'inviting' and 'requesting information' occurring after all the other acts imaginable, in other words a different definition for each place of occurrence.

On the other hand, if we distinguish between the communicative act *requesting information* and the interactive act *response*, the problem is greatly simplified. We can describe this exchange in terms of two structures, as shown in Table 2.

TABLE 2

Communicative	*Interactive*
1. inviting	opening
2. requesting information	response
3. informing	opening
4. accepting	response
(Defined in terms of illocutionary force and semantic and situational features)	(Defined in terms of interactional tactics)

There is a strong temptation to diagram this as in Figure 2

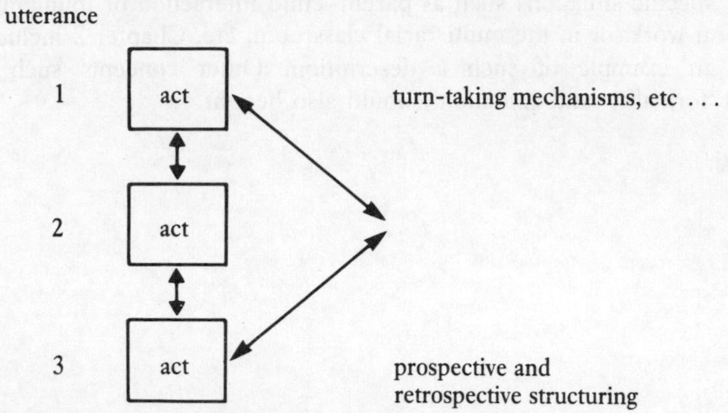

utterance

1 act — turn-taking mechanisms, etc . . .

2 act

3 act — prospective and retrospective structuring

FIGURE 2

but this would imply a 'tagmemic' relationship which our present state of knowledge does not justify (although Edmondson (1981) has done much to clarify and confirm this point).

I would now like to turn — very briefly indeed — to the possible applications of the type of model described in this section:

1. First, it seems to us that the system of address is a useful tool for the description of spontaneous small-group interactions. This means that for the first time we have found a way — an extremely simple but effective way — of coding utterances in conversation, for example. The implications for language teaching — starved of reliable discursive descriptions of almost any kind — are most encouraging.
2. We are now in a position to check on a range of observations and suggestions coming from psychiatrists. For example, there has been considerable comment by psychiatrists about the fact that families under treatment seemed to show a high incidence of simultaneous talking and interruption. Our first experiments in coding — though admittedly not carried out on pathological cases — are again most encouraging, though I certainly do not want to claim that we can do more than accurately describe symptoms. There are also obvious applications to studies of group structure and group dynamics.
3. Since the rules for turn-taking and address clearly imply rights to the floor, the sociolinguist now has a useful tool for the description (possibly even the definition) of interactive roles and status — especially when we take into account the concepts of

speaker/listener/hearer which can be considerably refined in specific situations such as parent–child interaction or immigrants at work, or in the multi-racial classroom, etc. Chapter 2 includes an example of such a description. Other concepts such as 'formality' and 'situation' should also benefit.

1 You did say 'oral interactive discourse'?

H. Holec

Introduction

Discourse analysis is a relatively new discipline, so it is hardly surprising that the discussions to which it has given rise include ambiguities, inconsistencies and even contradictions, which are due partly to a lack of precision in the definition of some of the basic concepts and partly to the inadequacy of the analytical tools which are used. But though these 'imperfections' may be sources of potential confusion, the problems they pose enable us to clarify and extend the discipline, in other words to make progress.

One such problem concerns the notion of interaction as it is applied to the distinction between oral discourse and written discourse. For some analysts, of course, this notion is not relevant and they are satisfied to subcategorize discourse into oral discourse and written discourse and leave it at that: but this attitude is becoming increasingly rare. Among those who think that this dimension is relevant, there are some for whom only certain types of oral discourse are interactive:

> . . . the term 'interaction' is used to describe a direct communicative exchange (the direct communicative exchange being a particular type of oral communication). (Gremmo, Holec and Riley 1978)

For others, both written and oral forms are interactive:

> Those working in written discourse have tended to analyse it as monologue and to ignore the fact that as he reads it the reader interacts with the text and thus an interactive model might also be appropriate to a written discourse. (Coulthard 1977, p. 180)

Still others, like Widdowson, suggest that

> in written discourse . . . there is interactivity without interaction. (Widdowson 1977, p. 259)

Such differences of approach show clearly that the distinction between the terms '*interactive*' and '*non-interactive*' is far from having been fully elucidated and it is the aim of this paper to contribute to that elucidation.

Since it is probable that these differences are as much due to differing interpretations of the terms 'discourse', 'oral discourse' and 'written discourse' as they are to the lack of precision in the distinction between interactive discourse and non-interactive discourse, it will be necessary first to recall just what the aim of discourse analysis is. I will then go on to propose a definition, and one that I hope is both clear and precise, of what is meant by oral discourse and written discourse. Finally, some examples will be taken for discussion which seem to throw light on the problem of interactive discourse.

Discourse

The first source of confusion which must be briefly considered, and which may largely explain why the notion of interaction is not universally regarded as relevant, is to be found in the definition of the very object of analysis, discourse. There are three types of ambiguity here:

'Discourse' is sometimes used as an equivalent of de Saussure's *parole* to refer to all the realizations of the underlying *langue*: in this sense, the object of analysis consists of all the utterances which speakers in fact produce, utterances which are then considered in terms of their relationship to *langue* (for example, the relationships between *langue* and oral discourse, or the relationships between *langue* and written discourse).

'Discourse' is also used to refer to the object of analysis of what British and American linguists call 'suprasentential linguistics' (Householder 1972); from this point of view, discourse is any series of utterances which are not simply juxtaposed, but which form part of a higher structure, being linked by semantic cohesion (whether this cohesion is realized grammatically, lexically, non-verbally, etc.).

'Discourse' is also used in a wider sense by linguists who try to analyse the communicative functions of language, such as Widdowson (1977), Sinclair and Coulthard (1975); here it is used to refer to the entity consisting of the text (verbal and non-verbal messages) and of the circumstances in which the text is produced and interpreted (who is the speaker, whom is he addressing, what is his communicative aim, etc.). For instance, a printed notice saying 'No Smoking' on the wall of a theatre is an example of discourse, but the same message, put away in a drawer, would be merely a text. From this point of view, then, the object of analysis is the text-in-situation (or the message in context and in situation) and the aim of the analysis would be, for example, to identify and describe the relationships between a text and the circumstances in which it is produced, or to define the structures of texts containing several messages.

In this third approach extra-textual parameters are also taken into account: indeed, the text is regarded as the product, realized verbally or non-verbally, of the psychological and sociological constraints and conventions which enter into a given situation. It is this approach alone that includes the idea of 'interaction', describing the collaborative production of a text by several different speakers. This, then, is the approach which will be adopted in what follows, the term 'discourse' being used to designate the verbal and non-verbal text used by an actor to address his interlocutor for communicative purposes.

Oral and written discourse

A second source of confusion is due to the lack of clarity in the distinction between oral discourse and written discourse: this can be seen when we talk about a written transcription of oral discourse as still being oral discourse, or when we say that a written text read aloud is still fundamentally a written text. This shows, at least, that the way we subcategorize discourse intuitively is not based on the differences between the various communicative channels. However, the distinction is not easy to make with precision.

It is not possible to define the distinction in question by taking actual examples of the two types and by describing those features which are characteristic of Type A and those which are characteristic of Type B, to avoid the terms 'oral' and 'written' for the moment. This impossibility arises because of one of the two following reasons:

Either the characteristics described in this way are not sufficiently precise for the distinction to be applied with any satisfactory degree of rigour or in any consistent fashion: this is the consequence of faulty methodology, since we start by intuitively separating the various examples of discourse into the two main sub-categories which it is our very purpose to describe, so that when we do later get round to describing them we run the serious risk of attributing significance to features which are not necessarily exclusive to one of the two types. For example, it may be found that a given formal feature occurs in all the texts of discourse type A and is therefore regarded as specific to that type, whereas in fact it cannot be proved that it can never be found in examples of discourse type B: what is improbable has been confused with what is impossible.

Or the simultaneous description of discourse along a number of different parameters gives us a cline where it is impossible to locate one and only one point where discourse type A can be separated from discourse type B.

The description of particular examples of discourse is not, therefore, especially helpful.

In the same way, psycholinguistic analyses of the differences between the encoding and decoding processes, although very illuminating as regards the ways in which texts of the two discourse types are produced and interpreted, do not, as things stand, provide an adequate basis on which to establish the distinction.

An examination of the differences between discourse type A and discourse type B in terms of 'why' rather than 'how' would seem to be a more rewarding line of investigation, in that it allows us to consider discourse as a *process* rather than as a *product*. We believe then that the distinction between type A and type B can be made acceptably explicit by analysing the conditions in which the discourse is produced.

If we take into consideration both the dynamic dimension of the production of discourse (a product being made) and the static dimension of its realization (a finished product), it is in fact possible to distinguish two types of discourse:

1. There is one type of discourse whose finished product, the text (a set of verbal and non-verbal messages), is constructed in real time and whose production cannot be dissociated from the linear passage of time. The structure of the text and the production of the text proceed 'abreast', concomitantly and in real time so that for every 'after' in production there is a corresponding 'after' in the text, the production of the text being continuous and irreversible: in this type of discourse, the text has an internal temporal structure.
2. In the second type of discourse, the structure of the text is not directly associated with the temporal linearity of the process of production: dissociated in time from the process of construction, the text proceeds parallel to it, but not abreast of it nor in real time, so that a 'before' in the text may correspond to an 'after' in the process of construction: in this case, the production of the text is therefore non-continuous and reversible and the text has no internal temporal structure.

In order to understand this fundamental difference between the texts in these two types of discourse, it may be helpful to compare them to pictures being drawn on two strips of paper: in one case, the strip would unwind continuously, while in the second, it would be possible to control the movement (to slow it down, stop it, to rewind, to start again, and so on). The pictures on the first strip would have an internal dynamic structure which would remain even if the strip was later unwound and read.

The presence or absence of internal temporal structure has many different effects on texts. For example, to mention only one of these effects — one which is extremely important but which has never been studied systematically — texts in the first type of discourse reflect the limits of human capacities for memorizing, anticipating, organizing, etc., in real time, which is obviously not the case in discourse of the second type: consequently, the content of texts of the first type tends to be organized gradually as the discourse proceeds — very often on the basis of chronological development — with frequent repetition, switching back, etc., and the longer the text, the more noticeable all this is.

Texts of the first type are usually, but not necessarily, realized acoustically as regards their verbal component and visually as regards their non-verbal component. When this is the case, we find, in addition to the characteristics related to their temporal structure, characteristics which derive from the ephemeral nature of acoustic and visual signals. For example, the limitations on human capacities mentioned above are made even tighter in this way.

Similarly, texts of the second type are usually but not necessarily realized graphically (by some lasting visual signals). One of the effects of this is an increase in the number of ways in which the text can be controlled. In addition to the freedom from temporal constraints there is the fact that the material realization is spatial in nature (which makes it possible, for example, to begin the realization of the text by the end as well as by the middle or the beginning). It is the spatial nature of such texts which explains the use (in meta-discursive comments on the structure of an argument) of spatial expressions such as 'above', 'below', 'in the pages which follow', etc. In texts of the first type the internal temporal structure results in the use of temporal expressions 'As I may show later on', 'As I was just saying . . .', 'I will go into this when we come to . . .'

Consequently, to use the term 'oral' to refer to the first type of discourse and the term 'written' to refer to the second is neither arbitrary nor incorrect, but simply insufficiently explicit to prevent ambiguity and misunderstanding. Since it is not possible simply to do away with such widely-used terminology, we will have to be satisfied with underlining the fact that by 'oral discourse' we mean discourse whose text is constructed in real time, and by written discourse we mean discourse whose text is not subject to this constraint. Obviously, it is also possible to distinguish between subcategories of oral or written discourse according to the type of situation (face-to-face/at a distance, 'live'/recorded transmission) or to the register (literary/scientific, academic/non-academic) and so on.

Interactive discourse/non-interactive discourse

Interaction

The notion of interaction would be of little use as the basis for a descriptive category if all it meant was that discourse is a phenomenon involving two or more participants influencing one another: if this were the case all discourse would be interactive by definition, as indeed would painting, sculpture, music and so on.

Nor can the notion of interaction be limited to the fact that one of the participants, the speaker, takes into account the presence of other participant(s), his interlocutor(s), either in the sense that he is guided by feedback or by his own construing of the situation: if such were the case, all discourse would be interactive and the most one would be able to do would be to analyse degrees of difference along the same parameter (type and/or degree of interaction); in any case, there would no longer be grounds for the distinction between interactive and non-interactive.

A definition of interaction, if it is to be used in discourse analysis, should be based on an analysis of the types of role played by participants.

In certain cases, the discourse is the mutual responsibility of all the participants, each contributing in turn to its realization and collaborating with the other participants to produce a coherent series of contributions (for further details on the way in which this alternation is carried out see Gremmo, Holec and Riley 1978, and Riley, this vol. pp. 50–2). This means that each participant constructs and realizes only part of the text, contributing a number of fragments in alternation with the other participants; the stretches of discourse which are realized by these fragments of text are usually, though perhaps incorrectly, called 'speaking turns'.

In other cases, a single participant is responsible for the whole of the discourse.

In the first case, we are dealing with interactive discourse; in the second, non-interactive discourse.

> By interactive discourse, we mean discourse which is the collaborative construct of two or more participants mutually engaged in other-directed communicative behaviour. (Riley, this vol. p. 50)

The clarity of this distinction notwithstanding, the analysis of authentic discourse does throw up a number of problematic borderline cases. For instance, since the degree of participation varies from individual to individual, how are we to handle discourse involving a number of participants but in the realization of which — in terms of speaking turns — only two actually take part: is such discourse less interactive than a discourse in which all present share the task? And what about the type of discourse which involves two participants but to which one participant makes only a single contribution, as is the case in certain interviews where the interviewer sets the ball rolling with a question and then makes no other contribution other than a brief expression of thanks at the very end? And does it make any difference if this contribution is very long — or very short? At a more general level, is it possible to talk in terms of degrees of interaction, non-interaction being just an extreme point on the scale? Only by analysing numerous examples of authentic discourse can we hope to answer these questions. The distinction between interactive and non-interactive as it has been defined above is important, even crucial in some ways, in the analysis and description of discourse, and it is this distinction which we are going to refine by applying it to both oral and written discourse: can both these types of discourse be both interactive and non interactive?

Oral, non-interactive discourse

There is no need to show that oral discourse can be interactive; the majority of oral discourses *are*, which is hardly surprising since this type of discourse is usually realized in face-to-face communicative situations which, for psychosocial reasons, generally require the interactive participation of all present (at least in Western cultures). In certain situations, however, the oral discourse which is produced is non-interactive: an example would be a political speech or a lecture.

As an example, then, let us take the following passage, translated from a lecture:

> This time erm we're again going to be working on a corpus er . . . a corpus which has to be worked out . . . and we've got both a prose and an unseen . . . This time it's Turkish . . . erm . . . For the prose and the unseen don't . . . don't go looking things up, right, do it on your own . . .

> without a grammar, without . . . because you can always find some . . . some people of Turkish nationality in this area of course . . . so do it on your own, eh? It's for your . . . if you do it on your own it's much better training for you, right, rather than . . . looking things up or getting someone to tell you the answers . . . So work as if you . . . er, if you already know some Turkish of course there'll be things you won't have to guess at or discover for yourselves . . . I'm going to give you the . . . that, that's the beginning (distributes stencilled copies of the texts).

There is no doubt as to whether this is oral discourse or not; the text is being constructed in the here-and-now along with the discourse; it is also non-interactive, since the teacher was the only participant to take the floor during this extract (and during the three-quarters of an hour which followed it — the last 15 minutes of these lectures being regularly given over to a discussion separated from the lecture by a long pause).

The differences between a text like this and a text from a written non-interactive discourse on the same subject (e.g., a lesson in a text-book on linguistics or a chapter in an introduction to descriptive linguistics) are so obvious that there is no need to enter into further detail here, except, perhaps, to note that this extract is essentially a recommendation to the students to do the exercises without outside help and that this would probably have been omitted in written discourse, or would appear in a general introductory chapter on working methods.

To illustrate more clearly these differences between oral non-interactive discourse and written non-interactive discourse, let us consider the two examples reproduced below. The first is an extract from a didactic discourse, showing how to use a video-cassette recorder, which we will regard as non-interactive, since it has all the relevant characteristics (this example is taken from Hutchinson 1978, p. 15); the second is an extract from the instructions for use booklet provided by the manufacturer.

EXAMPLE 1

> First of all, of course, we must put the cassette of tape into the machine. Well on the machine the first button here is labelled EJECT and this means that it ejects the cassette in its holder here. We press this button we see the cassette holder comes up out of the machine and this now enables us to put the cassette into the machine. We take the cassette with the label uppermost and simply feed it into the slot which is so exposed. We push the lid down firmly, make sure it goes right down and the cassette is now ready to play.

Hutchinson describes the lesson from which this extract has been taken as having in fact been recorded in the absence of any students: '. . . played direct to the camera with only film crew as audience' (p. 5), which further confirms the belief that it is non-interactive discourse. It should also be noted that the transcription has been considerably 'cleaned up' or 'idealized'.

EXAMPLE 2 (extract from the instructions for use: FIGURE 1)

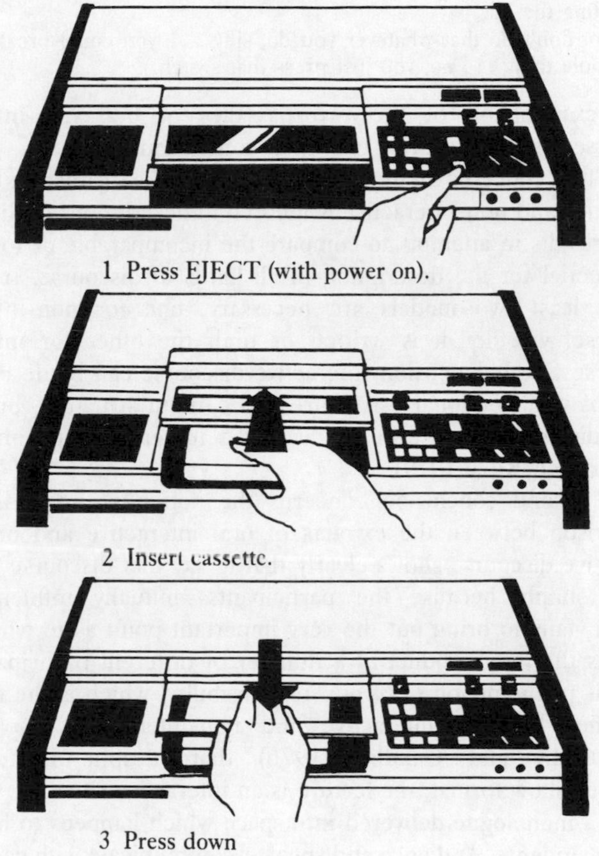

1 Press EJECT (with power on).
2 Insert cassette.
3 Press down

FIGURE 1

Finally, let us consider a third example, this time an extract from an oral interactive discourse on the same subject, which can be rendered in English as follows:

EXAMPLE 3

C: Show me how that works, will you?
A: What . . . that, the video recorder?
C: Yes, I can't remember how you put the cassette in (laugh).
A: Oh, that's not difficult, er, the cassette goes in there, er, in this compartment.
C: Yes, I know that, but how do you open it?
A: Well, you press that switch . . . the one where it says EJECT, there . . . you see, it opens by itself, it's simple.
C: Oh, right . . . I was trying to open it like this (laugh) . . . pulling . . . lifting the lid.
A: No, don't do that whatever you do, silly . . . you could break the whole thing . . . no, you just press that switch.

An examination of the two passages of oral non-interactive discourse leads us to draw two main conclusions:

The first concerns methodology: very often the distinction between interactive and non-interactive is ignored in descriptions of discourse, which results in attempts to compare the incomparable or to use the same model for the description of all kinds of discourse. It is clear that at least two models are necessary, one for non-interactive discourse, whether it is written or oral, the other for interactive discourse (see below); non-interactive discourse can be described in terms of its illocutionary structure and content structure, but interactive discourse must also be described in terms of its interactive structure (cf. Riley 1979).

The second conclusion concerns the notion of interaction: the comparison between the extracts of oral interactive and oral non-interactive discourse shows clearly that to say that discourse is interactive, simply because the participants mutually influence one another, fails to bring out the very important point as to whether or not it is the joint product of a number of different participants and it is this phenomenon of 'group responsibility' which is the essential difference between interactive and non-interactive. To say, as do Murphy and Candlin (1976) that 'despite its apparent one-man-show format, the lecture is an interactive situation. It is not simply a monologue delivered into space which happens to be occupied by students. Audience and speaker communicate with each other through eye contact, gaze direction, facial expression, etc . . . ' (quoted and discussed in Hutchinson 1978, p. 5) emphasizes the point that face-to-face oral discourse (such as the type of lecture referred to here) has certain characteristics which are not to be found in discourse where the participants are separated by a greater distance, but it tells us nothing about the difference between a lecture and a discussion.

Written interactive discourse

Just as oral discourse can be non-interactive, written discourse can be interactive. Reproduced below is an example, consisting of an exchange of letters between the organizers of a colloquium and one of the participants.

M. H. Holec 11th January 1979
CRAPEL
Université de Nancy II
23 Boulevard Albert 1er
54000 Nancy

Dear Henri,

I am writing to invite you to participate in an Applied Linguistics Colloquium to be held at the University of Berne from the evening of Wednesday 30th May to midday on Saturday 2nd June 1979 . . . the invited participants will present a paper at the Colloquium and agree to its being published in the proceedings.

Previous years have shown that it is an advantage to have papers bear on a particular theme; and this year we would like this theme to be discourse analysis and its application to language teaching.

If you would like to accept this invitation to attend I would be grateful if you could let me know very soon, and at the latest by 31 January 1979. Participants will be asked to let me have a copy of their papers by 12 March 1979 so that I can then arrange to have them duplicated and distributed to other members of the group well before the Colloquium takes place. There will, of course, be an opportunity to revise the papers in the light of discussion before they are submitted to press.

I look forward to hearing from you.

Yours,
H. G. Widdowson

Professor H. G. WIDDOWSON *Nancy*, *le* 25th January 1979
University of London *Le Directeur*
Institute of Education
Bedford Way
London, WC1H 0AL

Dear Henry,

Aren't I honoured and pleased at your invitation! Thank you mille fois, mon vieux.

I don't know much about language teaching and still less about discourse analysis, but this won't hamper my powerful cerebral machinery!

Looking forward (and upward!) to seeing you again.

Friendly-ly, Henri Holec

21st March 1979

Dear Colleague,

I wonder if I could remind you gently that I would like to receive a copy of your Berne paper as soon as possible so that it can be distributed before the Colloquium. So far I have only received 1 paper.

Best wishes.

Yours sincerely,

Professor H. G. Widdowson

Is this discourse interactive or non-interactive? Before we can answer this question, it is necessary to make clear exactly what we are talking about. Is each letter taken separately — in which case, we will have to reply that we are dealing with three different examples of non-interactive discourse? Or is it the set of three letters taken together — in which case our reply will be that we are dealing with a single, interactive discourse?

The analytical observations which follow show that everything points to the second being the case, these letters being three 'speaking turns' which form a whole.

1. AT THE LEVEL OF THE INTERACTIVE STRUCTURE

a) At the beginning of the exchange an interactive pair consisting of 'speaker' and 'addressee' is set up; the speaker selects himself and appoints his addressee. (Realizations include the name and address of the recipient at the top on the left, and the opening 'Dear Henri'.)
b) The addressee appointed replies to the speaker (the name and address at the top on the left; 'Dear Henry').
c) The third letter opens a new exchange, since the addressee is no longer just the Henri of the first letter but all the participants in the Colloquium who have failed to send in their articles.

The discourse is, therefore, interactively coherent (cf. Riley, this vol. p. 60).

2. AT THE LEVEL OF ILLOCUTIONARY STRUCTURE

a) The first letter includes, among other things, an invitation and two requests.
b) The second includes, among other things, an acceptance of the invitation and complies with one of the two requests (it is dated before the deadline stipulated in the first request).
c) The third letter includes, among other things, a repetition of the request which has not yet been complied with.

Therefore, despite extreme variations in the modalization of the illocutionary acts (formal/informal), the discourse is also coherent from the illocutionary point of view.

3. AT THE LEVEL OF CONTENT.

a) The invitation included in the first letter is an invitation to a particular colloquium, bearing on a particular topic.
b) The acceptance in the second letter is an acceptance to attend this same colloquium (by implication) on the topic referred to (which is repeated indirectly in the acceptance).
c) The request in the third letter deals with the same matter as the request in the first letter, the venue and date of the colloquium being repeated.

Therefore, at the level of content, the three turns are also coherent.

It is, then, the whole formed by the three letters which should be considered, and this is an interactive discourse containing three 'speaking turns'.

Of course, there are many differences between written interactive discourse and spoken interactive discourse, due both to the non-temporal nature of written text and to the communicative uses to which it is generally put, such as communication at a distance, which results in the 'speaking turns' being spaced out in time, which further means that each turn has a certain independence (it is not possible to interrupt, for example, and there is a tendency to include as much information as possible in one single turn). Generally speaking, the ways in which interactive structure is realized are completely different, so that written interactive discourse is not just a written transposition of oral interactive discourse.

Nevertheless, these differences do not mean that the written form excludes any possibility of interaction, even if written discourse is not usually interactive (just as oral discourse is not usually non-interactive). As soon as a certain number of conditions are fulfilled, such as the triple coherence which has been described above to show that the three different letters are parts of the same whole, written discourse can be produced interactively. But it must be emphasized that all these conditions have to be satisfied and not just any one of them: for example, it is not interactive simply because, at the level of content, a reference is made to the content of another discourse, as is often the case in scientific articles, say, where other writers and other texts are quoted. This is not sufficient to make it a 'speaking turn' forming a coherent interactive whole with the quotation. Below is an example translated from the letters page of the *Nouvel Observateur*, which clearly brings out what does and what does not form part of an interactive written discourse:

The cost of foot-and-mouth disease

Anyone who dares to claim that it is farmers who are the least affected by foot-and-mouth disease, as does Fabien Gruber in his article 'Cloven-footed fever' (*Nouvel Observateur N° 754*) is just revealing his own ignorance of what agriculture really is . . . Breeders do receive compensation after an investigation but do you really imagine that the owner of a quality herd, selected over a period of 20 years, is going to find a herd of similar value on the market? Never. So he will have to start again from scratch. And this is without taking into consideration the psychological shock . . . Do you realise that between 1962 and 1978, the price of a 75 h.p. tractor quadrupled, whilst agricultural prices — whether for corn or pork or beef — hardly changed? And the same is true for all materials and equipment (fertiliser, fuel-oil, etc.). I won't mention salaries: a shepherd in this area earns the minimum legal wage, but he works more than 60 hours a week. The only thing that consoles me is that this refusal to face up to agricultural problems is as prevalent on the left as on the right. 'Agriculture is petrol' but no one gives a damn as long as it holds out. Just how long will that be?

Olivier Giraud
L'Isle–Jourdain

(*Obviously you have to 'start from scratch' to re-establish a herd. But in the meantime, in addition to a payment for slaughtered stock, the farmers concerned also receive compensation for loss of earnings. So they are not as hard-hit as the others, whose stock has not been slaughtered but who are still cut off from the market and to whom no compensation is available* — F. G.)

The letter from the reader, addressed to the author of an article which has prompted him to write, forms, together with the author's reaction, an interactive discourse. But the article in question does not form part of this discourse: it is simply a referent, in the same way as the general situation of cattle-breeders is, for example.

2 Interactional structure: the role of role

M–J. Gremmo, H. Holec and P. Riley

Ralph . . . lifted the shell on his knees and looked round the sun-slashed faces.
"There aren't any grown-ups. We shall have to look after ourselves."
The meeting hummed and was silent.
"And another thing. We can't have everybody talking at once. We'll have to have 'Hands up', like at school."
He held the conch before his face and glanced round the mouth.
"Then I'll give him the conch."
"Conch?"
"That's what this shell's called. I'll give the conch to the next person to speak. He can hold it when he's speaking."
"But —"
"Look —"
"And he won't be interrupted. Except by me."
Jack was on his feet.
"We'll have rules!" he cried excitedly. "Lots of rules! Then when anyone breaks 'em —"
"Whee-oh!"
"Wacco!"
"Bong!"
"Doink!"

From *The Lord of the Flies*, by William Golding.

Introduction

The concept of communicative competence which has become so influential in language teaching in recent years has resulted in a new emphasis being placed on the nature of interaction. Teachers and textbook writers now ask themselves questions concerning the communicative needs of their learners: what types of interaction will they participate in, what will their roles be, what kinds of communicative act will they wish to perform? Clearly, if we can predict the answers to these questions we will be in a position to make our teaching far more effective and efficient.

But before these very important practical problems can be tackled, we need to establish some kind of descriptive system. That is, before we can get down to specifying the particular communicative needs and objectives of a particular group of learners, we need some overall framework for the description of communicative interaction and of its various components. Once this general description has been carried out, we can apply it to the particular types of interaction in which learners will be required to participate.

This paper is a contribution to that general description (see also Holec 1973; Riley 1976) although, as we show in the sample passage we have taken for analysis, it is one that has immediate practical applications and implications for both the applied linguist and the classroom teacher.

Status and role

In any interaction, the identities of the participants impinge on one another in a variety of different ways — physically, psychologically, socially and linguistically. As this process is one of enormous complexity, social scientists have tried to define and isolate the relevant variables, partly for descriptive purposes, of course, but partly just to break the problem down into manageable chunks. Unfortunately, this compartmentalization, however necessary, has resulted in a polarization between the approaches of those disciplines (such as sociology, politics and economics) which focus on *social structure* and those (such as linguistics, psychology and ethology) which concentrate on *social behaviour*. Despite the existence of hybrid disciplines such as social psychology and sociolinguistics, there exists a considerable conceptual gap between the two extremes. In particular, those concepts which prove most valuable for describing social structures seldom seem to provide insights into the nature of interaction: indeed, such concepts and categories often do not even seem relevant to the description and understanding of interactive events. The reverse is also true: descriptions of interactive events carried out according to the procedures of, say, linguistics, very rarely provide the commentary on underlying social structures which the sociologist is looking for, being limited to a relatively superficial analysis of the communicative code (Cicourel 1973).

A crucial example of this dichotomy is to be found in the literature on *status* and *role*. No definitions of these terms which are acceptable to, say, the sociologist, have ever been found of use to students of interaction, and vice versa. So confusing have been the results of trying to impose the definitions of the one discipline on the objects of the other, that some researchers (e.g. Coulson 1972) have seriously questioned their scientific validity, despite their generally-accepted intuitive and operational availability.

This seems to us rather like throwing out the baby with the bath-water, and in this paper we try to suggest why such confusion has arisen and, more ambitiously, what sort of model of social interaction might satisfy both students of social structure *and* students of social behaviour. We hope that we have done so with the minimum amount of damage to sociological sensibilities, but we would like to make it clear that our own interests lie strictly in the realms of discourse analysis and interaction: so that even if our definitions are rejected by the sociologists, we would claim that they still retain considerable internal validity as descriptions of formally observable behaviours.

The wide variety of definitions of status and role to be found in sociological discussion prevents us from doing more than sketching the main outlines of the debate:

Status is usually defined as a social position, as part of a structure. Many observers see it essentially as a feature of social order. Status relates the individual to the wider community with which he or she comes in contact, usually through other structures such as those based on kinship or occupation. Compared to role, status is relatively stable and static, and it is more institutionalized. It is based on norms accepted by third parties and is therefore sometimes described as a collection of rights and duties.

Role is usually seen as more dynamic and consequently more fleeting than status. It operates over a narrower set of relations and is dependent on norms set and accepted by the participants themselves.

Many writers see the two terms as poles of an opposition between *most* and *least institutionalized*: indeed, for some, status is defined as 'that class of roles which is institutionalized' (Goode 1960). However, even such a definition, susceptible as it is to an interactive approach, has failed to give rise to an investigation of those behaviours which might be regarded as bringing about the institutionalization. Again, neither term, it has been noted, has given rise to a theory for describing behaviour which rests on the distinction between them.

Another problem over which much sociological ink has been spilt concerns the descriptive perspective: are status and role to be described from the *observer*'s or from the *actor*'s point of view? In other words, to what extent should the observer's retrospective conceptualizations reflect the actor's options at successive points in the interaction? Closely related to this is the problem of observer effect:

to what extent is the description distorted by the observer's own prejudices (based on cultural differences between himself and the actor, for example) concerning role and status?

Our attitude to these considerable theoretical problems is brutally pragmatic: since we hope that our work will eventually produce pedagogical spin-off, we opt firmly for an actor's view of interaction. A highly sophisticated theoretical model — no matter how much more exhaustive, elegant and powerful — is not nearly as valuable to us as one which takes advantage of the experiences and intuitions of the learner.

Role in interaction

It seems to us that the most promising point of departure for any investigator of interaction is the distinction which some writers draw between status as a collection or bundle of rights and duties (Banton 1965) and role as the enactment of those rights and duties. Though by no means universally accepted, this approach has a number of advantages, in particular its potential for distinguishing between, yet accommodating, both structuralist and interactional perspectives, by placing status firmly in the purlieus of the former and role in the domain of the latter.

Of course, this approach can only be regarded as valid if we do indeed succeed in describing role in terms of interactive rights and duties. To do so, we need a model of discourse and interaction which goes beyond a relatively superficial categorization of acts, which is able to link patterns of interactional behaviour with other aspects of social behaviour, and which is able to correlate *types of participation* (in terms of acts) with *types of participant* (in terms of social structures). This approach, then, is the reverse of the 'sociological' approach, which tries to impose categories of social structure onto behaviour: rather, we set up categories of behaviour in their own right. Sometimes (though by no means always) our categories will be entirely congruent with those of the sociologist: when this happens, all well and good, but in general the correspondences between categories of social structure and categories of social behaviour provide insights into both sets of phenomena without conflating them.

It is for these reasons that we distinguish clearly between the sociological concept 'status' and the socio*linguistic* and interactional concept 'role'. Status lacks that dynamic and diachronic dimension which is necessary for relevance to interaction, although, along with other features of identity such as office and personality, it may be regarded as one of the parameters of role. Unfortunately, both in the technical literature on the subject and in everyday language, the two are often confused.

For us, then, role is to be understood and described as the enactment of privileges and duties, which may be either linguistic or non-linguistic. Non-linguistic privileges include, for example, the right of a barman to pour the drinks in a pub: perhaps regrettably, the customer cannot simply help himself. Again, a policeman has the non-linguistic right to arrest people. Such non-linguistic rights are usually correlated with *office*, another parameter of role.

Linguistic privileges and rights, on the other hand, are to be understood and described as being enacted in discourse: they are rights which are realized by various types of linguistic act. It goes without saying that the only way of isolating these linguistic acts is through the analysis of communicative interaction, since there is no one-to-one relationship between units of interaction and units of social structure.

Parameters of social identity: office, status and role

Before proceeding to investigate the types of linguistic act which realize role, let us summarize and exemplify the set of distinctions we have drawn: these concern the three parameters of *social identity* which have been labelled office, status and role:

By *office*, we mean that class of positions in the social structure which is usually ascribed by appointment, attainment or professional qualification.

Status is a more general term for a position in the social structure which is defined by a number of parameters of which office (although often the most important) is only one; others may include such things as wealth, personality and religion.

Role is the enactment of interactional privileges and duties which are realized by certain types of act. In very general terms, these acts fall into two main categories: *illocutionary* or communicative acts (Austin 1971; Holec 1973; Searle 1969) and *interactive* or discursive acts. Illocutionary acts include persuading, forbidding, agreeing, inviting and so on. Interactive acts include taking and giving the floor, interrupting, opening/replying/closing in an exchange, and so on. (n.b., although both illocutionary acts and interactive acts are clearly equally important as realizations of role privileges, in this paper we will focus almost exclusively on the interactive acts.)

It is clearly essential to distinguish role from *participant*, even though a role can only be enacted by a participant. A given role *may* depend on 'outside' parameters such as status, office, personality and religion; but a banker may or may not be taciturn, or a generally respected member of the community may or may not be talkative, so that their interactive roles cannot be automatically deduced from either office or status.

As an example, let us take three labels which are used indiscriminately for office or status or role: 'doctor', 'priest', and 'teacher'. Their offices are conferred by virtue of their possessing the recognized qualifications. Their status in society will usually be consistently linked with their office, but will also be subject to the influence of a number of other factors, which may be religious or economic, for example, but which may also relate to such factors as their perceived professional standing: a village G.P. and a Harley Street specialist may have an identical office, but they most certainly do not have identical status.

Again, similar status may be ascribed to the doctor, a faith-healer, a herbalist and a pharmacist, and there is the important point that we often talk about the doctor, the teacher and the priest in a village having 'the same status', which clearly shows a use of the term which is separable from office.

When the doctor, the priest and the teacher perform those acts which are usually only performed by people holding a certain office — removing appendices, marrying people, marking examination papers — it is very easy to conflate or confuse office, status and role, since there is a close 'downwards' congruence or overlapping between the three categories. Yet it is not difficult, even with such seemingly clear-cut examples, to find aspects of role which are shared by all three, and which therefore cannot be said to be distinguishing characteristics of office or status: they are role-behaviours and it is in these terms that roles should be categorized.

For example, all three might clearly indicate that an interaction (a consultation, let us say) is closed by saying, 'Right, well that's all for now, but mind you follow my advice'. It is their discursive privilege to terminate such encounters which interests us here, since it shows that a role-behaviour may be common to several statuses and offices. Unless we describe role-behaviour in its own terms, we fail to account for these important distinctions.

One sub-class of offices merits special mention: certain offices, instead of conferring the right to perform non-linguistic acts, like arresting, confer the right to perform a certain class of linguistic acts. In some cases, these are the *performatives* discussed by Austin (1962), but at least as often they are acts of *discourse control.* Such an office is held by the Speaker of the House of Commons, who has the right to declare sittings open and closed, to nominate speakers and to limit their speaking turns and the lengths of their speeches. The quotation from *The Lord of the Flies* which precedes this discussion is a perceptive comment on the operation of such an institution, where rights of address are given an objective correlative in the conch shell.

Since the negotiation for discourse control is, in varying degrees, a feature of a wide range of types of interaction (e.g. TV interviews, the language of the classroom, argument), it is only in those cases where the institutional authority is recognized by all participants that we can say for certain that we are dealing with rights and privileges conferred directly by office. It is typical of such offices that they are highly formalized and their privileges are usually strictly codified. Where this is not the case, the only reliable solution is to observe the actual discourse behaviour and to derive our categories from the data.

Categories of linguistic act: realizations of role

As we saw earlier, linguistic acts fall into two main categories: illocutionary (or communicative or speech) acts, and interactive (or discursive) acts. In very general terms, illocutionary acts can be regarded as a reflection of the actor's intention in performing that particular act: inviting, refusing, agreeing, etc. Sequences of illocutionary acts give us illocutionary structure, and, as we shall see, the distribution of such acts between different types of participant provides considerable insights into the nature of role. For the moment, let us simply emphasize the fact that the roles implied by illocutionary acts, such as *commanding*, are illocutionary roles, such as *commander.* They are not directly related to either status or office, though there may be extremely interesting correlations. They may, on the other hand, be directly related to participant: by stating the repertoire of a given participant's illocutionary acts in a given interaction, we are describing an important constituent of role in that interaction.

By interactional (or 'discursive') acts we mean those acts which realize and impose the interactive structure of the discourse. Fundamentally the interactive structure is to be understood and described in terms of who speaks to whom and when; that is, in terms of turns and their relative distribution. Basically, a turn is communicative behaviour which enters into the structure of the discourse. If a participant's contribution is unheard or deliberately ignored, it is not a turn. Turns may be realized both verbally and non-verbally: a nod of the head or the utterance 'yes' can both realize a turn.

In those types of interaction which we have been studying, turns fall into three main categories: *opening* (O), *replying* (R) and *closing* (C). This sub-categorization of turn is based on the concept of *address*: by address we mean that a speaker selects another participant or participants and imposes on him/them the right/duty to reply. Address may be realized verbally or non-verbally (Riley 1976); in small-group interaction it is almost exclusively non-verbal, being realized by eye-contact, gesture and orientation. An *opening* turn (O) is one in which a *speaker* (S) imposes on one or more other participants the right/duty to reply: they are the speaker's *addressees* (A). When the addressee avails himself of his right, his turn is a *reply* (R) (the addressee of an R-turn being, by definition, the speaker of the previous turn). An O followed by an R gives us the minimum unit of interaction, the *exchange*.

Once an exchange is completed, the speaker (i.e. the producer of the O turn) can either initiate a new exchange with the same participant, or he can change address (i.e. select a new addressee), or he can perform a closing turn, one in which no duty to reply is imposed. Change of address and closing both mark the boundary of the next-higher unit of interaction, the *transaction*, which therefore has the structure O, $R_{(1....n)}$ C

When we talk about discourse rights and privileges, then, we are referring in particular to the rights to perform Os, Rs and Cs, to the right to address and to the right to *interrupt*. These rights vary considerably from interaction to interaction and from participant to participant: by stating the repertoire of a given participant's interactive acts, that is the types of turns he performs, we are describing a second important constituent of his role.

Role in interaction: an example

As an example of this approach to the description and definition of role, let us take a brief passage for analysis. The passage in question, which is authentic, is an extract from a lesson being given by a teacher of French to a group of immigrant workers. The demands we make on our analysis and our model are stiff ones: can we, by describing the discourse, make generalizations about the teacher's role and the students' roles in this type of interaction?

In this passage, the teacher was preparing a dialogue with his group: this target discourse was:

Tiens, bonjour Bashir.
Bonjour Iovan.

(Bashir and Iovan are names of characters in the text book.)

Turn 1.	TEACHER:	Right then? I'm starting now. 'Tiens, bonjour Bashir.' You are Iovan, Ali.
Turn 2.	STUDENT 1:	'Tiens, bonjour Bashir.'
Turn 3/4.	TEACHER:	Very good. Now Bashir says to Iovan 'Bonjour Iovan'. You are Bashir.
Turn 5.	STUDENT 2:	'Bonjour, tiens bonjour Iovan.'
Turn 6.	TEACHER:	He doesn't say 'tiens', it's Iovan who says 'tiens, bonjour Bashir'. Now Bashir simply says 'bonjour'.
Turn 7.	STUDENT 2:	'Bonjour'.
Turn 8.	TEACHER:	What's his name?
Turn 9.	STUDENT 3:	Iovan.
Turn 10.	TEACHER:	(Gesture to student 2 to try again)
Turn 11.	STUDENT 2:	'Bonjour Iovan.'
Turn 12/13.	TEACHER:	Very good. Right, you're Iovan and you're Bashir. Carry on.
Turn 14.	STUDENT 4:	'Tiens, bonjour Bashir.'
Turn 15.	TEACHER:	Bashir.
Turn 16.	STUDENT 5:	'Bonjour Iovan'.
Turn 17.	TEACHER:	Very good.

Illocutionary structure

Turn 1. Framing — Performative — Modelling
Right then? I'm starting now. 'Tiens, bonjour Bashir.'

Nominating
You are Iovan, Ali.

Turn 2. Practising
'Tiens, bonjour Bashir.'

Turn 3. Evaluating
Very good.

Turn 4. Modelling — Nominating
Now Bashir says to Iovan 'Bonjour Iovan'. You are Bashir.

Turn 5. Practising
'Bonjour, tiens bonjour Iovan.'

Turn 6. Correcting
He doesn't say 'tiens', it's Iovan who says 'tiens, bonjour Bashir'. Now Bashir simply says 'bonjour'.

Turn 7. Practising
'Bonjour'.

Turn 8. Correcting
What's his name?

Turn 9. Informing
Iovan.

Turn 10. Nominating
(non-verbal communication: address and gesture)

Turn 11. Practising
'Bonjour Iovan.'

Turn 12. Evaluating
Very good.

Turn 13. Nominating / Directing
Right, you're Iovan and you're Bashir. Carry on.

Turn 14. Practising
'Tiens, bonjour Bashir.'

Turn 15. Nominating
Bashir.

Turn 16. Practising
'Bonjour Iovan.'

Turn 17. Evaluating
Very good.

Before proceeding with our analysis, we would like to make two points:

1. For the sake of argument, we ask the reader to accept the fiction that it is possible to make valid generalizations on the basis of such a small corpus.
2. We are well aware of the inadequacy of the labels we have used for the illocutionary acts; only after far more analyses of this type have been carried out will we have a more reliable taxonomy, and even then operational consistency (i.e. different observers using the same labels for the same acts) will probably be the most we can hope for, since our present state of knowledge does not allow of a rigorous definition of such acts. Our ignorance of the hierarchical ordering of illocutionary values is an especially serious handicap: in the passage in question, for example, should 'evaluating' and 'correcting' be related to some macro-function such as 'judging'? Or is 'nominating' more closely related to 'performing' (specifying an addressee) or to 'directing'?

Turning to the illocutionary structure of this passage as shown in our suggested analysis, we are struck first by the preponderance of teacher acts. Note that this is not the same thing as teacher-*talk*,

TABLE 1 Interactional structure

Participant / *Turn*	1	2	3	4	5	6	7	8	9	10	11	12	13	14	15	16	17
Teacher	S	A	S	S	A	S	A	S	A	S	A	S	S	A	S	A	S
Student 1	A	S	H	H	H	H	H	H	H	H	H	H	H	H	H	H	H
Student 2	H	H	H	A	S	A	S	H	H	A	S	H	H	H	H	H	H
Student 3	H	H	H	H	H	H	H	A	S	H	H	H	H	H	H	H	H
Student 4	H	H	H	H	H	H	H	H	H	H	H	H	A	S	H	H	H
Student 5	H	H	H	H	H	H	H	H	H	H	H	H	A	H	A	S	H
	O	R	C	O	R	O	R	O	R	O	R	C	O	R	O	R	C

Exchange (turns 1–2) — Transaction (turns 1–3)
Exchange Exchange Exchange Exchange (turns 4–11) — Transaction (turns 4–12)
Exchange Exchange (turns 13–16) — Transaction (turns 13–17)

Legend: S = speaker A = addressee H = hearer
O = opening (a speaker turn in which a participant is addressed, i.e. the duty to reply is imposed on him)
R = reply
C = closing (a speaker turn performed by the same participant as the opening, but in which no duty to reply is imposed)

which has always been measured in purely quantitative, chronological terms. The realizations of acts may be of very different lengths (compare 6 and 8, for example). Nonetheless, the ratio of teacher acts to student acts in this passage is exactly the same as that generally given for teacher talk to student talk, i.e. 2 to 1: of the 22 acts in this passage, 15 are performed by the teacher, 7 by the students. If we look at the passage in terms of types of act, we see that the teacher performs seven different types (framing, performing, modelling (2×), nominating (5×), evaluating (3×), correcting (2×) and directing), whereas the students perform only two types of act (practising (6×) and informing).

As can be clearly seen, almost all the teacher acts involve some form of control over the learner's behaviour. The importance of this aspect of role is underlined by the fact that *none* of the types of act performed in this passage are common to both teacher and student. Nothing could be a clearer example of role as the right to perform acts. The reader is invited to test this against his or her own experience: it is just unimaginable that in a traditional class such as this, one of the students should start evaluating or correcting, or indeed performing any of the acts performed here by the teacher. He simply would not have the right: it is not his role.

When we examine the interactional structure of this passage (Table 1) we are immediately struck by the teacher's degree of discourse control. This is directly related to his right of address; he and he alone can select speakers. The students cannot initiate an exchange, they have to wait until they are addressed; their right to interrupt is correspondingly non-existent. They have extremely limited rights of address. They cannot even address one another; they can only address the teacher. Consequently, only he can produce opening and closing turns. One consequence of this is his centrality: since all the discourse must go via the teacher, his share will be far greater than that of the students. All decisions concerning the activity are in his hands — when to begin and end a new phase of some kind, selection of participants, specification of their participation. The teacher's task of classroom management is clearly reflected in his task of discourse management. The most direct form of role-challenge possible in this situation would be to try to wrest the control of the discourse away from the teacher, which explains why teachers have traditionally been so opposed to talking in class. Of course, role is relationship. The norms on which the behaviour we have been studying rests have to be accepted by all participants. The roles of teacher and student, that is, are mutually defining because, we would claim, they are defined by and in interaction.

3 When communication breaks down; levels of coherence in discourse

P. Riley

Introduction

As the movement towards 'communicative' teaching grows, it becomes more and more common for language teachers to say 'I only correct (interrupt, etc.) when communication breaks down'. This reaction against the incessant nit-picking which characterizes so much teaching is a healthy one: at least it encourages the learner to try to speak, rather than penalizing him every time he opens his mouth. But it also glosses over a very real and important problem: how do we *know* when communication has broken down?

The classroom teacher's answer to this question is usually a simple one : 'Communication has broken down when I do not understand what the learner is trying to say.'

Now this is a good rule-of-thumb — but it has no diagnostic or remedial value whatsoever. Moreover, it imposes the sort of either/or decision — a particular attempt at communication is judged to be either a complete success or a complete failure — of which case-hardened applied linguists tend to be very suspicious. They prefer to deal with clines, with degrees of difference, rather than with black and white opposed categories.

This is particularly true for the linguist who looks back at the dossier on grammaticality, and who sees the way in which early attempts to build up a case of unacceptability against certain doubtful sentences were outwitted by fast-talking semanticists, and alibis were found for suspicious constructions. Once bitten, twice shy: this time we'll start by taking a more flexible line by talking in terms of degrees of . . .

Of what? As Malcolm Coulthard (1978) has pointed out, in the description of oral face-to-face interaction, there seems to be no discourse equivalent of the concept of grammaticality: 'a next speaker always has the option of producing an *un*related utterance'. This might well seem to be discouraging to linguists whose aim is to describe the relationships holding between utterances (or, rather, between communicative acts). If anything goes, what is the point of trying to establish neat little Newtonian models? What are the rules of anarchy?

> A: What is your name?
> B: Well, let's say you might have thought you had something from before, but you haven't got it any more.

This example of schizophrenic's talk (from Labov 1970; also cited by Coulthard 1977), has become the *locus classicus* for the problem of appropriateness. But whereas it is usually taken to exemplify discourse in which communication has completely broken down, it will be argued here that the very fact that B made a contribution to and took a turn in the discourse shows that this is not the case: however attenuated, some form of communication has taken place. And then, at the opposite extreme, there is the very real sense in which *all* dyadic discourse is schizophrenic — it is the product of two personalities, however well they succeed in communicating.

What we need, then, is some way of describing degrees of 'discoursality'. This paper is a very tentative step in that direction. It argues that if we distinguish between *interaction, illocution, content* and *realization* (a similar distinction is made in Widdowson 1977) we can show that a given communicative act may be acceptable discourse at one or more of those levels but not at another or others. By pinpointing why and how an 'utterance' is unacceptable, the degree to which it is deviant, the linguist is once again back in business as a discourse analyst, since he is now able — he hopes — to establish a model which can give a chain-exhaustive account of discourse as a series of *relatively* related utterances.

This does not mean, though, that he can claim to be describing all the factors which enter into the structuring of discourse: the psychology and motivations of participants in an interaction will remain outside his competence, as will their social roles. Although his observations may shed an indirect and interesting light on such factors when they have linguistic correlates — by drawing certain distinctions (e.g. that between linguistic and social roles) or by providing descriptive tools (see pp. 42–6) — the linguist restricts himself to those aspects of the structure of observable communicative behaviour which can be shown to be rule-governed. In other words, a model for the description of discourse is not an overall theory of communicative behaviour, nor is it a theory of either communication or behaviour: it is an attempt to account for discourse, i.e. the linguistic aspects of interaction. This may mean the linguist casting his net much wider than he has previously done, to include non-verbal behaviours, for example, (Riley 1976) but this does not alter the fact that such a demarcation line has to be drawn somewhere. Here we will concentrate on two fundamental distinctions: between interactive and non-interactive discourse, and between interaction and illocution.

A second aim of this paper is to show that work at present being carried out in discourse analysis is relevant to language teaching in an immediate, fundamental and detailed way. As the boundaries of linguistic science have grown wider still and wider, giving rise to a large number of hybrid applications — sociolinguistics, neurolinguistics, psycholinguistics — and to exciting developments in fields as disparate as philosophy, language acquisition and semiotics, the language teacher tends to feel that applied linguistics is very interesting and all that, but hardly relevant to his needs and interests. This is one of a number of papers based on the work of a C.R.A.P.E.L. research team consisting of M–J. Gremmo, Henri Holec and the author in which we have investigated the pedagogical applications of discourse analysis. Earlier papers have considered applications of our own research to the evaluation of audio-visual teaching materials (Holec 1975), to problems in communicative language teaching (Riley 1977; Gremmo, Holec and Riley 1978), to the study of the teacher's role (see pp. 35–46) and to contrastive analysis (Riley 1979). Here we try to outline an approach to the description and understanding of communicative error or failure. Readers already familiar with the earlier work are asked to excuse a certain amount of repetition, but newcomers need to know the story so far.

1. Interactive versus non-interactive discourse

There is no generally accepted typology or taxonomy for discourse; so far, workers in the field have been kept busy enough simply identifying the relevant parameters and resources, a task which is still by no means complete. Among the oppositions and clines which have already been identified are: spontaneous/prepared; oral/written; formal/informal; authentic/non-authentic. It can be and has been shown that variations along any of these parameters will result directly in corresponding variations in the discourse type. In what follows we will be discussing *spontaneous, oral, authentic* discourse.

A further such opposition — but one which has been largely ignored until very recently — is interactive/non-interactive. By interactive discourse we mean discourse which is the collaborative construct of two or more participants mutually engaged in other-directed communicative behaviour. To put it more simply: is the discourse produced by one person or more than one? How many sources or contributors are there?

The defining characteristic of interaction, then, is *alternation*: whatever the relative length or frequency of individual contributions, verbal or non-verbal, there must be this 'floor-sharing' if contributions from more than one participant are to be integrated into the discourse. To be adequate, a description of discourse must account for alternation, for the rules governing the transition from speaker–state to hearer–state: this includes not just turn-taking, but rights to the floor, which is why descriptions based on the 'ideal speaker–hearer' necessarily lack a social and interactive dimension.

It should be noted that we are here using the term 'interaction' in a restricted sense, to refer to one particular aspect of communicative behaviour. By interaction, we mean the set of actions and reactions which are realized by *turns* ('taking the floor'), in other words the give-and-take which characterizes this particular category of oral communication. We are dealing here with *interactional tactics*: who speaks when and to whom; in other words, how the turns are distributed. We are not concerned for the moment with *what* participants say, only with the fact that it is, or is not, their turn to say it.

Participants regulate their interaction by *address*, that is, the transition in real time from one turn to another. The rules of address decide whose turn it is, and whose turn it will be next. The timing of turns is determined by the turn-taking signals (most of them non-verbal, particularly *key, orientation* and *gaze*) which are emitted by the participants (Kendon 1967; Duncan 1972).

When a participant makes the transition from one turn to another when (for example, he 'hands over the floor', or he 'takes his turn') he enacts an *interactive role* which can be described in terms of functions and acts. Interactive roles are not to be confused with social roles (see pp. 38–42): they define the nature of the individual's participation in a given minimal interactive structure, the *return*.

In very general terms, four such roles are available to participants:

1. The role of *speaker* (S), who initiates and closes the minimal unit of interactive structure , the *return*.
2. The role of *addressee* (A) which consists in the acceptance of the turn-taking restraints imposed by S.

3. The role of *talker* (T), normally available only to the A of the previous turn and which differs from S in that there is no choice of interactive partner, who must be the previous S.
4. The role of *listener* (L), which might at first seem to be a purely negative role, since it consists in participating in an interaction without taking the floor, but of course any listener is a potential speaker or addressee, to say nothing of the ever-present possibility of interruption (such as floor-taking out-of-turn, not anticipating one's turn). Moreover, listeners have an indirect influence on the interaction via the continual stream of information which they communicate to S or A (approval, impatience, boredom, etc.) verbally or non-verbally.

These interactive roles are realized by the performance of interactive *acts*, or particular types of turn. There are three basic types of act: *opening* (O), *closing* (C) and *reply* (R). Acts combine to form interactive structures which may be hierarchically ordered as in Table 1:

TABLE 1 Interaction

Turn	*O,R,C*
Return	O + Rn + (C)
Involvement	[O + Rn + (C)] + [O + Rn + (C)]n
Encounter	{[O + Rn + (C)] + [O + Rn + (C)]n} + {[O + Rn + (C)] + [O + Rn + (C)]n}n

In reading this table, the following points should be kept in mind:

1. *Turns* are 'acts', but of course this is a nonsense, communicatively speaking; 'What is the sound of one hand clapping?' They do not enter *inter*active discourse as there is no alternation.
   Return is the minimal structure. The end of a return is signalled by a C and/or by a change of addressee.
   Involvement is the intermediate structure. The end of an involvement is signalled by a change of speaker.
   Encounter is the maximal structure. Above this, we would be dealing with situationally-defined *events*.
2. A dyadic interaction, even one of considerable length, might well be limited simply to a series of returns. That is, this model distinguishes between interactions involving two and three or more participants.

1.1 An analogy

It might help the reader to understand what is meant by 'interaction' here if it is thought of in terms of a game of tennis, a rule-governed activity which also requires a minimum of two participants. There, too, we find an alternation in the turns which players have: *rallies* may be of any length, but players must take it in turn to play their strokes. When it is my turn, I can play one of several kinds of stroke: a service (if it is my turn to start), a reply (if my opponent has just hit the ball into my side of the court) or out (if I fail to return the ball to my opponent's side).

In each rally, then, there is only one service (S). This may be followed by any number of replies (R). The end of a rally is signalled by:

1. An out;
2. The cessation of alternation: if the same player plays two consecutive strokes, the second must be a service.

The minimal structure for a rally, then, is S + Rn + (O). A minimum of four rallies gives us a game, the end of which is signalled by a change of server. The analogy can be continued through set and match, but we'd better not push things too far. For the moment, let us just note that the description of tennis resulting from this approach makes no reference to many aspects of the game: psychological factors, such as the will to win, physical factors such as fitness and speed, formal differences between strokes (lob, volley, smash, etc.) — all these are consciously omitted to enable us to see starkly one particular aspect of the game, the work rate or distribution of turns.

1.2 Rules of performance

One of the conclusions to which the investigator of interaction (as understood here) is driven is that there are some rules of performance which are based not on some underlying linguistic competence but rather on the physical nature of the activity and the medium in question.

Space, time and the materials which occupy them are subject to physical rules which are inherent in their nature. These rules impose certain restraints on the development and growth of all materials. Although very simple in themselves such restraints often result in extremely complex patterning. For a full discussion of these matters, see Stevens 1974, from which the following quotation is taken.

Suppose you make a small disc of clay. It is obvious that with a rolling

> pin you can spread the clay into a larger disc. Under the action of the rolling pin, the clay spreads evenly in all directions — just like the space in which it lies.
>
> Now, suppose you press or flatten only the center of the disc. You can do that by manipulating the clay with your fingers. Flattening the center causes the center to spread and grow faster than the perimeter, and the disc naturally takes the shape of a bowl. You can also squeeze the perimeter of the disc so that it grows faster than the center. Again the disc will not lie flat. Instead, it thrusts itself simultaneously both forward and back to make a saddle. The saddle comes about just as naturally as the bowl. The clay is not moulded into those forms but the forms arise naturally, depending upon where you press the clay. From playing with the clay, we are led to the discovery of a fundamental rule: if the center and perimeter grow at the same rate, the material spreads in a plane; if the center grows faster than the perimeter, or the perimeter grows faster than the center, a bowl or a saddle results.
>
> The reason for those transformations lies in the nature of space. The transformations have nothing to do with our intentions to make one form or another. Nature too is similarly constrained. She makes cups and saddles not as she pleases but as she must, as the distribution of material dictates. Take an oyster shell, for example. Since the perimeter of the shell grows at a faster rate than the center, the perimeter curls and wrinkles. No genes carry an image of how to place the wrinkles; no genes remember the shape of the shell; they only permit or encourage faster growth at the perimeter than at the center.
>
> Similar differences of growth lead to the development of more complicated structures, like the outer shell of the human ear. The convolutions of the outer ear arise like the convolutions in a piece of paper that has been sprinkled with water. The living tissue and the paper both bend and warp in accord with the differential expansion of their surfaces.

The same type of argument can be applied to the description of meanders, to branching growths — and to face-to-face interaction. Now it is true that it is possible to give highly abstract descriptions of forms of such structures — the wavy edge of the oyster shell, for instance. But we must not make the mistake of thinking that our abstraction is the underlying structure: it is only a description of the results of certain physical constraints. It is those constraints which govern the structure and evolution of the material. Similarly, the series of abstractions which we call *langue* or *competence* must not be thought of as the *only* rules or constraints governing the structure and evolution of communication: face-to-face interaction is also a physical phenomenon subject to the constraints imposed on the various media by space and time. Alternation, for example, which we have seen to be the most fundamental characteristic of interactive discourse, is imposed by the physical nature of communication (cf. C. F. Hockett's 'design features of language') which makes it nearly impossible for two acoustic messages to occupy the same acoustic space at the same time and which prevents us from acting as emitters and receivers simultaneously. Indeed, we can go further and say that this is why so many behaviours regulating interaction are in fact non-verbal. If we ignore this physical dimension of face-to-face interaction — if we preserve a neat competence/performance opposition, where performance is itself a level of abstraction — we misrepresent some of the most important features of this type of discourse. For example, there seems good reason to believe that many of the 'I hereby's' of speech act theory are only verbal paraphrases for the interactive act of floor-taking. In face-to-face interaction, 'I hereby' by taking my turn, by performing an interactive act, by taking the floor and contributing to the discourse. That I usually do so non-verbally is neither here nor there: by concentrating on the purely verbal aspects of communication, speech act theorists are obliged to try to account for all aspects of discourse in verbal and illocutionary terms alone. This leads to the circularity of giving a verbal label to the act of taking the floor, which has to be integrated into the deep semantic structure of the utterance, only to be deleted later because there appears to be no 'surface realization'. But there is in fact and it is related not just to an underlying competence but to the physical laws governing the distribution of the object, discourse, in time and space.

1.3 Analysis of a passage of classroom interaction

Consider the following passage; it is an extract from a transcription of a language class given by a native speaker of American English to a group of four learners.

Turn 1.	TEACHER:	er, Mr P, er what's the man doing . . . he's sitting, but what's he doing with his hand?
Turn 2.	MR P:	She's pointing their hand.
Turn 3.	TEACHER:	Pardon?
Turn 4.	MR P:	He is pointing his hand.
Turn 5.	TEACHER:	OK, he's pointing his hand and what —
Turn 6.	MR P:	and he is showing the seat in front of him.
Turn 7.	TEACHER:	OK, he's pointing his hand and what —
Turn 8.	MLLE X:	the menu . . . the menu . . .
Turn 9.	TEACHER:	The menu or (gesture) look at the picture, look at the picture . . . he's pointing at his watch. Why

is he pointing at his watch?

Turn 10. MR P: Because she's late.

Turn 11. MR D: (?) She's she's late.

Turn 12. TEACHER: OK, the girl is late and perhaps (gesture) he's been . . . what? (drums hands on desk imitating impatience) he's been . . .

Turn 13. MLLE X: Wait wait . . .

Turn 14. TEACHER: Waiting.

Turn 15. MLLE X: He has waited . . .

Turn 16. TEACHER: He's been waiting . . .

Turn 17. MLLE X: waiting many many times . . .

Turn 18. TEACHER: Many times? (French gesture for doubt) Many times?

Turn 19. MLLE X: Some times . . .

Turn 20. TEACHER: Some times (gesture)

Turn 21. MLLE X: No.

Turn 22. TEACHER: No, he's been waiting for (gesture) for a (gesture — 'fisherman's tale' = long) . . .

Turn 23. ?: A lot of time.
?: A long time.

Turn 24. TEACHER: A long time he's been waiting for a long time.

Turn 25. TEACHER: er, let's look at the text and, er, Mr D, will you read the text please, the text on the next page?

Turn 26. MR D: Julia had a date a date with her new boyfriend in this restaurant at 8. He came on time but she she did not. She came in only a moment ago. It is 9. 'Have you been waiting long?' she asked him when she came in.

Turn 27. TEACHER: She what?

Turn 28. MR D: when she came in . . .

Turn 29. TEACHER: She *asked* him, she *asked* him . . .

Turn 30. MR D: She asked him, she asked him when she came in. 'Yes I have', he is saying: he is rather angry.

Turn 31. TEACHER: Rather. He's he's, what? He's rather *angry*, he's rather *angry* (writes on blackboard).

Turn 32. MR D: Because he has been waiting for an hour.

Turn 33. TEACHER: An hour (correcting pronunciation).

Turn 34. MR D: An hour.

Turn 35. TEACHER: Yes, for an hour.

Turn 36. TEACHER: Yes, what time is it now on the picture?

Turn 37. MLLE X: It's nine o'clock

Turn 38. TEACHER: Yes it's nine o'clock . . . and when did this er man arrive when did he arrive in the restaurant when did he get to the —

Turn 39. MR P: He arrived at 8.
MLLE X: (?) At eight . . .

Turn 40. TEACHER: 8 o'clock. OK. (writes on blackboard)

Turn 41. TEACHER: Miss E, can you ask a question with 'how long'?

Turn 42. MLLE E: How long ago . . .?

Turn 43. TEACHER: 'How long' and 'the man'?

Turn 44. MLLE E: How long ago did he arrived?

Turn 45. TEACHER: Mmm be careful . . .

Turn 46. MLLE E: No, how long did he . . .

Turn 47. TEACHER: Er, ask me a question with 'how long has'.

Turn 48. MLLE E: How long has he arrived?

Turn 49. TEACHER: What happened at 8 o'clock, what happened . . .

Turn 50. MLLE E: He arrived at 8 o'clock.

Turn 51. TEACHER: OK, he arrived, huh, and what's he doing right now?

Turn 52. MLLE E Now he waits.

Turn 53. TEACHER: Now he's . . .

Turn 54. MLLE E: Now he's waiting.

Turn 55. TEACHER: Now he's waiting . . .

Turn 56. MLLE E: How long has he wait he wait . . . wait?

Turn 57. TEACHER: How long has he waited, or when did he start waiting? When did he begin waiting? When did he begin waiting, when did he start waiting . . .

Turn 58. MLLE E: At 8 o'clock.

Turn 59. TEACHER: At 8 o'clock. OK, at 8 o'clock he was waiting and now he's waiting and that that's been continuing, huh, so how long has he has has he what what can we put here (gesture indicating sentence on blackboard)?

Turn 60. MLLE E: In the restaurant, in this restaurant.

Turn 61. TEACHER: I wanted you to I want you to change something with this with wait. OK, at 8 o'clock he was waiting, now he is waiting, how long has he (whistle to indicate blank that they have to fill in) look at the text, look back at the text, look back at the text, look at Julia's question . . .

Turn 62. MR D: What exactly is that question?

Turn 63. TEACHER: No look at her question, Mr D. Look at the question what is the, what is the question?

Turn 64. MLLE X: / MR D: } She asks when he came . . .
Turn 65. TEACHER: No, no, look at the text, not not the question, look at the question.
Turn 66. MR D: Have you been waiting long?
Turn 67. TEACHER: Yeah have you been waiting long?
Turn 68. TEACHER: Mmm. OK, now this question is very similar , you can change this question so that it's it's looks like . . .
Turn 69. MR D: } How long has . . . waiting long.
MLLE E: } Has be been . . . wait.
Turn 70. TEACHER: How long has be been . . .?
Turn 71. MR D: Waiting.
Turn 72. TEACHER: Waiting. Do you see that he started waiting at 8 o'clock, he's still waiting now and he's he's been waiting for an hour. He started an hour ago and it's continuing, he has been waiting for an hour . . .
Turn 73. TEACHER: Right.

If we apply our system of analysis to this passage we obtain the description in Table 2 (see over).

Since most of the signals or behaviours which realize address — and which enable us to assign symbols to utterances — are non-verbal, this analysis could only really be justified by providing the reader with a copy of the videotape and by annotating each separate turn with a description of the relevant non-verbal communication. In the absence of any satisfactory notation, this description would have to be verbal and lengthy and therefore no attempt has been made to provide this detailed information here. Nonetheless, certain turns and their attributions to particular participants probably need further clarification.

How do we decide, for example, that Turn 1 is an O produced by the teacher as S? Our reply would be that he takes the floor, which is vacant, spontaneously; that is, no other participant was occupying the floor and he himself was under no interactive obligation to do so (he was no one's addressee). He initiated this stretch of interaction by taking the floor and choosing his addressee, his interactive partner: 'er Mr P' (an example here of address being realized verbally). When Mr P fulfills his interactive duty in Turn 2 he is a talker not a speaker precisely because he did not initiate this return and because he has no choice of addressee: he must reply to the teacher. As long as this particular interactive S and T partnership continues we are dealing

TABLE 2

Turn No.	Teacher	Mr P	Mlle X	Mr D	Mlle E	Act	Return
1	S	A	L	L	L	O	
2	A	T	L	L	L	R	
3	S	A	L	L	L	R	
4	A	T	L	L	L	R	return 1
5	S	A	L	L	L	R	
6	A	T	L	L	L	R	
7	S	A	L	L	L	R	
8	A	L	S	L	L	O	
9	T	L	A	L	L	R	return 2
10	S	A	A	A	A	O	
11	A	T	L	T	L	R	
12	S	A	A	A	A	R	
13	A	L	T	L	L	R	
14	S	L	A	L	L	R	
15	A	L	T	L	L	R	
16	S	L	A	L	L	R	return 3
17	A	L	T	L	L	R	
18	S	L	A	L	L	R	
19	A	L	T	L	L	R	
20	S	L	A	L	L	R	
21	A	L	T	L	L	R	
22	S	A	L	A	A	O	
23	A	A, L not identifiable				R	return 4
24	S	L	L	L	L	C	
25	S	L	L	A	L	O	
26	A	L	L	T	L	R	
27	S	L	L	A	L	R	
28	A	L	L	T	L	R	
29	S	L	L	A	L	R	
30	A	L	L	T	L	R	return 5
31	S	L	L	A	L	R	
32	A	L	L	T	L	R	
33	S	L	L	A	L	R	
34	A	L	L	T	L	R	
35	S	L	L	L	L	C	
36	S	L	A	L	L	O	
37	A	L	T	L	L	R	return 6
38	S	A	L	A	A	O	
39	A	T	T	L	L	R	return 7
40	S	L	L	L	L	C	
41	S	L	L	L	A	O	
42	A	L	L	L	T	R	
43	S	L	L	L	A	R	
44	A	L	L	L	T	R	
45	S	L	L	L	A	R	
46	A	L	L	L	T	R	
47	S	L	L	L	A	R	
48	A	L	L	L	T	R	
49	S	L	L	L	A	R	
50	A	L	L	L	T	R	
51	S	L	L	L	A	R	return 8
52	A	L	L	L	T	R	
53	S	L	L	L	A	R	
54	A	L	L	L	T	R	
55	S	L	L	L	A	R	
56	A	L	L	L	T	R	
57	S	L	L	L	A	R	
58	A	L	L	L	T	R	
59	S	L	L	L	A	R	
60	A	L	L	L	T	R	
61	S	A	A	A	L	O	
62	A	L	L	T	L	R	
63	S	L	L	A	L	R	
64	A	I	T	T	L	R	return 9
65	S	L	L	A	L	R	
66	A	L	L	T	L	R	
67	S	L	L	L	L	C	
68	S	A	A	A	A	O	
69	A	L	L	T	T	R	
70	S	L	L	A	L	T	return 10
71	A	L	L	T	L	R	
72	S	L	L	L	L	C	
73	S	A	A	A	A	O	return 11

S: speaker T: talker A: addressee
L: listener O: opening R: Reply C: closing

with the same return. This partnership is dissolved in Turn 8, where Mlle X takes the floor without having been the addressee of the previous utterance, in other words, she performs an O. In terms of the interactional structure, she has performed an opening or initiation, whereas in terms of the illocutionary structure it is a reply, the second element in an exchange.

Turns 9 and 10, although forming one utterance, are separate interactive acts, Turn 9 being in reply to Mlle X, Turn 10 marking a change of address and, consequently, the beginning of a new return: it is an example of *general address*, where the speaker imposes the duty to reply on several or all of the other participants. In this case, the transition from address to Mlle X to address to the whole group was marked by gaze, key, posture and gesture: he looked all round the group, went from low to high key, took up a step-back stance and held out his right hand palm upwards. A speaker who has signalled a general address has the choice of continuing to do so as in Turn 12, or of 'narrowing down' his address to those participants who reply, as in Turn 14. At the end of that same return, though, the process is reversed: here (21, 22) the teacher switched his address from Mlle X to the rest of the group. In such cases, the change of address almost always implies the exclusion of the previous addressee (it is a form of evaluation or sanction of Mlle X's performance) which is the reason for coding her role in 22 as listener and not including her in the general address.

Return number 4 contains a closing (24). The teacher, who was the addressee of the previous turn, fulfills his interactive duty by taking the floor but does not himself choose an addressee, that is, he does not impose on any of the other participants the duty to reply. This C is signalled by a drop to low key, by the teacher's breaking off eye-contact and by a pause before the selection of a new addressee (in 25, the opening of a new return).

2. Interaction versus illocution

The major aim of the discourse analyst is to describe communicative behaviour in terms of the constraints placed by participants on other and subsequent contributors to the discourse. This is a complex task, since there are many types of constraint. There are the interactive constraints which we have just been looking at which, roughly speaking, oblige a participant to speak or to keep quiet. Other kinds of restraint, though, can be placed not on a participant's right to speak, but on what he says: a speaker can impose the duty to reply at the same time limiting the choice of his addressee as regards the illocutionary value and the propositional content of his reply. Interactive acts, then, such as taking or giving the floor, are to be distinguished from the illocutionary values which messages occurring at those points in structure may happen to have: an opening turn may be occupied by a greeting, requesting information, ordering, etc. The relationship can be seen as a tagmemic, or slot-and-filler one: in each interactive slot there is at least one illocutionary filler. At the same time, sequences of illocutionary act give us illocutionary structure.

The adjacency pair can be cited as an extreme example of illocutionary constraint. Normally, *requesting information* is followed by *informing, greeting* by *greeting*:

Good morning.	Greeting	Exchange
Good morning.	Greeting	

But we can also attest

Good morning.	Greeting	
You're late.	Remonstrating	

It is obviously not going to be possible to set up hard-and-fast rules for discourse structure based on illocutionary forces alone or their positions of occurrence alone. We do not need to take the extreme case of schizophrenic discourse cited earlier to show that any illocutionary force may be followed by any other, although there are of course statistical correlates.

This presents the discourse analyst with an insuperable problem if he thinks that illocutionary constraints and structures are the only ones there are. But if he recognizes interactive structure, he can show that although the second exchange may be 'deviant' at the illocutionary level, it is perfectly coherent at the interactive level.

A: Good morning.	O	Return
B: Good morning.	R	

A: Good morning.	O	Return
B: You're late.	R	

The same would hold true even for pathologically deviant sequences:

A: What is your name?	O	Return
B: Well, let's say you might have thought you had something from before, but you haven't got it any more.	R	

We are dealing, then, with two 'parallel' structures. As it happens in these examples there is a congruence in the units of those structures — the boundaries of the illocutionary exchange and the interactive return coincide exactly. But this is by no means always the case: let us look back at the long return between the teacher and Mlle E which occurs between Turns 41 and 60 in the passage we took for analysis. This is one return because it is an unbroken stretch of interaction between two participants: there is no change of speaker nor of his addressee. At the illocutionary level, however, it is a very different kettle of fish: in his (ultimately unsuccessful) bid to get a particular answer from Mlle E, the teacher initiated a long series of seven illocutionary exchanges (Table 3).

TABLE 3

	Interactive		Illocutionary	
	Turns	*Acts*	*Moves*	*Exchanges*
	41	nomination, elicit	initiating	eliciting exchange 1
	42	reply	responding	
	43	elicit	initiating	exchange 2
	44	reply	responding	
	45	evaluation	follow-up	
	46	reply	responding	
	47	elicit	initiating	eliciting exchange 3
	48	reply	responding	
	49	elicit	initiating	eliciting exchange 4
	50	reply	responding	
Return 8	51	evaluation, elicit	initiating	eliciting exchange 5
	52	reply	responding	
	53	evaluation	follow-up	
	54	reply	responding	
	55	accept	follow-up	
	56	reply	responding	
	57	elicit	initiating	eliciting exchange 6
	58	reply	responding	
	59	accept, comment, elicit	initiating	eliciting exchange 7
	60	reply	responding	
	61	comment, elicit	follow-up	

This is an attempt to apply the Sinclair–Coulthard system of analysis — rather a ham-handed one, as we are not always sure that we apply their categories as they understand them. Questions of detail aside, though, one thing is clear: there is no one-to-one relationship between their units of illocutionary structure (act, move, exchange, transaction and interaction) and our units of interactional structure (turn, return, involvement and encounter). The Sinclair–Coulthard system gives an analysis of the sequences of illocutionary acts which occur in the language of the classroom and of the constraints which participants place on one another at the illocutionary level. As such it is different from, but perfectly compatible with, the interactive analysis we looked at earlier.

We have here, then, a series of 20 interactive turns which form one interactive return: the same passage (approximately) includes 26 illocutionary *acts* forming 20 moves, forming 7 exchanges. Just as an utterance may include more than one interactive turn (72, 73) so it may also include more than one illocutionary act (59). Moreover the boundaries between units may coincide but they may also occur at quite different points; the final eliciting exchange, for example, continues beyond the end of the interactive return.

2.1 *Interruptions*

An interesting aspect of discourse on which much light is shed by the interaction/illocution distinction is the problem of *interruption*. A purely illocutionary description such as the Sinclair–Coulthard model does not distinguish between contributions which are *in turn* and those which are not: it assumes that every successive utterance was in turn. Our intuitive awareness that this is not the case is a major justification for recognizing the interactive dimension of discourse. For example, in the passage we have taken for analysis, the teacher addressed Mr P in turn 7, but it was Mlle X who replied. It was not her turn to speak, yet she was clearly answering the teacher's question. A full description of discourse must account for both these facts: it must show that there is a lack of coherence here at one level— interaction — but that the discourse is acceptable at another level — illocution.

We can now see that it is also perfectly possible to have an interruption at the level of illocution in an interactively well-formed passage:

What's the time?	O	Return
Why do you want to know?	R	
Well it's for my bus . . .	R	
Oh, I see. It's 6.30.	R	
Thanks.	R	

We have here an adjacency pair whose members are not in fact adjacent, yet any speaker of English can pair them off. It clearly cannot be position of occurrence alone which justifies his doing so — which is a further reason for distinguishing the turn from the message.

In the interruption exemplified by Turn 8, the interrupting speaker addressed the interrupted speaker. This seems in some sense to be less of an interruption than one where the interrupting speaker addresses the original addressee (i.e. the participant whose turn he has just taken), and this in turn is less of an interruption than would be the case if the interrupting speaker were to address a previous listener. This would be bordering on 'talking in class'. All these interactive interruptions may or may not coincide with illocutionary and content interruptions: to take just one example, the interrupting speaker who addresses a previous listener may suggest an answer or he may talk about last night's football match. In this case the discourse is incoherent at the levels of interaction, illocution and content — and the 'talking in class' has become a separate but simultaneous discourse.

By looking at who is the speaker of an interrupting O, then, and who is the addressee, we are able to describe degrees in interactive coherence which go from the over-enthusiastic floor-grabbing of the learner who answers a teacher's question out of turn, but whose participation in the same discourse cannot be questioned, to the 'aside' remark.

3. Realization and content

Two further levels of structuring are posited in the model of discourse presented here: *realization* and *content*. Neither will be discussed in detail since, although both levels present considerable problems to the analyst, at least the distinctions which they summarize are pretty generally accepted, which is not the case with the interaction/illocution opposition.

For the moment, then, we will limit ourselves to a few brief and rather general observations:

By *realization* we mean the set of message-bearing elements (verbal, paralinguistic, non-verbal) in a situation. These elements have substance and are realizations of various systems and structures whose organization can be described in terms such as class, units, structure and distribution. The textual function of such elements is described in terms of their internal relations, and without reference to the meaning they carry.

We use the term 'content' in the sense of 'propositional content'. For our present purposes, the important thing is to distinguish between the illocutionary value and propositional content of utterances; there is nothing new in this, of course, it is fundamental to the whole concept of the speech act. It is easy to show that content and illocutionary value can vary independently, that the 'same' content can be present in acts having different illocutionary values (and vice-versa):

1. A: I forgot to give John his car keys back and I can't get them back before tomorrow.
   B: I'm going to John's for dinner tonight.
2. A: Do you fancy dropping round for a game?
   B: I'm going to John's for dinner tonight.

The semantico–logical or pragmalinguistic operations which allow us to understand and label B's utterances as, say, 'offering help' and 'refusing' have been the subject of intense study recently (in particular, see Cole and Morgan 1975) and we do not feel competent to enlarge on them. However, two fundamental points need to be kept in mind:

1. If illocutionary force and propositional content can be shown to vary independently, they should, as far as is possible, be described separately. To describe illocutionary acts uniquely in terms of their relationship to content or information is to privilege the purely informative and verbal elements of communication at the expense of the psycho-social, pragmatic and dynamic aspects.

2. If we separate content from illocution, interaction and realization, and if within content operations we distinguish between implications, presuppositions and notions, we have at our disposal a further set of tools for the description of communicative breakdown. It is most unfortunate that almost all the work which has been carried out so far in this area is based on artificial, isolated and decontextualized examples, and is therefore useless from our point of view. We can do no more here than hint (Table 4) at the sort of approach which might be adopted for the description of *misunderstandings*.

TABLE 4

	Interaction	Realization	Illocution	Content	
A: What's the time? B: 6.30.	✓	✓	✓	✓	1
A: What's the time? B: I like fish and chips.	✓	✓	✓	✗	2
A: What's the time? B: Why?	✓	✓	✗	✗	3
A: What's the time? B: nurdlenurdle.	✓	✗	✗	✗	4
A: What's the time? B: __________	✗	✗	✗	✗	5
A: What's the time? C: 6.30.	✗	✓	✓	✓	6

1. is coherent both as an interactive return (OR) and as an illocutionary exchange (requesting information, informing). It is also realized by well-formed sentences and the propositional content of the reply is that requested in the elicit.
2. is coherent as an interactive return (OR) and as an illocutionary exchange (requesting information, informing). It is realized by well-formed sentences but the propositional content of the reply is not that which was requested in the elicit.
3. This is a coherent return, consisting of two well-formed utterances. But the illocutionary adjacency pair is interrupted, so that we have a request for information followed by a request for information.
4. Here B makes a complete hash of his reply. It is, therefore, incoherent at the level of realization, illocution and content. But a reply has been made, the turn taken, so that at the interactive level we still have a coherent return.
5. Here, B fails to reply. Interaction has broken down and the discourse is incoherent at all four levels.
6. An interruption. It was not C's turn, so the interaction is incoherent. But a request for information has been satisfied, so that

at the levels of illocution, realization and content the discourse is coherent.

This is sketchy in the extreme and an enormous amount remains to be done, particularly in the definition of illocutionary forces and in content and topic analysis (columns for inferencing operations could be added, for example — cf. the discussion of 'cross-cultural pragmatic failure' in Thomas 1983.). Nonetheless, we feel that this approach has much to offer the applied linguist and the language teacher interested in the description of communicative error.

Reading and communicative competence

> L'auteur de ces lignes se souvient d'un de ces vieux maîtres qui, quatre mois après le début de son enseignement , n'avait pas atteint la lettre T dans la bibliographie qu'il dictait, de façon fort distincte il est vrai, et dans une langue très classique, à des étudiants venus chercher non un répertoire par ailleurs accessible sur les rayons d'une bibliothèque, mais une méthode d'utilisation de ce repertoire. Le maître qui accable sous le poids d'une bibliographie dont on peut statistiquement constater, comme l'a fait dans un autre domaine le Professeur Escarpit, qu'une vie humaine ne saurait l'épuiser, même compte tenu des espérances que nous ouvrent les progrès de la science médicale, s'est il jamais assuré que ses étudiants savaient lire?
>
> *Yves Châlon*

Meaning and reading[1]

One of the most common assumptions regarding learning to read is that first the mechanisms have to be mastered and only then can problems of comprehension be tackled. Independent of the particular methodology employed, this ordering of objectives is well-nigh universal, both in mother-tongue and in second-language reading programmes. But there is increasing evidence to show that the reverse is often true; that reading is, to a considerable extent, a recognition process, and that we cannot recognize what we do not already know. Moreover, it is a matter of everyday experience that it is perfectly possible to go through the motions of reading without achieving any worthwhile degree of comprehension: small children, for example, are often quite capable of transposing a written text into its phonic equivalent — 'reading aloud' — without having any understanding of what they have 'read'. That is, their recognition has been restricted to the low-level processing of formal items.

Clearly, at any higher levels this process of recognition is related to the activation of knowledge stocked in the reader's memory, short- or long-term. What types of knowledge, though, are relevant to

[1]For an excellent and more detailed discussion of the topics mentioned here, see Sprenger–Charolles 1982a and 1982b.

reading comprehension? *Mutatis mutandis*, we may postulate the same three major categories as were suggested for the interpretation of oral discourse: linguistic knowledge, knowledge of the world and knowledge of the rules for relating the two.

1. *Linguistic knowledge* includes the graphemic system of the language, vocabulary and syntax. The correspondences between the written and spoken forms at all levels, but above all at the graphemic/phonemic levels, are not a particularly important part of the reading skill; it is perfectly possible to understand a text without being able to read it aloud. However, in cases involving alphabetic scripts where the learners have already mastered the spoken form — as is the usual situation for children learning to read their mother tongue in Europe, for example — the graphemic/phonemic correspondences do provide a useful if superficial basis for the evaluation of performance.

For foreign learners, however, especially for adults with specific needs of some kind, it makes far more sense to base at least part of the training received in reading on a grammar of the written language. Materials produced in this way will start out from a particular written form ('-ing', '-ed', '-s', etc.) and try to provide the learner with the necessary information and techniques for distinguishing between the different morphosyntactic functions which these elements can realize: when, for example, does '-s' signal 'plural', 'third person singular', 'present simple', 'genitive', etc.? See for example, Abé and Duda 1974. However, for reading purposes, it will not be necessary to train the learner in the different pronunciations (/s/, /z/, /iz/) involved. As Marie–José Gremmo argues, though, (in Chapter 4) this ability to decipher the linguistic code is a necessary but by no means sufficient condition for comprehension to take place.

2. *Knowledge of the world*: when we are engaged in computing the intended meaning of a written text, we do so on the basis of hypotheses whose validity we check against our knowledge of what is and what is not possible in the world we live in and in particular as regards our knowledge of the particular topic we happen to be reading about. It follows that reading is a highly idiosyncratic process, since the knowledge we bring to bear on the text is the sum of our previous experience (or at least, what we have learnt from it!), a sort of epistemological autobiography. To a greater or lesser extent, all readings differ; this is not just true of poetry, it can be true of even the most 'scientific' discourse. If, for example, we come across the following sentence (kindly provided by David Brown)

> The geologically younger estuaries of the Pacific coast tend to lack the native estuarine fish, oysters, large crabs, and large prawns common to temperate estuaries.

our interpretation of its meaning will depend to a great extent on previously acquired geographical knowledge. Only if we already know whether or not the area in question is included in the category 'temperate estuaries' can we decide between two contradictory interpretations.

This dialectic between individual knowledge and text, between memory and discourse processing , is one of the liveliest fields of current applied linguistic research. How do we select and retrieve the particular items of knowledge which a particular element in the text calls on, in order to construct meaningful discourse? More specifically, how do we select from among the various potential meanings which an item of knowledge may articulate that which seems to be textually and contextually appropriate? That is, what is the relationship between cognitive structure — the way in which our knowledge is stocked — and remembering — the process by which we locate, activate and retrieve that knowledge and relate it to aspects of the situation?

Models of cognitive processing based on the earlier versions of information theory have proved inadequate in that they fail to account for the flexibility of the systems involved; in crude terms, they describe retrieval but not interpretation. Remembering can only be compared to finding a book in a library if we also include the process of reading the book.

3. *Rules for relating 1 and 2*: more recent models, drawing on the work on inferencing procedures mentioned above and on research into artificial intelligence, suggest that as well as distinguishing between short and long-term memory, we should distinguish *semantic memory* from *episodic memory* (Quillian 1974; Schank 1975; Tulving 1976; Sprenger–Charolles 1982a). In our semantic memory we stock knowledge in the form of concepts, whilst our episodic memory contains 'schemas' or 'scripts' for the accomplishment of conventional or routine activities (ordering a meal or making a phone-call) and 'plans' for less familiar sequences. The term 'plan' is also used to describe aspects of the organization of the semantic memory. This apparent terminological confusion is in fact the reflection of a hypothesis concerning the nature of the operation of memory as a whole, namely that it is organized into networks which allow the same nodes

to be reached *by a variety of different routes*. The importance of this idea for the linguist is two-fold.

First, it is a strong challenge to models of memory based on componential semantic descriptions, where cognitive structure is pictured in terms of sets of categories and sets of distinctive features; these 'branching diagram' models provide one and only one correct route for reaching a given node. (As far as I am competent to judge, this issue is by no means settled. It suffices for the psycholinguist to show that an individual can possess more than one categorization system and the 'branching diagram' model becomes just as flexible as the 'networks' model. Moreover, the componential semantic model does seem to account more convincingly for the existence of certain types of malfunction in the reading process (Sprenger–Charolles 1982a; Lavorel 1982) where alexic subjects either 'take a wrong turning' — 'rose' instead of 'orchid' — or fail to reach their destination — 'plant' instead of 'flower'.)

The second implication of the 'network' hypothesis is that its functional flexibility allows us to search for and select the information which seems most relevant (the 'salient point') to a particular situation and context. We have already seen that the nature of reference in natural languages means that most linguistic items are polysemic and multifunctional. If there were only one route to each node, we would have to run through all the possible meanings of every item: clearly, this is not so, a fact which seems to indicate that there are differing routes to the 'same' item, so that the information selected and retrieved at the node-point varies according to the line of approach, that is, the hypothesis on which the sender is proceeding. When the information selected fails to match expectations, in other words, when the meaning is not consistent with previous knowledge, a different line of approach is tried. This problem of *semantic opacity* is particularly acute, therefore, in cases where the reader does not possess either the variety of approaches to a point or the background knowledge for testing his hypotheses, as is often the case with small children and second-language learners. An excellent and well-illustrated discussion of this problem is to be found in Lee, Whitburn and Winter (1982). Basing their argument on Clark and Clark's (1979) work on innovation and on Clark and Carlson's (1981) discussion of the role of context in comprehension, they make three main points:

1. As an expression can be categorized from denotational (fixed sense and denotation), through indexical/deictic (fixed sense and denotation, but shifting referent). to contextual (shifting sense and denotation), so the degree of cooperation required from the listener/reader is increased.

2. Interpretative skill depends on the ability to recognize the salient points in a given context. This ability . . . is linked to the degree to which generic knowledge of the world is similarly ordered in the minds of the speaker and listener (writer and reader):
   "In using 'brick', a speaker intends to denote the kind of object that fits his theory for bricks. For this to succeed, speakers and listeners must share the same generic theory for bricks". (Clark and Clark 1979, p. 790).

For concrete objects the authors postulate that these generic theories specify the object's physical characteristics, its outgoing and its potential roles. The 'predominant features' of the definition are the limited number of features necessary to distinguish the object in question from all other objects. In an 'unmarked' use, the *predominant* features are also *salient* (we can consider predominance to be an aspect of the definition and salience to be an aspect of the context).

3. The accessibility of information is crucial to ease of compatibility (understanding). This implies not only the question of salience and prominence but also the concept of *common ground*.

Lee, Whitburn and Winter make two further points which are important for the teaching and learning of reading. Firstly, they argue strongly in favour of a systematic L2 approach to 'cultural opacity', that is, an approach based on a principled selection of reading comprehension problems which would favour the acquisition of 'common knowledge' and of strategies for identifying salient features. Secondly, they show that the linguistic and psychological criteria for making that selection are already available. Taken together with research into the pedagogical exploitation of authentic materials (see pp. 321–31) with their potential for activating knowledge which the learner already possesses (pp. 305–8) this work promises to be both insightful and helpful in the teaching and learning of reading comprehension at discourse level.

Reading and communicative competence

Comprehension is as much a part of communicative competence as is expression. This includes written comprehension, a point which needs to be emphasized since there is a clear tendency in modern language teaching discussion to equate communicative competence with oral expression.

Reading is a communicative act, the transformation by an individual of text into discourse; therefore both text and context need to be taken into account in any description of reading which aims to go beyond purely formal linguistic or mechanical observations. Reading, then, is a creative act, in the sense that all texts demand a skilled response from the reader.

When a reader recreates discourse from a written text he performs the act of reading. It is the nature of this act which is the topic of Marie–José Gremmo's paper (Chapter 4). The term 'act' is aptly chosen here, since it underlines the importance of the reader as an individual in a given situation, an individual whose behaviour is the expression of personal intentions, needs and habits. Reading is not a disembodied information retrieval process identical for every performer: it is an essentially private activity involving the negotiation of personal meaning. We may all 'read' the same text, but no two people ever 'read' the same discourse because they never bring exactly the same knowledge, expectations and contexts to bear on the text. These discrepancies between readers are likely to be particularly wide between native and non-native readers, but not necessarily for linguistic reasons: if the situational features of non-native readers are not taken into account (either by themselves or by the teacher), then their reading will remain a matter of decoding text and will never be personally interpreted as discourse.

In Chapter 5, Carolyn Henner–Stanchina demonstrates some of the practical implications and applications of the model of discourse and the approach to the study of reading which have been discussed. It will come as no great surprise to primary school teachers the world over that it is possible to transfer from 'reading' to 'writing acts'. What is interesting is the use of this approach with a heterogeneous ESL group of adults, and the very explicit use which was made of the taxonomic model in question. Of course, Henner–Stanchina was dealing with a group who all shared the same basic aim — to get into college — and this certainly justifies her very 'cognitive' approach to the problem, and to some extent at least explains its success. However, it is worth pointing out that traditional handbooks on style are just as 'cognitive' and are by and large considerably less successful.

This last point brings us directly to the heart of Odile Régent's paper, Chapter 6, since she shows that there are discursive structures which have eluded traditional approaches to stylistic description, as well as more recent linguistic models. Although her paper is an illustration of a methodology for the contrastive analysis of specialized discourses, she makes an important point of general validity. She shows that, contrary to popular belief, scientific discourse is not based on some universally accepted model of philosophy, that there is what might be called an ethno-discursive level of organization which takes precedence over 'objective' scientific demonstration.

The implications of this for teachers in the field of languages for special purposes are considerable: above all, it can be taken as a telling criticism of much current work in English for Special Purposes. ESP specialists often seem unaware of the resentment which the ethnocentricity of their materials and methodology has aroused, regarding accusations of cultural and economic imperialism as reactionary misunderstandings, whereas they are in fact real if simplistic protests against this aspect of their work. Indeed, non-British and non-American specialists in this field often claim that this narrowness of approach in the materials is reflected in the lack of interest shown by ESP experts in LSP in general. To take a recent example, here is a quotation from Max Gorosch's review (Gorosch 1982) of Pauline Robinson's *ESP: the Present Position* (1982).

> In the Introduction the statement is made 'that ESP of a slightly different kind has been in existence for longer in Europe, although it may not have been until comparatively recently that the term ESP was used to describe it'. To many non-English speaking readers 'slightly different' will seem a typical English understatement. What is now termed ESP was an essential part of the scientific study and practical teaching of *Fachsprache* in the German-speaking countries since the 1930s, and of *langue de la spécialité* in France since the 1960s.

4 Learning a language — or learning to read?

M–J. Gremmo

The increasing use of English in written documents of every kind, read by vast numbers of people from every imaginable linguistic background, has led to considerable interest in the learning and teaching of reading. This interest has been particularly lively among language teachers: indeed, it has always been seen as a language-teaching problem. However, our experience of teaching reading in English to speakers of French has led us to call such an analysis into doubt and to wonder whether we are dealing with language learners (people who are learning English) or with apprentice readers (people who are learning to read).

For reasons which are discussed below, we believe that this problem can only really be tackled by recognizing the highly specific nature of the process of learning to read a foreign language. The foreign language learner who is learning to read is not merely an apprentice reader: he is not in the position of a small child encountering the written form for the first time. But neither is he merely a language learner; there are many aspects of the written form of the foreign language which differ from that of his mother tongue. He knows how to read in the sense that he knows how to select and implement strategies which are suitable for particular documents in his mother tongue. What he needs to learn if he is to become an efficient reader of a foreign language is how to make that selection for these new types of document.

Analysing and discussing the reading process therefore involves considerations drawn from three separate domains. These are:

1. *The linguistic organization of the written language* ('linguistic' in the widest possible sense), which can be described in terms of the different levels of extended discourse (morpho-syntax, rhetorical structure and communicative aim) and which can in turn be used to determine various pedagogical objectives;
2. *Reading strategies*, which, although they seem to be universal in western culture, do vary as regards the details of their application

to specific languages;

3. *The learner* himself or herself, whose educational background and cultural and professional situation all need to be taken into account in a general way and who also has precise, short-term objectives which have to be met in a particular learning situation of some kind.

This process, then, involves a specific combination of all these factors, which calls for a specific methodological response. The learner is not just learning to read, nor is he just learning the language: he is learning-to-read-a-foreign-language.

What is reading?

Does the teaching process actually tackle the problem of learning to read, which is, after all, the main aim of our learners? To be in a position to answer this question we first had to ask another: what *is* reading? To find out, we turned not to the linguists, but to the psychologists and psycholinguists who have long been involved in investigating the reading process.

Although there are a number of different schools of thought, some of which the specialist will find contradictory, the language teacher can still find descriptive tools which are useful for his or her purposes. These are summarized by the psycholinguist K. S. Goodman (1973) when he says, apropos of the language-comprehension process, 'Receptive language processes are cycles of sampling, predicting, testing and confirming.' Two of these cycles — sampling and confirming — are related to the eye, that is, they are cycles of visual information in which the eye plays an active role. Researchers studying eye movements (Javal 1905; Tinker 1965) have shown how the eye functions during reading. Their analyses have underlined the importance of the time-span between eye-movements; a good reader manages to take in a relatively high number of letters per fixation. Moreover, these fixations occur at regular intervals of time and distance and — and this is crucial — almost exclusively forwards in the text. In other words, a good reader knows how to choose the rhythm and length of fixation which suit him, and his progress through the text is such that he understands it satisfactorily. A bad reader, on the other hand, does not manage to find the right speed and is forced to keep going back, which slows down and complicates his progress. The authors cited also distinguished between slow reading and a slow reader, showing that a good reader has a wide range of reading rhythms at his command which he is able to adapt to the particular document with which he is confronted. Finally, they have shown the importance of recognition; a reader is able to recognize a letter or a word which is only partly available. Memory, practice and experience provide the reader with a system of recognition factors which increase his speed of perception.

The other cycles, predicting and testing, are related to what F. Smith (1971) has called 'non-visual information,' that is, information which the brain provides. During the two ocular cycles, it is the eye which transmits information from the written document to the brain. During the other two phases the process is reversed: it is the brain which provides the eye with information and controls its movements.

What these researchers have revealed is the preponderant role of mental mechanisms in the reading process. The brain does not just record and compile: it controls the eye's movements by providing it with all sorts of non-visual information, drawing on its own knowledge of the language and of those aspects of reality which are dealt with in the text. It is this knowledge which enables the brain to construct hypotheses on and about the content of the text, hypotheses which are then compared with the typographical text; in other words, the eye now enables us to confirm or disprove these hypotheses by calling on the visual information provided by the written text. Once this check has been carried out, the brain can proceed to a new phase, making predictions based on the visual and non-visual information available to it. The eye is, therefore, highly dependent on the brain during reading. We could even say that it only sees what the brain wants it to see.

The hypotheses which the brain constructs are based on three types of clues or markers: graphic, syntactic and semantic. These clues are to be found at different levels in the written text. The first are the result of a detailed study of the words themselves, the second are related to the rules of structure of a language and the third call on the reader's powers of reasoning. Research in this field has shown that it is this third category, the semantic clues, which are the most useful, even though they are the least 'visual.' A good reader therefore prefers this strategy, because it helps him to understand a passage more easily.

This brings us to a further important concept, that of *strategy*. The texts with which a reader finds himself confronted at different times are not constructed identically: different words are used; the syntactic structure may be more or less complex; the relationship between the text and the reader will also vary, according to whether the topic is or is not familiar to the reader, whether he is for or against the ideas the author is discussing and whether he has plenty of time or not. In each case the reading task will be different. For this reason he will need strategies which will enable him to use the three types of clues available to him in the way which is best suited to the task in hand.

Learning to read a foreign language: a matter of learning to read?

What use are these different approaches to reading to the foreign language teacher who wishes to improve his learners' reading ability? In other words, should he regard his learners as 'apprentice readers'? Before we can answer this question we must be able to say just what an apprentice reader needs to be able to do.

The research which has been mentioned above shows the importance of mental activity in the reading process. It also shows that when it results in the construction of non-visual information, this activity is partially rooted in the document itself. The reader uses his external knowledge (external to the content of the document) to 'read' the document, that is to extract from it the type of comprehension he is looking for. This 'reading' will be unique and will depend on the relationship holding at a given moment between reader and document.

The teacher should therefore think of the language learner as a *reader*. Of course, he cannot talk about reading without taking into account what is going to be read and who is going to read it. As we saw above, he first has to define the types of document which the learner–reader should tackle and the types of strategy he will use.

For example, a learner–reader whose reading in a foreign language is imposed by his profession differs from a reader who freely chooses what it is he is going to do. Again, the scientist who has to use publications in English to keep up with the research being done in his field, does not read for the same purposes as an information officer in a research centre, whose main aim is to establish a catalogue which is as complete and as efficient as possible. In the same way, technicians who are obliged to refer daily to documents drawn up in English — because they are using some American technique, for example — do not deal with them in the same way as an executive working for a multinational company handles the numerous memoranda which come his way daily. Finally, students who have to improve their reading ability simply because it is an obligatory part of the syllabus and is going to be examined, but who otherwise have no real need to be able to read, are very different readers from adults whose professional competence may be very closely related to their foreign language reading competence.

Moreover, the different documents which these different types of readers will have to read are not all built on the same model, because they do not all fulfill the same functions for their readers. These various functions provide us with a means of categorizing the different written documents which were available to our learners, though obviously such a list — omitting as it does religious texts, for example — is far from exhaustive:

Documents with an extra-linguistic purpose

In this category would be included, for example, the documents which technicians use on the job and which aim at making the reader do something. They therefore require a non-linguistic response of some kind: 'when you have operated the blue switch, press the yellow button', for instance. These are mostly documents such as instructions for use, maintenance instructions or lists of mistakes, all of which teach the technician to acquire a particular piece of know-how. The basic function of such documents, then, is to transmit orders, advice and warnings which the reader has to assimilate if his work is to proceed correctly. In addition, there are often pictures or diagrams which present the task to be carried out visually.

Informative documents

The main aim of this type of document is to provide the reader with all or part of the information regarded as true in the present state of knowledge, as in the case of some types of scientific documents — descriptions of apparatus, textbooks, popular articles — and of certain newspaper articles whose content is accepted by the experts. These documents aim first and foremost at giving the reader the information which the author, usually a specialist, judges to be both necessary and sufficient if the reader is to have a full understanding of the subject in question. The information content in such documents is usually highly organized and its structure is made quite explicit to make it as accessible as possible for the reader.

In both these types of text, the relationship between writer and reader is a pupil–teacher one. The author possesses knowledge or know-how which he transmits to the reader. In the two types of text which we are now going to look at, on the other hand, reader and writer are on an equal footing.

Argumentative documents

Such documents differ from informative documents in that they do not present information which is generally regarded as true within a particular field. On the contrary, they aim at revising or at completely changing that information, or even at creating new information by bringing together various pieces of information as part of a process of rational argument. Most scientific articles are included in this category: scientific knowledge progresses on the basis of argumentative discourse of this kind, where opposing theories are confronted and researchers construct the generally-accepted models of information which, later, form the basis of the 'informative documents' described above. Contrary to what one might expect, one also finds articles from the daily press, such as editorials, included in this category. Journalists working in the thick of topical events obviously cannot claim to be providing information on which there is general agreement. The information which they publish is in fact an analysis of those events, and for this very reason necessarily reflects the journalist's or the publication's own point of view. But not all journalistic discourse is argumentative: we often find in the specialized press, for example, 'popular' articles which are informative in nature.

Literary documents

It is obviously very difficult to define just what is meant by a literary document. One possible approach might be to say that unlike the three categories of document already discussed, literary documents have no utilitarian aim. Such documents are not the means towards an end, they are the end in themselves. We read them for their own sakes and not as a key to unlock some aspect of extra-linguistic reality. Such documents therefore leave the reader a considerable degree of liberty (unless he happens to be a professional critic or literary scholar). Few literary texts were found amongst the documents which our learners provided us with.

These different types of texts create different reading needs. For this reason, a reader should be able to recognize what sort of document he is tackling even before he starts reading it. A final point is that the reader has to take into consideration the situation in which the document was published: is it an article from a popular magazine, a photocopy of an internal company report, or a manufacturer's instruction manual for a machine? Such factors have an influence on the type of document and although one might think, as far as a French learner of English is concerned, that there was little difference between French and English documents in this respect, certain of them do pose problems: the 'Sunday papers', for example, have no real equivalent in France and, faced with one of them, a French reader has trouble finding his way around.

In the first place, then, it is the writer who defines the nature of a written document, since he is the one who decides on the aim, the potential readers and where the document will be published. It is these choices which determine a document's main characteristics, which explains why two documents which are based on the same 'conceptual content' can still be very different indeed. However, a second series of choices is made by the reader, who defines the nature of the document in terms of his personal reading objectives. So the same document — a scientific article published in a specialized journal, say — is read differently by a researcher looking for confirmation of a particular point and a librarian making out a catalogue card. Similarly, the same reader can read the same document with two different objectives in mind: he may read a novel once for personal pleasure and then, a couple of months later, re-read it analytically, having in the meantime chosen it as a research topic. So the first thing a reader does, even before he starts actually reading, is to decide on his reading objectives and on the strategies which he is going to use to attain them and he does this on the basis of the knowledge he has of the different characteristics of written communication which we have just looked at.

What are the implications here for language teachers and learners? They should never lose sight of the fact that the main aim of a language learner in the sort of situation we are discussing is to become a reader, that is, someone who is capable of independently exercising these choices, not just of deciphering the lines on a page. He is, therefore, a learner–reader and ought to develop this reading know-how. This means that he should approach every text as a reader, even one that is written in a foreign language. All too often, the relationship between the reader and the document is completely neglected by the syllabus, yet since this relationship is specific, unique even, to every case, it should be dealt with explicitly at the beginning of every written comprehension exercise.

The aim of the exercise should not just be to teach people 'reading' but to help them practise certain aspects of the complex skill which makes up the act of reading. The learner's objective should, therefore, always be precisely defined: reading for pleasure, reading to find a particular piece of information (the description of an experiment, for example) or reading to have an overall idea of a document.

If the learning objective of the exercise is *linguistic* (such as the acquisition of the vocabulary of behaviourist psychology or the use of the passive in operating instructions) it will be unrelated to the act of reading in the fuller sense, and will therefore have no claims to teaching, let alone practising it. It is for these reasons that some teachers, including ourselves, prefer to see the learner as a learner–reader and have therefore concentrated on methods of improving the reading capacity as such. Since the objective is learning to read, we give our learners materials whose explicit aim is to teach them to read better.

What are the weaknesses of the learner–readers? For most of them, undertaking the study of reading in a foreign language seems to bring on a phenomenon of regression at both the intellectual and psychological levels. This is largely due to the learning situation in which they find themselves. These days, when someone sets out to learn a foreign language, they assume — and so does everyone around them — that they are going to learn to *speak*. The layman's conception of a language is often limited to its oral aspects. Moreover, it is precisely in the field of teaching the spoken language that most developments in educational technology have taken place (tape-recorders, language laboratories, video-recorders, etc.), developments which teachers themselves use for their publicity value. All this tends to make it seem that the spoken language is somehow superior. This leaves people who are thinking of learning to read a foreign language with the impression that educationally they are second-class citizens: they are *only* learning written English, they don't *speak*. This attitude tends to lower the value of what they are learning in their own eyes. Moreover, their study materials are both more traditional, since they consist mostly of written documents (they could hardly be anything else!) and duller, since they lack the variety, novelty and flexibility of audio-visual materials. All this means that the learners themselves do not approach the task of learning to read in a foreign language with the same enthusiasm and willpower with which they tackle the spoken language. They themselves are often unaware of this, since they are convinced that what they are learning is useful, but they do not find it easy to reconcile business and pleasure.

The main source of this regression, though, is to be found in their own ideas about learning. Every learner is influenced by his ideas concerning what his course should include. In the case of the teaching and learning of reading in a foreign language, few learners think of this problem as anything but a linguistic one. Yet many of the learners we deal with are at an advanced level in purely linguistic terms: they have little difficulty in understanding the sentences with which they are confronted. It is only when they have to find their way around a longer document that they start to have difficulty. It is for this reason that we say that it is their *method of reading* which is inadequate; but in their own minds they are convinced that they know how to read. For this reason, they cannot see that the problems they are having with their written texts are reading problems: so they must be linguistic. In the same way, beginners analyse their needs only in linguistic terms, so even though their objective is to improve their *reading ability* in a foreign language, most of them seek above all to improve their *linguistic competence.*

These ideas about learning give rise to certain attitudes when learners are confronted with foreign language documents. Firstly, they have a tendency to exaggerate the importance of vocabulary. It seems that for them, a text is a series of words and that they have to know the meaning of each one of them. To do this, they turn constantly to their dictionaries: this tool thus becomes an indispensable crutch without which they can do nothing. We have often come across this attitude, which leads people to refuse from the start even to try to read normally: they say that when they do not have a dictionary available, they do not know the meanings of all the words and when they do not understand every single word they claim to understand nothing at all.

Moreover this constant use of the dictionary often leads them astray since they use it clumsily. To use a dictionary properly, the reader should analyse the syntactic and semantic context of the unknown word before he even opens it. In other words, he should already have some idea about what it is he is looking for, because it is only this analysis which is going to enable him to choose the entry and the sense which correspond to the passage in question. These learner–readers get the wrong end of the stick, because they think they cannot carry out this analysis while there are still unknown words in the passage. This leads them into a vicious circle from which they are unable to escape (Heddesheimer 1971).

Another common characteristic is linear reading. This characteristic is also related to the exaggerated importance given to the dictionary. Faced with a document in a foreign language, most learner–readers adopt the same sort of linear approach: armed with their dictionary and a pen, they rush straight to the beginning of the text and then patiently decipher word after word, sentence after sentence, writing down the dictionary meanings of the unknown words. This 'myopic' reading, this process of decipherment, prevents them from having a more global view of the document and from discovering the main points or ideas it contains. Moreover, they forget to make use of all the other elements which make up a written text: headlines, subtitles, graphs, diagrams, photographs, etc. They are often quite unable to give the title of the document they are reading, or to describe its lay-out or even to say how many diagrams etc. accompany the part they have read. For them, reading in a foreign language is a sort of line-by-line translation and this translation precedes any 'direct' act of comprehension on their part.

So great is the importance which they attribute to these linguistic features that they seem to forget that they have any actual reason for reading. Moreover, the effort which this meticulous decoding of details demands leaves them confused. They cannot see the wood for the trees and forget what it is they are looking for. If they ever do reach their objective it usually takes them far too long for their reading ever to become an efficient professional tool. It is for these reasons that they often feel that they have read something — because they have looked up the words in a dictionary, making a linear translation, which takes hours — without really understanding anything they have read. They often even forget their own specialized knowledge. One English teacher who was giving a reading course to a group of chemists, people who were already specialists in the field, found that it was like teaching a group of beginners in chemistry. Time after time, they could have solved the linguistic problems their documents contained if they had made use of their knowledge of chemistry, but this never seemed to occur to them: they seemed to think that everything should be included in the text, and even went so far as to criticize the teacher for not being able to explain the chemistry of passages which in their mother tongue they would have found absolute child's-play!

What are the reasons for this poor level of performance? If we apply the criteria drawn from the research articles discussed at the beginning of this paper (p.76), we can see that our learner–readers make such poor readers because they almost never use either those most powerful of markers, the semantic clues, or the non-visual information stored in their memories. It is as if the document in a foreign language had come from another planet about which they know nothing whatever. The document is a world in itself, cut off from any external reality, and has to be explained in linguistic terms alone. This therefore obliges the reader to rely heavily on the visual information, and this, as we have seen, is not dealt with adequately.

Yet these foreign language learner–readers are all competent readers in their mother tongue: some are better than others, of course, but all of them are perfectly satisfied with their performance and none of them is anything like as weak as he is in the foreign language. So the central problem which learners and teachers have to solve together is one of transferring know-how from the mother tongue to the foreign language, something which does not happen automatically. Learning a new linguistic code is not in itself enough to give the learner the confidence necessary to tackle a document in the foreign language as he would one in his mother tongue. The most efficient and economic way of giving him that confidence is, in our view, by practising those very techniques which he has already mastered in his mother tongue (though in varying degrees, of course). If this is done explicitly, he will be in a position to adapt his reading processes to a new linguistic code.

One important way of doing this is by *sensitizing* learners to the ways in which they read in their mother tongue. This brings home to them a number of important points such as the fact that they would normally never dream of reading with a dictionary to hand, even though certain texts contain words they do not understand. In such cases, readers make use of 'avoidance strategies' or 'repair strategies'.

A second important step is to recognize the notion of *reading task*. For example, the learner–reader can be asked to define a reading objective for each of his foreign language documents and also to decide on the most suitable technique or techniques for that particular task. In this way, teacher and learner soon make up a list of the different reading techniques which are available. From these it is not difficult to develop a series of exercises in which each of these techniques is practised systematically: we ourselves used a list which had been developed by an English colleague who had tried to organize different categories such as 'scanning', 'skimming' and 'search reading' (A. K. Pugh in Latham 1975) and to describe their main characteristics.

Predicting is also an important aspect of reading, as we saw above, and various exercises can be used to encourage this activity. For example, learner–readers can be asked to complete a truncated text. Other exercises emphasize the importance of typographical lay-out in predicting by asking learner–readers to forecast the content of an article on the basis of the title, sub-titles and diagrams alone. Again, students can be asked what ideas and information come to their minds when they read a particular heading or title: the resulting discussion often provides them with details which are useful in their reading. This sort of exercise helps make learners aware of the mass of information they already possess on a subject before they start reading about it.

Another important dimension is that of *evaluation*: if the learner is to be weaned away from word-by-word decoding, he has to be convinced that he can read well using other techniques, that is, he has to know how good a foreign language reader he is. He sees the problem in terms of 'How do I know whether I've understood properly?' He has to be helped, therefore, to evaluate his own performance. We tried to suggest exercises which showed learners that they understood properly when they *read* properly; when, for example, they compared summaries or they used reading techniques first and then checked on their results by a more linear reading translation.

We also saw that a good reader makes use of visual information. By using foreign language documents to train eye-movements the learner–reader is more fully prepared for the task in hand. The techniques which have been developed for 'rapid reading' (Richaudeau, Gauquelin and Gauquelin 1969) can be useful here, since they aim at improving eye-movements. Different exercises are suggested for reading with the different types of movement: learner–readers practise to improve their reading speeds, to increase their field of vision, to reduce their number of fixations per line and to use their faculty of recognition.

In the different exercises and materials which we have just described, the learner is seen as an apprentice reader who has to 're-train' his foreign language reading ability (as defined at the beginning of this paper). However, our experience as teachers has shown us that the transfer of skills which this approach leads us to expect does not always take place satisfactorily. In our opinion, this (relative) failure is due to the fact that the learner–reader remains a language learner.

Language learner?

Written language has specific characteristics which allow us to construct a text by the hierarchical ordering of information, by the realization of communicative aims and by signalling the rhetorical structure of the discourse. A reader knows these specific characteristics of his mother tongue in its written form, which are different from those of the spoken form, and uses this knowledge when he is reading to establish and select his reading strategies. When we put a reader of a foreign language in the situation of an apprentice reader, we are asking him to make use of these same characteristics. This is one of the sources of difficulty: when a foreign language reader performs badly, it is not because he does not know about these special characteristics of written language (because he is a competent reader in his own language) but because he does not know just how this specificity is manifested in the foreign language. This ignorance prevents him from adapting his personal reading process to the specific linguistic characteristics of the foreign language. When he uses the techniques described above, he comes up constantly against obstacles which are insuperable since he does not possess the tools which are necessary if he is to take the important steps of selecting the relevant clues, of identifying the structure or of perceiving the communicative aim of the text. To check his hypotheses, he is obliged to keep on referring to a linguistic analysis — lexical or syntactic — of the passage in question. This gives him the impression that the process in question is far longer, more tedious, less systematic and much less efficient than a linear reading. The structure of the written document is no longer something he recognizes at first glance. His knowledge of the language is incomplete: although he is a learner–reader he is still also a language learner.

He is, however, a language learner of a particular type, and it is interesting to examine his characteristic features. Firstly, in terms of language skills, it is clear that his objective, which is to improve his reading capacity, is one that only involves the skill of written comprehension. The whole pedagogic approach should therefore be built around this skill: only those aspects of the language which play a role in this area should be taken into account. Teaching content and teaching strategies should focus on the characteristic features of the written form.

For many teachers the foreign language is a whole, all of whose characterisitics have to be learnt by the learner, whatever the situation in which he will actually use the language. The spoken and written forms are taught together: for example, the written form (spelling) and the spoken form (pronunciation) of a word are taught simultaneously, and learners are taught to write down extracts of the spoken language ('dictation') and to read aloud written passages. For some teachers, it would seem nonsense to try to teach a language without referring to aspects of its oral form, such as pronunciation or intonation. They would feel that they were only half doing their job, since they would be giving the learners only a very limited idea of the foreign language. But in fact by binding the oral and written forms of the language together in this way, the teacher gives the learner a distorted view of the language, since it is one which prevents him from recognizing the differences between the two. Just as a foreign language learner should learn to use the system of that language independently, without reference to his mother tongue, so he should learn to use the written system without reference to the oral form. The two systems use different channels and neither teacher nor learner should forget this. The teaching should, therefore, reveal the nature of this difference.

Let us consider an example. To transmit a certain piece of information, the oral system has available a number of techniques which make use of the acoustic channel. The techniques of the written system, on the other hand, make use of the visual channel. Work which aims at helping the learner to read should therefore train him in using the various graphic signs to find his way around the document and to understand it. The learner ought to learn to recognize the various typographical signals which serve to structure a written document — things like punctuation marks and the use of different kinds of typeface. Since this aspect is often neglected, learners conclude either that it is unimportant or that it is the same as in their mother tongue, neither of which is necessarily true. Language teaching which aims at improving learners' reading ability should include work which will help make them aware of the role of these tools in the structure of a written document.

It would, however, be wrong to say that all teachers refuse to tackle the teaching of the written form on the basis of a methodology which is specific to that form. During the last ten years or so many have recognized the necessity to do so. This approach, whose main objective is to base teaching on language learners' specific needs, is particularly common amongst teachers working in the field of language for special purposes (such as ESP and *Français fonctionnel*). The syllabuses which have been developed for their learners have emphasized the characteristic features of the written system of a language. Those features which were the first to be noted were the lexical, morphological and syntactic elements peculiar to the written form, in other words the 'structural' elements.

This approach has been fruitful, because it has allowed us to develop an independent methodology for the teaching of the written form and of the language skills related to it. However, it has still not solved all the problems which learners have: even though it concentrates on a specific linguistic domain, it still neglects an important aspect of that domain and consequently it fails to encourage, or sometimes even runs directly counter to, the reading strategies being tried out by learner–readers.

Take, for example, the grammatical approach developed in a number of written comprehension teaching materials (Abé and Duda 1974). Materials of this kind aim at helping the learner acquire the ability to identify the surface structure of the English sentence, so that he can segment a sentence in the foreign language and, consequently, understand it. In this way, the learner acquires a detailed and close knowledge of the morpho-syntax of the language whose written form he is studying. This has the advantage of enabling the learner to find his way around a written text.

However, by plunging the learner into the deep water of morpho-syntactic analysis, this procedure leads him to rely constantly on the visual information provided by linear reading. It also implies that grammatical analysis precedes comprehension. The learner gets into the habit of 'taking to bits' or segmenting every single sentence in his text before making any attempt to understand it (although, as in the case of the C.R.A.P.E.L. course mentioned, global comprehension exercises are sometimes introduced as a balance to the enormous quantity of grammatical work.) This means that the learner gives priority to what he gets out of the visual information, putting off comprehension of the meaning to a later stage. He is also forced to concentrate on graphic and syntactic clues which, as we have seen, are the least valuable to him. For these reasons, this procedure does not really help the learner to develop real reading strategies; indeed it encourages the development of techniques which may act as a brake on or even prevent an acceptable reading performance. This is why such an approach should not be confused with an approach based on the acquisition of reading skills.

Other, more recent, teaching methods using the insights provided by pragmalinguistic analysis do allow us to give learner–readers a clearer idea of the nature of written communication and of those features which are specific to it. These methods are based on the fact that many learners have a formal knowledge of the structure of the foreign language (knowledge which they have acquired in 'written comprehension' courses) but are still unable to use this knowledge to recognize the roles which these grammatical structures play in the communicative structure of an extended text. They therefore concentrate on the elucidation and acquisition of the rules which govern communicative structure.

These procedures are very similar to what happens in a real reading situation, but they still are not on their own entirely sufficient for improving reading. As we saw earlier, reading strategies often rely on the *discursive* dimension of a document, particularly as regards the search for semantic clues. It is this discursive dimension of a document which reveals a text's structure and which transforms a succession of words or sentences into one continuous semantically unique entity in which each sentence enters into relationships with the sentence or sentences which precede or follow it. These relationships allow the various types of information contained in the document to be hierarchically ordered. For the learner to be able to grasp the discursive framework of a document, he has to be able to analyse the relationships which hold between the different elements of the discourse and to be aware of the different levels at which these relationships may operate. To do this, he has to know how the higher levels of the conceptual organization of discourse are constructed; but this problem is never dealt with in this sort of methodology, which limits its attention to the relationships between sentences. Very often the highest level of structure is the paragraph. Short texts, containing only a few paragraphs, are used. Now the documents which our learner-readers need to read are often several pages long: it is at this point that the discursive organization begins to play a really important role, its linguistic markers helping the learner to structure his reading process.

Reading-related language teaching should therefore include work which helps the learner become aware of the nature of *extended* discourse (that is, of the way in which a semantic whole is constructed in the foreign language) and which helps him develop tactics for recognizing the relevant organizational markers. It is these markers (of which lexical markers such as coordinative adverbs are only one category) which will help at those times when he is trying to improve his reading capacity.

Let us consider two examples. Research carried out at the C.R.A.P.E.L. (described in Abé *et al.* 1975; Gremmo 1977) has shown the importance of the discursive role of what we call *positing sentences*. These sentences are distinguished by the fact that they are not directly related to the sentences which precede or follow them; they correspond to a higher level of the organization of the information contained in the text. They posit the information on which part or all of the subsequent text is based. An adequate summary of a text can often be obtained simply by putting together the positing sentences it contains. We have therefore included in our courses activities designed to sensitize learner-readers to the existence and role of such sentences.

Our second example concerns what we have called *discourse performatives*, sentences in which the author reveals in an explicit way the discursive organization of a text by saying what he has done or what he is going to do. An example would be:

> The classification of the main types of porosity will now be discussed and followed by a description of the commoner varieties of pore.

Performatives such as this, then, also allow the reader to select his reading strategy and to structure his reading. Some of them, such as the example given here, are obvious enough, but others are more difficult to recognize. Here, too, the learner–reader will need help.

We also believe that it is helpful to introduce a contrastive element, since the improvement of reading capacity involves the re-learning not only of techniques based on linguistic features, but also on other types of knowledge. For example, the impression of confusion with which many French scientists are left after reading a specialized text in English seems to us to be due to the fact that the conceptual structure of such works is different in the two languages. Our work has brought home to us the importance of rheme and theme, the distribution of new and old information, in this context, and although we have not carried out any really rigorous contrastive investigation, it does seem to us that French prefers the order theme–rheme, whilst English tends to favour rheme–theme. A French reader will therefore tend to look for new information in the second part of an English sentence, applying techniques which work well enough in his mother tongue but which are the opposite of those procedures which are specific to English.

We mentioned above the importance of typography, which plays a far from negligeable role in the global structure of a text. Odile Régent (pp. 105–20) working on a corpus of medical texts in French and English, has shown that French texts use typographical markers such as titles, subtitles, headings, indentation, and heavy print to a far greater extent than English texts.[1] The French reader, used as he is to texts in which typography and lay-out make a considerable contribution towards structuring a text, therefore feels at a loss when faced with an English text which is far less varied — and far more foreign — from this point of view.

Contrastive analysis of the characteristics of written discourse in the two languages concerned highlights those aspects of the reading process on which attempts to improve reading capacity should focus.

[1] *Translator's note*: It is interesting to note that the French original of this paper contains 85 paragraphs, whilst in this translation there are only just over 50.

5 From reading to writing acts

C. Henner-Stanchina

Background and justification of the approach

The development of the approach to writing to be described in this article was prompted by several factors.

The first was three semesters of observation of the writing problems of intermediate ESL learners at Queens College (City University of New York). These problems proved to be not only of a grammatical nature, but more often of an organizational one. Learners were unable to write coherent paragraphs providing supporting details for one given topic sentence, a term which is taken to mean a restricted generalization which 'expresses the main idea on which a paragraph is based and developed' (Di Pippo 1971). This is an especially important task for our learners, as it is part of the final exam which determines their eligibility for college. Further analysis of their writing showed an unawareness not only of cohesion/coherence techniques but of the very relationships between sentences; an ignorance of the hierarchization of information in a text, an unawareness of the levels of generality within a text — that is, an inability to differentiate between the general and the specific; in short, an overall lack of knowledge of the rhetorical conventions which constitute normal written discourse. It should be noted that because rhetorical conventions are culturally linked, these problems varied with each national group. Needless to say, there was the occasional student to whom rational discursive development came naturally, but, this being the exception, the problem of making this explicit and helping learners to adopt certain patterns remained. For even though 'what appears as a logical sequence of main and supporting ideas by our rhetorical traditions is the result of our cultural conditioning' (Dubin and Olshtain 1980) college professors will expect ideas to be dealt with in ways traditional to English, and we therefore must accept this imposition of 'culturally conditioned rhetorical traditions'.

The second factor was observation of a general emphasis in composition manuals and classroom teaching practices either on strict sentence construction or on descriptive and narrative writing. Unfortunately, as J. F. Green has pointed out (1967), it is expository writing which is so necessary for college, while 'imaginative, narrative, or informal personal writing is rarely required'. This emphasis, then, must be construed as a failure to recognize learners' needs and prepare them adequately for the demands of college writing, as a babying tendency in the nature of the tasks we expect learners to be able to perform, and, as such, as a perpetuation of the gap that now exists between ESL writing and writing for a real university situation. Moreover, the exclusion of preliminary reading tasks from descriptive and narrative writing exercises automatically eliminates the need for training in the critical analytical processes — that is, practice in the interpretation and re-structuring of information culled from reading materials, and the re-incorporation of this selected information into a new piece of expository writing. Again, the ESL writing–college writing gap looms before us.

The last factor was learners' involvement in two other types of activities, which seemed to set the stage for the introduction of this approach to writing:

1. *Reading comprehension using authentic materials*: at the beginning of each term, learners were given a choice as to the type of reading texts they would prefer: recommended commercial ESL readers or materials taken from newspapers, magazines and college textbooks. In spite of repeated warnings that the latter would necessarily be a more challenging choice (due to the uncontrolled nature of the authentic text, the absence of grading of difficulty, the lack of grammatical progression, proliferation of new vocabulary, idioms, cultural references, etc . . .), an overwhelming majority of learners each term opted for authentic materials. (Perhaps their choice should serve as an indication to ESL teachers that the learners themselves perceive the gap between ESL work and college work mentioned earlier, and that their motivation is greatly increased as this gap is narrowed.)

For the purposes of this paper, a detailed description of all the reading comprehension exercises accompanying these texts would not be appropriate. Suffice it to say that learners were asked to read carefully each text at length, at home, and work in groups on various exercises in class.

Each text was then discussed extensively in order to ensure total comprehension before proceeding to summarize the text.

The assumption upon which the summarizing was based — simply that by selecting for each paragraph a topic sentence and supporting details, learners could then string the topic sentences together to form a summary — is discussed by M–J. Gremmo (1977).

> At the macro level of the discursive organization of the text, it appears that for a student to fully understand a text, it is vital to identify the sentences fulfilling the role we have termed positing (taken here as synonymous with topic sentence). The positing sentences are differentiated by the fact that they are not related to the directly preceding or succeeding sentence but correspond to the hierarchization of the information carried through a text. They often could start a text on their own. The positing sentences of one particular text, grouped together, can serve as an 'acceptable' summary of the text.

A similar approach seems to be suggested by Dubin and Olshtain (1980, p. 360): '(ESOL learners) need to know that most paragraphs have a single controlling idea usually recoverable in a topic sentence. They need to look closely at how the other sentences of the paragraph support the topic sentence', although their goal is to use 'the plan of the written material as a tool for better reading', and not, as is the case here, to use the reading material as a means to achieving better writing. The present study would seem to suggest that Dubin and Olshtain's (1980) model, writing process → text → reading process, is a reversible one.

2. *Exposure to speech acts*: A parallel component of the learners' training consisted of listening to recordings of authentic interactions between native speakers, with the aim of first identifying the communicative functions manifested in these interactions, and then of reproducing acceptable utterances at the appropriate times. They had, thus, already acquired a repertoire of categories or 'speech acts' along with specific realizations of each act, either provided by the teacher or derived from listening to these taped interactions. An example of a speech act and some of its realizations would be:

speech act:	giving advice
realizations:	If I were you, I would . . .
	Why don't you . . .
	Try + ing
	You could always . . . etc.

If, then, this notion of categories could merely be transferred to writing, the labelling of the categories being changed to suit the purposes of writing, the learners should be able to repeat the process of first identifying the discursive categories, or *writing acts* obtained by summarizing the reading texts, and then reproducing realizations of these acts in appropriate situations. In doing so they would be considering each text not simply as a linear sequence but as a hierarchical arrangement, with certain acts linked to form the main propositional development and others playing a supporting role.

The course aimed not only to encourage effective acquisition of writing skills, but more so, to provide these learners with the methodological tools with which to continue improving these skills beyond the boundaries of the classroom and without the direction of a teacher. For even when these learners have passed the exams required for college or university entrance they are still sometimes burdened with several semesters of English, often containing composition courses (regardless, it would seem, of their intended fields of study). The politics, economics, or ethics behind these rigid requirements for foreign students are, no doubt questionable and worthy of investigation, yet such is not the purpose of this paper. The problem at hand is that of showing learners how to use the media materials which are readily available to them, how to conform to the concrete norms of already published materials (and whatever complaints one may lodge against published writings today, one must assume that if these have, in fact, been accepted for publication, then they do fulfill certain conditions) instead of to some abstract notion of writing which may or may not be shared by the community of teachers whose job it is to judge their writing. In other words, the attempt first to instill in learners an awareness of how authentic texts are constructed, and then to demonstrate to them some of the possible techniques for reproducing acceptable texts, stemmed from the desire to make them more autonomous — less dependent on the classroom, on didactic materials and on the teacher for providing tasks, models, for correcting and evaluating (in sum, for teaching!).

This approach to writing, then, was merely a logical extension of the training learners were already getting in reading comprehension and speech acts, a response to their writing problems and condition as foreign students anxious and impatient to enter American universities, and an attempt to implement an autonomous learning strategy in a new setting.

Description of the methodology

The text below on brainwashing, extracted from a college psychology manual (McNeil and Rubin 1977), was chosen by two learners as the basis for their reading comprehension project. Their exercises were subsequently re-used by the entire class and summarized, the topic sentences and writing acts being determined. Prior to this analysis, learners had been given a list of writing acts including:

generalization (usually, for our purposes, the topic sentence)
exemplification
consequence/result
explicitation (becoming more specific, narrowing down of information)
elaboration (extending, expanding, widening of information)
giving reasons (telling *why*)
explanation (telling *how*)
classification
definition
description
characterization (partial definition)
statement
restatement
thesis statement
reformulation (re-stating in different words a preceding proposition)
evaluation (writer's interjection, opinion)

The function of each of these acts was discussed, in order to give learners an initial understanding of the framework within which they would be analysing their texts.

In most cases, the sentence was taken as the unit, mainly because it was a more convenient one when transferring from reading to writing. There were, however, occasions where larger chunks of discourse were taken as the unit and assigned one particular function, as can be seen in the analysis of the text below, arrived at through discussion among the learners in small groups and consultation with the teacher. (This group work did yield variations in the analysis of the text, a problem which is discussed in pp. 102–3).

BRAINWASHING

[1] The term 'brainwashing' is a loaded one, with different meanings for different people. [2] For some, it has come to mean almost any case of a person's being persuaded to do or think something that he or she later regrets having done or thought. [3] For example, consumers complain that they are brainwashed into buying products they don't really want. [4] For others, the term 'brainwashing' has a sinister ring to it, with connotations of tortures, mind drugs, and brain stimulation. [5] Most accurately, however, brainwashing refers to a set of techniques that are used in an attempt to change a captured person's basic attitudes

and values.

[6] These techniques do not depend on physical tortures, drugs, or gadgets.

[7] Rather, they are based on a recognition of the social foundations of attitudes; [8] they work (when they are successful) by tearing down the existing social foundations of a person's attitudes and erecting new ones in their place.

[9] The word 'brainwash' comes from the Chinese expression *hsi nao*, which literally means 'wash brain'. [10] The Chinese Communists devoted a lot of effort to developing these techniques as part of the program of thought reform that followed their takeover of mainland China in 1949. Brainwashing techniques were used to convert Chinese young people and intellectuals, and similar techniques were also applied to Westerners in China and to American prisoners captured by the Chinese during the Korean War.

[11] Brainwashing has two major phases. The first is to destroy the person's existing group ties and, in so doing, to break down his or her sense of identity. [12] This may be done by isolating prisoners from other people, by restricting communication to them, and by making them feel guilty for their actions. [13] For example, the Chinese would deliver American prisoners their mail only if it contained bad news. [14] And they told the prisoners that their failure to receive mail proved that their loved ones at home had abandoned them (Schein 1957).

[15] The second phase of brainwashing is to give the prisoner a new set of relationships, tied to the new ideals that the brainwashers want the prisoners to adopt. [16] Edgard Schein (1957) reports that Chinese 'instructors' sometimes lived with American prisoners for long periods of time in order to establish close relationships with them. [17] And they offered the prisoners special privileges if they would make public confessions or engage in other propaganda activities. [18] By inducing the prisoner to engage in public behaviors that betrayed their old group and ideas, the brainwashers hoped that their private attitudes would change as well.

[19] Brainwashing was back in the news recently when Patricia Hearst was placed on trial for taking part in a bank robbery while she was a captive of the militant radical group called the Symbionese Liberation Army (the SLA). [20] One of the witnesses in Patty's defense was Robert Lifton, a psychiatrist who had done extensive research on Chinese brainwashing techniques. Lifton claimed that the SLA employed many techniques with Patty Hearst that came right out of the Communist Chinese's book. [21] They toppled Patty's sense of self by locking her in a closet for weeks, and they created feelings of guilt and self-blame by branding her as 'the daughter of a ruling class family, the Hearsts'. When Patty emerged from the closet, they induced her to take steps to renounce her old identity, such as making a tape on which she publicly called her parents 'the pig Hearsts'. And the bank robbery itself (which, Lifton claimed, Patty was forced to take part in) further cut off her links to the past.

Instead, Patty took on a new name ('Tania') and a new identity, as a member of the group that had captured her.

[22] In spite of the power of these techniques, it is extremely difficult to brainwash someone successfully.

Schein found that although the Chinese were successful in obtaining behavioral compliance and collaboration from many of their American prisoners, they produced very few ideological conversions. [23] People's attitudes and ideals are rooted in decades of training in their original groups, and breaking down these strongly held attitudes is no easy matter. Nevertheless, there is no doubt that by systematically destroying and replacing people's group supports and self-image, lasting changes in beliefs and attitudes can be produced. [24] During the Hearst trial, Robert Lifton was asked whether there is any system that would enable a prospective victim to avoid being brainwashed. His answer: 'There is none. [25] If one's captors are sufficiently determined, they can break down anyone' (reported by Turner 1976).

[1] thesis statement
[2] definition
[3] exemplification
[4] definition
[5] definition
[6] negative explicitation
[7] positive explicitation
[8] explanation
[9] definition
[10] exemplification
[11] classification
[12] explanation
[13] exemplification
[14] exemplification
[15] classification
[16] explanation
[17] explanation
[18] statement/consequence
[19] exemplification
[20] elaboration
[21] description/elaboration
[22] restatement
[23] explanation
[24] elaboration
[25] restatement

The following summary was proposed for this text:

The term 'brainwashing' is a loaded one, with different meanings for different people. For some, it has come to mean almost any case of a person's being persuaded to do or think something that he or she later regrets having done or thought. For others, the term 'brainwashing' has a sinister ring to it, with connotations of tortures, mind drugs and brain stimulation. Most accurately, however, brainwashing refers to a set of techniques that are used in an attempt to change a captured person's basic attitudes and values. The word 'brainwash' comes from the Chinese expression *hsi nao*, which literally means 'wash brain'.

Brainwashing has two major phases. The first is to destroy the person's existing group ties and, in so doing, to break down his or her sense of identity. The second phase of brainwashing is to give the prisoner a new set of relationships, tied to the new ideals that the brainwashers want the prisoners to adopt.

In spite of the power of these techniques, it is extremely difficult to brainwash someone successfully.

Nevertheless, there is no doubt that by systematically destroying and replacing people's group supports and self-images, lasting changes in beliefs and attitudes can be produced.

Having thus sensitized the learners to the hierarchical interlocking of writing acts in authentic discourse, the focus was then shifted to individual writing acts. Definition and classification, well-represented in this text, were chosen as the basis for the first writing exercises or 'pastiches'.

A. Definition

There are many ways to define a word, but the example of this category of act in the text in question was: 'For some, it has come to mean almost any case of a person's being persuaded to do or think something that he or she later regrets having done or thought. For example, consumers complain that they are brainwashed into buying products they don't really want'. That is: definition (restricted generalization) + exemplification.

The text below was taken from *Future Shock* (Toffler 1970).

> Culture shock is the effect that immersion in a strange culture has on the unprepared visitor. Peace Corps volunteers suffer from it in Borneo or Brazil. Marco Polo probably suffered from it in Cathay. Culture shock is what happens when a traveler suddenly finds himself in a place where yes may mean no, where a 'fixed price' is negotiable, where to be kept waiting in an outer office is no cause for insult, where laughter may signify anger. It is what happens when the familiar psychological cues that help an individual to function in society are suddenly withdrawn and replaced by new ones that are strange or incomprehensible.

Once comprehension of this text was established, learners were given the skeleton of the paragraph:

> Culture shock is the effect that immersion in a strange culture has on the unprepared visitor. It is what happens when the familiar psychological cues that help an individual to function in society are suddenly withdrawn and replaced by new ones that are strange or incomprehensible.

They were then asked, working in small groups, to substitute three new examples of culture shock taken from their own personal experiences of life in New York City. (Elements such as the physical layout of cities, the conception of time, dating rules, greetings, waiting in line, etc. were suggested, but numerous others were mentioned.) Whether or not they chose to repeat the same sentence structures as those in the original text was entirely up to them.

This exercise provided learners with a framework for definition — leaving them only to supply appropriate support in the form of examples. Subsequent exercises dealt with the writing of definitions from scratch, using this same model, and others.

B. Classification

This writing act was chosen not only because a realization of it had appeared in the text on 'Brainwashing', but also because it had become evident, as suggested by Henry Widdowson (1978, pp. 111–143) that the use of non-verbal representations for classification was extremely instrumental in getting learners to distinguish — through visualization and mapping on diagrams — levels of generality. The following text was used first for reading comprehension.

> The positions which the child assumes in utero may be divided into two general classes: longitudinal and transverse.
>
> In the longitudinal the spinal column of the child is parallel to the spinal column of the mother; in the transverse it is at right angles to that of the mother, forming a cross with it. The former is normal, accounting for more than 99%; while the transverse position is rare, occuring in less than 0.5%.
>
> These two general classifications of the fetal position may be subdivided into more exact groups. We term these more specific positions presentations: this refers to the precise part of the fetus which presents over the bony birth passage, the pelvis. At term, 96% of fetuses present by the head; 3.5% with the buttocks; and in less than 0.5% the child lies transversely, a shoulder presenting. (Guttmacher 1956).

Comprehension having been checked, learners were asked to fill in the diagram shown in Figure 1 using the information given in the text.

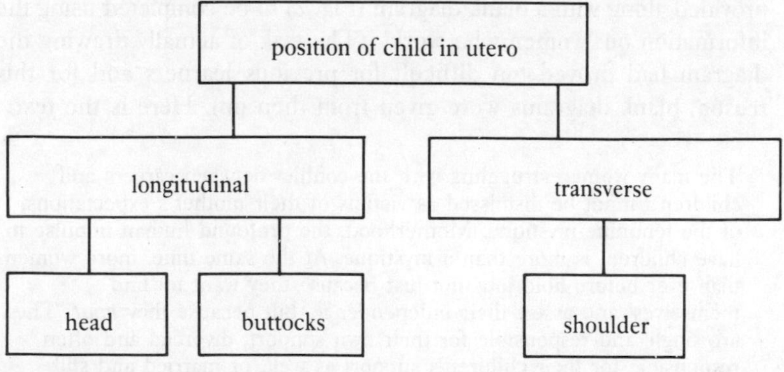

FIGURE 1

At this point, learners were asked to glean from the text the expressions typically used for classification. The expressions:

X may be divided into two general classes . . .
These two general classifications of X may be subdivided into more exact groups . . .

formed the beginning of a list which was later supplemented with others such as:

X can be broken down into . . .
X can be classified according to whether . . .
There are . . . groups of X . . .
X is composed of . . .
X is made up of . . .
X comprises . . .
X constitutes . . .
X consists of . . .
X includes . . .
X contains . . .

The question of what to do about grammar has most likely arisen by this time. The answer is simply that whatever grammatical structures were needed to carry out these writing tasks (for example modals or passive voice) were introduced at the appropriate times; that is, before or after the writing task had been completed, according to the needs of these intermediate learners. Grammar, it should be stressed, was dealt with as a means to an end, and not as an end in itself.

Next, a second text, extracted from their reading material, was provided along with a blank diagram (Fig. 2) to be completed using the information on 'women who work'. (The task of actually drawing the diagram had proved too difficult for previous learners and for this reason, blank diagrams were given from then on). Here is the text:

> The many women struggling with the conflict between careers and children cannot be dismissed as victims of their mother's expectations, of the feminine mystique. Motherhood, the profound human impulse to have children, is more than a mystique. At the same time, more women than ever before hold jobs not just because they want to 'find themselves' and assert their independence, but because they *must*. They are single and responsible for their own support, divorced and often responsible for their children's support as well, or married and still partly responsible for their families' support because one paycheck is not enough in this era of inflation. (Friedan 1979)

Figure 2 shows the diagram which was provided:

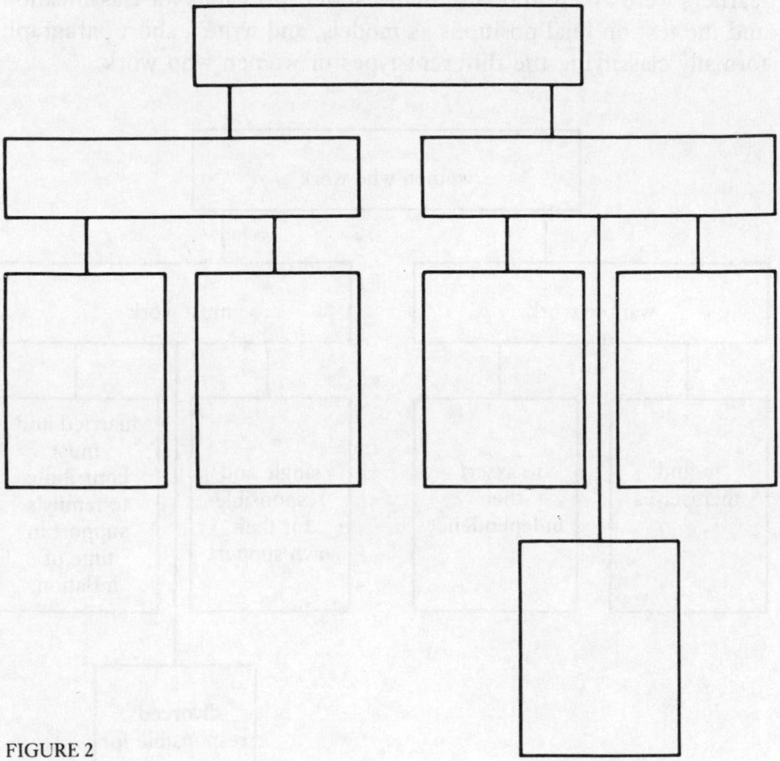

FIGURE 2

Here again, careful attention had to be paid to the levels of generality in the text, so as to avoid something like Figure 3, which was often the first interpretation rendered.

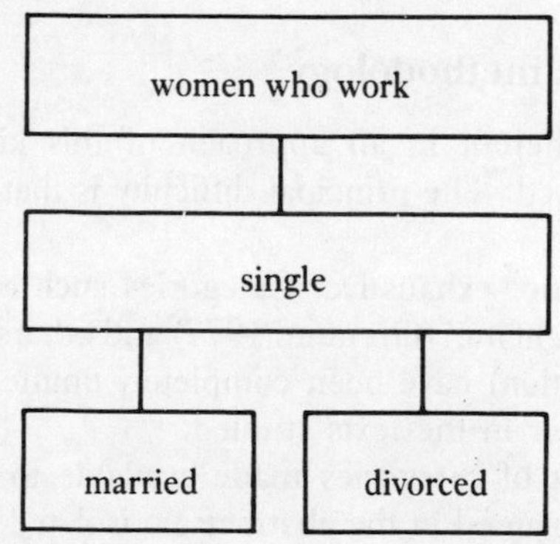

FIGURE 3

Finally, having successfully completed the diagram as in Figure 4, learners were asked to re-use their list of expressions for classification and the text on fetal positions as models, and write a short paragraph formally classifying the different types of women who work.

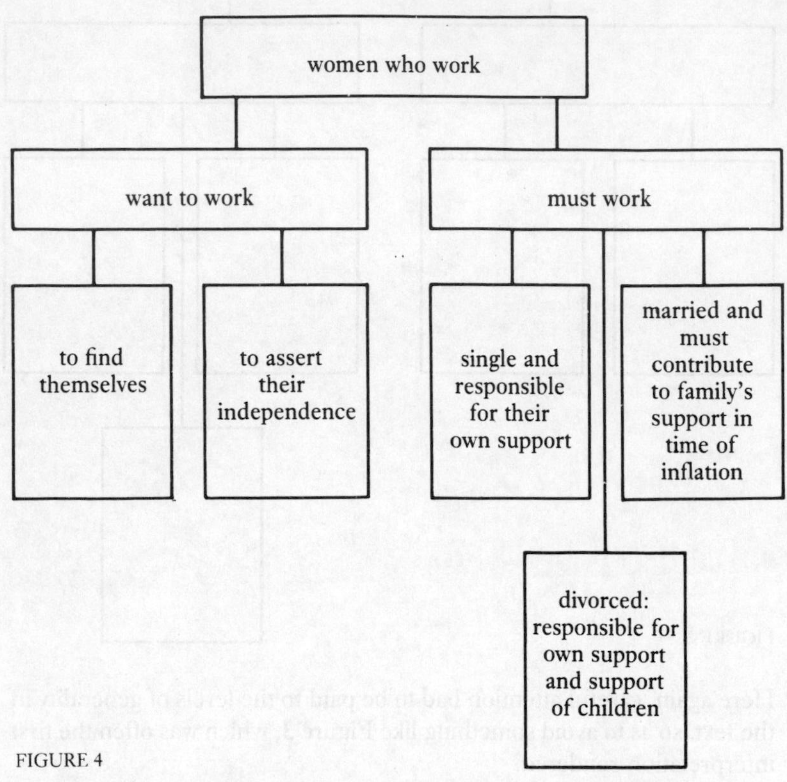

FIGURE 4

Critique of the methodology

The problems inherent in an approach of this kind are far from having been resolved. The principal difficulty is that of the categories themselves.

First, they are not exhaustive. Categories such as 'performatives', 'deduction', 'referencing' (Gremmo 1977) and others (comparison and contrast, qualification) have been completely omitted simply because they did not appear in the texts studied.

Second, the set of categories made available to the learners was presented and explained in the abstract; no isolated examples of each act were initially provided. This obviously would have facilitated recognition of the acts in the reading texts.

Third, these categories at times overlap, allowing for various interpretations of the same sentence. For example, the text on brainwashing contains the following segment:

> They toppled Patty's sense of self by locking her in a closet for weeks, and they created feelings of guilt and self-blame by branding her as 'the daughter of a ruling class family, the Hearsts'. When Patty emerged from the closet, they induced her to take steps to renounce her old identity, such as making a tape on which she publicly called her parents 'the pig Hearsts'. And the bank robbery itself (which, Lifton claimed, Patty was forced to take part in) further cut off her links to the past. Instead, Patty took on a new name ('Tania') and a new identity, as a member of the group that had captured her.

Is this:

a case of explanation?	(how they toppled Patty's sense of self)
a case of explicitation?	(of 'The SLA employed many techniques with Patty Hearst that came right out of the Communist Chinese's book')
or a case of description?	(of the brainwashing techniques)

In sum, there is no authoritative analysis to which a teacher or producer of materials can refer, and consequently the analyses arrived at by teachers and learners may well be debatable or completely erroneous. Whether or not this flaw negates the value of the exercise is the question which must be raised here. In other words, is it the process itself or the definitive result which is of most importance to the learner?

Perhaps the very difficulty of the analysis, coupled with discussions of suggested variations, will sufficiently sensitize learners to the hierarchical nature of texts and to the various discursive functions of their components, thereby fulfilling the goal of enabling them to develop more effective writing styles which will meet the requirements of the American universities they seek to enter, and spare them endless semesters of reading and writing courses. Some of the remaining questions are:

1. What are the formal devices or markers (the position of a topic sentence in a paragraph, cues signalling specific writing acts, etc.) which could be emphasized so as to aid learners in recognizing and reproducing these acts, and how, for example, can the logical connectors (however = qualification; therefore = consequence) be introduced in such a way as to reinforce this general approach?

2. Is there a recurring sequencing of these acts of which learners could be made aware?

To the extent that this approach sheds light on the inner workings of a text (allowing for re-integration of the communicative values of the text), it affords learners the confidence and ability to deal with real-life texts, and equips them with a set of categories which can be expanded at will, and analytical techniques which can render them more autonomous in both reading and writing skills. The approach, however tentative, does offer many possibilities to learners, and on that count alone, would seem to merit further study and elaboration.

6 A comparative approach to the learning of specialized written discourse

O. Régent

Recent work on written communication and reading has emphasized the importance of individual variation in comprehension. The reader is no longer seen as the passive recipient of a discourse which has only the meaning its author intended, but rather as the performer of a communicative act who has to discover the particular meaning that the discourse he is reading has for him. In other words, once a text has been written it no longer belongs to its writer: the reader also creates meaning. The reader constructs his own meaning in terms of his knowledge of the world and of the gaps in it which he is trying to fill in. The comprehension process is, therefore, closely linked to the reader's culture and personal background.

In intercultural written communication, whether we are talking about reading discourse in a foreign language or writing discourse for a different community, the degree of efficiency of the communication is dependent on the knowledge of the differences between the cultures and the thought-patterns of the interlocutors. That is why someone reading a foreign language who applies his mother-tongue reading techniques and knowledge of the world to the interpretation of a discourse encoded in another culture and having a different rhetorical system often has difficulties in comprehension. He reads more slowly, because he cannot grasp the overall meaning; the information he is looking for is not in the place where he expects to find it nor in the form in which he expects to find it. The problem is even more acute for the person wishing to write in a foreign language for a foreign audience. If he merely translates his text, his foreign audience, used to having information presented in a different way, is likely to have trouble understanding it. If his text is to be fully readable in the foreign language, it has to be constructed on the lines of the foreign rhetorical system. This is why it is necessary to undertake contrastive studies of the rhetorical system of discourse in general, in order to solve the problems in intercultural written communication encountered by foreign language learners. Some language-teaching specialists are already aware of this necessity:

> Our preconceived notions about what constitutes a fact or an identity or a concept or a relationship spring from our culture, of which language is the core. And this observation leads us to the conclusion that contrastive rhetoric is necessary to teach writing in ESL. Bilingualism implies biculturalism. To be a cultured person in a second culture requires the knowledge of a second rhetoric. (Palmer 1980)

Equally to the point is the work of R. B. Kaplan (1972) who has shown how it is possible to recognize the structure and rhetoric of oriental stories in the English essays written by students from that part of the world. Scientific discourse has rarely been approached from a contrastive point of view. It has long been thought that science in the west — and in other countries whose universities are based on the western model — has always sprung from the same roots. Modern scientific communication has been an international phenomenon for a long time and people have leapt to the conclusion that there must be universally accepted models for the organization of scientific knowledge and, therefore, of scientific discourse (Widdowson 1975). In support of this argument, it is pointed out that the logical and rhetorical models which western societies use in scientific discussion can all be traced back to Aristotle. Language teaching specialists have tended to concentrate above all on the lexical and syntactic aspects of specialized discourse, with occasional references to rhetorical or sociolinguistic considerations. Most publications in this field deal with one particular type of specialized discourse in one particular language, since they are written by language-teaching specialists for foreign students who are staying in the country whose language they are studying, or who have to use a major language in order to pursue their studies. In all such cases we are dealing with people who need the second language as a tool for the acquisition of a scientific specialization and whose main reading material is the relatively unspecialized textbook. The discourse contained in works of this kind is simplified when compared with that to be found in top-flight scientific publications: its communicative function is to instruct the reader on a topic about which he is ignorant. Information is presented as simply as possible and in general polemic is avoided. Under these circumstances it is not surprising that scientific discourse seems to possess characteristics of its own, independent of the particular language in which it happens to be written. This is what Widdowson (1975) calls 'the philosophy of science', universal in that it seems to be independent of any particular form of expression:

> We can define scientific discourse, then, as the verbal and non-verbal realisation of the communicative system of science. Now this system *has* been described under the name of the philosophy of science, and any systematic description of scientific discourse in English must therefore take account of this philosophy, which represents the basic principles of scientific enquiry.

However, when we turn to the study of scientific discourse which is *not purely didactic*, the universality of the philosophy of science becomes far less obvious. The fundamental concepts which make up the different disciplines may well be the same in a great number of languages, but the various types of scientific discourse used in professional circles often show clear differences in cultural attitudes to science and research. They contain none of the uniformity nor the simplicity of the expository discourse to be found in school or university textbooks. If we are to train professional people to participate in international communication in their field we need to know something about the organization of the specialized discourse in both the languages in question. For example, a research worker who wants to read a foreign language in order to keep up with developments in his field needs to be able to find the information he is looking for in discourse which is organized differently from his own. To do so, he may well have to modify his usual reading strategies to take into account forms of presentation or organization which are unfamiliar to him. If, on the other hand, he wishes to publish in a foreign language, he should know how to organize his discourse in such a way as to catch the interest of his foreign colleagues and to convince them of the relevance of his work; that implies having a good knowledge of the discursive and illocutionary strategies characteristic of the foreign language and culture.

True, there exist any number of handbooks on style for the use of university scientists and one might have expected them to reveal all the secrets of rhetoric and the organization of specialized discourse in a particular language. Were this the case, all one would have to do would be to study two such handbooks. Unfortunately, they make disappointing reading. If one compares, for example, English, French and American handbooks, one finds that the content is much the same. An outline of Aristotelian rhetoric is given, with a sprinkling of common-sense advice on sorting out and classifying one's ideas for presentation, rounded off by a list of common mistakes. They always place great emphasis on the virtues of clarity and brevity, virtues which they naturally think they themselves possess, of course. Yet the end-products are different: scientific English discourse is not constructed in the same way as scientific French discourse. Obviously, then, this has nothing to do with the handbooks of style; rather it is a matter of a sort of consensus between writers who belong to the culture. The model has not been learnt, it has been assimilated by each writer without ever having been explicitly described.

Only by studying the organization of the discourse in the specialized texts themselves can we isolate and describe the features which characterize the textual competence for each type of discourse in a given language. Contrastive descriptions of discourse of the same type and drawn from the same area of specialization may help us to understand problems experienced when reading or writing a foreign language. The examples which follow are an attempt to illustrate the methodology of a contrastive analysis of specialized discourse for didactic purposes. They are selected from a study of a corpus of sixty articles taken from medical journals in French and English, all of them on the same subject: hepatic complications in Hodgkin's disease. Only the language of publication was used to distinguish between the two groups of articles: not only would it be very difficult to establish the origins and nationality of each author, the world of medical research being a highly mobile one, but the object of this study was medical discourse as it actually appears in technical journals. The fact that an article has been accepted by the editorial board of such a journal is enough to show that it satisfies the criteria in question.

Surface organization

Iconic characteristics

If we first consider the texts from the visual point of view, studying their iconic characteristics, we find there is one striking difference: the typography and layout of an article in French are much more varied than those of an article in English; we notice how fragmented the page in French seems when compared with the more compact look of the English page. The French writer makes great use of all the typographical markers available: heavy print, capital letters, dashes, italics and sub-headings with or without A, B, C. In this way the text is divided into a series of hierarchically ordered units which reflect the care the writer takes to emphasize certain scientific data: 'rechutes et incidents', 'récidives', etc. Sometimes the same typographical markers are used to give prominence to quite different types

COMMENTAIRES

A. — Tolérance de la chimiothérapie

L'incertitude de nos connaissances sur l'association chimiothérapie–radiothérapie élargie justifiait, a l'époque, notre prudence vis-à-vis de la chimiothérapie qui a été très modérée ici, expliquant la bonne tolérance. Nous n'avons observé, à ce jour, aucune néoplasie non hodgkinienne, aucune leucémie, mais les délais sont encore trop courts (17). Il semble que le traitement au long cours par la Vinblastine favorise, par immunodépression, l'acquisition et la persistance de l'antigène Australia et la constitution d'une hépatite chronique persistante, ceci chez des sujets en état de guérison apparente de leur maladie de Hodgkin (18).

B. — Appréciation des résultats

En ce qui concerne les données de la littérature, quelques essais d'association ont été faits dans les stades localisés de la maladie mais les schémas sont tous différents, et la chimiothérapie n'a jamais été très intense (19, 20, 21, 22, 23, 24, 25, 26). Les résultats sur la survie à long terme sont dans l'ensemble légèrement en faveur de l'association quelle que soit la place de la chimiothérapie par rapport à la radiothérapie. L'absence de série témoin, dans notre essai, ne permet aucune conclusion quant à la supériorité éventuelle de l'association chimiothérapie–radiothérapie vis-à-vis de la seule radiothérapie. Il n'existe pas de différence en ce qui concerne la survie avec d'autres séries étrangères traitées par la seule radiothérapie.

— *Parmi les rechutes et incidents*, des 6 reprises en bordure de champ, 4 sont liées a une irradiation médiastinale trop économique.

— *Les 6 récidives* in situ en territoire irradié sont peut-être en rapport avec un étalement un peu long de l'irradiation. Le pourcentage de ces récidives est cependant comparable à celui d'autres séries (25) utilisant un étalement de 4 semaines. La chimiothérapie choisie ici ne parait donc pas avoir amélioré le rendement local de la radiothérapie, même si en diminuant le volume tumoral elle en a facilité souvent l'application.

— *24 malades initialement atteints de lésions sus-diaphragmatiques* ont rechuté dans la région lombo–aortique (50% de l'ensemble des rechutes). Dans la moitié de ces cas une laparotomie a montré l'existence d'un envahissement splénique massif associé aux atteintes ganglionnaires lombaires avec une atteinte hépatique dans 3 cas. Ceci confirme bien la fréquence de l'atteinte splénique sans doute précoce et passée inaperçue dans cette série, et l'insuffisance probable de la chimiothérapie associée.

— L'efficacité du traitement d'entretien n'apparaît pas nettement: 80% des rechutes ont eu lieu dans les 3 premières années, contre 85% dans les 2 premières années pour Kaplan (27).

C. — Conclusions pratiques

Malgré son caractère limité, cet essai nous a apporté divers enseignements.

— *En premier lieu*, il nous paraît nécessaire et possible d'intensifier la chimiothérapie associée à la radiothérapie. Aussi avons-nous effectué un essai randomisé de janvier 1969 à avril 1972 avec 2 séries, l'une témoin avec irradiation immédiate (Rx), l'autre (Ch/Rx) avec 3 cures de Mopp préradiothérapique. Après l'irradiation un entretien de 3 ans a été entrepris par Vinblastine mensuelle ou Vinblastine mensuelle et 1 cure type Mopp tous les 6 mois. 228 malades ont été inclus dans cet essai dont l'exploitation est en cours.

— *En second lieu*, si cet essai confirme l'intérêt pronostique des signes généraux (A, B), notion admise par tous (6, 28, 29), il montre aussi que l'existence d'anomalies biologiques /β/ (6) confère un pronostic plus mauvais aux formes 1 A: la fréquence des incidents est significativement différente, dans ces formes, entre les groupe. 1 Aa (3/41) et le groupe 1 Ab (8/20), $p < 0.01$ (*fig. 2*).

— *Enfin. l'étude anatomopathologique* dégage deux caractéristiques péjoratives. La première est la déplétion lymphocytaire, qu'il s'agisse du type IV ou du type 11 avec déplétion lymphocytaire (13); Sur 11 malades pour l'ensemble de ces groupes, 10 ont rechuté. La seconde concerne l'existence de lésions vasculaires, quel que soit le type histopathologique. Sur les 16 malades qui avaient des lésions vasculaires dans la biopsie ganglionnaire initiale, nous avons observé: 5 échecs du traitement avec diffusion rapide, 7 rechutes sous-phréniques avec rate pathologique, 4 bons résultats. En définitive, 78% des malades ont eu une évolution sévère.

CONCLUSION

L'association radiothérapie–chimiothérapie nous paraît utile dans le traitement de la maladie de Hodgkin, même dans les stades localisés, à condition d'intensifier la chimiothérapie d'attaque précédant la radiothérapie. Dans cet essai, l'utilité du traitement d'entretien n'est pas démontrée.

of unit. For example, in Section B the dashes followed by italics signal that a process of classification is taking place; in section C, on the other hand, they only serve to emphasize discursive operators, not the classification and ordering of the data. In contrast, the absence of typographical markers and the resulting solid look of the page in English (see over) do not reveal at a glance what it is that is being emphasized. The only typographical marker is indentation and even that is used sparingly, so that the paragraphs are relatively long, there being in general between three and six per page. Nonetheless, this solitary marker provides an accurate guide for both reading and for the

DISCUSSION

Previous reports of splenectomy in Hodgkin's disease have revealed high incidence of morbidity and mortality. The mortality rates approach 40 per cent in previously reported groups, and there is approximately 50 per cent incidence of complications due to infection. These reports dealt with patients who presented with hypersplenism as a complication of Hodgkin's disease. Since hypersplenism is usually a late complication of Hodgkin's disease, these reported patients are assumed to have been suffering from general debilitation, often with bone marrow involvement, and limited cellular and immune responses to infection. The patients in this study, in contrast, were in comparatively good health. The presence of Hodgkin's disease did not appear to result in excessive surgical morbidity rates.

Since the negative aspects of the exploration are clearly limited, the positive aspects deserve great emphasis. As was noted, staging data were altered in 50 per cent of the patients undergoing such exploration. Twenty-four of the patients, or 35 per cent, had more severe involvement than suspected. The resultant treatment of these previously undefined areas of disease, we believe, will result in higher over-all cure rates for these patients.

Removal of spleen involved with Hodgkin's disease has the additional advantage of avoiding high dose radiotherapy to the left upper quadrant. The radiotherapists at this center prefer to avoid such therapy to this area because of the risk of radiation pneumonitis of the lower lobe of the left lung and radiation nephritis of the left kidney. Marking the splenic pedicle allows identification and treatment of those nodes without blind extension of the treatment field into the left upper quadrant.

location of information because each paragraph develops a new idea and marks a new stage in the writer's argument. Reading the first sentence of each paragraph tells us what sort of argument is going to be developed there.

It seems, therefore, that the visual impression made by the printed page is related to different attitudes towards science; in French, the *data have precedence over reasoning*. The discourse and its presentation on the page are organized around the data. For the sake of clarity each important piece of data is indicated by some typographical device and separated from the rest of the text by spaces round the headings and between the paragraphs. Paradoxically, this concern for clarity sometimes results in complete confusion; when a page is overflowing with typographical and iconic markers, the essential information is lost because nothing really stands out. In English, on the other hand, the overall look of the page may be very austere, but since the composition of the paragraphs follows stricter rules and since the writer develops his argument throughout the whole of the length of the text, the reader has no difficulty in following his line of thought or in identifying the data at whatever stages in the argument they may occur.

A unit of rhetoric

As we saw above, the paragraph has a different status in English and in French. Consequently, there is a problem as regards the choice of a unit of analysis for the comparison of the two languages. Given the pedagogical applications which we have in mind, the sentence is too small a unit. Larger units are section and sub-section. In biology there is a plan for the structure of articles which includes three parts headed 'Materials and methods', 'Results' and 'Discussion'. This plan, following as it does the chronology of the events involved in the empirical method, is recommended by all medical journals and followed by all writers of original articles, English and French. This common framework determines high-level units within which it is possible to identify comparable discursive sequences even if the content of each section is not precisely defined (certain items may occur either under 'Results' or under 'Discussion' and the relative size of the two sections depends on the authors). The discursive sequence can be defined as a unit of thought consisting of the introduction of a topic, development and termination. In English, the limits of the sequence and those of the paragraph coincide fairly often, but in French the sequence may be contained within one single paragraph or spread out over several.

Discursive sequences

The 'Introductions' of research articles have a discursive structure which is more or less the same in both languages: the theme is established in a general way by a *topic sentence* (or '*énoncé-thème*'). In the next step, *focalization*, the writer defines those aspects of the overall theme on which his study concentrates and, finally, he uses a *performative* to state just what it is he is doing or is going to do in the article which follows ('We wish to report our experience with...'; 'Nous versons à ce dossier déjà fort nourri une contribution...'.) Within the article proper, there are two major types of discursive sequences to be found: descriptive sequences, which are especially common in the 'Materials and methods' section, and interpretative or evaluative sequences which tend to occur under 'Results' or 'Comments'.

Descriptive sequences

The subject of a descriptive sequence may be static (a particular patient or group of patients, for example, or a physical organ) or it may be dynamic (e.g. a process, or the carrying out of an operation). Descriptions of static subjects are very similar in both languages, consisting of a series of operations including quantification, qualification, inclusion and elimination. A comparison of the descriptive sequences dealing with dynamic subjects, on the other hand, reveals some interesting differences. Below are two examples taken from the sections headed 'Apparatus and Method' and '*Matériel et Méthodes*' of articles in which the authors describe the methods they used to carry out laparotomies on a particular group of patients.

> All of the referred patients were considered for laparotomy. One patient did not undergo laparotomy because of a positive bone-marrow biopsy. The remaining 30 patients had no unequivocal clinical evidence of disseminated visceral disease, and all underwent exploratory laparotomy and splenectomy. During surgery, we attempted to biopsy those lymph nodes which appeared abnormal on lymphangiography. When the lymphangiogram was normal and no nodes appeared to be enlarged at surgery, one of the left periaortic nodes was biopsied. In most cases, the iliac and mesenteric nodes were biopsied routinely. The porta hepatis was explored, and enlarged nodes were biopsied. Splenectomy and wedge biopsy of the liver were performed. Silver clips were used to demarcate all biopsy sites as well as the splenic pedicle and the lateral extent of any massive retroperitoneal disease. Bilateral oophoropexy was performed in 12 young females.

The English writer organizes his description into a single paragraph which is connected with the preceding paragraph by the anaphoric expression 'all of the referred patients'. The first topic-sentence introduces the subject of the paragraph and all the other sentences are subordinate to it. Before the description itself is entered on, the topic is specified more exactly ('one patient did not . . . The remaining 30 patients . . .'). The beginning of the description is signalled by a repetition of the topic, 'During surgery'. The various operations carried out are then enumerated, but none of them is given any particular prominence. The description is in the past tense. All the verbs except the first ('We attempted') are passive.

> PROTOCOLE OPÉRATOIRE
>
> La voie d'abord a été, 48 fois sur 50, une laparotomie médiane dépassant l'ombilic vers le bas.
>
> La rate est explorée, aspect de sa surface, volume et consistance. La splénectomie est réalisée en liant les vaisseaux au plus près dans le hile. S'il existe à ce niveau des adénopathies, elles sont prélevées.
>
> L'exploration du foie apprécie sa surface, son volume, sa couleur et

> sa consistance. De larges biopsies sont effectuées au bord antérieur du foie gauche (segment III) et du foie droit (segment V). Un prélèvement électif est réalisé s'il existe un nodule pathologique visible.
>
> Les aires ganglionnaires sont explorées à l'étage sus-mésocolique (ganglions cœliaques au bord supérieur du pancréas, ganglions du pédicule hépatique), dans le ligament gastrocolique, le grand épiploon et le méso-côlon transverse; à l'étage sous-mésocolique (ganglions du mésentère, ganglions des chaines lombo-aortiques, iliaques et hypogastriques). Les ganglions d'allure pathologique et les ganglions suspects sur la lymphographie sont prélevés.
>
> Des clips sont mis en place sur les zones prélevées et sur les masses ganglionnaires manifestement tumorales et fixées. Dans certains cas des ganglions rétro-cruraux ont été prélevés par une incision inguinale séparée.

The French writer puts a sub-heading above his text, which is divided into five paragraphs. There is no linking between this and the preceding passage, nor are the paragraphs here connected in any way, they are simply juxtaposed. Each paragraph describes a step in the operation and introduces a different topic: '*La voie*', '*la rate*', '*le foie*', '*les aires ganglionnaires*' and '*les clips*'. The topic, laparotomy, is divided into five sub-topics which are introduced in chronological order and which, for this reason are linked by a zero-operator: the sequence of acts to be performed is already known to the reader and is expected by him in that order. The paragraph here is a unit which divides the topic into sub-topics, while in English it is a unit of thought which includes everything related to the topic. There are two changes of tense within the sequence: the first and last sentences are in the past, all the others being in the present tense. It is these changes of tense at the very beginning and end of the sequence, which seem to delimit the passage as a unit which is not signalled by any kind of typographical marker. This is the unit which corresponds to the English paragraph, the sub-heading forming its topic-sentence. As in English, the verbs are in the passive: the focus is on the scientific approach. There is no personal reference to the writer. The use of the French present tense gives the description a 'timeless' aspect never to be found in English.

Interpretative and evaluative sequences

The act of interpretation consists of a writer's relating the facts which he has described to a body of concepts which is already known, or of reorganizing those concepts in the light of the new data which he has revealed. He gives his opinion of the *significance* of an earlier sequence. In an *evaluation* the writer gives his opinion as regards the *value* of an earlier sequence. He classifies the facts in question along a scale of values such as negligible, essential, necessary, etc. Interpretations and evaluations almost always have an illocutionary value of *assertion*. One of the communicative aims of the discourse is to arrive at these assertions. This is why these discursive operations often appear as the conclusions of an argumentative sequence. Below are two examples taken from passages headed 'Discussion':

> [1] *Cette étude confirme l'activité remarquable du protocole H2 65 dans le traitement des formes diffuses de la maladie de Hodgkin,* [2] elles peuvent guérir par la seule chimiothérapie, plus de 6 fois sur 10, par l'association polychimiothérapie, irradiation par grands champs près de 7 fois sur 10, avec des réinductions plus de 8 fois sur 10. [3] Ces résultats montrent les progrès réalisés dans les formes diffuses de la maladie; par l'irradiation seule, Vera Peters obtenait en 1951, 10% de survie dans les stades III et IV à 5 ans; Kaplan en 1965, après classement par laparotomie obtient 62% de survie à 6 ans dans les stades III et 40% dans les stades stades IV à 3 ans.
>
> [4] Nos résultats se comparent à ceux obtenus avec le même protocole (sans chimiothérapie d'entretien, de réinduction ou d'irradiation) par Canellos et De Vita: 67% à 59% de survie respectivement à 4 et 6 ans: [5] *ils confirment les études de Frei sur la nécessité d'un traitement d'entretien et ou la pratique des réinductions, sur l'intérêt d'une irradiation complémentaire à la rémission* (irradiation par grands champs ou irradiation sur les territoires initialement les plus atteints).

Both these paragraphs are built around an evaluation: the first begins with the evaluation and then develops it, the second concludes with it. The discursive operations associated with evaluation are *explicitation* (the clarification of the preceding proposition) and *reference* (reference to a statement contained in another text). The function of these other operations is to bring in arguments in support of the evaluation which has been proposed. The argumentative structure formed by the continuation of these discursive operations can be diagrammed in this way:

TABLE 1

discursive operations	*argumentative operations*
1. *Topic sentence/evaluation*	*assertion*
2. Explicitation (quantification)	argument 1 (figures)
3. Reference	argument 2 (progress)
4. Reference/comparison	argument
5. *Evaluation*	*assertion*

Now here is the English passage followed by an analysis in diagram form:

> [1] The single patient with biopsy-proved hepatic involvement also had a positive spleen. [2] This is in accord with the original observation of the Stanford group, who reported no instance of hepatic involvement without concomitant splenic involvement. [3] The liver scan was primarily responsible for 8 of 9 false-positive liver evaluations. [4] *We conclude that, as with the spleen scan, the liver scan has little value in the initial staging of Hodgkin's disease.* [5] Since liver function tests are also unreliable,[6] *it is clear that open biopsy is necessary in order to evaluate the liver* more definitively. [7] Even the latter technique is subject to the limitations of sampling procedures. [8]One patient (M. H.) died of an acute myocardial infarction three months after staging laparotomy with negative liver biopsy. Hepatic involvement was found at autopsy.

TABLE 2

discursive operations	*argumentative operations*
1. Topic sentence: specification	argument: conjunction
2. Reference: comparison	
3. Explanation	argument: cause
4. *Evaluation*	*assertion*
5. Explanation	argument: addition
6. *Evaluation*	
7. Restriction	
8. Exemplification	

In this passage, the acts of evaluation which form the culminating point of the argumentation come after the argumentative operations which underpin them. The sequence specification reference/comparison–evaluation is the most common evaluative sequence in English. (*Specification* is the provision of additional descriptive detail. The topic-sentence refers back to a case mentioned in an earlier descriptive passage, adding a further piece of information.) It follows the logical order of operations; the relevant fact is noted, then correlated and compared, and the writer then deduces from it an interpretation or evaluation. With the aid of the operators 'since' and 'also', the second assertion is presented as a consequence of the first. 'Also' signals the conjunction of this proposition with the preceding one and 'since' establishes a causal relationship between those two propositions and the one which follows. If we examine the modalization of these two assertions, we notice that the second is much stronger than the first. In the first, 'we conclude that' indicates an evaluation for which the authors accept full responsibility. In the second, 'it is clear that' introduces an evaluation which cannot be contested: the reader is almost bullied into accepting the proposition.

The relative paucity of discursive operators in these two texts is also worth noting. The French writer only uses the colon, an indication that a conclusion is about to be reached. In the English text, the operators 'since', 'also' and 'even' are clustered around the main assertion which is the final goal of the discourse. They bring together the terms of the argument and make explicit the causal relationships and the correlations which lead to the assertion. The first propositions, on the other hand, are merely juxtaposed. Their role in the argument is only to be found by examining their contents, although their position in the sequence is also relevant: it is the accumulation of these facts which allows the writer to draw his conclusions ('we conclude that').

There is an absence of modalization in the passages containing these two evaluations. While interpretation is almost always modalized ('*il semble que*', 'there appears to be a tendency for', etc.) this is practically never true of evaluation. Writers are more willing to commit themselves as regards to the value of the work carried out than as regards its interpretation.

Illocution

Assertion

As we have just seen, the aim of the discourse is an assertion and the whole of the discourse is constructed with this in mind. Assertion is used here in the sense given by Searle. It has the following characteristics: the speaker has proof of the truth of the proposition; it is not obvious that his interlocutor knows this proposition; the speaker believes the proposition; the proposition represents an existing state of affairs. The aim of the article is to inform and convince; indeed, the article could be defined as the distance between an initial assertion and a final assertion. In fact, the majority of topic-sentences are also assertions, but they are weak assertions where the wish to persuade is not essential, whereas in final assertions it is crucial, as can be seen by the presence of explicit performatives such as 'we believe that' or '*d'après nous*'. English articles tend to be more closely argued, with stronger final assertions. The illocutionary point of many French articles seems to be limited to giving information: they finish with a recapitulation of the main points, but without any kind of evaluation or any strong final assertion as if nothing had happened between the beginning and the end. They leave the discussion open, whereas a final assertion closes it temporarily.

Other illocutionary acts

It would obviously be impossible to give an analysis of all the illocutionary aims which can be identified even in a single article. We can only mention *justification* which is often associated with the discursive operation *explanation*. It is clear that writers try to defend themselves from potential criticisms, but it is often difficult to know whether an explanation is a necessary piece of information or whether it is the expression of a wish to justify something. Similarly, polemical intentions may be associated with acts of *criticizing*, although this is rather unusual in research articles. Criticism is far more likely to occur in other types of writing, such as editorials, letters to the editor or review articles. A certain number of *directives* — advice, warnings and even orders — can also be observed.

Context of situation

Three actors participate in the situation presented by medical discourse: these are the reference, the object of scientific study (the illness or the organs affected), the writer of the article who has carried out the study or the experiment described in it, and the patient — the subject of the study or experiment. A systematic study of the verbs and subjects in all the articles in the corpus reveals regular patterns for focusing on one or other of these actors. As in many types of scientific discourse, writers rarely allow their own personality to intrude and the passive is used very often indeed; at different times, this serves to focus on the object of study or on the patients. In French, the passive form may alternate with '*on*', but this is an individual variation, some writers using only the passive form, others alternating. The use of the passive is not necessarily an indication of self-effacement on the part of the author, either in English or in French: the writers are not the only ones to work on experiments and the tasks which they describe may well have been carried out by people whose names do not appear. Patients are sometimes referred to by their initials, when it is necessary to single out one from a group or series, but the rest of the time they are simply 'patients' or '*cas*', '*malades*', or '*sujets*'. They are most frequently the subjects of passive verbs. In both languages there are only a limited number of verbs in the active voice of which they can be the subjects and these are both more numerous and more frequent in English, in particular the verb 'to note', which writers use to mean that the patient notices the onset of his symptoms. In French 'one' notices for him, or the symptom 'appears'. This may be the expression of a very different philosophy of medicine; it is generally agreed that French doctors hide the seriousness of their condition from patients, whilst doctors in the English-speaking world are more open with them, leaving them, as it were, a greater degree of responsibility.

A study of verbs and subjects occurring in the different parts of the articles in English reveals that the focus shifts according to a regular pattern.

TABLE 3

	Verbs	*Subjects*	*Focus*
Introduction	passive/active	inanimate	object of study
Equipment and methods	passive	inanimate/animate	object of study
Results	active/passive	animate	patients
Discussion	active/passive	animate/inanimate	object of study/author

Articles in French are not nearly so regular, although, of course, the focus does vary according to the illocutionary aims of the writers at any given moment. Compare the two brief passages which follow, both of which are from the same article and refer to the same facts, the first in the Introduction, the second from the Discussion:

1. Des centaines de patients venus consulter pour un problème ganglionnaire cervical, parfois apparemment très circonscrit, se sont vus, depuis une dizaine d'années, proposer d'accepter une laparotomie, et ont été privés d'une rate parfois pathologique, assez souvent saine.
2. Nous avons enlevé une rate malade chez 40% de nos malades, ce qui veut dire aussi en contrepartie que nous avons enlevé une rate indemne chez 60% de nos malades.

At the beginning of the article, the authors focus on the '*patients*' who are the subjects of passive verbs. By playing with different connotations here the writers are able to obtain certain expressive effects presenting the patients as innocent victims. At the end of the article, however, the focus is on the writer: '*nous*', which is the subject of verbs in the active voice. In this way, the writers accept full responsibility for these often untoward incidents. This kind of striving for expressive effects is fairly common in the French texts in the corpus. The descriptive passage quoted above (pp. 112–13) illustrated the use made of the present tense in the description. Particularly striking is the use made of changes of tense in case studies, where the patient's history is made up like a narrative, with flash-backs in the past and glances forward in the future tense.

> M. X est hospitalisé ... Lorsque nous l'examinons, nous trouvons ... La température, modérée à l'entrée, va en réalité s'élever progressivement ... L'amaigrissement dans les deux derniers mois a été important ...

Expressive effects of this kind do not occur in English, where the rules governing the sequence and use of tenses tend to be fairly strict. Only the past tense is used for the description and for any reference to past events in general; the present tense only occurs in the Introduction and the Discussion, where it is used to refer to facts which have already been established, or to state conclusions.

Conclusions — implications for language learning

Everything that has been said above leads us to the conclusion that the organization of medical articles in English is based on a model which is far stricter than for the French equivalent, for which, indeed, no real model exists. There is no generally agreed way of writing such an article in French, although there is now a tendency on the part of a certain number of writers to follow the English model. The fundamental difference — and it is one which probably explains all the others — resides in the relative importance accorded to the different elements which make up the article. For the French writers it is the scientific facts which have to be communicated, and the whole of the discourse is organized around the data to be presented. The line of argument, if it exists at all, is secondary.

In English, on the other hand, it is precisely the line of argument which is of prime importance. The article is organized on the basis of a thought process which starts with a proposition and ends with an assertion and the data is put in when it is relevant to this argumentative structure.

Reading in a foreign language

Reading a scientific article is above all a matter of looking for information. Now the organization of the discourse in the two languages shows that the writers, and therefore *a fortiori* the readers, do not have the same ideas as to just what the essential information is. For this reason a French reader, used to seeing the main facts and figures stand out on the page, tends to look for them in English texts too, where they are not given the same prominence. In the same way, an English reader has a hard time following the line of thought in a French article where there is no clear unit of rhetoric such as the English paragraph. A contrastive study of discourse organization thus enables us to identify the source of certain reading problems and to sensitize learners to the differences in methodology and philosophy revealed by that study. This enables us to suggest ways in which mother-tongue reading strategies need to be modified for reading in the foreign language.

Written expression in a foreign language

The above discussion clearly shows that writing an article in a foreign language is most certainly not simply a matter of translating an article organized in conformity with the conventions of the writer's own culture. The result would most likely be quite unreadable for members of the other community. Rather, this study suggests that the article as a whole must be taken as the basic point-of-departure unit in any learning programme, the composition of smaller units — paragraphs, sections and subsections — only being dealt with later. This is especially true for speakers of French wishing to write in English; some of them need to learn to reorganize their discourse completely and to recategorize their data so that it can be integrated into an article which follows the thread of an argument. Learning discourse organization could be done separately from the learning of the more narrowly linguistic skills, since it involves a particular type of competence which can be developed parallel with linguistic competence.

Part Two
Learning

> La religion du savoir est une forme de l'esprit d'enfance. Il ne s'agit plus dans un monde en perpétuelle évolution d'enseigner un contenu, mais les moyens autonomes d'acquisition de ce contenu et surtout l'approche critique qui mettra constamment en cause ce contenu, en le relativisant. C'est pour celui qui étudie la première étape sur le difficile chemin de la liberté d'apprendre, car. . . on a jusqu'à présent posé les problèmes pédagogiques en termes d'enseignement et pas en termes d'apprentissage.
>
> *Yves Châlon*

There has been no shortage of 'models of learning' in recent years. Ever since the territory was opened up, there has been a sort of academic gold-rush to stake out claims. An exceptionally wide range of disciplines have sent out their scouts and settlers who have poured forward into new areas with an enthusiasm which is in itself a potent criticism of the rule of behaviourism. Among these disciplines there are three whose interests overlap considerably and whose relevance to our present interests is particularly important: educational psychology, psycholinguistics and applied linguistics.

Even if we limit our attention for the moment to contributions made by researchers in these fields (omitting the work being done in other disciplines by, among others, Bruner *et al.* 1966, 1973; Neisser 1976; de Mey 1982; Grossberg 1982), we shall find ourselves dealing with a rich and varied literature. The very briefest of surveys would have to include references to Schumann's (1978) 'acculturation' model; to Selinker and Lamendella's work (1978) on neuro-functional aspects of second-language acquisition; Corder (1967, 1971) and Hatch (1979) on 'input' and the work of the personal construct psychologists (Kelly 1969; Fransella 1977; Bannister and Fransella 1977). For more detailed discussions, see Clark and Clark 1977; Schumann 1979; Sajavaara 1981. In addition, there is a rapidly increasing literature on discourse processing (Seliger 1977; Lehtonen and Sajavaara 1980; see also pp. 7 and 11) and on learning strategies (Tarone 1974; Bialystok 1978; Faerch and Kasper 1983; Candlin and

Breen, forthcoming) which is in turn closely related to 'interlanguage' studies (Selinker 1969, 1972; Richards 1971, 1973; Sridhar 1981; Corder and Roulet 1977).

When we consider that each of the references given here is only the tip of an iceberg of research and publications, any attempt to discuss these matters from an overall point of view seems daunting, foolhardy even. But we need some kind of compass to help us find our way across such broken and varied terrain: this is why there is such a strong temptation to impose order on the mass of chaotic data by means of relatively simple, clear-cut verbal oppositions, as is the case with Krashen's 'Monitor' model (1981), but where the dangers of hypostatization of pre-theoretical concepts are greater than ever.

The problem is, of course, that however dangerous it may be to generalize, it is essential to do so, since it is only on the basis of hypotheses which can be formulated, debated and tested that any theoretical or applied progress can be made. After all, overgeneralization has long been recognized as an essential step in the learning process.

One such generalization which is both interesting and insightful for language teachers and which provides the conceptual starting-point for most of the papers included in this selection is the following: all these lines of investigation have emphasized the crucial role in the learning process of some aspect of the learner's previous knowledge and experience. This observation is not a new one, though recent work has confirmed its importance as well as its relevance to a far wider range of psychological, social and linguistic phenomena than was at first realized:

> If I had to reduce all of educational psychology to just one principle, I would say this: the most important single factor influencing learning is what the learner already knows. Ascertain this and teach him accordingly. (Ausubel 1968)

There seems now to be a general consensus that the learning process is ecological rather than structuralist, accumulative and systemic rather than discrete. Let us consider, then, very briefly and in the simplest possible terms, just what it is that a learner can be thought of as knowing and, more specifically, what it is he or she brings to the process of learning a second language.

The first and most obvious thing — and possibly the most important — is the mother tongue. Many people, both linguists and laymen, have drawn a double conclusion from the apparent ease with which the L1 is learnt: firstly, that the L2 would best be learnt the same way and, secondly, that it should be learnt without any use of or reference to the L1. In very broad terms this is the rationale behind the various brands of 'Direct Method'. There is, however, a flaw in the reasoning: you cannot, by definition, learn your first language twice. Certain cases of bilingualism apart, when we come to a second language, the first is already there — our individual identity is there — to act as a filter. Our 'capacity' to learn the second language, both in the quantitative and qualitative senses of the word, will vary according to the particular combination of experiences which makes up that identity.

Moreover, we need to distinguish between learning in the sense of '*what* has been learnt' and learning in the sense of '*how* it was learnt'. If we do so, we quickly see that extrapolations from L1 to L2 learning are never simple and rarely valid. For example, 'how it was learnt' also includes two very different considerations: on the one hand, there is the learning *situation*, on the other the learning *strategies*. Only in the special circumstances of 'natural second-language acquisition', is there an analogous relationship between the situations of L1 learners and L2 learners. In the foreign language classroom the learners are older, they are proportionately far more numerous than their models, and they are exposed to the target language for only a tiny fraction of the time which a child spends on learning its mother tongue. (See Singleton 1981 for an excellent survey of age as a factor in language learning and acquisition. However, it should be remembered this is by no means the only difference between children and adults as far as language learning is concerned.) Work on learning strategies, however, although only in its early days, seems to indicate that there is considerable overlap between L1 and L2 learning in this respect — as well as considerable problems of transfer.

This brings us directly to the problem of learning as what has been learnt. The learner possesses the knowledge, albeit unconscious, of the structure and functioning of his L1, including its phonology and morpho-syntax, lexis, notions, functions and semantic and pragmatic rules. The extension of linguistic descriptions to include these later topics has provided a fillip to contrastive studies (Fisiak 1981) as well as to studies of interlanguage and communicative and learning strategies.

Apart from this usually unconscious linguistic knowledge, there is also the knowledge which the learner possesses *about* language (in general), about his language, about other languages and about language learning. From the technical applied linguistic point of view, much of this knowledge may be erroneous or apocryphal: nonetheless it is relevant to language learning since it will clearly influence the learner's learning behaviour. Indeed, this type of knowledge can be seen as a sub-category of the learner's knowledge about himself, both as regards his own social identity and his self-image as a learner (Morris 1980). Obviously this image will influence his choice of learning strategies in the narrow sense but it will also predetermine to a considerable extent the whole nature of his learning programme and of his participation in it. If I think that the only way to learn a language is with a teacher and a grammar book in a classroom — and that, anyway, I am 'no good at languages' — my learning behaviour and the results I achieve are likely to reflect those beliefs. As a number of papers in this collection show, the learner's role and the learner's image are mutually defining: moreover role — defined as the right to perform certain categories of act — is the dynamic manifestation of competence, or social knowledge.

Finally, there is the extra-linguistic knowledge, the learner's knowledge of the world and of social reality, of geographical, physical and historical events, or people. Each individual brings this knowledge to bear on a text or interaction, and it is on this basis that he selects the information and constructs the intersubjectivity which is essential to discourse. The categorization and perception of situation, as well as the nature of his participation, is defined in terms of a dialectic process between his extralinguistic knowledge and the communicative activity in question. In a simple yet profound sense, *all* discourse is a learning process and our identity is what we know. Part of the fascination of second-language learning is that it heightens our awareness of both.

Language teachers and applied linguists have long been in the habit of pointing out to anyone who would stop to listen that 'language is a tool for communication'. Unfortunately, despite the undoubted sincerity with which this conviction is held, most methods and materials have always concentrated on the construction of the tool itself rather than on the uses to which it can be put. The full implications of the term 'communication' have never been assimilated, either conceptually or methodologically, into our language-teaching practices.

Only relatively recently — since the beginning of the 1970s, approximately — have detailed and systematic attempts been made to investigate the nature of communicative (as opposed to linguistic) competence, and to apply this knowledge to the second-language learning situation. This has partly been the result of developments within the field of theoretical linguistics, especially in discourse analysis and speech act theory, and in allied disciplines such as ethnography and sociology, which will be discussed in more detail below. It is also partly due to the world-wide interest in languages for instrumental purposes. The adjective 'pragmatic' has been cheerfully if somewhat ambiguously used to describe the main thrust of both these developments.

In Europe, in particular, the 'functional' or 'communicative' approach has aroused considerable interest, largely because of its adoption by the Council of Europe's project on modern languages and its propagation through their publications such as *A Threshold Level, Un niveau-seuil* and *Un Nivel Umbral*. Few textbooks or language-teaching materials of any kind are now published which do not at least claim to be 'functional'. However, between these two types of publication — that is, between those which specify the aims and contents of communicative syllabuses and those which contain actual materials for teaching/learning activities — there is a gap. Relatively little systematic study has been made of the methodological issues involved. That is, we have no heuristically established criteria for selecting one activity or set of materials rather than another, for justifying our choice didactically. To put it bluntly, we may know what we want to teach, but we do not have much idea of how to go about it: the present jumble of simulations, role-plays, games, dramatic techniques, etc. is no substitute for a principled approach to sensitization, presentation, practice, acquisition and use, even if such activities seem, intuitively, to be somchow 'more communicative'.

This is no place to attempt a hard and fast definition of the term 'methodology'; but I feel I should give a general idea of what I mean by it (I think it is what *most* people mean, but just in case. . .). It is one of the three main constituent areas of any learning programme, the others being 'objectives' and 'contents'. Where they deal with the questions Why? and What?, methodology considers How?. How, that is, are we to process these contents if we are to meet those objectives? A methodology, though, is not simply a list of activities, any more than a selection of tunes is the chromatic scale. It is a rationale: a set of organizational and operational principles underlying the selection and implementation of those processes and activities which, it is believed, will facilitate language acquisition.

We need, then, to know why we do what we do; we need to know whether it works; and we need to know how to do it better. Many present-day learning materials and activities are attractive, imaginative and effective — and many are not. We ought to be able to tell the difference. In other words, we need theories and techniques of learning, evaluation and interaction which take communicative considerations into account.

A useful point of departure is provided by the literature on the language of the classroom, in particular those studies which use functional or interactive categories (Cazden, John and Hymes 1972; Sinclair and Coulthard 1975; Stubbs 1976; Allwright 1977; Kramsch 1981), but so far little work has been done on applying those observations directly to problems of communicative methodology. There is a gap between the theoretical literature and actual teaching materials; even those items which deal explicitly with methodological issues do so at a high level of abstraction, as practical implications of theoretical considerations rather than as the results of experimentation, observation and application (Widdowson 1978; Breen and Candlin 1980; Johnson 1982; Moirand 1982).

Given the epistemological ancestry of the communicative approach, this opposition between theory and practice is hardly surprising. On the one hand we have the contributions made by the linguistic philosophers (Frege 1892; Strawson 1952, 1964; Austin 1962; Russell 1940; Apel 1976) who have been interested in the definition and description of speech acts, or perhaps more accurately in functions of language other than the truth-values of propositions, in the 'happiness' conditions for their successful performance, in their taxonomic relationships, in presuppositions and in the relationships between semantics and pragmatics in general. On the other hand, linguists (Katz and Postal 1964; Ross 1970, 1975; Fillmore 1971; Sadock 1975; Wunderlich 1976, and the contributors to Cole and Morgan 1975 and Wunderlich 1975) have been mainly interested in the correspondences between sentence structures and sentence uses, that is, in the pragmatic potential of sentences, in presuppositions and in the relationships between syntax and semantics in general. It is convenient to group these two 'bottom–up' approaches together under the label *speech act theory*.

However, there exists a very different approach to the study of language use and extended texts: scholars from many other disciplines, interested in language as it affects them have found that linguistics and philosophy have little or nothing to offer. They found that language impinged directly on their central objects of investigation and turned to linguistics only to discover that its descriptions concentrated on the internal structure of language and not on the external uses to which it was put (Hymes 1964; Holec 1973). Their common characteristic is an interest in the *speech event*: they include anthropologists (Gumperz and Hymes 1972), sociologists and sociolinguists (Allen and Guy 1974; Burton 1980; Stubbs 1976), linguists (Labov 1972; Sinclair and Coulthard 1975), ethnomethodologists (Sacks 1971, 1972; Sacks *et al.* 1974; Schegloff 1968; Garfinkel 1968; Sudnow 1972), applied linguists (Candlin *et al.* 1976; Allwright 1975; Gremmo *et al.* 1977; Holec *et al.* 1980; Riley 1980) and investigators of behavioural strategies (Goffman 1959, 1971; Berne 1964; Candlin and Breen forthcoming). All these investigators share an interest in the description of extended texts, working 'top–down', that is, from categories of communicative events down to the types of functions which characterize them, and it is this trait which justifies our bundling them together under the label *discourse analysis* (see the Introduction to Part One of this book).

Applied linguists have been aware of this opposition, which tugs them in opposite directions (Widdowson 1977). However, the only article I know of which deals explicitly with its pedagogical and methodological results is by Daniel Coste (and who better than one of the authors of *Un niveau-seuil?*) It is 'Analyse de discours et pragmatique de la parole dans quelques usages d'une didactique des langues' (1979), a thoughtful and perceptive study of the situation in France, but which seems to me to be of more general validity. Coste summarizes his viewpoint as follows:

Speech act theory	*Discourse analysis*
oral	written
expression	comprehension
speech event	text
onamasiological perspective	semasiological perspective
paradigmatic	syntagmatic
specification/appropriateness	cohesion/coherence
'everyday' communication	specialized fields

> It would not be difficult to show that, in France at least, language teaching has tended to pair off speech acts with the spoken language and discourse with the written, but I am not going to start giving examples of this tendency here. We need only recall that when the concept of 'speech act' spread – very rapidly – throughout language teaching circles, it was almost always introduced by means of examples such as 'asking (the time)', 'asking (your way)', 'identifying yourself' and 'introducing yourself', whose realizations were prepared and varied orally. It seems to me that this is what happens not only in the works by Wilkins and Roulet which aim at a wide public, but also in a number of the publications of the Council of Europe dealing with the setting up of threshold levels.

After discussing possible reasons for this polarization. Coste mentions some of the factors which might have brought about a reconciliation between the two approaches: the work of Benveniste, Jakobson and Ducrot in linguistics, the work of the CREDIF on reported discourse and the section on 'speech acts' in *Un niveau-seuil*. He finds that the influence of discourse analysis has been much weaker than that of speech act theory because

> It's as if we always needed a 'teaching material' cut up into bits which can be counted, labelled and listed. Now from this point of view, discourse is at a disadvantage: it can't be easily reduced to lists like vocabulary or to branching diagrams like grammatical structures. On the other hand, speech acts or notions, in the cut-and-dried versions of certain descriptions, easily replace the old syllabuses.

(The same point is made forcibly in Candlin 1976). Among the causes of this state of affairs, he identifies tradition, but

> Inertia doesn't explain everything, since language teaching has also shown itself to be quite capable of taking over certain aspects of pragmatics, such as those applied in the works of the Council of Europe's project on Modern Languages. 'Taken over', it is to be feared, in the sense that tools such as *Un niveau-seuil*, which give considerable space to a typology of acts and to lists of notions, may, despite all the precautions taken, be read and used as check-lists of items which should be included in a functional–notional syllabus. Willy-nilly, such lists encourage a fragmentation of the 'teaching material' and keep the discourse aspects of language use in the background.

This polarization, then, is also dangerous because it reinforces the tendency, to which language teaching is very prone, to isolate and privilege one aspect of language at the expense of others which may well be just as important. Partly this is because language teachers tend to be (have to be) enthusiasts, partly because certain pedagogical concepts such as 'progression' or 'unit' encourage approaches based on simplified, controllable models. Whatever the reason, it seems clear that the 'communicative approach', as practised if not as preached, has resulted in an emphasis being placed on the teaching of functions at the expense of, for example, other features such as propositional content, affective and interactive factors, and negotiation. It is significant that the term 'speech act' is often used both by linguists and language teachers as if it were synonymous with 'illocutionary force', rather than as a superordinate term including all those other factors which have been mentioned. Admittedly, I am being wise after the event here: our own work at the C.R.A.P.E.L. began with 'pure' communicative teaching based on single acts, but we were gradually forced to take propositional content and interactive features into account. But by all means let us be wise after the event — as long as we are sure we are being wise! It is no good teaching our learners to request information if they are not also aware that there are strict limits on the number and topics of the requests they can make in different situations and interactions. In a travel agency I can produce a long series of such requests: but in a train with a stranger the limit is probably as low as two or three, *unless* the stranger shows that he wishes to prolong the interaction by making his own request. Similarly, the information I can ask for differs: I can ask the agent how much a holiday in Costa del Plonque costs — but not a stranger who is just on his way there.

There are, then, a number of weaknesses in our present approach, weaknesses which have immediate methodological repercussions.

First, there is the fact, mentioned above, that publications of the Threshold Level type are not materials: they are lists, repertoires, source-documents for reference. They contain no methodological instructions or criteria. Nonetheless — and this is the source of weakness — it has to be recognized that they have often been used as materials. This is a travesty of the authors' intentions, although the proliferation of 'levels' (Threshold, Waystage) can only aggravate the misunderstanding. Attempts to 'repair the damage' such as Roulet's '*mode d'emploi*' for *Un niveau-seuil* are as much as a symptom as a cure.

A second objection to the 'Threshold Approach', indeed to all approaches based on Speech Act Theory, is that they are atomistic: by 'teaching' separate 'acts', such as 'inviting', not only do we make things *more* artificial, we also fail to give the learner any glimpse of the highly systematic nature of language functions. Mitchell (1980), speaking of the communicative movement has said that it has

> offered the teacher communicative syllabuses without first specifying for him in a systematic, comprehensive and explanatory fashion what overall body of linguistic knowledge we now consider it appropriate for him to teach. The 'notional syllabus' which is the only reference material relating to communicative language teaching that is currently available to the teacher, is presumably intended as a checklist whose purpose should be no more than to provide a rough and ready reminder to the teacher of some of the items he might include in his teaching, *it being assumed that the teacher will already possess an understanding of how the various artificially discrete items it contains are interrelated within an overall system, i.e. the grammar of the language.* (Editor's italics.)

Mitchell is making two points here: the first is that a speech act taxonomy is like a thesaurus, it *presupposes* the knowledge it contains. It assumes that the user will be able to recognize why an item has been categorized in a particular way ('faintly polite refusal'). A speech act taxonomy or a thesaurus is a description of the native speaker's competences. But this does not mean that a given native speaker uses them all; we vary in our degree of social competence, in our domains of specialized knowledge, interests or skills, in our preferences or personalities and in the roles we are called upon to play in our daily lives. Our individual communicative competence is only a selection of what is recognized as socially acceptable, so that when we find ourselves in an unfamiliar situation we don't know what to say! For the non-native speaker/teacher the problem is obviously all the more acute. This brings us up against two of the most crucial, practical problems: does the communicative approach imply the use of native speakers (only) in the classroom?; is the linguistic model for a communicative approach necessarily that of the native speaker?

The importance of these problems and their implications can hardly be exaggerated (for example, employers in France now often refuse to employ non-native teachers 'for communicative reasons') but neither can they be dealt with in the time and space available here.

It is essential to recognize, however, that works such as *A Threshold Level* are neither exhaustive nor objective. They are the result of selections and choices, and the criteria on which they are based include *social* criteria. Underlying such works is a model of the language learner/user. In most cases, it seems to me, this is a middle-aged, slightly old-fashioned professional man. To what extent this model corresponds to the reality of the individual learner is a moot point: but it cannot be suitable for *all* learners.

Mitchell's second point is that speech act descriptions and taxonomies are *paradigmatic*. It is this point which justifies his claim that most grammatical descriptions of 'functions' and 'acts' are in fact grammars of notions. Such grammars are therefore semantic rather than sociolinguistic: they lack the interactive, syntagmatic, social dimensions of discourse. How do we link speech acts? What are the categories and operations for inferencing and interpretation (notions, functions, presuppositions, implications.) How do we, that is, go from what is said to what is meant?

There can be little doubt that the notions of *strategy* and *procedural rule* will be central to discussion of the communicative approach during the next few years. As was remarked earlier, these notions provide an epistemological bridge between the theory of knowing and the theory of action, essential in any worthwhile account of interaction. Moreover, an actor-based model of communicative behaviour would seem to be a prerequisite of any learner-centred approach to language acquisition. The concept of strategy brings a rich inheritance of insights with it from games theory, mathematics and psychology. As some indication of the central position it now occupies it is worth noting that it is widely used in psycholinguistics, including work on child language acquisition and caretaker talk (Clark and Clark 1977), inter-language studies including foreigner-talk (Tarone 1980; Faerch and Kasper 1983), discourse processing and interpretative strategies (Widdowson 1980) and learning strategies (Holec 1980). It is obviously quite impossible to foresee all the implications of this work for communicative methodology but several important general points can be made.

1. It may well prove to be the case that psycholinguistic strategies *are* communicative strategies *are* learning strategies (they are all different aspects of the negotiation of meaning (see pp. 2–10). This would be a considerable argument in favour of the communicative approach in general, but might be taken as indicating a far less cognitive methodology than is often used at present.
2. The problems related to the identification of 'discrete units' for teaching purposes (discussed above in the quotation from Coste) are seriously aggravated.
3. A considerable amount of contrastive work will have to be done at discourse level to identify cross-cultural differences in communicative strategies. There is no point in teaching what is universal, but at present we simply do not know where the differences are. Topics which need to be studied include realizations and sequences of speech acts, modalization, negotiating and inferencing procedures. In the meantime authentic documents will remain a valuable tool for sensitization to these problems (Bates 1976; Blum–Kulka 1981; Kramsch 1981; Larsen–Freeman 1980; Sinclair 1980).

A further criticism of Threshold-level type materials and repertoires is that they concentrate almost exclusively on the verbal aspects of communication. No indications are given as regards facial expression, gesture, kinesics, proxemics, etc. Such features can be shown to be intrinsic to the meaning of face-to-face interaction (Riley 1976) but even their importance pales before that of the various vocal prosodies; above all, intonation and key.

> Rien n'a été prévu pour la prosodie, bien que le rôle de *l'intonation* soit particulièrement évident dans la réalisation des actes de parole. (Coste *et al.* 1976)

Given that intonation and key also play major roles in the structuration of discourse and in the transmission of information, the development of teaching and learning techniques to deal with this problem would seem to be a major pedagogical priority. Such a task would be daunting in the extreme were it not for the fact that there is already a clear and relatively simple description of the discursive role of intonation in English, *Discourse intonation and language teaching* by Brazil, Coulthard and Johns (1980). The difference between their model and 'grammatical' descriptions of intonation is much the same as that between a functional description and a syntactic description of the verbal component.

Specific techniques for the teaching and learning of these features will therefore have to be developed: in very general terms, they will deal with the transmission and expression of information and attitudes. It is not difficult to develop such techniques, but in both cases the problem of a metalanguage remains acute, for teachers and learners alike.

The psychology of learning versus learners' psychology

> Enseigner le latin à John, c'est sans doute connaître le latin, mais c'est surtout connaître John.
>
> *Yves Châlon*

Chris Brumfit once told the story of a mother who went to see her son's teacher to find out why he was not to be allowed to do French at school, even though he was very keen to do so. The teacher's answer was that he thought her son was not clever enough, to which the mother replied 'Well why can't you teach him the sort of French which stupid French children speak?'

Most psychologists would agree that the mother had quite a point, as, indeed, would most teachers. Language learning does not seem to be correlated with IQ. In fact, we are painfully ignorant about what it *is* related to. There is motivation, of course, but that is just the sort of 'subjective variable' which much modern psychology has either ignored or trivialized: ignored because it is not susceptible to objective measurement, trivialized (like the idea of intelligence itself) by being reduced to what can be measured.

For teachers, though, it is a matter of constant personal and professional experience that language learning and personality (in the widest sense) are intimately related. This really does not seem so extraordinary when we consider the basic fact that language teaching and learning involve trying to change the way people think and behave, that it is an attack on the personality. The two papers in this section investigate, in very different ways, aspects of that relationship. Collin and Holec report on observations made within a classic heuristic paradigm, and their results are a clear demonstration of individual variation in the learning process. They show that it is perfectly possible to study that process with the methodological tools available. Their investigation is traditional science, but they have carried out a crucial shift of focus, so that the conceptual perspective of their work is a new one. The question they ask seems simple, obvious even: what do learners get out of teaching? Surprisingly, such studies are in their infancy. Almost all the previous literature on didactics addresses the question 'What do teachers put in?'. However, such work is still clearly of more interest to the writers and to other researchers than it is to the learners.

In the second paper, on the other hand, we have an account of a form of psychological investigation which is part and parcel of the learning process, which can be carried out and used by the learners themselves. The charge of introspection is met head-on, it being argued that subjective variables can only be described within the terms of an individual's cognitive system and that such an investigation cannot be carried out within the traditional scientific paradigm. The very 'subjectivity' of this approach is one of its main attractions for the applied linguist interested in the negotiation of personal meaning.

7 Foreign language acquisition processes in a secondary school setting: negation

A. Collin and H. Holec

The movement away from the behaviourism of the late 1950s and 1960s towards a cognitive approach to the study of human behaviour has led to a certain number of empirical studies of first and second language acquisition processes. These studies have shown:

1. That the model proposed by Skinner in the 1950s in which language learning is seen as the mechanical learning of a series of reflexes, one after the other in a linear fashion and therefore analagous to the ways in which animals learn to behave, cannot account satisfactorily for language acquisition.
2. That the language acquisition process is, in fact, a cognitive process in which data are checked by the construction and testing of hypotheses and that the process involves the increasingly complex development of what were originally simple elements, the acquisition of each new element entailing the reorganization of all previously acquired elements.

These same studies have also shown that the fundamental characteristic of language acquisition is *variability*.

1. *Internal variability*: the acquisition process is a continuum in a state of permanent flux, so that at any moment stable elements are to be found alongside unstable elements and what is acquired develops in a non-linear way, first advancing, then stagnating or losing ground.
2. *External variability*: each individual learner has his or her own continuum, since the periods of stabilization and destabilization do not occur at the same time for everyone, nor do they concern the same elements.

It was with these ideas in mind that we undertook a year–long study of the way in which negation in English was acquired by a group of first-form beginners. Among the aims of this study were the following:

1. We hoped that it would show us
   a) at what point in the year each pupil could be regarded as having acquired negation in English (i.e. at what point stabilization of correct productions occurred).
   b) how each pupil developed to reach this stage (i.e. what path he followed in terms of variable production, sometimes correct and sometimes incorrect).
   c) how to detect any cases of fossilization which might occur (i.e. consistent production of incorrect forms).
2. The above data would enable us to compare the pupils amongst themselves on these different points.
3. Finally, we hoped to be in a position to make a certain number of inferences concerning foreign language acquisition processes in a school setting.

The study

The study we undertook consisted, firstly, in the collection of data concerning the acquisition of negation by real live learners working in real learning conditions. Secondly, we analysed and categorized these data with a view to interpreting them.

Observation

The public consisted of beginners, first-form secondary school pupils (average age eleven years). In the class taken for observation there were 24 pupils but the productions of only twelve of them were taken for analysis, the others being pupils who were repeating the year or who were absent or whose productions simply were not numerous enough for generalizations to be made about their development. The teaching of negation faithfully followed the textbook in use in the class. It included:

5 October:
Negation of 'be', copula. Examples, grammatical explanation, exercises on 'it isn't'.
3 November:
Revision; exercises on 'he isn't', 'she isn't'.
13 November:
Revision; exercises on 'we/you/they aren't'.
12 December:
Negation of present continuous; examples, grammatical explana-

tions, exercises on 'be + n't + V-ing'.
1 March:
Negation of 'there is/are'; examples, grammatical explanation; exercises on 'there isn't/aren't any'.
29 March:
Negation of the modal auxiliaries 'can' and 'must'; examples, grammatical explanation, exercises on 'can't', 'mustn't'.
28 May:
Negation of 'have': examples, grammatical explanation, exercises on 'hasn't/haven't'.
1 June:
Negation of present simple: examples, grammatical explanation, exercises on 'doesn't/don't'.

The corpus of oral productions consisted of tape recordings of all the English lessons these pupils had during the year. The written part of the corpus consisted of all the written work they carried out during the same period (mostly classwork, plus a few exercises done at home).

The analysis and categorization of productions

For analysis, the problem of negation was broken down into seven constituent features (see below). Each of these features has to be mastered for there to be acquisition and, conversely, failure to master any of them can result in error. These features are the following:

1. *Form* (notation: f). Negation is realized verbally by a certain number of different forms. Those taken into account in this study (cf. the textbook analysis above) were the following:

no (whether followed by an affirmative structure or not), e.g. 'Is that a pen?' 'No, it's a book'.
not, n't e.g. 'It is not red' or 'It isn't red'.
no + not, n't e.g. 'No, it is not red' or 'No, it isn't red'.
not, n't + any e.g. 'He hasn't any books'.
no + not, n't + any e.g. 'No, he hasn't any books'.

2. *Environment* (notation: e). *No* can occur alone, but *not* must be accompanied by *be* or *have* or by an auxiliary (*be, can, must, do*) and in neither case should the accompanying verb be repeated ('She's isn't French').

3. *Place* (notation: p). The negative form or forms cannot be placed

just anywhere in a sentence. *No* should be placed at the beginning of a negative reply, *not* must be placed after the verbs *be* and *have* and after the auxiliaries *be*, *can*, *must*, *do*.

4. *Syntactic structure* (notation: s). The syntactic structure of a negative sentence is either Subject + Auxiliary + *not* + Verb, or Subject + *be/have* + *not*.

5. *Orthography* (written form only. Notation: g). Contracted *not* is written *n't* and attached to *be*, *have* or the auxiliary verb, e.g. 'No, it isn't'.

(Note: it was not possible to take pronunciation of the negative form into account in this study: the recordings were made with a single tape recorder for the whole class and the quality of the sound was not good enough for any kind of phonetic analysis to be made).

Moreover, at a more general level, the correct use of negation (i.e. its complete acquisition) also supposes:

6. that the notation of negation is not abused (notation: a), a negative utterance being produced instead of an affirmative one:
'Is it a boy?' (pointing to Mary).
'No, it isn't a girl.'

7. that there is no non-negation or omission of negation, an affirmative utterance being produced instead of a negative one:
'Is it a girl?' (pointing to Mary).
'No, it is a girl.'

The pupils' productions were, therefore, analysed in terms of 'correct'/'incorrect' for each of these seven features. They were then categorized on the basis of the following parameters, which were considered to be relevant to any kind of interpretation.

1. *Written/spoken*
2. *Types of exercises*. Each type of exercise which elicited negative utterances from the pupils consisted of a different type of verbal task: this parameter therefore provided a useful basis for the analysis. Going from least to most spontaneous, the types of exercises included the following:

Oral: Oral comprehension (notation: A).
Reading aloud (B).
Structural drills (C):
substitution exercises (C_1).
transformation exercises (C_2).

Exercises using visual materials (D): oral composition with the felt-board, games, mini-dialogues, etc.
Question-and-answer exercises (E):
where the answer is provided (E_1).
where no answer is provided (E_2).
Activities involving spontaneous production (G): games.
simulations.

Written: Dictation (notation: a).
Pairing words or sentences (b).
Replying to questions (e):
with a model or with the book open (e_1).
without model, without book (e_2).
Activities involving spontaneous production (g), such as creating dialogues, different kinds of essay-writing, etc.

3. *Time*. There are at least three different possible approaches to the analysis of acquisition as a function of time. The first possibility would have been to take into consideration only the beginning and end of the learning period, that is, the beginning and end of the school year, comparing the earliest performances with the latest. This would have given only the crudest sketch of learning development and would not even have enabled us to distinguish between rapid development (where acquisition was complete before the end of the year) and slow development (where acquisition was only completed at the end of the year).

A second possibility would have been to note down the exact time in each lesson of every single performance; but since not all the pupils necessarily produce simultaneously performances which illustrate all seven features of negation for all types of exercises, oral and written, this procedure would not have made it possible to compare the ways in which different individuals developed; moreover, the picture given of each individual pupil's development would have been a distorted one because of the irregular distribution in time of performances exemplifying each of the features, in every type of exercise, written and spoken.

A third possibility was to break the learning process up into periods of equal length, each of these periods being regarded as a moment of acquisition. It was this approach which was in fact followed, each period being 12 lessons in length, this being the minimum if each was to contain a satisfactory number of productions. This gave fourteen consecutive periods between 5 October and 19 June.

Interpretation

In order to interpret the data we also collected a certain amount of complementary information about the pupils, concerning their personality and their performance in other subjects. In order to compare their development, a separate interpretation was established for each pupil and then for the group as a whole.

Results

We will begin our analysis of the acquisition of negation by referring to Tables 1 and 2 which show whether each pupil's productions during each period were all correct (stable correct: S) or all incorrect (stable incorrect: Si) or sometimes correct, sometimes incorrect (variable: V), taking all the different features of negation and all the types of exercise together. These tables are followed by histograms which show the level of acquisition reached by each individual pupil at each stage, this level again being expressed in terms of stabilization (stable correct: S; stable incorrect: Si) and variability (V), all features and all types of exercises, written or oral being taken into account.

Secondly, since acquisition and the elimination of errors obviously go hand in hand, we will try to determine the manner in which the different errors of all types gradually disappear.

Thirdly, we will be making some general comments about the acquisition of both the written and the spoken forms from both the overall point of view and from the point of view of the relationship between acquisition and particular types of exercises.

Acquisition, taking into account all features of negation and all types of exercise

Table 1 shows that, as regards the spoken form, pupils B, C, D and G did not acquire the mechanism of negation: at the end of the learning period (that is, in periods 12 to 14) their productions had still not become stable and correct. Pupil F had not acquired this mechanism either, since all his productions were still incorrect (Si) during period 13. There are also strong reasons for doubting whether pupil A's performance — variable in periods 12 and 13, stable in periods 11 and 14 — is truly stabilized.

There are, therefore, six pupils (A, B, C, D, F, G) (50%) who had not acquired negation by the end of the academic year.

Pupils H, I, J and K made no further mistakes from period 8

TABLE 1 The development of oral acquisition, based on all features of negation and all types of exercise

period	1	2	3	4	5	6	7	8	9	10	11	12	13	14
exercises	BC_1D	C_1C_2BD	BDE_1	E_1C_2BG	$E_2E_1C_2$	GBE_2C_2	C_1GBE_2 AC_2	GE_2	C_1C_2	GE_2C_2	GC_2	GE_2E_1	DE_2AC_2	GE_2
pupil A	S	S	V	V	V	S	V	V	V		S	V	V	S
B	S	S	S	S	S	S	Si	V	S				V	
C	S	V	S	S	V	S	V	S		S	S		V	
D	S	S	S	S	S	S	V	S	S		S		V	
E	S	V	S	S	S	S	Si	V	S	Si			S	S
F	S	S	S	S	V	S	Si	S	S		S		Si	
G	S	S	S	S	S	S	Si		S	S	S	S	V	
H	S	S	V	S	Si	S	Si	S	S	S	S	S	S	S
I	S	S	S	S	S	V	V	S	S	S	S	S	S	S
J	S	S	S	S	S	S	V	S	S	S	S	○	S	S
K	S	S	S	S	S	S	V	S	S	S	S	S	S	S
L	S	S	S	S	S	S	S	S	S	S	S	S	S	S

onwards, that is, from about the beginning of the second term. Pupil E's performance became stable at the end of the year (in periods 13 and 14). Pupil L understood how negation worked in this foreign language right from the very beginning and his productions were correct throughout the whole of the experiment.

It is worth noting that it was those pupils who provided the greatest number of productions who were the quickest to become stable. The question is, though, whether a large number of productions results in stabilization or whether stabilization gives rise to a large number of productions.

Table 2 shows that, in the written form, pupils A, B, C, D, E and F had not acquired the mechanism of negation by the end of the

TABLE 2 The development of written acquisition, based on all features of negation and all types of exercise

period	1	2	3	4	5	6	7	8	9	10	11	12	13	14
exercises	$e_2$ab	g_1	e_1e_2	e_2g_2a	e_2g_2	e_2g_2c	e_2b	e_2g_2	e_2e_1	g_1g_2	e_2	g_1e_2	$e_2g_2e_1$	g_2e_2
pupil A	V	S	S	V	V	V	S	V	V	V	S	V	V	V
B	V	S	S	V		Si	S	V	V		S	V	V	V
C	V	S	S	V	S	V	S	V	V	V	S	V	V	V
D	V	S	S	V	V		S	V	S	V	S	S	V	V
E	V	S	S	V	S		S	V	V	S	S	V	V	V
F	V	S	S	V	S	V	S	V	S	V	S	S	V	V
G	V	S	S	V	V		S	V	V	S	S	V	V	S
H	V	S	S	V	V	Si	S	V	V	S	S	V	S	S
I	S	S	S	V	S	V	S	V	S	V	S	V	S	S
J	V	S	S	V	S	Si	S	V	S	S	S	S	S	S
K	V	S	S	S	V	S	S	S	S	S	S	S	S	(V)
L	S	V	S	V	S	S	S	S	S	S	S	S	S	S

learning period. There are strong reasons for doubting whether the stabilization of pupil G's performance in period 14 is really definite. Although the productions of pupils H and I also only become stable in periods 13 and 14, it seems reasonable to suppose that, since oral acquisition had been stable from period 8 onwards, written acquisition in period 13 will also be definitive. Pupils J, K and L acquired the mechanism of negation in periods 9, 6 and 5 respectively.

The histograms in Figure 1 show that pupils A, B, C, D, E, F and G did not acquire overall negation (i.e. for both spoken and written forms). Pupils H and I did so in period 13 (cf. above); pupil J is stable overall from period 9 onwards. Pupil K is stable from period 6 onwards (it seems that the performance in period 14 may well have been due to an accident) and pupil L from period 5 onwards. These three pupils, therefore, all quickly acquired overall negation.

FIGURE 1 Histograms showing the development of each pupil's acquisition for all aspects of negation and all exercises, written and spoken

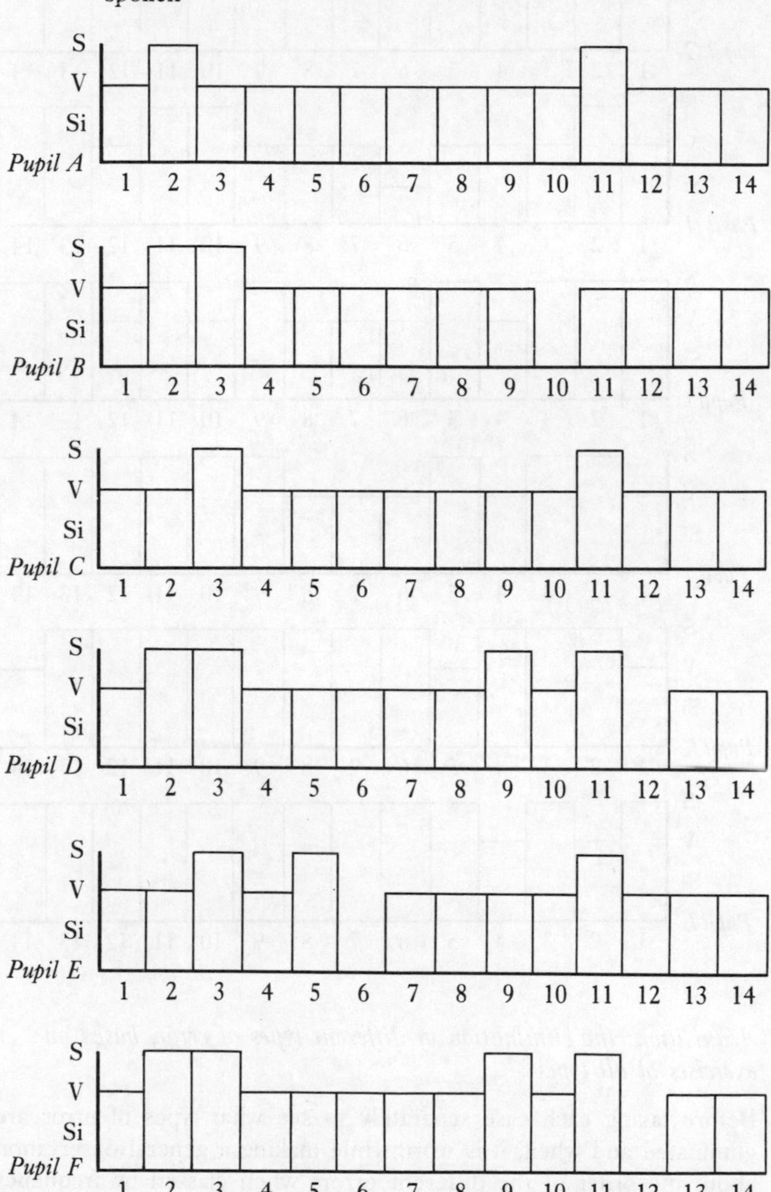

Figure 1 continues

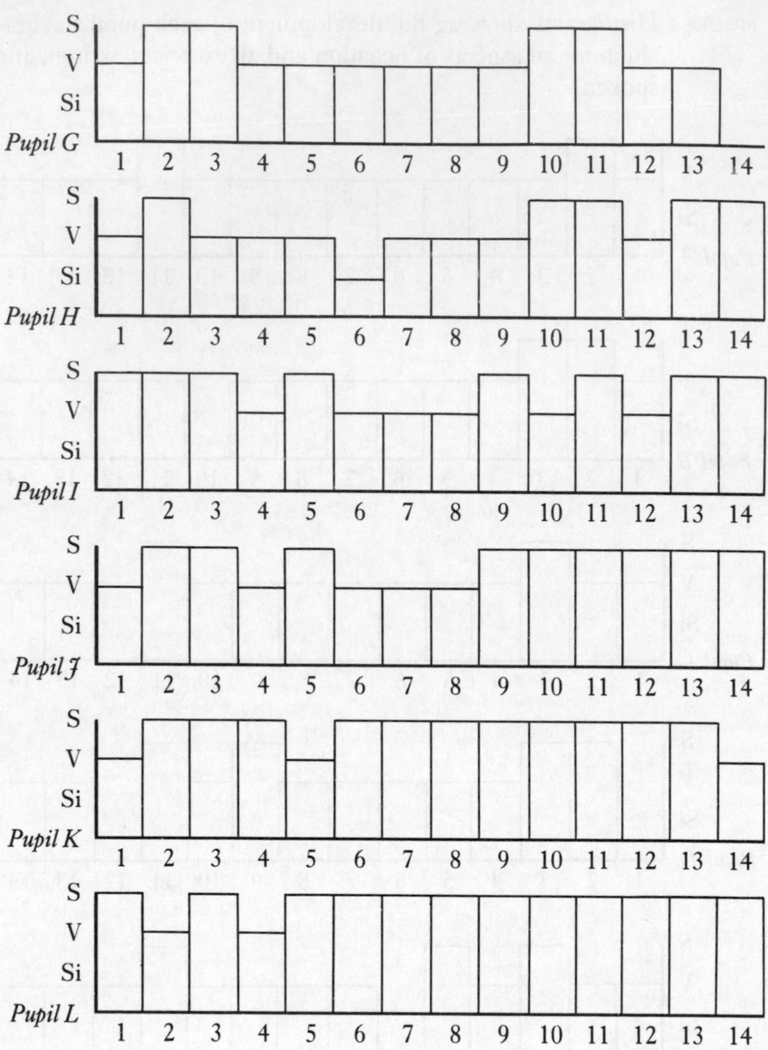

Acquisition: the elimination of different types of error, based on exercises of all types

Before taking each case separately to see what types of error are eliminated and when, it is worthwhile making a general observation about the order of the different errors when classed by frequency (which is also the inverse of the order in which they are eliminated). It is errors of form which predominate and which are the last to be eliminated. Next come errors of environment and syntax. Finally, there are errors of omission of place, which do not appear at all in the oral productions and only very little in the written ones.

For pupils A, B, D, F and K formal errors are not eliminated. They are eliminated for C in period 5, for E in period 13, for G in period 14, for H in period 13, for I in period 13, for J in period 9 and for L in period 3.

For pupils A, B, D, F and K environmental errors are not eliminated. They are eliminated for C, E and G in period 14 and for H in period 13.

Errors of omission of negation are eliminated for A in period 1, B in period 14, C in period 13, D in period 14, E in period 14 and H in period 6.

Orthographical errors are eliminated for A in period 2, D in period 6, E in period 9 and H in period 13.

Since the other types of error were rare, they will not be entered into in detail here.

Observation shows that in the written form combinations of errors occur. But in fact these rarely concern other than formal errors or environmental errors, which do clearly seem to go together (for example, 'no, he likes fish' instead of 'no, he doesn't like fish').

Progression in the acquisition of both the spoken and written forms of negation, for each pupil and at each stage in the learning period

If we represent progression in the acquisition of the spoken and written forms by pairs of graphs, we notice that no pair is ever identical: for every learner, learning takes place differently (Fig. 2). Two pairs of graphs (those for pupils L and C) are typical in the sense that they seem to represent extremes in the relationship between progress in speaking and progress in writing. These graphs also show that in general the acquisition of the written form is more irregular (in terms of the number of 'highs' followed by 'lows') and slower than oral acquisition.

General remarks on the relationships between acquisition and types of exercise

There does not seem to be any correlation between particular types of error and particular types of exercise. Similarly, speed of acquisition is independent of type of exercise. We have calculated the percentage of stable correct pupils for each type of exercise, and the results are expressed in Figures 3–6.

FIGURE 2 Progression in the acquisition of both the spoken and written forms for each pupil

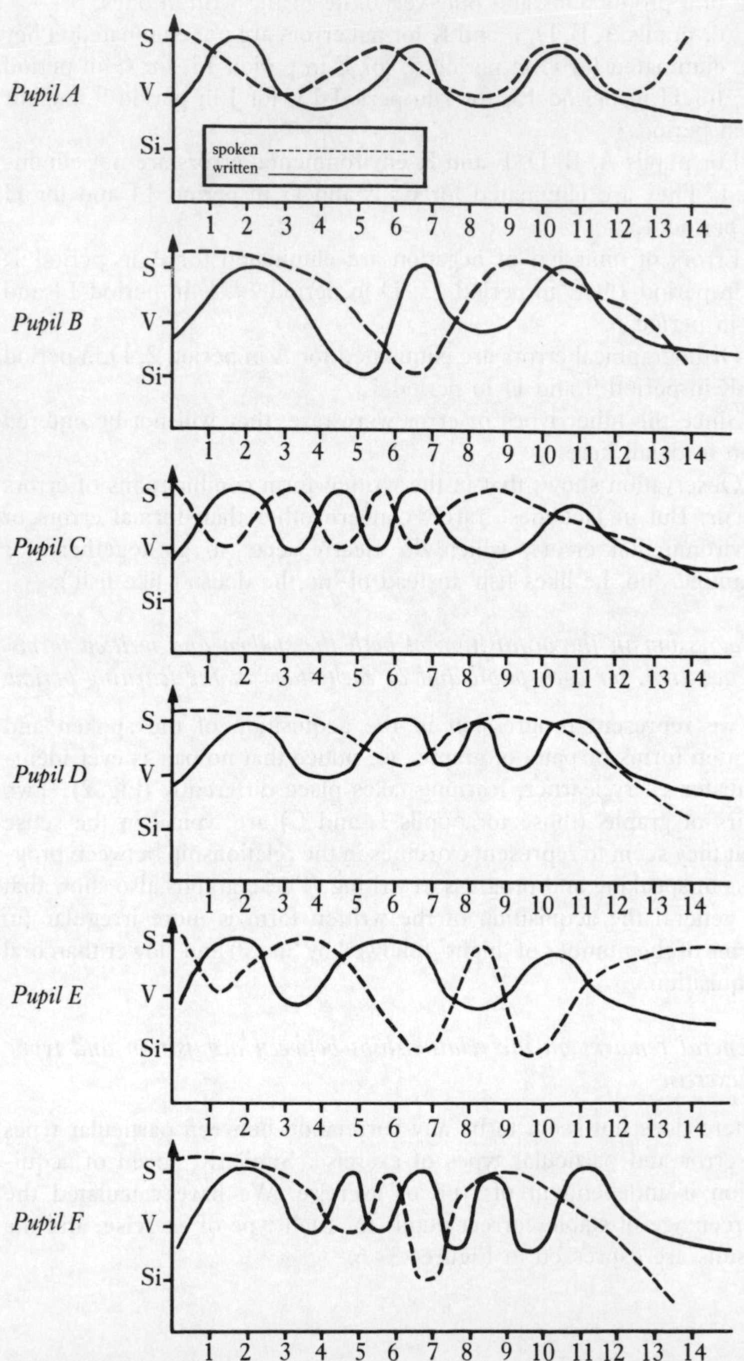

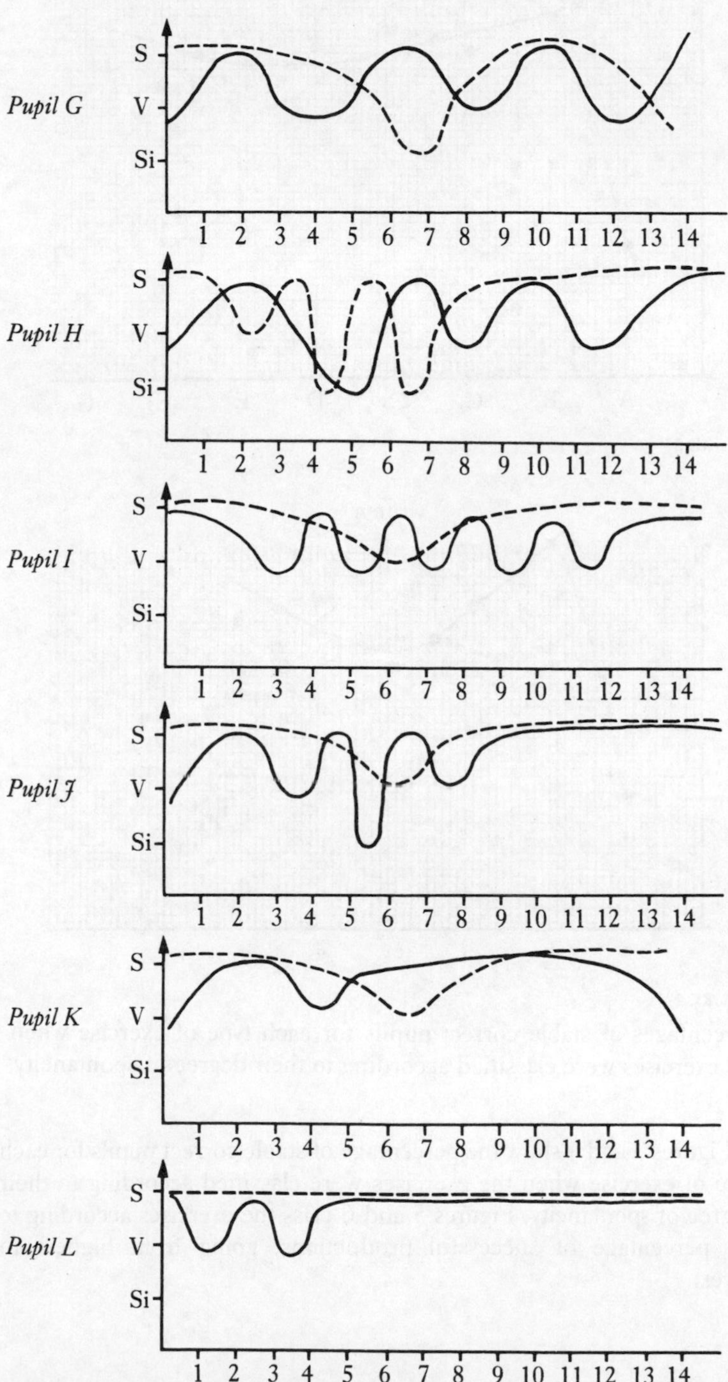
Pupil G
Pupil H
Pupil I
Pupil J
Pupil K
Pupil L
S
V
Si
1 2 3 4 5 6 7 8 9 10 11 12 13 14

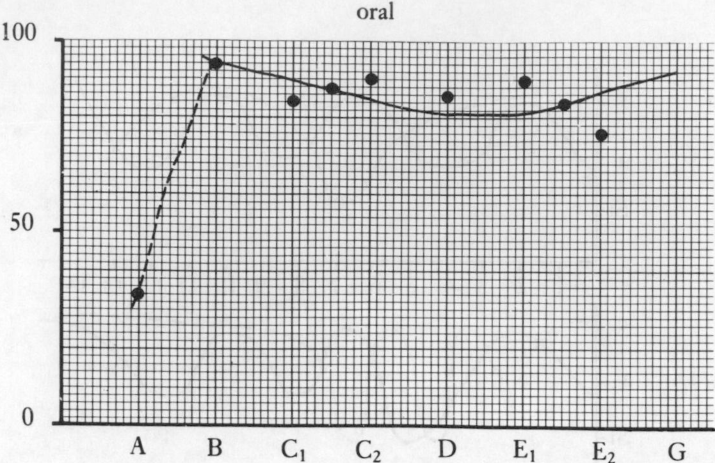

FIGURE 3

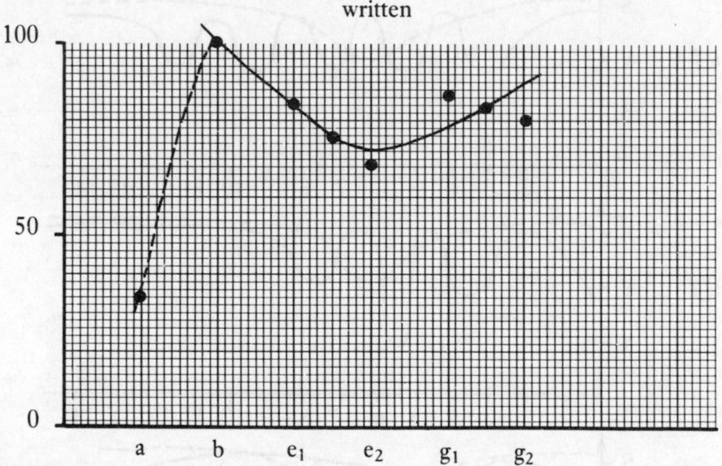

FIGURE 4
Percentages of stable correct pupils for each type of exercise when the exercises were classified according to their degree of spontaneity

Figures 3 and 4 show the percentage of stable correct pupils for each type of exercise when the exercises were classified according to their degree of spontaneity. Figures 5 and 6 class the exercises according to the percentage of successful productions, going from highest to lowest.

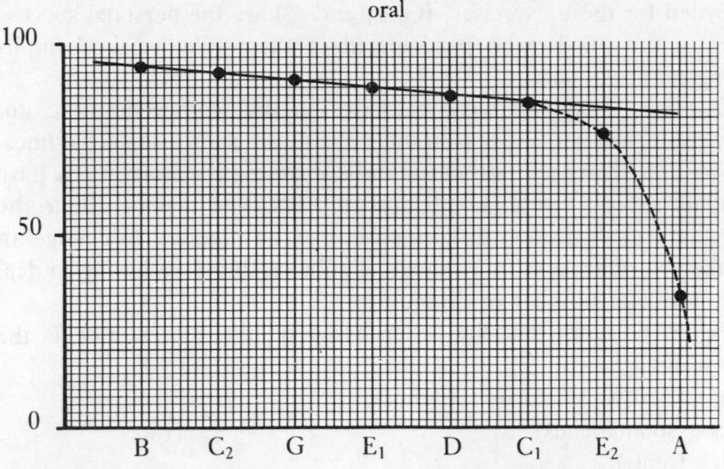

FIGURE 5

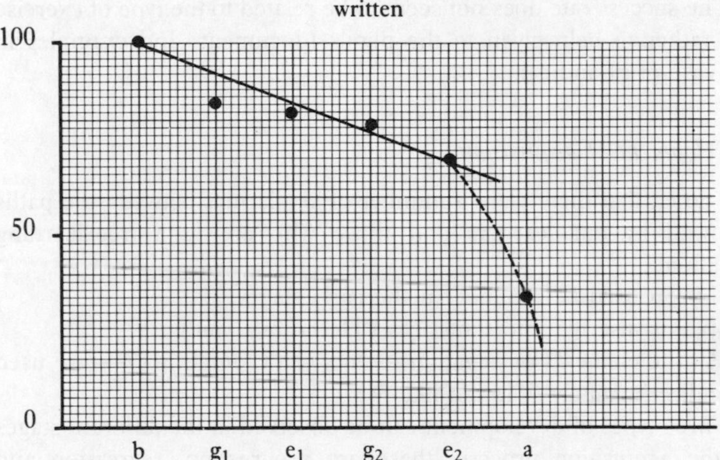

FIGURE 6

Exercises classified by percentages of successful productions

As can be seen, Figures 3 and 4 follow much the same pattern even if 3 (oral) is less concave than 4 (written). The success rate decreases as the degree of spontaneity increases. Nonetheless, an improvement in the success rate can be seen for the purely spontaneous exercises; this can in part be explained by the fact that the 90% success rates recorded for these exercises, (G, g_1 and g_2) are the personal success rates of the pupils who participated in them (the 'weaker' pupils taking no active part).

Exercises A and B were exercises in oral comprehension, not expression, and for this reason their results are shown as dotted lines.

Figure 5 shows that structural drills involving transformations have a higher success rate than substitution drills. This may be due to the fact that in substitution drills a pupil may be required to change an auxiliary verb because of a change of subject, therefore having to deal with a greater number of difficulties.

Figure 6 shows that the order based on the success rate is the following:

b (pairing words or sentences)
g_1 (spontaneous)
e_1 (reply)
g_2 (spontaneous)
e_2 (reply)

The success rate does not seem to be related to the type of exercise but rather to help given to the pupils (documents and examples in the case of g_1 and e_1).

Development of acquisition

We noted that there were a number of similarities between the paths followed by our learners and those who are in a free-learning situation:

1. 'No' is used before 'not' in the early stages.
2. 'No' is inserted into sentences ('He no bite you').
3. All the elements of negation — 'no, can't, don't, not' — are used indiscriminately ('He not like fish').

Three types of development can be observed in the different stages of the acquisition process: these are progression, regression and fossilization. Only the 'very good' pupils make progress in a clear, straightforward way. In Tables 1 and 2, where the pupils were put in order going from 'poorer' to 'better' (on the basis of an end-of-year overall judgement), the earlier a pupil occurs in the table the later his or her progress towards a state of stable correctness. Indeed, the 'weaker' pupils even tend to regress after a stable correct period at the beginning (for instance, B, D and F in oral work). Regression is manifested by a transition from stable correct to variable, or stable correct to stable incorrect. It occurs for all the pupils from A to J. In oral work such regressions are only temporary.

ORAL

Pupil A: a period of regression occurs in period 3. The two first learning periods are stable, as is the case for the majority of the group, the lexical items to be acquired being limited to a few nouns and the grammar to 'it is', 'it's' and 'it isn't'.

Pupil B: regression in periods 1 and 8.

Pupils C and E: both undergo a period of regression after periods 1 and 2. This coincided with the first mechanical exercises — substitution drills, transformation drills and felt-board exercises. It is interesting to note that these pupils also had problems learning mechanical mathematical operations. Pupil E made mistakes in periods 5 to 7 when doing these types of exercises and during period 9 he produced nothing at all.

Pupil D: went through a period of regression from period 6 to period 8. This pupil has serious comprehension problems in all subjects. She therefore failed the type A exercise. In period 8 she was questioned, but did not reply, being again prevented from doing so by her failure to understand the question which had been put.

Pupil I: went through a period of regression after period 5. It was during this period that he made his only formal errors. It is also worth noting that during this same period he participated in every type of exercise which was given.

Pupil G: seemed to regress between periods 6 and 8 (stable incorrect and no productions). These were the only times when this pupil had any problems, and they followed an attack of jaundice: fatigue was perhaps therefore the cause of regression, since this pupil was otherwise always stable.

Pupil F: seemed to regress from period 12 onwards. When questioned, she did not answer. Though by no means a dull child, towards the end of the school year she just did not seem motivated.

Pupil H: regressed between periods 2 and 3, 4 and 5, 6 and 7. This regression was due to formal errors in different types of exercises which always involved the acquisition of 'be' in the negative. What tends to confirm the fact that this pupil was actually going through a period of acquisition is that she never produced any negative forms spontaneously (spontaneous productions being better evidence of what has really been acquired). It was only from period 8 onwards that this pupil began producing spontaneous utterances.

Pupil J: like the eleven others, she regressed between periods 6 and 7 in the Type A exercise.

WRITTEN
Pupils A, B and C clearly regress in period 12 onwards. For A, B, C, D, E and G there are temporary periods of regression preceded by long periods of fossilization in the 'variable' state.

For pupils H, I, J, K and L the acquisition process goes through periods of regression to the variable state, alternating with periods of stabilization which decrease in length the lower in the table one goes. This is a sign of constant self-monitoring.

Fossilization can occur either in the variable or the stable incorrect states. There are no examples here of either temporary or permanent fossilization in the stable incorrect state. Our observations show that those pupils who enter a stable incorrect state only remain there for *one* learning period. It seems reasonable to argue that this is simply a temporary hold-up in development. A brief fossilization in the variable state occurs in the written work during the second half of the year (period 8 onwards) for pupils A, B, C, D and E, those who had the most difficulty in other subjects.

Conclusion

Although limited both as regards the number of learners and because it concentrates on the acquisition of a single phenomenon, this study does allow us to confirm and evaluate certain general features of foreign language acquisition in a school setting, in particular:
1. that acquisition develops differently from one learner to another;
2. that it develops differently in the written and spoken forms;
3. that development of acquisition does not correspond to the progression which the learning programme attempts to impose;
4. that the production of errors does not seem to result in the learning of errors (there is no fossilization in the stable incorrect state).

However, we must be careful not to push our generalizations too far: this study was carried out in a particular pedagogical situation (a school setting) and with an audio–oral course that follows a very strict progression; it was carried out by the teacher responsible for the class in question and could only consider the linguistic input which actually occurred in the classroom. Before any kind of exact conclusions about the acquisition process in a school setting could be drawn, this study should therefore be repeated with other learners and teachers. It would also be necessary to compare the different types of acquisition — grammatical, lexical and phonetic — which occurred in one and the same year, in order to evaluate the types of relationship which hold between them, to see, for example, whether or not the form of an individual learner's acquisition corresponds to the divisions imposed by the teaching programme.

In the short term, though, this has at least enabled us to describe an aspect of the actual acquisition process of real pupils in a real learning situation and is, for this very reason, an important first step in a field which remains almost unexplored.

8 Mud and stars: personal constructs, sensitization and learning

P. Riley

> Two men looked out through prison bars
> One saw mud, the other, stars.

Introductory note

This paper is a kite-flying exercise: it tries to relate certain recent developments in psychology with a particular pedagogical practice. But the psychological approach in question — Personal Construct Theory — is virtually unknown in applied linguistics circles, and the pedagogical practice — Sensitization — has never, as far as I know, been the subject of any serious investigation. The result is therefore both programmatic and sketchy, though where possible I have tried to give concrete examples, and may turn out simply to be a resounding statement of the obvious. But after all,

> A child, when it begins to speak,
> learns what it is that it knows.
>
> (J. H. Wheelock)

On descriptions

> A rose is a rose is a rose.
>
> (G. Stein)

The meta-theoretical point which will be made in this section is neither complex nor new: it is simply that theoretical descriptions are not to be identified with the objects they describe. It follows that the theoretical descriptions of the constituent parts of complex objects are not freely interchangeable.

Now the description of any complex object requires that a minimum of the constituent parts be recognized: for the complex object 'language', terminology varies considerably, but it is common to recognize three constituents which will here be labelled *capacity*, *process* and *product*.

Theoretical descriptions of *products*, then, are to be distinguished from theoretical descriptions of *processes* and both are to be distinguished in turn from theoretical descriptions of *capacities*. As Andrew Chesterman (1977) has pointed out, much of the confusion in psycholinguistics has been due to precisely this failure to observe these meta-theoretical demarcation lines.

If we distinguish, then, between the study of language as

A: a *capacity*, that is, whatever it is 'inside their heads' which enables people to speak,

B: behaviour, i.e. what people do when they communicate, the communicative *process*,

C: a *product* of capacity and process,

we must also distinguish between

A^1: a description of capacity,

B^1: a description of process,

C^1: a description of product.

Chesterman (1977) argues convincingly that the 'Psycholinguistic Fallacy'

> was to mistake C^1 for B^1 and A^1 — to assume the formal processes used by the grammar actually represented the productive and perceptive processes of language behaviour (B) and that grammatical constructs like deep structure actually existed in peoples' heads.

Such confusions have only been encouraged by the Chomskyan notion of *competence* which, Janus-like, looks to intuitions based on capacity A to help formulate the terms of the description A^1, glossing over the differences. Yet earlier Chomsky (1965) seemed to warn against this line of reasoning:

> A generative grammar is not a model for a speaker or hearer . . . when we say that a sentence has a certain derivation with respect to a particular generative grammar, we say nothing about how the speaker or hearer might proceed, in some practical or efficient way, to construct such a derivation.

It is difficult to square this with his notorious 'systematic ambiguity' whereby grammatical descriptions B^1, C^1 are actually identified with capacities and processes A, B. Indeed, Chomsky insists (private communication, 1978) that transformational generative grammar 'has led to some rather striking insights into principles of mental representation and mental computation'.

Of course, this is only one particular instance of a failure to observe the set of distinctions which Chesterman has so lucidly set out, but the objection is one which can be generalized to all such epistemological short-cuts.

The line of reasoning being followed here has a number of important theoretical and practical implications, but from the point of view of our immediate interests — the pedagogical description and presentation of language — there is one which is absolutely crucial, namely that theoretical linguistic descriptions of, say, products are not to be confused with descriptions of capacity — and even less with psycho-pedagogical descriptions of the acquisition of capacity. All too often, the term *pedagogical grammar* is used in ways which reveal this underlying confusion.

To a considerable extent this underlines the point that applied linguistics is not merely linguistics applied, that a wide range of situational, social and personal factors — ranging from company policy to the weather — will influence who learns what, where, when and how. It also hammers in the point that theories of teaching are not theories of learning: they describe different objects, which in turn have different loci. Finally, it emphasizes the danger of imposing units developed for the description of one object on a second and different object; units of grammar are not units of learning — we must distinguish between the conceptual tools and operations which a learner uses in the process of second-language acquisition and those which the linguist uses in the description of the product (Candlin 1973).

In the light of the above discussion, it is possible to formulate some *fundamental requirements for an adequate psychological model of second language learning*, though this list will not, of course, be anything like exhaustive.

Such a model should be learner-centred: this should be pleonastic but unfortunately, as we have seen, it is not, although recent discussions of the Input-Intake-Output distinction have done much to clarify matters (Corder 1967). Secondly, it should focus on the learning process not on the activity of teaching, and thirdly it should describe that process in terms of the learner's own categories and operations, not those of the observer. At the risk of labouring the point, it is worth noting that neither the theorist nor the teacher has the slightest choice about this, since they cannot learn on behalf of the learner. Since these categories and operations differ from individual to individual, the model should be sufficiently powerful to generate descriptions for different individuals and to generalize from them, to account for both minds and mind.

To perform this task of generalization, without which the model cannot be said to exist except in some inchoate, introspective way, it is necessary both to have access to the individual learner's cognitive categories, and to render them observable.

These dual requirements have hitherto been regarded as completely incompatible, since all that is 'subjective' has been taken as unobservable and all that is observable fails to account for 'subjective' categories. It is this which has given rise to the major rift between the 'Humanistic' and 'Behaviouristic' schools of psychology: Humanistic psychology is criticized by the Behaviourists because it is unscientific, Behaviouristic psychology is criticized by the Humanists because it is trivial.

This is where Personal Construct Theory comes in, it seems to me, since it offers both a model and a method for the observation of subjective variables. The pioneering work which has been carried out at the Centre for the Study of Human Learning, Brunel University, seems to confirm this (though none of that work has concentrated specifically on *language* learning). So, too, does our work at the C.R.A.P.E.L. — although it has not been consciously carried out as research into Personal Construct psychology. As yet, therefore, no work has been done on adapting the techniques of Personal Construct psychology to the investigation and furthering of the language-learning process.

Nonetheless, work on autonomous learning (Holec 1980) and on self-assessment (Oskarsson 1980) shows such a high degree of congruity in methods, aims and interests that there is every reason to be optimistic about the prospects for the development of a psychological model of second-language learning.

Personal Construct Theory

Orthodoxy is my doxy: heterodoxy is another man's doxy.

(Warburton)

It is obviously impossible to summarize a psychological theory in a couple of paragraphs. The interested reader is therefore referred to the various works included in the bibliography: what follows here is an attempt to give a very general idea of the intellectual stance involved in this approach, although even this incurs the risk of caricature.

Personal Construct Theory is a 'total psychology', by which I understand its proponents to mean that it is both a theory of the person and a theory of knowing: it is, then, a *meta-theoretical epistemics*, a theory of the ontogenesis of meaning, in that it studies the individual's apprehension and categorization of knowledge. Knowledge is knowledge of order, the order created by the individual when he imposes the organization of his cognitive categories on the chaos which surrounds him. The focus of Personal Construct Theory, then, is the individual, his forms of appraisal and his construing of events: the aim of Personal Construct psychology is the identification, observation and extension of his cognitive categories and their operations.

Personal Construct psychology, is, therefore, essentially relativistic. Its epistemological pedigree is a long one, going back, I suppose, to Protagoras: 'Man is the measure of all things'. But it was George Kelly who founded, formulated and systematized the modern school. Kelly brought to his psychological studies the interest in relativity which has been one of the outstanding characteristics of the intellectual history of this century. Names like Sapir, Whorf, Heisenberg, Einstein, Mead, and Lévi-Strauss, testify to the extent and importance of this trend.

As was to be expected, Kelly's work was completely ignored by the Behaviourists: there is a clear parallel here with the reception given to the ideas of Sapir and Whorf (1956) by Bloomfield and the Structuralists. They were also rejected as being 'unscientific', since they involved unobservables. Although Whorf and Kelly have a great deal in common, there are also considerable differences between their approaches. In particular, the Sapir–Whorf Hypothesis involves external, social categories — those of the language — which are imposed on our perception of reality (much the same is true for the work of later linguists such as Bernstein and Halliday). Personal Construct Theory, on the other hand, deals with the personal selections, operations and interpretations which an individual makes on the basis of the (social) options available to him.

Nonetheless, Kelly seems to have exercised a great influence on such thinkers as Rogers (1972), Illich (1970) and Pirsig (1976) as this quotation will show:

> I have raised the question as to whether psychology will remain a narrow technological fragment of a science, tied to an outdated philosophical conception of itself, clinging to a security blanket of observable behaviours only; or whether it can possibly become a truly broad and creative science, rooted in subjective vision, open to all aspects of the human condition, worthy of the name of a mature science.
>
> (Rogers, quoted in Giorgi 1977)

Ironically, Kelly criticized Rogers and the Humanists because they were insufficiently scientific, since they did not develop any rigorous techniques for observation.

Kelly's rejection of the physical sciences paradigm as a model for psychological investigation is a direct result of his emphasis on the relativity of individual cognition. He argued that not only is the empirical method not the only way of doing science, but that it is the wrong way to develop a science of the person, its very objectivity being an insurmountable barrier; a psychology which imposes 'objective', external categories — whether they are Freud's or Skinner's — falls into Chesterman's fallacy, by confusing the units of a description of one object with those of another. Freud's categories for describing and analysing my behaviour are not *my* categories: to understand my own cognitive processes, I need to know the bases on which I go about construing my world, what categories I use — 'Know thyself' — and the same holds for anyone who wants to understand me, rather than explain me. It is well worth while asking how it happens that Freudian analysts always get 'Freudian' patients, Jungian analysts 'Jungian' patients, and so on!

This radical shift in perspective obliges us to reconsider and redefine just what we mean by 'scientific' and 'scientific method'. For the applied linguist who is afraid of getting out of his depth, there are at least two important sources of encouragement: the first is that in the physical sciences themselves the concept of relativity and the view of scientific definitions as semantic constructs is now a commonplace. Clearly this springs from the work of Einstein and Heisenberg, but both the methodological and epistemological implications have been systematized by Bachelard (1934). Secondly, we should be aware that, from the historical point of view, such shifts in perspective are by no means unusual; indeed the development from heresy to scientific orthodoxy so richly documented by Kuhn (1962) is itself sufficient reason to take a relativistic attitude towards even the most objective scientific knowledge.

A direct consequence of this rejection of the physical sciences paradigm is the changed role of the *experiment* in Personal Construct Theory, where it is seen more as *une expérience* in which the scientist actively participates along with the other participants. The problem of 'alienation' or 'observer effect' has long been recognized, above all in the social sciences (Rosenthal 1963), where it has been shown time and again that the more controlled the experiment the more trivial the results. The position of the Personal Construct Theorists is, in a nutshell, that since they cannot prevent 'observer effect' from occurring, it is far more scientific to acknowledge the fact and subject their own behaviour to the same scrutiny as that of the other participants. Too bad if the social scientist loses his aura of Olympian objectivity: he never really deserved it anyway.

This necessity to study the nature of the involvement of the investigator in the experimental activity, above all his relationships with and influence on the other participants, has produced a considerable literature on conversational heuristics (Fransella 1977) since this is obviously the 'interface' between observer and observed and indeed is often the actual locus of the experiment. In many ways this overlaps with the work dealing with the role of the helper or counsellor in autonomous learning schemes (Rogers 1972; Henner–Stanchina, this volume pp. 191–205). But the conversational tools and techniques which the Personal Construct psychologists have developed seem to me to have no counterparts in language teaching or learning. Insofar as these tools aim at helping the learner to learn by making him conscious of his own motivations, priorities, interests, attitudes, etc., they are of immediate and practical interest to us. Whether they will be directly transferable to *language* learning in a more detailed way remains to be seen.

In Personal Construct terms, an individual learns when he extends his personal system of meaning, that is, when he adds to or refines his set of personal constructs. Amendments to this cognitive map come about, consciously or unconsciously, through experience 'as constructs which are hierarchically organized into a system within which meaning is attributed, sorted and applied' (Harri-Augstein 1977). Lewis Carroll's map paradox is delightfully appropriate here:

> 'That's another thing we've learned from *your* Nation,' said Mein Herr, 'map-making. But we've carried it much further than *you*. What do you consider the *largest* map that would be really useful?'
> 'About six inches to the mile.'
> 'About six inches!' exclaimed Mein Herr. 'We very soon got to six *yards* to the mile. Then we tried a hundred yards to the mile. And then came the grandest idea of all! We actually made a map of the country, on the scale of a *mile to the mile*!'
> 'Have you used it much?' I enquired.
> 'It has never been spread out, yet.' said Mein Herr: 'the farmers objected: they said it would cover the whole country, and shut out the sunlight! So we now use the country itself, as its own map, and I assure you it does nearly as well.'
>
> (Quoted in Hughes and Brecht 1975).

Since each individual has his own cognitive map and will add to it idiosyncratically, the most powerful aids to learning will be those which reveal to him the nature of his map, which provide him with a model of his world. The development of such aids has been a major aim of Personal Construct psychology: they include variations on a number of familiar tools — different types of interview and 'learning conversation', games, role-playing, problem solving and so on — but also a number of content-free interactive computer programmes and grid techniques.

To illustrate this approach, I have chosen the very simplest grid technique of all, since it seems to me to bring out most clearly what is meant by Personal Constructs, how they might be elicited and recorded for observation, how this might help in the process of learning (to learn) and the role of the observer. In this case, learners were being helped to improve their reading ability and efficiency, but it can easily be seen that the same technique could be used for analysing, say, their reasons for learning a foreign language or their needs in that language. (The example is taken from Thomas and Harri-Augstein 1979.)

THE GRID TECHNIQUE

The grid is a vehicle for exploring the experiential world (thoughts and feelings) of an individual. The grid elicitation interview consists of two phases. In the first phase, the participator is asked to name a range of "elements" which would define a "universe of discourse". In the study, the universe of discourse was "purposes for reading". Interviewing techniques were used to guide the participant into really exploring his or her own reading until he or she could name vivid examples of different purposes from within this experience. Eliciting reading purposes can be aided by talking the subject through a diary of reading events, covering a day, week or month. Each event can be explored to identify a reading purpose.

When a representative sample of elements (purposes) has been elicited the subject is then moved into the second phase of the interview. This is concerned with eliciting "constructs" and assigning elements to the poles of these constructs. Specifically, each purpose for reading is written on a card and the subject is offered three cards at a time. He or she is asked to think about the three purposes holistically and to decide which two out of the three are most alike. Again, sensitive interviewing can enhance the quality of the response. When a similar pair has been identified the subject is asked to describe the nature of the similarity. This description constitutes one pole of the construct. A description of how the third card or "singleton" differs from the pair is then elicited. This constitutes the second pole of the construct.

For example, Sybil (Table 5) offers the following three purposes among her 10 elements:—

(i) Because it was recommended,
(ii) Revision for exams,
(iii) For reference.

Sybil decided that "for reference" and "because it was recommended" were more alike each other than "revision for examinations". She

TABLE 5 Sybil's raw grid purposes for reading.

✔ ✓ × X	1 Own interest, independent of set work — Specific set work	2 No aim, no reason — Set work with reason and purpose	3 Curiosity from own desire for knowledge — Curiosity induced by others' ideas	4 Pleasure, for knowledge and satisfaction — Anxiety, never feel to have learned anything	5 Influenced by others' ideas by choice — Set work under pressure	6 Choice but not necessarily pleasure — Set work	7 No aim, not hoping for results — Aim and purpose, to gain knowledge
1 Interest/curiosity	✔		✓	✔	✓	✔	×
2 To pass time		✔				✔	✔
3 Examination revision	X	X		×	X	X	X
4 For reference	✓		X	✓	✔	✔	X
5 Ought to, but don't feel like	×	✔		X	×		
6 Knowledge of subject	✓		✔	✓	✓	✔	X
7 Set for discussion	X	X		×	X	X	X
8 Because recommended	✓	×	X	×	✔	✔	
9 Essay/seminar	X	X			X	X	X
10 For pleasure		✓	✔	✔	✓		✔

describes the similarity between the pair as "influenced by other people's ideas and choices" and the difference as "set work under pressure". Thus, one of Sybil's constructs was:—

Pole 1	Pole 2
Influenced by other people's ideas and choices	Set work under pressure

Once the two poles have been elicited, the subject is asked to imagine a five point scale, ranging from:—

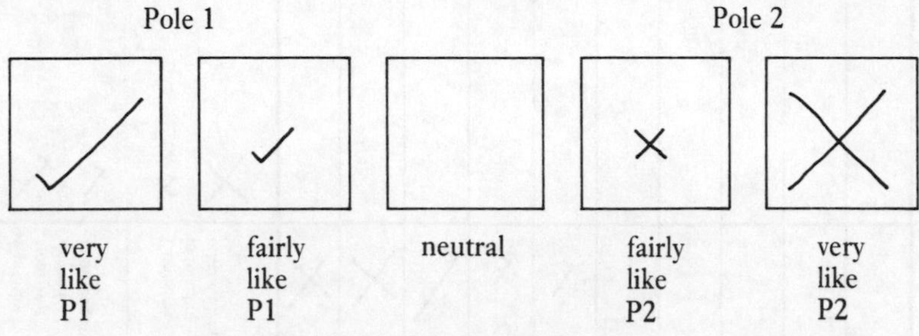

This defines the five point scale. The subject assigns each element to a position on this scale. For example, Sybil rates each of her ten purposes for reading as:—

1	2	3	4	5	6	7	8	9	10
✓		╳	✓	×	✓	╳	✓	╳	✓

on the basis of her construct.

Using fresh sets of three elements, written on cards, Sybil continues to identify constructs, and to rate all elements on each construct, until her repertoire of constructs is exhausted. A systematic randomising technique is used for selecting each fresh "triad" or set of three elements. This ensures that no one pair of elements is repeated more often than any other in the combination sequence.

Thus, the repertory grid technique makes explicit a subject's views of significant elements in her thinking and feeling about a topic and the dimensions in which the topic is thought about. Constructing this raw grid is a useful exercise in itself. The subject becomes immediately more aware of the topic and of the framework in which she perceives it. However, focusing the grid produces a more powerful awareness raising experience for the participant. Elements are correlated with elements to produce a total "relations matrix". This in turn can be cluster-analysed to reveal 'what goes with what' in the subject's thinking. Constructs can be similarly clustered. The Thomas focusing technique displays the grid responses more meaningfully by re-ordering the elements and constructs in cluster sequence (Sybil's focused grid Table 6).

TABLE 6 **Sybil's focused grid purposes for reading.**

	3 Curiosity from own desire for knowledge / Curiosity induced by others' ideas	4 Pleasure, for knowledge and satisfaction / Anxiety, never feel to have learned anything	1 Own interest, independent of set work / Specific set work	5 Influenced by others' ideas by choice / Set work under pressure	6 Choice but not necessarily pleasure / Set work	2 No aim, no reason / Set work with reason and purpose	7 No aim, not hoping for results / Aim and purpose, to gain knowledge
8 Because recommended	X		✓	✔	✔	x	
4 For reference	X	✓	✓	✔	✔		X
6 Knowledge of subject	✔	✓	✓	✓	✔		X
1 Interest/curiosity	✓	✔	✔	✓	✔		x
10 For pleasure	✓	✔		✓		✓	✔
2 To pass time					✔	✔	✔
5 Ought to but don't feel like		X	x	x		✔	
9 Essay/seminar		x	X	X	X	X	X
3 Examination revision		x	X	X	X	X	X
7 Set for discussion		x	X	X	X	X	X

The example given here is only one of a number of different grid assembly and interpretation techniques. Although they vary considerably, above all in statistical sophistication, the principle underlying all of them is that they provide the learner with an 'objective correlative' of his cognitive categories in a particular area — a sort of 'psychic mirror'. Since grids can also be exchanged and integrated in various ways, they provide a useful basis for comparison between learners and for the investigation of various aspects of group behaviour.

Sensitization

If I don't know I don't know, I think I know.
If I don't know I know, I think I don't know.

(R. D. Laing)

Mais — vous voulez dire qu'il y a des verbes irréguliers en français!

(French adult learner of English)

As we have seen, with their common emphasis on learning and the learner and on autonomy, there is a considerable amount of overlap between Personal Construct Theory and certain tendencies in applied linguistics. It is therefore interesting to ask whether there are already language learning techniques which are based — not in name, but in principle — on the elicitation and use of the learner's personal constructs.

Not surprisingly, this does in fact prove to be the case; each time we ask learners to try to define or analyse their own motivations and needs, or to evaluate their own techniques and results, we are trying to get them to make explicit their cognitive categories, however fuzzy they may be around the edges. And the ESP teacher who gives his students a text on their specialization and asks 'Well, what don't you understand?' is also allowing them to use their technical knowledge as a basis for hypotheses about meaning. Another example, and one which is far more widespread than either of those already mentioned, is *sensitization*.

By sensitization we mean the pedagogical technique whereby examples drawn from a learner's L1 are used to help the understanding of certain characteristics of the L2. As such it is not really susceptible to rigorous definition; it lies between the two extremes of translation and a fully-fledged meta-language. It is a form of metacommentary, yet one which avoids many of the problems posed by linguistic terminology, since it reduces the number and technicality of terms which need to be used, relying on demonstration and intuition.

Since it is a technique which directly and explicitly involves the use of the L1 in the acquisition of the L2, it is one which touches on a number of psychological and methodological problems. The role of the mother tongue in foreign language learning continues to be the subject of heated debate. On the one hand, there are those who favour the various types of 'direct method' and who forbid all reference to and use of the L1. On the other, there is the grammar-translation type of approach, which is essentially an explicit set of terms and rules for the reformulation of L1 structures as L2 structures. The 'direct' method is based on the dubious hypothesis that one can learn one's first language twice, with no intermediate process of conceptual categorization, while the grammar-translation approach involves the use of a detailed meta-language which 'predigests' all the material to which the learner is exposed.

In principle, then, there is little in mainstream language-teaching theory which would seem to favour recourse to sensitization as a regular pedagogical practice: one would expect it to be regarded as a dangerous source of either interference or imprecision. But in fact it is one of the most common practices imaginable and the teacher who makes no use of it for even a lesson is a rare bird indeed. Whether it is a rough-and-ready analogy ('It's a bit like when you say . . . in French') or a kind of grass-roots contrastive analysis, sensitization seems to be the expression of some deeply-felt beliefs concerning the nature of *explaining*.

This being the case, it is very surprising to notice how little serious attention has been paid to sensitization: is this because it is somehow 'ideologically' unacceptable to most researchers? My impression, after talking with a number of teachers, is that they feel that sensitization is somehow letting the side down, making things too easy and they have a niggling feeling that it is different from other techniques.

Insofar as sensitization calls on the knowledge and experience of the learner, it is a special case in a teacher-centered pedagogy: perhaps this is why teachers feel uneasy about it. It enables the learner to use his own set of intuitions and notions, not those of the teacher. Of course, this is what all learners do anyway: it really is rather pointless ordering a group of beginners to 'try to think in English'. So in a sense we are making a virtue of necessity, trying to divert the process of interference to profitable ends. In the discussion of the examples which follow, I will try to suggest how this might be done and what the conditions are for a valid transference of this kind.

EXAMPLE 1

A teacher trying to explain the nature and role of *segmentation* in phonetic discrimination for listening comprehension (and having great difficulty trying to avoid just this sort of vocabulary!) suddenly takes the example of the way in which the title of the TV *Collaro Show* appears in a number of different 'arrangements': *Colle à rôt chaud; col a rot chaud; collard au chaud*, etc. . . . The teacher later also explained how homophones are disambiguated in context by taking a series of French examples (*vers, vert, vair, verre*, etc.).

EXAMPLE 2

This is the translation of the first page of a module aimed at sensitizing learners to the ideas of

1. different realizations for the same function,
2. different registers or styles.

INTRODUCTIONS AND HOW TO REPLY TO THEM

Introductions made by a third person.

0 A: Mr Carver, may I introduce you to my wife? Simone, Mr Carver.
B: How do you do?
C: Pleased to meet you.

– A: Oh, Denis, this is my sister, you know, the art student.
B: Oh yes. Hello.
C: Hi.

+ A: Come and let me introduce you to my colleague, Mr Rossi, who will be responsible for showing you around the firm. Mr Rossi, this is Mr Davids, who has come to discuss our project.
B: How do you do?
C: How do you do?

0 A: Sue, this is the new French *assistante*, Sylvie.
B: Pleased to meet you.
C: And I'm very happy to meet you, I hope you're going to like it here.

Two people introducing themselves to one another.

0 A: My name's Martin Brown.
B: I'm Ann Ford. How do you do?

0 A: Excuse me, but you're not Mrs Mount, are you?
B: Yes, I am.

A: How do you do? I'm Catherine Laver. I've come to meet you.
B: How do you do? That's very kind of you.

EXAMPLE 3

A small group of specialists due to attend a medical congress were having great difficulty understanding the authentic recordings with which they had been provided. Discussion with the teacher showed that at least part of the problem was at discourse level: in particular, they were unable to recognize references or quotations which were usually signalled by changes in key and tempo. By taking a similar recording in French, the teacher was able to draw their attention to these characteristics and their level of understanding seemed to improve considerably.

Almost every aspect of language can be illustrated in this way. During my own teaching recently I have found myself using sensitization to explain such things as the differences between comprehension and expression (e.g. the choice of the article is made for you in the one case but not the other), the differences between the spoken and the written forms at the syntactical level (greetings, etc., in letters, the simple past) and differences in sequences of functions (you don't say 'thank you' if someone pays you a compliment in French).

Conclusion

The French for London is Paris.

(Ionesco)

This quotation illustrates a major objection to the use of sensitization: it risks giving the learner the impression that the L1 and the L2 are 'really' the same, resulting in something like word-for-word translation. This danger should certainly not be minimized, but neither is it going to be eliminated simply by refusing to use sensitization since, as we have seen, the learner can only use his own personal constructs; again, it is a danger which can in fact be countered by sensitization, as in Example 2, where one of the points being made is that, as there is no one-to-one relationship between structures and functions in the L1 there cannot be a direct correspondence either between those of the L1 and L2.

To the extent, though, that 'universals' do exist there seems to be no logical or pedagogical reason for ignoring them. This should not be taken as implying that sensitization should only be used for 'high-level' linguistic phenomena (e.g. at discourse level) since clearly a concept such as 'segmentation' is highly abstract. One of the main advantages of sensitization is this avoidance of meta-linguistic problems: this is particularly true of Example 3, where the sheer weight of linguistic terminology and theory necessary to describe the discursive functions of certain prosodies would completely crush the learner.

After a very brief period of observation, it seems to me that sensitization serves, as the name suggests, to make the learner aware of the nature of the problem he is faced with. In Example 1, the effect of the teacher's explanation was certainly not to make his learners suddenly capable of perfect phonetic discrimination and oral comprehension. But it did seem to help them understand what it was they had to learn, and the same is true for the other examples given. In other words, sensitization is most valuable as a way of encouraging learning–readiness, or of creating the conditions for learning. This seems to be confirmed by recent work on bilingualism (Skutnab-Kangas and Toukomaa 1976) which shows that a category acquired in the L1 will be 'sought for' and rapidly acquired in the L2.

We need to investigate a wide range of different topics if the relevance and use of Personal Construct psychology and sensitization in language teaching and learning are to be evaluated and understood. Topics which come immediately to my mind are:

1. 'Natural' metalinguistics or occurrences of sensitization: parent–child, helper–learner discourse, etc.
2. Techniques for the elicitation and recording of learners' needs, motivations, attitudes, etc.
3. Language aptitude, in the sense of judging the probability of success for a given learner in a particular pedagogical situation, such as an autonomous learning scheme.
4. Learning techniques.
5. Discourse categories: it seems possible that recent approaches to the description of aspects of discourse, such as Brazil *et al.* (1980) on intonation or Burton (1981) on conversational strategies, might be susceptible to Personal Construct/sensitization techniques, since they operate with relatively simple, limited conceptual categories.

Finally, this work might also provide a useful counterweight to some of the less healthy forms of interest in subjectivity at present proliferating in language teaching.

Autonomous learning schemes: principles and organization

> En dépossédant le maître de l'exclusivité du pouvoir d'enseigner on investit l'élève d'une responsabilité nouvelle, celle de s'enseigner; l'opération ne va pas sans difficulté, tant est lourd le poids des conditionnements antérieurs, tant est sécurisante l'autorité magistrale. Les perspectives que la pédagogie rogérienne ouvre à l'enseignement des langues restent généralement inexplorées. Il faudra dans les années qui viennent experimenter aussi loin qu'il sera possible dans ce domaine, et à tous les niveaux. La démythification du maître s'accompagnera de la démythification de l'étudiant, et chacun, rendu à son ignorance, pourra en tâtonnant découvrir des voies nouvelles.
>
> *Yves Châlon*

Almost every society worthy of the name has counted independence of thought and action amongst its highest ideals. It is, therefore, pointless trying to trace to any single historical source the concept of autonomy as it is understood in current educational discussion. It is a concept, too, which has deep and tangled roots which stretch out into the fields of philosophy, psychology and politics.

The task of disentangling them will have to be left to some future historian of ideas. Nevertheless, we can be confident that he or she will identify the decades immediately following the Second World War as a period of special interest to the investigation. Between 1950 and 1970 (let us say) a number of social and political currents of thought converged to produce an intellectual climate that stressed the value and interest of individual experience.

Partly this was a reaction against the materialistic behaviourism which had effectively reduced the study of human psychology to a sort of contrastive physiology, happily extrapolating from experiments on rats, rabbits and pigeons to mankind, but completely incapable of addressing aspects of human behaviour (such as language) which are species–specific. Workers in a wide range of vocations and disciplines, finding that contemporary academic psychology was almost totally irrelevant to their interests, turned to more therapeutic models or, and this was a crucial point, were forced to develop their own psychological models. Philosophers, educationists, linguists, sociologists, even physicists and mathematicians found themselves hammering out 'their' approach to psychology. Not only did this produce a new interest in and understanding of the relativistic nature of cognition, but the lessons learned from this exercise in free thought themselves became an important part of the psychology. As one might expect, this is particularly clear in the writings of those whose work touched on what we might rather loosely call the philosophy of education; Paulo Freire, Ivan Illich, Carl Rogers and George Kelly all contributed in their different ways to a reaffirmation of the individual, to a re-awakening of belief in the value of individual experience and to a corresponding wariness of institutions and institutionalized thought and behaviour. Our future historian of ideas may well come to the conclusion that what are now being called the cognitive sciences owe at least as much to these sources as to 'official' psychology. He or she will no doubt also point out that the concept of autonomy, with its almost protestant insistence on individual responsibility and its consequent activism, is the polar opposite of the determinism encouraged by behaviouristic psychology. Minority rights movements of every kind, but especially feminism, drew their dynamism largely from these sources, as did the ecologists.

These ideas have been influential in the field of adult education just about everywhere. Among those to further them in Europe were the educational reformer Bertrand Schwartz and the applied linguist Yves Châlon. Châlon's direct role in developing and spreading the concept of autonomy was twofold: he was founder of the C.R.A.P.E.L. and a leading member of the Council of Europe's Modern Languages project. Through these institutional channels and through his own extraordinary gifts for personal relationships, he was able in turn to inspire a number of teachers with his interests and ideals. Research into aspects of autonomy and autonomous learning schemes has been a permanent and major feature of the C.R.A.P.E.L.'s work since its inception.

As we hope the papers in this section will show, autonomy is not just a theory, but it does have a coherent intellectual basis. The main outlines of this epistemological framework are set out by Holec in his paper 'On autonomy', but he never loses sight of the didactic implications. This is followed by a relatively early article describing the functioning of an autonomous learning scheme, though it is one which is still operating along the lines described here.

Probably the most common objection to autonomy which is made by teachers is 'well that all sounds very fine, but it'd never work in my school/firm/college.' True, it is impossible to introduce schemes of this kind into a completely hostile institutional environment, but if the institution is anything less than that we usually find that something can be done. Moulden's paper describes just such an experimental scheme, complete with handouts, questionnaires — and breast-beating. Again, the scheme is still going strong.

If self-directed learning schemes hand over many of the teacher's tasks to the learners, what do the teachers do? Clearly, their role must shift radically unless the change to self-direction is one in name only: they must become 'helpers'. In their paper, Gremmo and Abé, who are both experienced teachers and experienced helpers, describe and discuss the differences between the two roles by relating them to the different types of learning scheme.

The final paper in this section is a synthesis of extracts from different articles on various aspects of autonomy.

9 On autonomy: some elementary concepts

H. Holec

The concept of autonomy has played the role of catalyst in language teaching in recent years and this is an extremely promising development for a number of reasons: not only has it helped a certain number of educationalists to bring out into the open and clarify what would otherwise have been just unknown approaches or sporadic intuitions, but it has also helped these and other teachers to become more aware of the educative nature of the pedagogic work in which they are involved, an aspect of their work which has gradually been hidden from view by the increasingly technocratic line along which language-teaching methodology has been developing. For both these reasons, the continuing debate to which this concept gives rise has contributed at least as much to progress in education as have its practical applications.

However, we should not allow the potential applications of autonomy to make us forget that it is essentially a conceptual tool and that to be used properly it must first of all be used as such: this is why anyone intending to 'use' autonomy needs first of all to have a clear idea of just what it involves. The aim of this article, therefore, is to improve our awareness of the ramifications of what might be called the autonomous approach.

The main lines of development of this approach, which has been under investigation at the C.R.A.P.E.L. since 1972, are based on a three-way distinction: self-directed learning, the acquisition of autonomy by the learner and the relationships between autonomy and self-directed learning. This applies strictly to the autonomous approach, of course, which is only one amongst many others which are practised at the C.R.A.P.E.L. — individualized teaching, distance teaching, etc. The autonomous approach is just one of a range of options available to the learner and is in no sense a path which has to be followed. In what follows, though, 'approach' will be used to refer only to the autonomous approach.

Self-directed learning

This term refers to the way in which the various modalities of the learning programme are determined: objectives, contents, method, place, time and pace and evaluation. For the learning to be self-directed, it is both necessary and sufficient for these operations to be carried out by the learner himself, to be his own responsibility. The nature of this responsibility can be described in the following ways:

General characteristics

First, the responsibility can be regarded as something *static*, as a finished product:

1. The learner may be responsible for defining every aspect of his learning programme, or some, or none; it is quite possible to imagine different learning programmes based on completely different combinations going from complete self-direction to complete 'other-direction', or anything in between. This variability in the degree of self-direction is worth noting for two reasons: firstly, we recognize that this is not an all-or-nothing choice, it becomes possible to envisage a progression towards self-direction (see below). Secondly, it becomes possible to undertake empirical research to determine which of the theoretically possible combinations are in fact feasible, which allows us to establish a hierarchy of the different operations involved in defining the learning programme, and this in turn would help with the diversification of learning systems.

2. Accepting this responsibility means that the learner has to determine for each of the operations in question the nature of the decision which has to be taken and that he then takes it (in fact these two tasks, though quite distinct, can be carried out more or less simultaneously, even if the one must precede the other in purely logical terms). For example, as regards the definition of the contents of his or her learning programme, the learner has to:

   a) *select* from among all the possible contents those which will help him to attain the objectives which he has defined and then make a further selection of those which he will in fact include in his learning programme;
   b) *organize* these contents, by examining the different progressions possible and choosing one of them.

3. Taking on this responsibility is not necessarily something the

learner does on his own. It can be done together with other learners (compare the experiment in self-directed group learning reported by Riley and Sicre in this volume, pp. 275–82) or with outside help. In this last case, the outside help might be provided directly, by a teacher for example, or indirectly, through materials such as books, recordings or specialized audio-visual documents: the learner is not helped to take the decision by someone else taking the decision for him (that would, by definition, be 'other-direction', not self-direction) but rather is helped to make the decision himself by being shown what the decision involves. To go back to our example of the learner who is trying to define the contents of his learning programme, the help he received might consist of being shown all the different contents which would help him attain his objectives, together with advice as to how to make his choice — but the choice would be his own.

Secondly, accepting responsibility for the learning programme can be seen as something *dynamic*, as a process which develops and changes between the beginning and end of the programme. From this point of view:

1. The transition from other- to self-direction can be made progressively, the learner taking over more and more of the decisions; he might start by defining the contents and the pace for example, and then go on to define his objectives, finally carrying out all the operations, including evaluation.
2. Similarly, the amount of outside help given may gradually decrease, both as to the number of operations concerned and as to its importance in any particular operation.

Specific characteristics

Regarded as something *static*, this acceptance of responsibility can be seen as consisting of carrying out the following operations:

1. Both the intermediate objectives and the ultimate objective or objectives to which they lead need to be defined. This will not be done on the basis of a description of native-like communicative competence but on a communicative competence defined in terms of the language needs of which the learner himself is aware. These personal needs may well bring out further highly specific needs such as being able to make people laugh, understanding the stock market report on the radio, rapid reading, summarizing a foreign language text in the mother-tongue and so on. They also incude the com-

municative needs of the learner *qua* learner, going from the linguistic strategies which help him improve his own performance (asking for metalinguistic help, for example) to those which are necessary for dealing with the many problems a foreigner has to face (various ways of repairing failures in comprehension, for example, or of compensating for gaps in vocabulary, or simply of indicating to the speaker that one has such or such a problem, so please be patient and understanding). Generally speaking, when the learner takes over the definition of his own objectives, the result is that he takes into account needs which are personal or even unique, and this is equally true for all the other operations.

2. The definition of contents is at the interface between the definition of objectives and the definition of working methods and techniques. Taken in hand by the learner, it allows him to make an efficient use not only of his motivation and interests — fields of specialization, personal, cultural and social values, interests in current affairs, etc. — but also of those materials which he himself prefers — authentic and/or didactic, audiovisual and/or oral and/or written, video and/or films and/or slides, cartoons, etc.

3. The learner needs to think of all the different sources which are available to him: textbooks and other commercially published materials, his own previous experience of learning or that of other learners he knows, etc. In the light of his learning objectives he will select from this range of possibilities those types of activity which:

a) correspond to his personal expectations, that is, to his preferences as regards work techniques and methods (analytic/synthetic; implicit/explicit; inductive/deductive; mostly oral/mostly written; personal involvement/impersonal; one strictly linear progression/a variety of progressions)
b) can best be reconciled with the various constraints imposed on him by his learning situation (the total amount of time available to him; how it is distributed; financial resources; whether or not he can work with others).

If necessary, he also needs to discover methods and techniques other than those which he already knows, so that he can adapt his programme to his personal learning situation: he could do this either by asking himself whether there might not be activities which he has come across when studying non-language subjects which could be transferred to his present situation (in particular, any extra-scholastic learning which he may have done) or by simply using his imagination.

4. The main result of the learner's choosing his own time and place of learning is that it becomes possible to take into account not only the 'orthodox' times and places but many others (a journey by car, for example), the important thing being to choose those which are the most conducive to learning either because the learner is freer from distractions, or because he is more at ease, or because the material conditions are better.

Being responsible for the rhythm of learning means essentially:

a) planning the distribution in time, especially when external pressures (a journey abroad, an interview for a job) fix the date by which the learning programme has to be completed;
b) deciding when a particular aspect of the work should be started, continued or interrupted and doing so while taking into account parameters such as the speed with which knowledge is integrated, the necessity to vary learning activities, the necessity to keep the learning programme balanced, etc.

Depending on the learner's personality, decisions concerning the pace of the learning programme may be more or less strictly adhered to (and may or may not give rise to personal learning contracts) and they may be reviewed occasionally, regularly or continuously.

5. Self-assessment is of two types: the first concerns acquisition of the language, the second the learning process itself.

Evaluating acquisition consists of judging any progress made, by comparing the extent to which knowledge *acquired* corresponds with knowledge *sought*. Such an evaluation can be based on the analyses of performances realized during any of the learning activities, including 'authentic' activities (contacts with authentic documents and/or native speakers) and not just on those performances which are produced during tests (which, for this very reason, are no longer obligatory). It is the learner himself who is responsible for choosing which performances he wishes to analyse.

The analysis itself is carried out on the basis of criteria which the learner himself has defined and which are in fact what he considers to be the important features of a particular type of communication or of a single successful utterance; consequently, these are criteria for judging an idiolect or personal communicative competence. For details, see 'Taking learners' needs into account in self-directed learning', Holec, this volume pp. 263–75.

As to judgements concerning how much progress has been made, they will be relative to a psychologically acceptable threshold which the learner sets himself for each of the features specified by his criteria:

this threshold will vary depending on whether he is a perfectionist or easy-going, on the relative importance for him of the different features and on the model of reference which he chooses (a native speaker, a foreigner, himself). In general, it is this variability in sampling, criteria and thresholds which is the main characteristic of learner self-assessment.

Assessment of the learning as such consists of the learner's evaluating the results of his taking over the responsibility for defining the different aspects of the learning programme.

a) Have the objectives been correctly established? By examining the extent to which knowledge acquired corresponds with knowledge required, for example, it is possible to determine whether the learner's needs have been correctly analysed, whether they have been correctly interpreted in terms of final objectives and whether the intermediate objectives which have been chosen do in fact facilitate progress towards these final objectives.
b) Is the choice of contents satisfactory? The evaluation of what has been learnt should give results whose interpretation would allow the learner to spot, for example, a lack of fit between his objectives and the contents.
c) Have the right places, times and pace been chosen? Comparing the estimated 'profitability' of each learning session with an overall assessment of what has been learnt should help the learner realize if he has made any mistakes in this respect.
d) Has the evaluation of what has been learnt been carried out satisfactorily? The learner can answer this question retrospectively without any outside help, by reviewing his evaluation after a fixed lapse of time, for example: but there is nothing to stop him from using outside sources of information (provided by a teacher, a native speaker or a more advanced learner, etc.) provided that this information is regarded as simply one kind of feedback among others and not as a substitute for his own evaluation.

Seen as a *dynamic* phenomenon, the learner's taking charge of each of the operations involved in defining his learning programme proves to be largely flexible and adaptable: the decisions are never made once and for all or at fixed times and can, therefore, be revised whenever the learner wishes.

There is nothing, for example, which obliges the learner to define his final objectives at the very beginning of his learning programme; he might first carry out an analysis of his needs which will give him an idea of the general lines his programme will follow and then gradually refine it as he discovers more exactly just what learning a language for communication really means, developing his own 'theory' of communication, so that he is in a better position to describe his needs in terms which can be used in defining his learning objectives, for example. It may also happen that, as time passes, his needs change, because of some change in his circumstances (a new job, for example) or because he himself changes (new interests, maybe, or progress in his language studies).

Everything that has just been said above, about revising decisions as and when the learner wishes, applies equally to contents, methods and place/time and pace of learning. The learner can proceed by trial and error, modifying his choices as he goes along, learning from experience, and he will be able to do this without any great inconvenience — provided he carries out regular and frequent evaluations of his learning programme.

The determination of the criteria and thresholds to be used in evaluation also continues throughout the learning programme, along with the definition of objectives but also in accordance with any possible changes in the learner's personal requirements. The choice of criteria and thresholds can, in fact, be reviewed every time an evaluation is carried out, and so can the type of performance taken for analysis. The learner can decide not to judge such-and-such an aspect of his knowledge except in such-and-such a type of performance, postponing its evaluation in more 'difficult' cases until later, for example.

In a word, the quality of the learner's work in carrying out these decisions can improve as time passes and as the learner simply gets better at doing it. For a learner to be able to undertake a self-directed learning programme of some kind, therefore, it is not a necessary prerequisite for him to be already perfectly competent in these respects.

Self-directed learning: conclusion

Self-direction is an important aspect of the autonomous learning scheme practised at the C.R.A.P.E.L. Like every learner-centred approach, ours aims at the greatest possible degree of fit between learner and learning. This means that other types of learning programme will have to be defined which, if they do not replace our present ones, will complement them, thereby producing a diversification of the possibilities available to the various types of learner. It seems to us that the principle of self-direction is the one which is most likely to meet this need: because of the multiplicity of forms which it can take we believe that it can provide types of learning programmes which are truly learner-centred.

Again, the first concrete result of any pedagogical approach is to modify the behaviour of the participants involved: our approach as a research centre is to use self-directed learning to redefine the roles of teacher and learner and to specify new objectives for learning materials.

Finally, it seems to us that the best way for the learner to acquire the capacities necessary to his new role is simply to practise self-directed learning and to think about his practice.

The acquisition of autonomy by the learner: 'autonomization'

The acquisition of autonomy by the learner is the fundamental goal in the C.R.A.P.E.L. approach, and it is important to underline from the outset that it is a tendency, a dynamic process with a future, not a stable condition, something which develops — hence the neologism 'autonomization'.

This process can be seen from three different points of view:

From the point of view of the learner, it is a matter of acquiring those capacities which are necessary to carry out a self-directed learning programme.

From the point of view of the teacher, it is a matter of determining those types of intervention which are conducive to the learner's acquiring those capacities.

From the institutional point of view, it is a matter of creating those conditions which allow the learner and the teacher to put these aims into practice.

The learner and the acquisition of autonomy

The ability to direct one's own learning programme includes a certain number of skills and a certain amount of knowledge which can be deduced from a description of self-directed learning. As an example, here are some suggestions concerning the sorts of knowledge and skills which are related to each of the operations involved in defining a learning programme, though the list is by no means exhaustive:

1. DEFINING OBJECTIVES

a) The learner needs to know that a description of those communicative activities which he wishes to be able to perform can serve as a basis for defining his learning objectives.

b) He needs to be able to describe those activities in relevant terms, which implies a model of analysis, however rudimentary . . .

c) . . . and he needs to be able to refine that model.

d) He needs to know how to organize the parameters of analysis into a personal hierarchy.

e) He needs to know how to break down the terminal objectives into intermediate objectives.

f) He needs to know how to use the results of an evaluation as a basis for defining a new set of objectives.

2. DEFINING CONTENTS

a) The learner needs to be able to express his objectives in terms of linguistic elements to be learnt, which implies either a certain amount of descriptive knowledge, or knowledge of where to find it.

b) He needs to know how to establish a corpus of learning materials.

c) He needs to be able to gauge the degree of relevance of items in the corpus to the achievement of his different objectives.

d) He needs to be able to judge how difficult his materials are, if not straight away at least after a trial attempt.

3. DEFINING MATERIALS AND TECHNIQUES

a) The learner needs to be able to determine the objectives of commercially published courses.

b) He needs to be able to evaluate the degree of efficiency of those learning activities which are known to him.

c) He needs to know that no material or method is good in itself, but that it only has advantages or disadvantages with respect to the user and his aims.

d) He needs to be able to build his own 'course' by selecting items from a variety of textbooks, etc.

e) He needs to know that every type of learning activity, scholastic or not, linguistic or not, is potentially useful.

4. DEFINING THE PLACE/TIME AND PACE OF LEARNING

a) The learner needs to know that for every learner certain conditions of learning are more suitable than others.

b) He needs to be able to determine those circumstances in which he works best.
c) He needs to know that the pace of learning varies according to the content and type of learning and he has to be able to vary it as and when necessary.

5. EVALUATING WHAT HAS BEEN LEARNT

a) The learner needs to know that self-assessment is both necessary and sufficient.
b) He needs to be able to determine his own personal evaluation criteria.
c) He needs to know that his evaluation thresholds can vary according to the particular aspect of performance which is being evaluated, the time when the evaluation was carried out, etc.
d) He needs to know how to keep a record of earlier evaluations so that his progress can be measured, etc.

In general, there are very few learners indeed who already possess this knowledge and skill when they set out to learn a language: the ability to execute one's own learning programme is not innate, and whatever people may say it is not one of the objectives of an institutional education. In the majority of cases, therefore, the learner has to acquire this capacity; he has to learn to learn, to set off a process which will eventually enable him, if he is successful, to execute his own learning programme. Like every other learning programme, his may vary in length, difficulty and in its degree of success.

The problems this type of learning programme gives rise to, some of which are similar to those encountered in other types of learning, are essentially psycho-sociological in origin and are, for most learners, connected with the radical change in the learner's role and his perception of it. Obviously, the acquisition of new knowledge and skills also involves technical difficulties of all kinds, related to the discovery process which the learner has to set in motion if he is to become autonomous and not simply increase his stock of knowledge.

Providing yourself with the means to undertake your own learning programme presupposes that, at the very least, you think it is possible to be both 'producer' and 'consumer' of such a programme. This runs counter to the usual attitudes of members of our modern consumer society; indeed for the individual it means withdrawing from it to some extent, since the usual procedure for acquiring 'goods' (in this case competence in a foreign language) is not a creative one. Moreover, this withdrawal is accentuated by the demands that the producer should satisfy the client's demands fully and immediately: from the moment someone applies to an institution to 'obtain' a foreign language, the institution is expected to provide the product required to the full satisfaction of the client. All this is aggravated by the idea that not only can the producer fulfil these needs, because he knows how, but he is the only one who can do so. Obviously, all this puts a powerful brake on any movement towards automony.

Another brake on the acquisition of the capacity to manage one's own learning programme, one which is related to the notions of specialization and expertise, is the social distribution of knowledge and power. There is nothing in his earlier learning experiences, nor in his professional environment, for example, which might lead the learner to think that the surest way of reaching his objectives is to do away with this compartmentalization of different fields of competence to acquire knowledge and skills which lie outside his own field. Just as he would never dream, even for a moment, of taking over from his doctor when he is ill, so it never enters his head that he might take over certain of the teacher's functions when he wants to learn a language.

It is interesting to note that this applies just as much to language teachers: among them are to be found the learners who are the most convinced of the necessity of calling on a specialized teacher if one wishes to learn a language, perhaps because of the threat to their status which any other attitude would imply.

More generally speaking, the tendency towards the acceptance of responsibility implied by autonomization may in itself be a sort of social gamble for the learner. Where will this first bet lead to? Is this activity, limited to language learning for the moment, compatible with the way he behaves in other circumstances? These are just two of the problems the learner has to face immediately. The act of taking responsibility is indissociable from the social environment in which it is taken and with which it forms a whole from which the learner cannot escape.

At the psychological level, the self-examination involved in the acquisition of autonomy can also be a considerable obstacle. It means that the learner has to modify considerably his notion of what learning is and of the various behaviours related to it. Like any task of destructuration/restructuration, this is difficult in itself both intellectually — because it necessitates self-criticism and the tools appropriate to self-criticism (see Harri–Augstein and Thomas 1980) — and affectively, since it involves putting up with the fear of the unknown, hanging onto one's self-confidence, admitting one's weaknesses, being strong-willed and perservering, etc. Clearly the learner's personality has to be taken into account both as regards the process of self-examination and as regards the tasks it involves, just as it has to be taken into account in the language-learning process itself.

For the moment, then, all we can say — since not enough empirical research has been done into the psycho-social aspects of the acquisition of autonomy — is that much of the difficulty it involves for the learner is related to the different social and personal braking mechanisms which each of us brings into the learning situation. Individuals are no more equal before the laws of learning here than they are anywhere else (we are in complete agreement with the ideas expressed in Porcher 1981).

The teacher and the acquisition of autonomy

From the teacher's point of view, there is the problem of knowing just what types of intervention in the process of acquiring autonomy are legitimate and necessary. Quite obviously, it would be impossible for the teacher to bring to the process of learning-to-learn the functions which he has traditionally performed in language teaching: 'learning-to-learn' and 'making someone learn' are completely contradictory. And even if this contradiction could be somehow got round methodologically, the teaching in question would have to be tutorial in type, with the tutor taking into consideration details about the learner of which the learner himself is unaware (he would have to teach him what his needs are, for example, or teach him his own personal criteria for evaluation).

For this reason, the only possible sort of intervention is *support*. Indeed, in the light of recent second-language acquisition studies, which show that there is no direct relationship between teaching and learning — i.e. that teaching does not directly produce learning — it is worth asking whether support is not also necessary in every language-learning process which is not the complete responsibility of the learner.

As has already been pointed out, the nature and amount of support given by the teacher do not remain constant throughout the period of acquisition of autonomy: for this reason, the teacher's contribution cannot be planned in detail at the outset, but has to be continuously adapted to the learner's state at any given moment.

Broadly speaking, there are two types of support: technical and psycho-social.

1. *Technically*, the learner who is learning to learn needs to discover what decisions have to be taken if he is to direct his own learning programme, how to take them and how to evaluate the decisions he has made. The support will, therefore, consist of:

a) Helping analyse the decision: for example, as regards the definition of his objectives, the learner has to clarify the terms of the decision which is to be taken with the aid of a framework of analysis which has to be based on a 'theory' of communication: this 'theory' may, for example, see communication in terms of comprehension and expression, writing and speaking, communicative acts, verbal and non-verbal types of meaning, etc. If this is the case, the framework of analysis will include those parameters and the learner will describe his needs and learning objectives in terms of a competence whose elements will be based on particular values of those parameters. The support might consist of sensitizing the learner, by means of a personal study of the mother tongue, to the relevance of certain communicative parameters: the relationships between text, speaker and addressee, between text and situation or between text and communicative aim, for example (this most certainly does *not* mean that pre-established categories or jargon have to be used: it is far preferable if the learner provides the categories and the metalanguage). Or it might consist of explicit information provided by the teacher or drawn from some other source — or implicit information contained in documents of all kinds — concerning certain aspects of verbal communication (the distinction between the roles of speaker and hearer, for example). Or again, it might take the shape of a discussion with the learner aimed at eliciting and clarifying his personal 'theory', etc. However, there can be no question of anyone's analysing the decision on the learner's behalf.

b) Helping the learner to take the decision: the first few times decisions are taken, this will consist of sensitizing the learner to the fact that there is no reason why he should regard his decision as irrevocable, that it can be modified as and when he wants, that consequently a mistaken decision cannot invalidate the whole of a learning programme; that in any case, proceeding by trial and error is perfectly respectable and that he should therefore take decisions even when he is not entirely satisfied that they are the right ones.

c) Helping the learner with the regular evaluation of his learning — not by taking his place, but by helping him clarify and interpret his observations (by providing him with complementary information in the form of descriptions of other learners' experiences, for example) or simply by listening, which allows the learner to 'think aloud'.

2. At the *psycho-social* level, the teacher's role is essentially one of encouraging the learner to commit himself to the acquisition of autonomy and, once this is done, to spur him on in moments of uncertainty, to help salvage his self-confidence when he is discouraged and generally to support him in his efforts to overcome the obstacles we have mentioned. It is clearly this aspect of the teacher's intervention which is most problematic. How can you support someone without creating the kind of dependent relationship which would vitiate the whole process? How can you go about creating the sort of relationship where support is accepted? What do you do about the inevitable bouts of aggressivity? In addition to these problems there is the temptation for the teacher to think that his solution for such and such a problem is the best one and that he can help the learner save time by suggesting it right from the start, or simply to take over control of the whole process — in order to speed things up, say — by steering the learner in a particular direction rather than by letting him find his own way. Finally the teacher, like the learner, has to modify his conception of the teacher's role, which means that he too is susceptible to the psycho-social problems which such a change brings about: just as the learner has to learn to learn, so the teacher has to learn to help the learner to learn, and this brings us to the institutional problem of teacher-training.

The institution and the acquisition of autonomy

The institution which wishes to encourage the acquisition of autonomy has to create conditions which will allow teachers and learners to carry out the appropriate sorts of activities. Generally speaking, this means that the institution has to play a double role, since it has to provide a learning environment which is suitable both for learning a language and for learning-to-learn. In fact, of course, the acquisition of autonomy can never be achieved 'theoretically' or in isolation, it has to be connected with learning something, it has to be applied. The institution, therefore, has to plan and put into operation educational systems which meet these two aims.

Such systems are necessarily very varied, partly because of the variety of situations in which they may be set up, partly because of the diversity of possible types of public and of the practical constraints which have to be taken into account. At the C.R.A.P.E.L., for example, we offer the following possibilities:

Self-directed learning with support

In this system, learners are in charge of their own learning programme right from the beginning, but 'helpers' are available, by appointment, for help (see pp. 191–205).

Evening classes

Within this traditional structure, which operates during the academic year, self-directed learning activities which are conducive to the acquisition of autonomy are introduced as part of the course.

'One-off' systems

These are *ad hoc* systems, created with the constraints of a particular group in mind (see pp. 299–320).

Setting up and putting such systems into operation implies:

1. An infrastructure of appropriate materials and resources. The materials may be extremely varied both qualitatively and quantitatively, and have to be chosen, produced or acquired as particular needs arise: it is not so much a matter of having to have a vast stock available before the system starts operating as of the progressive accumulation of resources, and this applies not only to the technological hardware but also to the written and recorded documents, to types of activities, etc.
2. Teachers trained in providing support: this training, which would not necessarily have to be completed before they got down to work, can only be self-directed — after all, the principles which govern the acquisition of autonomy apply just as much to the teachers as to the learners they are supporting. This can be done in the institution itself or elsewhere by observing self-directed learners receiving support — or, indeed, by observing any kind of learning whose objective is the acquisition of autonomy — by practising and by analysing and thinking about one's practice and experience and that of other people, together with them or alone, with or without a 'trainer'.
3. Informing potential users of the system: since the acquisition of autonomy is not a very widespread objective, it is important to make it known and to have it recognized in the fullest sense. This is not simply a matter of advertising, in fact, the main arguments in favour of autonomy, such as 'accepting your responsibilities', are likely to be counter-productive. At the C.R.A.P.E.L., we have not really solved this problem; we deal with each case at it arises by handouts and by personal interviews with the institutions and

individuals concerned once they have approached us (as far as the learners are concerned, this procedure has the advantage of being a first step towards autonomy). However, as other institutions begin to set up similar systems the problems are sure to decrease.
The institutional problems faced by the teacher who tries to set up autonomous learning schemes in a 'hostile environment' will not be touched on here. See, however, the paper by Moulden (pp. 206–32).

The acquisition of autonomy is a fundamental aspect of the C.R.A.P.E.L. approach: it is the objective, just as self-direction and support are the methodology. This choice, which is dictated by our desire to make the learning as learner-centred as possible, helps us to get away from the 'traditional' choice between adapting the learner to the teaching and adapting the teaching to the learner. By becoming autonomous, that is by gradually and individually acquiring the capacity to conduct his own learning programme, the learner progressively becomes his own teacher and constructs and evaluates his learning programme himself. The pedagogical problems which arise are truly educational ones which concern the learner, both as an individual with his own personality, and as a member of society.

The fact that our objective is acquisition of autonomy and not simply a self-directed learning programme is the result of our conception of the institution's responsibility to the learner.

Autonomy and self-directed learning

Being autonomous, the end result of the process of acquiring autonomy, is the capacity to run one's own learning affairs: it is a capability, a potential. Self-direction, which results in self-directed learning, is a skill, an ability, a know-how — in this case, knowing how to realize that capacity. The logical relationship between the two is clear: doing something implies knowing how to do it, but the reverse is not always true.

To some people, the fact that we aim at autonomy rather than at self-directed learning might seem to be a dereliction of our pedagogic duty, a refusal to pursue the process to its logical conclusion. But this is to forget that what separates *being able to do something* from *doing it* is *the will to do it*, and that the will in question belongs to the learner: it is the learner who acquires autonomy, the learner who is involved in self-directed learning, the learner, therefore, who has to decide whether or not he wants to start or continue self-directed learning of a language. Is it possible, for example, to imagine a set-up where the institution or the teacher would pre-empt the learner's choice in this matter, forcing him into self-directed learning by simply not offering any other options? After all, are there not already large numbers of learners who have no other choice but self-direction for all sorts of other reasons, such as the constraints arising from their professional life taken together with the unsuitability of the distance teaching materials available?

These questions can only be answered by analysing the situation which would be created if this were done.

Firstly, the imposition of self-direction would entail the imposition of autonomy. But this is a contradiction in educational terms which produces an insoluble problem: how can you reconcile obedience to an external authority with the idea of the personal acceptance of responsibility? It would merely be replacing one kind of bondage with another. It would also mean ignoring the various psychological obstacles to the acquisition of autonomy, which is tantamount to saying that a number of learners would be banned from learning.

Secondly, it has to be remembered that there are a number of sociological obstacles to self-directed learning: to some people, for example, it does not seem to be particularly worthwhile or good for their self-esteem (it is second-best to a course with a 'real' teacher). Again, it might be completely incompatible with other aspects of the learner's behaviour, his way of life or his personality: some people are conditioned (by nurture, not nature) to the idea that they are incapable of taking on such responsibilities or disciplining themselves, and feel the need to delegate such tasks to others. In the face of such obstacles, trying to force people to be self-directed would be irresponsible — or it would mean first undertaking wide-ranging changes in society.

It is for all these reasons (as well as reasons of a more philosophical nature which we will not enter into here) that we have decided at the C.R.A.P.E.L. against making self-direction our objective. Obviously, though, not forcing people into self-direction does not mean that we actually forbid it. If a learner who is truly autonomous decides to direct the rest of his learning programme himself, he ought to be capable of doing so. This implies making certain practical arrangements, creating an infrastructure which will help self-directed learners by reducing their task to manageable proportions so that they are not prevented for psychological or practical reasons from learning in this way. Such an infrastructure would include a lending system for materials of all kinds, the provision of information of various types about learning or learning objectives, and the chance to meet other learners, native-speakers, or indeed anyone who might be of help in some way.

However, if the choice between self-directed learning and other sorts of learning is to be a real one for the learner, it is also necessary to ensure that all these types of learning are on an even footing. In the short term, this means avoiding giving preference of any kind, implicit or explicit, to any particular type or types; to do so would bias the learner's choice: he would choose the 'better' type without really thinking about it, or would feel somehow guilty for having chosen second-best. In the medium and long term, ways have to be found of equipping all learners psychologically and socially to enable them to make this choice (the problem is similar to that encountered when dealing with the acquisition of autonomy). Even if it is only in terms of research projects which have been or will be undertaken, the relationships between autonomy and self-directed learning are taken into consideration in the C.R.A.P.E.L. approach and therefore form an important aspect of it. It is true that the institution should not impose its authority on the learner but neither, if it is aiming at autonomy, should it neglect to provide conditions in which the learner is able to exercise a free choice.

Conclusion

The C.R.A.P.E.L.'s approach to autonomy is based on the three options we have just described: the choice of the acquisition of autonomy as objective, the choice of self-directed learning with support as the means of reaching this objective and the choice of making self-direction possible but not obligatory. Although many problems remain, and many others remain to be discovered, this approach is a viable one, as experience has shown; moreover, it has the advantage of making it possible to carry out a real evaluation based on that experience, of a pedagogical strategy whose educational value is certainly not limited to language learning, thereby making a contribution to pedagogics in general.

As Louis Porcher has emphasized (1981), autonomy has to be won, by learners, teachers and institutions working together and, like any new conquest, it is full of ambushes and pitfalls, internal and external: not to be careful would be foolhardy, but not to participate would be cowardly.

10 Two years of autonomy: practice and outlook

C. Henner-Stanchina

Introduction

At the close of its second year of experimentation, the autonomous learning scheme for adults (first described by Abé, Henner-Stanchina and Smith 1975) has grown in that it has increased its number of learners, expanded the range of learning experiences it makes available to those learners, and provided some interesting insights into the problems involved in running autonomous learning schemes.

The first experimental group involved 26 learners. Within two years, taking account of the inevitable turnover in this type of strategy, 56 people (18 women, 38 men) had at one time (and for whatever length of time) been part of the strategy. It is worth noting, although this perhaps does not attest to any real, widespread change in attitude towards self-directed learning, that interviews carried out over the two-year period reveal a progressive decrease in the proportion of people who choose autonomy for lack of any other solution, in favour of those who consciously prefer the opportunity for autonomous learning. Of the 30 learners in the second year, 10 had already had experience with some kind of class or group set-up elsewhere, be it an intensive language session or extensive evening courses. These 10 people, along with numerous others who had not had previous group experience, rejected the classroom solution either on the grounds that it was (or would be) inadequate in meeting their very specific needs, that working in a group simply did not appeal to them, or that they felt entirely capable of learning English on their own, and all the more effectively, providing the C.R.A.P.E.L. could give them the material means to do so.

Figure 1 represents the entire autonomy scheme as it is operating now. All its potential components are centred around the learners who, as the arrows indicate, move outward towards a variety of avail-

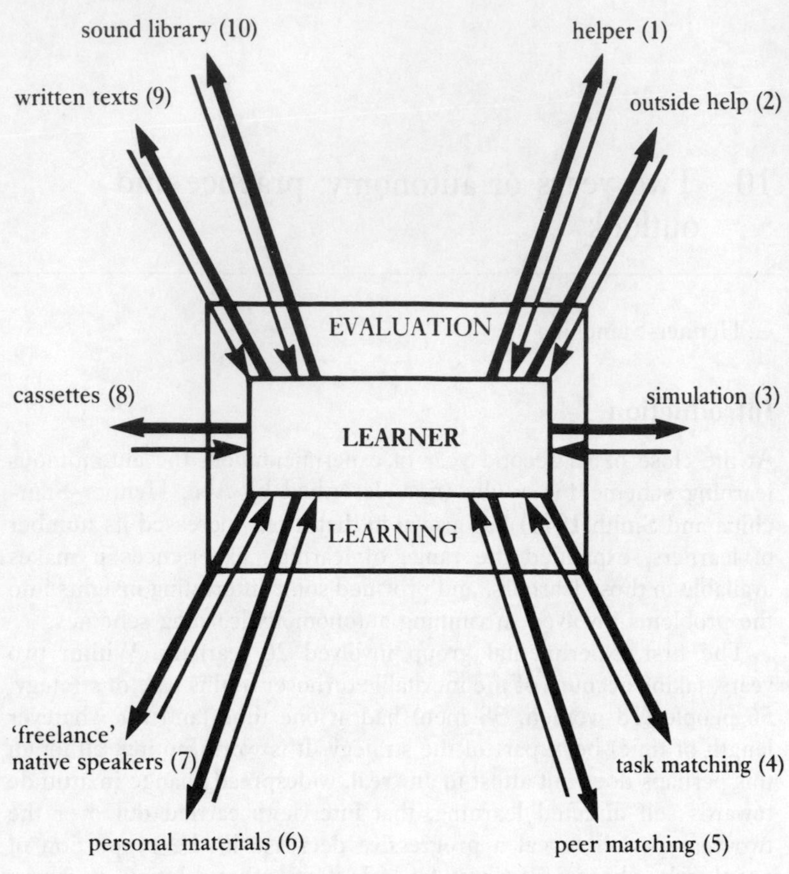

FIGURE I

able resources, choosing the ones most appropriate to the attainment of their language goals. The helper is simply one of the optional resources in this set-up, just like all the other services provided by the C.R.A.P.E.L. The fact that there is no centre for dispensing knowledge indicated on the diagram is, obviously, in no way an oversight, since the notion of teacher competence has been revised and the final responsibility for learning left to the learners themselves.

In order to illustrate exactly how learners with either general or very specific language needs can combine these ten elements in various ways to form total learning experiences, and to elucidate the respective roles of the learner, the helper and the institution involved this paper will briefly recount three case studies.

Mr D

Mr D, a brewery engineer, was overwhelmed by the heap of technical texts he had to read regularly in English. He recognized the inadequacy of his reading skills when what he thought he understood was in contradiction with what his technical knowledge told him to expect. His goal, then, was to develop accuracy, as well as speed in reading these documents, and to do so as quickly as possible.

Mr D began by choosing elements 1, 6 and 9 (see Fig. 1) as the basis of his learning experience; that is, the freedom to consult the helper when necessary, the use of his own technical documents and the use of the C.R.A.P.E.L.'s beginner's course in written comprehension. Had time permitted, Mr D would have gone through an initial stage of deciphering more general English, using the beginner's course, then passing through a second stage of applying the morphosyntactic rules he had learned to his own personal materials. However, since he was pressed for time, he decided to skip course element 9 and get right down to his texts.

The first session with the helper was devoted to examining several pages of one of these texts, so that Mr D could point out those elements he would usually stumble on. This exercise revealed his most urgent problems as being:

The complex noun phrase;
The reduction of relative clauses and passives;
Procedures of substitution and ellipsis, and discourse reference;
Semantic value of verbal forms.

Successive sessions, therefore, dealt with these points in particular. All examples were taken from Krebs 1975.

1. *The complex noun phrase*:

'the membrane covered oxygen electrode'
'a negative going linear voltage ramp'
'a sufficiently stable and repeatable reference potential'
'a gas permeable, ion and protein permeable, membrane'
'a special stainless steel reinforced Teflon–silicone rubber composite.'

Mr D used these examples, and others, to practise identifying the head (moving towards the far right), and pre-modification components (post-modification being far less common in the texts).

2. *The reduction of relative clauses and passives*:
   'conductive residues *left* in connectors after autoclaving or remaining after liquid has splashed in the connector . . .'
   'typical current-potential curves or polarograms *obtained* with the solution *stirred* at a constant rate and *equilibrated* first with nitrogen, then room air, and finally pure oxygen are *presented* in fig. 2.'
   'A negative going linear voltage ramp is *applied* to the platinum and the current generated *measured*.'
   'Oxygen at high concentration levels is *required* during the early stages of the brewing cycle . . .'
   'Data *obtained* with the IL 530 Brewery oxygen electrode system and with other IL oxygen electrodes *will be included*.'

Once Mr D had been shown the structures of relative clauses and passive forms, he was able to restore the elements necessary for comprehension.

3. *Procedure of substitution and ellipsis, and anaphoric reference:*
   ' . . . by utilizing an anode material which has a potential close to *that* of the optimum operating voltage . . .'
   'The diffusion later acts as a greater impedance to the transport of oxygen to the cathode than *does* the solution flowing past the layer.'
   'the "blood gas" electrode has the smallest cathode, the "alarm" electrode has the *largest*.'
   'Flow sensitivity is observed when Zr becomes significant, as it *can* in dissolved oxygen measurements . . .'
   '*This* has created a need . . .'
   '*This* establishes a concentration gradient between the level of oxygen in the sample and *that* at the cathode . . .'
   'Clinical investigators have been more acutely aware of and sensitive to the *above* limitations . . .'

The most effective way of re-establishing those various 'pro' forms, once they had been identified, was to go back over the text to do a more detailed reading of it, in order to determine the antecedents. Mr D did just that, meeting the helper afterwards to verify his hypotheses.

4. *Semantic value of verbal forms*:
   'If the condition for planar diffusion of oxygen to the platinum

cathode *were to be met*, the current, in the complete absence of stirring and convection, *would be found to* decrease to zero with the reciprocal square-root of time.'

'*Should Ep (actual) "slide"* over the edge of the current plateau, the output current sensitivity will decrease and vary with the electrode current.'

'*As long as "d" remains* constant the observed current *will be* proportional to the oxygen level . . .'

'*If K were constant* for all combinations of solvent, solute, and temperature, the relationship between the oxygen partial pressure and concentration *would be simple*.'

'An electrode which *is not to experience* extremes in either pressure or temperature, such as the IL Blood Gas electrode, is simple to design.'

The hypothetical value of the subjunctive in the first extract and of the inverted word order in the second had to be pointed out to the learner. Similarly, the compound conditional conjunction in the third extract, the inference of an unreal condition in the fourth and a command in the fifth had to be made explicit, for the learner was misinterpreting them. Having reviewed these structures once, he was then well equipped to recognize and understand them in other texts.

Besides the purely structural or grammatical problems examined, the concept of communicative acts was also approached briefly, focusing on such functions as *defining:*

> The platinum is the cathode inasmuch as it is the electrode at which reduction (that of oxygen) takes place. The chlorided silver sheet is the anode, since the corresponding oxidation reaction
>
> Ag + C1 —— e ——— Ag C1
>
> occurs at that electrode.

and *instructing*:

> Therefore, following an abrupt change in environmental temperature, time should be allowed before the electrode either is calibrated or data acquired in order for the thermistor to arrive at the new temperature.

A third problem that was only touched upon was that of training to skim, that is, to get a general idea of the text so as to be able to determine whether or not it is of interest, and if so, how it can be approached. In a well constructed scientific article, signals such as:

'This paper will attempt to: first . . . second . . . and third . . .'

'The more common techniques employed for oxygen analysis can be divided into three main categories: physical, chemical, and electrochemical. Physical methods include . . . Chemical methods in-

clude . . . Electrochemical methods are based on . . .'
'The electrochemical methods can in principle be subdivided into two categories: (1) . . . (2). . . These are discussed in the next sections . . .'

can be of great help to the reader who has to locate his information as fast as possible. 'Skimming', as defined by Pugh (1975), implies 'obtaining for its own sake an overall impression of certain features of a text (e.g. surface information, structure, tone)' and 'obtaining advance organization of a text which has to be known but which presents difficulties'. Unfortunately, lack of time made it impossible to deal with these last two problems in any more than a superficial way.

This case serves as an example of how the helper, who may or may not understand the actual content of the articles to be deciphered, can supply the tools necessary for analysing them. From there on the learner takes over, using those tools, along with his technical background, a dictionary and any other reference work he might have at his disposal, to plough through these documents with increasing speed and accuracy.

The next case-study again illustrates both why the emphasis should be placed on methodology rather than on content, and how a learner may be led to develop adequate learning techniques.

Mr C

A professor of organic chemistry, Mr C had been invited by an American professor to give a keynote speech at a conference. He needed practice in understanding American English and in speaking. Moreover, he had already decided that he would not stand up before his audience and read a prepared paper. He preferred to be able to deliver a more spontaneous talk (as he would do in French), using slides to illustrate his comments. Although he did intend to write out a full text of one possible version of his speech in English, this would certainly not represent a final polished version of his actual presentation. This situation, then, militated against the type of work that concentrates on the perfection of a finished product. What this learner needed was not to know how to read his paper without flaws, but rather to learn to approximate a natural style of delivery that would satisfy him, and be understandable to his audience. He organized his learning experience accordingly.

He began writing up his paper, and in the interim worked with cassettes at home. Within a month, he had gone through the entire intermediate course (*Cours Intensif d'Anglais Oral*), and had started on two higher level courses (*Colloquial English* and extracts from the *Cours Avancé de Compréhension Orale*, presenting a variety of American accents) as well as on authentic recordings (*Crosstalks* series) provided by the U.S. Information Service (Voice of America tapes). He was granted the use of these tapes throughout the summer. He was also introduced to an American living in Nancy, with whom he was able to spend several hours in natural conversation.

Once his paper was written, an entire session was devoted to reworking those parts the helper felt would be unclear to an American audience. The paper was then recorded by the helper, again less as a model to imitate than as an indication of one possible presentation. The most useful aspect of this exercise was the emphasis on certain semantic combinations such as 'to perform ', 'to carry out a reaction' (the learner decided that he would continue to search for these combinations while reading specialized texts in English), and on the pronunciation of technical terms such as 'tetrahydrofuranne', 'teramyloxide ', 'dihalogenocyclopropane', 'spectroscopy', 'benzene', and even more common terms like 'indulgence', 'substitution', 'activating agent' and others, where gallicized vowels or misplaced stress could hinder the comprehension of an American audience, or in any case, render their listening more taxing. Using this tape as a guide, Mr C practised recording himself several times at home. Finally, when he felt sufficiently prepared, a simulation of his speech was carried out, slide projector and all, and his presentation was tape-recorded. It was originally planned that Mr C would present his speech and slides before a competent audience — that is, members of his own research laboratory — likely to ask questions, make comments and stimulate the kind of interaction he would later be involved in. This, unfortunately, was not possible in the short time available.

The resulting tape was then analysed by the learner — who took notes on everything he felt needed improvement — in the presence of the helper. In this way, he gained confidence in his ability to evaluate his own performance, at the same time recognizing this as a tool which would allow him to go on practising his presentation in the absence of the helper, becoming more comfortable with it.

One activity that Mr C was also anxious to try was a 'task match'. The helper, therefore, tried to set up a task matching session between Mr C, who was to simulate his slide lecture before a competent audience, and Professor A, a doctor preparing to act as chairman at an international cardiology conference. Needless to say, there was no connection whatsoever between the two fields of speciality: organic chemistry and cardiology. This simulation could nevertheless have allowed each learner to play his respective role — Mr C delivering his speech, answering questions from the floor, and Professor A carrying out the more general functions of a chairman, making opening and closing remarks, giving instructions to speakers and to the floor, handling questions. The more specific functions Professor A had to practise (bringing back to the point, taking up a point) were so closely linked to the subject matter of his own conference that it would have been impossible to work on them out of context.

This task match never actually took place, for the simple reason that the two learners were unable to make their time schedules coincide. The idea of the task match for learners with highly specific needs remains, as well as the hope that the occasion will arise to coordinate other task matching sessions.

Mr R

For Mr R, a learner with no very specific needs other than the desire to improve his aural comprehension and oral expression in English, the learning experience consisted of elements 1, 2, 5, 7 and 8.

Given the *Cours Intensif d'Anglais Oral*, a course composed of spoken texts and structural exercises, Mr R insisted upon writing out translations of all the sentences, first into French, to make sure he really understood them, and then back into English, to see if he still remembered the given structures. Devoting approximately eight hours a week to his task, he naturally had little time left to use the recorded material provided him to practise aural comprehension and oral expression. When this was brought out to him, he explained that this was the only way he felt he could learn and retain anything. Discussion revealed that he judged his memory to be very poor, and what, in fact, he was unconsciously striving for was to memorize the course book. The helper suggested trying to elaborate a system of *fiches* or index cards that could eventually serve as a reference guide to the structures and vocabulary he had studied, while relieving his memory of those elements inherent to the course material and perhaps less likely to come up in real situations. Having thought this idea over, Mr R did decide to abandon most of his translating (except for some vocabulary) and began making index cards instead. However, when he had produced the first few and showed them to the helper, two flaws were discovered. First, the cards were not cards, but little pieces of torn paper that could never have lasted long enough to serve as a reference document. Second, index cards such as those shown below

to deserve : mériter
by the way : au fait
to be off = to take off

I can't help thinking
To give back
to dare
scarce

What have you come for ? :
Que venez-vous faire ?
Do they work overtime ?
A teaspoon is to stir your tea with
. . . for stirring your tea.

would certainly have been very difficult to exploit and would have been ineffective as a study guide mainly because the various elements were all grouped together in order of appearance in the course, and there was no way of knowing where to look for anything, and no guarantee that Mr R could ever find what he was looking for. By making this observation and showing Mr R the following examples of index cards being elaborated by another learner in autonomy, the helper led him to develop a much more usable system.

Emploi de GOT :
même chose que avoir dans le sens de posséder, avoir
(HAVE GOT
(HAVE
I have got = I have
have you got = have you
I haven't got = I haven't

Present perfect continue :
to be + verbe - ING +
for / since
(présent perfect)
indique une action qui a commencé dans le passé et qui n'est pas terminée.
- FOR : indique la durée, le temps écoulé depuis que l'action a commencé.
- SINCE : indique le moment, la date de début de l'action.

Venir de ...
Sujet + avoir + just + verbe
présent part. passé
présent perfect

Prétérit simple :
exprime une action définitivement passée.

Examples of Mr R's second, usable version of index cards (classified in alphabetical order by structural heading on card, or by first letter of verb or vocabulary word studied, and placed in a small filing box for future reference) are given below.

Gérondif
- My father is talking to my mother.
- That is one of the most interesting and serious questions that you could ask.
- Plenty of brushing improves your hair.
- A teaspoon is for stirring tea.
- I'm very fond of fishing.
- The church choir is practising.
- I was just setting off when it started raining.
- She's wearing an expression of happy anticipation.

As
- I don't feel so hungry as I did 10 minutes ago.
- His excitement grows and grows as they get closer.

This satisfied Mr R as a remedy for a failing memory and a substitute for translation, and allowed him more time to concentrate on the oral and aural skills he was, in fact, trying to improve.

However, this attitude exhibited by Mr R, that a language is a *savoir*, that is, a combined set of grammar rules and vocabulary to be ingurgitated before that language can actually be put to use, led him initially to postpone or reject the meetings with native speakers that were offered and encouraged by the C.R.A.P.E.L. He wanted, first, to store up all the structures presented in the course materials, then to move into an application phase (conversations with native speakers), and then to come back to another storage phase. He could not conceive of combining those phases of storage and application, because he did not recognize language as a *savoir-faire*, a communicative tool that may be used at all levels of proficiency.

This problem was handled in three stages. Since his readiness to test his communicative competence in an authentic situation did not come naturally because he was too self-conscious, afraid of making ridiculous mistakes and nervous about the contact with a stranger, Mr R preferred to meet the helper, a native speaker of English, for conversation. The second intermediate stage which was useful in building the learner's confidence in his own performance was the 'peer match'. Mr R was introduced to another learner who was at approximately the same proficiency level (and who, in the helper's opinion, was likely to have something in common professionally or personality-wise with Mr R). Their discussion dealt with their respective jobs, general topics of current interest, and especially with aspects of autonomous learning.

Since in many cases, autonomy has become synonymous with a

certain dose of solitude, this peer matching system provides an excellent opportunity for learners to commiserate with each other, one might say. Thus, they compared study habits, discussed their perceptions of their own strengths and weaknesses, while each took advantage of the situation to measure his performance against the other's. The helper was present at this session, acting as an objective observer, and recording the conversation to enable the two learners to re-examine their own performances.

The final stage of this progression is generally, of course, the actual meeting with a native speaker. It is here that learners can test their general interactional competence — how well they understand what is said to them, as well as how sensitive they are to non-verbal signals coming from their interlocutors, and how effectively they respond.

Mr R went through the first two stages being so obsessed with grammatical correctness that his part of the conversation would resemble a sort of stream of voiced hypotheses on each particular sentence. Obviously, this absorption led him to become totally insensitive to signals from his interlocutor indicating that he had already made himself understood and was therefore rather unconducive to spontaneous interaction, to say the least. At the end of the second stage, this was brought out to him by the helper. A discussion of the minimum adequate level of competence at which he was beginning, and of the differences between grammaticality and acceptability, ensued. This enabled him to work towards freeing himself from his self-imposed constraints, and to engage in more natural interactions with native speakers.

He later hired (with the aid of the C.R.A.P.E.L. acting as a placement agency) an English-speaking assistant for his office, thereby multiplying his opportunities to speak English in authentic communication situations.

In Mr R's case, as in countless others, the helper not only transmitted a fixed body of linguistic knowledge to the learner, but also discussed the efficacy of certain techniques in view of priorities and objectives.

The discussion of these three cases has, I hope, shed sufficient light on the organization and operation of an autonomous learning scheme. The one component of this scheme which did not receive much attention here is the sound library (element 10).

Conclusion

Because of the newness of the autonomous learning strategy, and the

Recapitulative chart

Learner		Helper	Institution
Understands role: maintain motivation; take on responsibility for defining needs, goals, priorities, selecting materials, organizing learning experiences (program developer), determining pace, time devoted to study, diagnosing learning difficulties, developing adequate learning techniques, self-monitoring; guiding and planning the learning process.		*Understands role*: not a private tutor; may assist learners at any stage of the learning process, acting as an objective observer, open to discussion, sharing ideas, giving advice when asked, assuring methodological preparation by helping learners develop techniques and use them as tools for analysing their documents, evaluating their own performances, and using media and people as learning resources; being available, assuring technical preparation.	Flexible structure, making such experimentation possible, providing a special place for helper – learner sessions. Making the rapid reproduction of materials possible (fast cassette copier, xeroz photocopier).
Self-assessment.	↔	Provide learners with opportunities to receive feedback in authentic situations.	
Furnishing materials, when possible.	↔	Furnishing materials, when possible.	Furnishing materials (tape archives, collection of dossiers, newspapers, magazines).
Devising descriptions of English.	↔	Helping to set up those descriptions in function of learner's degree of linguistic sophistication.	Lending equipment (cassette players, cassettes).
Determining level of perfection sought in function of personality.			Making simulations in studio possible.
Manifesting a certain willingness to accept change, both		Manifesting a sincere care for learners, adopting an attitude and creating an atmosphere that are condu-	Facilitating contacts with native speakers residing in Nancy;

cognitive and affective (attitudinal changes) if confronted with attitudes or techniques that are recognized as more beneficial.	cive to and supportive to autonomous learning. Assuring psychological preparation, providing an environment that will encourage attitudinal changes when these are advantageous for learners.	establishing a network of freelance native speakers of English.
Determining frequency of sessions with helper.	Intermediary between learners.	Dealing with material problems; paying helper; establishing registration fees; paying for a certain number of 'conversation' hours, which represent a socially embarassing situation to learners.
	Coordination: peer-matching, task-matching, preparation of material (cassettes, other documents, simulations).	
	Keeping detailed notes on each learner: knowing what cassettes they have, which experiences they have chosen, which resources they have used, where they are as far as the development of learning techniques is concerned, how they have fared in authentic communication situations, through contact with native speakers who have met them for conversation.	
	Awareness of research being carried out in the field of language learning; further research into the acquisition of each of the language skills.	
	Ultimate production of learning materials for learners with less specific goals.	

dynamic nature of the relationships existing between learner and helper and institution, it would be virtually impossible to prescribe roles for everybody involved. What can be drafted, however, is an admittedly non-exhaustive list, noting the roles the respective parties have so far assumed in the context of this particular experiment, showing where these roles overlap, where they differ, and in any case, leaving them open to suggestions. Such a list would look something like the recapitulative chart on pp. 202–3.

The results obtained in these two years seem to be positive: 15 dropouts out of the total of 56 learners — surely no worse than the grim statistics on dropouts from evening classes, perhaps better. And the causes for dropping out are different. People drop out of evening classes for any number of reasons: personality clash with the group or animator, the heterogeneity of proficiency levels, needs that are not met by the course, reluctance to participate in group activities because of shyness or dislike for these activities, missing two or three classes in a row, all lead to abandon.

In autonomy, giving up is attributable to a lack of time, lack of sufficient motivation, or to the unsuitability (demanding nature) of the strategy itself.

It is obvious that the C.R.A.P.E.L. autonomy set-up will have to undergo various degrees of modification in order to be workable in other contexts, with other helpers, other learners, in other institutions. The main concern is to work towards the autonomization of learners, and all steps in that direction are significant, at whatever level. However, this movement can most definitely be thwarted by institutional regulations.

Having broken down the autonomous learners into professional categories, it was found that in the two years of the experiment, 24 people had the legal right to request that their employers pay their registration fees. In the first year, 6 actually did so; in the second year 7 did so, a total of 13 out of 24. The remaining adults who were theoretically entitled to some type of continuing education through their employers either never requested or never received those benefits.

The employers who flatly refused their employees did so because this new autonomy scheme seemed too expensive for 'students' who were to be 'doing all the work by themselves'. In other instances, the companies wanted to hold out for a while to make sure that the operation was a serious one, and learners therefore paid their own fees, usually never to be reimbursed.

As for people holding positions in universities, they invariably financed their own learning experiences.

In all thirteen of these cases, then, it seems reasonable to presume that even if the French law on continuing education had never come into existence, these people would nevertheless have been offered the opportunity to learn English by their firms — who apparently will readily invest in continuing education providing, of course, they can directly reap the benefits of this education, as was true here. Moreover, not only has the law on continuing education failed to increase the numbers of potential candidates for autonomy, it has also served to discourage them by stipulating that an attendance certificate is obligatory.

It is obvious that employers are sceptical of innovative strategies like autonomy. They have never heard of it before, and cannot easily judge its validity because the work accomplished cannot be expressed in terms of class or teaching hours. Neither can the learner's sincerity, interest, progress, participation, level of attainment be expressed by an attendance certificate, a requirement which poses an absurd contradiction in an autonomous learning strategy.

If, then, autonomy is to become more widespread, some compromise will undoubtedly have to be reached between those who finance the learning and those who promote it.

11 Extending self-directed learning of English in an engineering college

H. Moulden

The experiment

The job of the English department of the *Ecole Nationale Supérieure de la Métallurgie et de L'Industrie des Mines* in Nancy is to prepare budding engineers for the social and professional communicative tasks which they may have to perform in English in later life. During the whole of their three year stay at the E.N.S.M.I.M. those students who, on entry, do not have a satisfactory level in English are required to study it for three to four hours a week. In any given year about 130 students out of a total of 210 or so will be doing English. The teaching staff available for coping with them consists of one *assistant*, two *lecteurs* and four to six part-time teachers (*vacataires*). All are native speakers. Most of the work done takes the form of 1½ to 2 hour classes in groups (beginners, intermediate, advanced) of about twelve students.

Although the bulk of English teaching at the E.N.S.M.I.M takes place in the classroom, self-directed learning (SDL) is coming to play a more and more important part.

SDL has, in theory, advantages over traditional teacher-directed learning. Thus, the former should, assuming adequate autodidactic competence and motivation, be more efficient than the latter. The self-directed learner learns only what he needs to learn, using the materials and techniques chosen by himself as being best adapted to his tastes and requirements. He works when and where it suits him best, at the pace which suits him best. The teacher-directed learner, however, is more or less completely at the mercy of the teacher as regards syllabus, material and methods. In addition, he is expected to work at fixed times in a fixed place with people of varying attainment level, aims and attitudes towards learning.

Our faith, at the E.N.S.M.I.M., in the superiority of the learner-centred approach has led, over the past few years, to the introduction of the following facilities (see Abé, Henner–Stanchina and Smith 1975; Duda 1978):

A self-service sound library open to all students and staff for four 1½ hour periods (one evening, three lunchtimes) per week; a choice of self-instructional courses (oral expression and listening comprehension) at all levels. Wide choice (500 items) of recordings of authentic English and a booklet of methods for exploiting them as listening comprehension material. Handouts on various communicative functions available. Small collection of books, magazines and newspapers in English. English-speaking monitor on hand to advise on choice of material and to provide conversation in English for those wanting it.

A cassette and cassette player loan service open to all students and staff. Cassettes duplicate sound library stock. Advice on choice of material and its exploitation available but no help beyond this.

Television room open at the same time as the sound library. Recordings of British, American and German programmes screened.

Counselling session of one hour per week for staff who wish to learn or improve in English. Native speaker available for individual advice on materials and methods in self-directed learning and to help with problems arising in the course of learning.

Classroom listening comprehension practice in third year intermediate and advanced groups replaced by semi-autonomous work on cassettes. Students choose cassettes from sound library stock and are given a booklet describing possible exploitation techniques. Teacher and student meet for half an hour once a fortnight to assess progress and deal with problems.

The first four activities, none of which is compulsory, have been successful insofar as they have attracted and continue to attract a fair number of customers. This seems to indicate that a need is being catered for. The compulsory semi-autonomous listening comprehension practice in third year, while having produced no startling increase in motivation among the seemingly incorrigibly uninterested minority, has however been very favourably received by the others, many of whom have spontaneously asserted that they found it much more profitable than classroom work. It should be pointed out, however, that this venture has led to a 50% increase in the teaching hours allocated to these students.

The success of these learner-centred facilities prompted an examination of the possibilities for further experiment in this direction. The first question which came to mind was that of how far autonomization of English learning could go. Emptying all the classrooms and packing each and every one of 130 students off to learn English on his own would not be immediately feasible. For a start, there was nothing like the necessary quantity of pedagogical hardware and software available. In addition, unless the increase in teaching hours which had accompanied the semi-autonomization of third year listening comprehension practice could be avoided, there would not be enough teachers available either. Of course, it would not really be desirable to abandon completely the classroom, for even if SDL were installed right up to the hilt a certain amount of work in groups would still be necessary: necessary psychologically, as a cheering corrective to the rigours of cloistered communing with cassette recorders, and necessary pedagogically, as an occasion for realistic communication practice and for initiating, soothing and encouraging startled or unwilling newcomers to the fold. Even so, it did not seem likely that this mitigating factor would entirely solve the problem of extra teaching hours. At any rate, as far as the immediate future was concerned, the number of cassette recorders available would limit further experiment to just one group of students. But while waiting for some horn of plenty to send an abundance of hard, soft and personware thudding about our ears we could, within this one small group, take SDL a little further than we had before. The experience gained should stand us in good stead at the happy epoch alluded to above and might lead, in the interim, to further modest extensions of SDL.

In what way should SDL be taken a little further, then? The majority of students being weakest in oral expression, it seemed logical to combine the already proven self-directed listening comprehension practice with an attempt to see what could be done in the way of applying SDL to the speaking of English. This might present more of a challenge than self-directed listening comprehension practice but might, on the other hand, fulfil a greater need if reasonably successful.

The choice of group on which to carry out the experiment eventually fell upon the second year intermediates. This gave a group of students who would not be totally unprepared (as might be first year students) for semi-autonomous work in English, since they would already have been exposed for a year to the *Ecole's* English teaching methods and to the necessity for private study imposed by the *Ecole's* teaching of technical disciplines. Moreover, their experience of the *Ecole's* normal English teaching methods would, at the end of the experiment, allow a comparison to be made between the relative efficacity of the latter and the self-directed approach. In addition, an intermediate group would, perhaps, suffer less from reduced supervision than a group at a lower level and would, we hoped, over a year, make clear progress, whereas with an advanced group progress might be less tangible.

The guinea pigs having been selected, it was now necessary to decide how to split the time available for this group between SDL and class work. Normally in second year, there was a course on Tuesday evening from 5 p.m. to 6.30 p.m. and another on Thursday morning from 9 a.m. to 11 a.m. Motivation being somewhat diminished, if not utterly extinguished, at 5 p.m., it was decided to scrap the Tuesday course and to have just one course per week from 9 to 10.30. At this hour, mind and eye should, it was felt, sparkle more brightly than at 5 in the evening. Apart from some instruction in SDL techniques where necessary, classroom work would, as far as possible, consist of activities aimed at making the students want to use English (games, simulations, problem-solving, etc.). This, it was hoped, would make them more conscious of any deficiencies that needed working on. As the group was to be given a completely free hand in designing its individual SDL programmes, classroom sessions could, in the event of mass neglect of important objectives, be used to rectify the situation discreetly.

This pruned timetable would relieve the teacher of two hours per week of classroom teaching, which he could now devote to giving individual help to the students in the group at the rate of 20 minutes each per fortnight (for a group of twelve) in the now empty Tuesday evening (5 to 6.30) and Thursday morning (10.30 to 11) slots. It would be important, however, bearing in mind that further extension of SDL within the present teaching hours allocated might be envisaged, to try not to exceed the allowance of 20 minutes per interview. The interviews would serve not only to help the students with their specifically linguistic problems but also to accustom them to planning and assessing their work themselves, i.e. in preparing them to deal, in later life, with any language-learning needs which might present themselves. From the point of view of oral expression, the interview time would be useful for carrying out simulations and would give everybody a regular opportunity of speaking English for an extended period. It was felt that this latter feature might be particularly useful for the kind of student who, for one reason or another, never opens his mouth in the classroom and might lead to more satisfying teacher--student relationships. The interviews would also provide a continuous and detailed check on each student's work and achievement level which, in view of the necessity of providing twice-yearly reports, should make this chore easier and lead to fuller, less superficial assessments.

The only decision now left to be taken was that on how to teach the students to work on their own. As they had never learned English in this way before, it was going to be necessary to give them at least some preliminary information on SDL, if not actual practice under supervision. Previous experience with self-directed listening comprehension practice had suggested that gradual preparations and rehearsals were not absolutely essential to painless transfer from traditional to self-directed learning, so it was decided simply to throw the requisite information at the students two weeks before starting the experiment and then to have a meeting to clear up obscure points. The information given to the students took the form of two home-made, twenty-page booklets entitled *Objectives in English* and *Learning English on your own* plus a short note of introduction.

Objectives in English contains lists of the sort of things which we thought future engineers should be able to do in English. These are classified under three headings: Reading Comprehension, Listening Comprehension and Oral Expression (Written Expression was omitted because this skill is reserved for the third year). The students were free to add and work on any objectives not appearing in the lists. Columns are provided in which they were invited to note how they rated themselves (0 to 5) for each activity. Space is also left for marking priorities and any progress made. In this way the booklet could be used not only to assess present standing in English (and hence what work needed to be done) but also as a work record which might give an encouraging sense of forward movement (see pp. 221–2).

Learning English on your own sets out the advantages of self-directed learning and gives advice on how to do it. The latter section contains the following titles: *Assessing yourself*, *Planning your work programme*, *Working on an objective*, *Deciding how close you have got to an objective*, *Work record*, *Interviews*, *Projects*, *Practising reading comprehension on your own*, *Practising listening comprehension on your own* and *Speaking English on your own* (see pp. 211–21).

At the end of the first year of the experiment described here, a questionnaire was devised to evaluate the effectiveness and organization of the scheme. This questionnaire is reproduced and discussed on pp. 222–31

Excerpt from 'Learning English on your own'

THE ADVANTAGES OF LEARNING ENGLISH ON YOUR OWN

These might be summarized by saying that working alone gives you the freedom to learn what *you* want in the way that suits *you* best. It is only fair to point out, however, that this individualization of the learning process also implies shouldering more responsibility and perhaps working a bit harder than usual.

Working on your own means that *you* design your *own* English course (priority of objectives, materials, methods, evaluation) and are free to work when and where you like at your own pace and rhythm.

Up to now, your English teachers have taken all or most of the decisions on objectives. From time to time this has probably led to you wasting time going over work you had already learned or learning new things which you didn't find particularly useful. But if you yourself decide on the content of your learning programme, this sort of thing should be obviated.

Up to now, your English teachers have done all or most of the choosing of learning material (course, reading matter, cassettes, tapes, etc.). You must surely have sometimes had difficulty in learning English when the learning was based for example, on a tape whose subject held no interest whatsoever for you. But if *you* choose the material yourself, this problem should disappear too.

Your teachers will also have imposed on you their methods of exploiting English material. You must have sometimes felt bored (and hence switched-off for learning) doing, for instance, detailed comprehension of a tape when you would have preferred to listen just for the general ideas. If you choose your own learning methods, however, you will be able to use those methods which you find the most interesting and profitable at any given moment.

So far, you have always been obliged to do your English at regular intervals, in a certain place, at a certain time and at a pace decided on by the teacher. It seems highly unlikely that anybody should *always* feel in the mood for English-learning in the same classroom every Tuesday from 9 'til 11 and that *everybody* in a class of 12 or so should feel like working, or even be capable of working, at the pace set by the teacher. But working on your own sets you free to work as often as you want to, where you want to, for as long as you want to, at the pace that suits you best. Working on your own at home can also provide better conditions for learning (less noise, fewer distractions). Admittedly, the human contact is absent, but there is nothing to stop you working in pairs or groups and there will also be an opportunity for a 20 minute interview with the teacher every two weeks.

These fortnightly meetings, which are intended to give you help with the problems you may meet, should result in you getting more individual attention than you have probably received so far. They will also give you a regular chance to speak English. In fact, the new system should result in everyone in the group having more opportunity to talk than before.

The meetings with the teacher are also intended to keep an eye on how you are getting on. A work record will be kept both by yourself and the teacher. This will allow you to see what progress you are making and what remains to be done. It is hoped that this arrangement will be more stimulating than just turning up for classes, sitting more or less passively through what the teacher offers and coming out with only a vague idea of what progress, if any, you have made.

If you feel by now that all this sounds suspiciously like harder work, you are very probably right. For those of you who *want* to learn English, however, it should lead to your learning becoming less haphazard and more efficient. And what you learn about learning English on your own here may be useful to you after you've left the *Mines*, whether in just keeping up your English or in acquiring on your own some very specific professional or social skill in English. And don't forget that autonomy is not English-specific; if you ever have to learn a new language or brush up on one you already know, there's no reason why you shouldn't do it on your own.

LEARNING ENGLISH ON YOUR OWN – HOW TO DO IT

The following points will be discussed:

Assessing yourself
Planning your work programme
Working on an objective
Deciding how close you have got to your objective
Work record
Interviews
Projects
Practising reading comprehension on your own
Practising listening comprehension on your own
Practising speaking English on your own

Assessing yourself

The first thing to do when starting to learn English on your own is to decide how good you are at English now. You can then decide what work needs to be done.

To get an idea of how good you are at English now, take a look at pages 1–5 of the booklet *Objectives in English*. These show you the *Mines* objectives in reading comprehension, listening comprehension and oral expression in English. For each objective, in the column headed 'Rate yourself 0 to 5', give an indication of how good you think you are or might be at that particular objective; 0 for no good at all, 5 for 100% successful, 1 for 20%, 2 for 40%, etc. There are two copies of *Objectives in English*. **Please fill in both copies.** One is for me. Pages 6–18 of *Objectives in English* consist of a detailed list of some of the things you need to be able to do in order to fulfil the oral expression objectives on pages 4–5 and need not be filled in immediately.

Planning your work programme

This involves deciding what objectives you are going to work on, in what order of priority and when.

First of all, what objectives are you going to aim at? The self-assessment you have just made should have shown you in which areas you are weakest. Theoretically these are the areas you need to work on. However, you may feel that you are not likely to need to *do* some of the things mentioned in the objectives list and consequently, that if you are weak in that particular area, you don't need to do anything about it. Fair enough — but you've got to be really *sure*. Conversely, there may be things you want to be able to do which aren't mentioned in the objectives lists. In this case, just add them to the list. The choice is up to you. Mark your choice by putting a dash (—) in the 'Priority' column against the objectives you wish to work on.

You will also need to decide on a rough order of priority. Theoretically, once again, the priority objectives should be those you are worst at, but no doubt personal taste will be a factor too. You probably won't be able to put all your chosen objectives in an accurate order of priority, but try to pick out the 5 or 6 objectives you need to work on most urgently and mark them 1, 2, 3, etc. in the priority column of the objectives list. Again, **please fill in both copies.**

Finally, when should you work? Obviously, this is a matter of personal taste and convenience. In theory, you should be working 2 hours per week on average (classwork having been reduced by 2 hours) less 10 minutes per week (fortnightly interview of 20 minutes) equals 1 hour 50 minutes per week on average. The time of day you do your 1 hour 50 minutes average and whether you do it in one session or in several shorter sessions or even in one monster 3 hour 40 minutes fortnightly session is entirely up to you. (Although 3 hours 40 minutes is probably a bit too long to be effective and anything under 30 minutes probably a bit on the short side.) The important thing is that the work should be done and done fairly regularly. N.B. If you feel like doing more than an average of 1 hour 50 minutes a week, nobody in the English department is going to stop you.

Working on an objective

As the objectives are numerous and varied, possible ways of attaining them can best be discussed on an individual basis at interviews. Only very general indications will be given here.

A little further on in this booklet you will find three sections[1] devoted to:

practising reading comprehension on your own
practising listening comprehension on your own
practising speaking English on your own

These give you information on where to find material to work on and suggestions for working methods. To give you an idea of how objectives may be worked on, an example will now be given from each of the three skill areas mentioned above.

READING COMPREHENSION

Objective: scanning a report or technical article. See *Practising reading comprehension on your own*. The section on *Materials* indicates that technical journals in English are available at the Library. Now see the *Methods* section. The subsection *Scanning* suggests methods for practising scanning.

LISTENING COMPREHENSION

Objective: grasping the essential points of a technical lecture. See the *Materials* section of *Practising listening comprehension on your own*. *Authentic English recorded on cassette* seems a likely place for finding technical lectures. If you now consult the list of cassettes mentioned under this title, you will find a *Technology* section which includes a number of lectures on technical subjects from which you can choose. Now see the *Methods* section of *Practising listening comprehension on your own*. Under *Global comprehension* you will find methods for practising extracting essential information from spoken discourse.

ORAL EXPRESSION

Objective: showing a visiting English-speaking engineer round a factory or a lab. This could be simulated by showing me round a laboratory you know at the *Mines*. First of all, however, you'd have to analyse what you needed to do in terms of vocabulary and functions. Under the *Vocabulary* heading in *Practising speaking English on your own* you would see that dictionaries, cassettes and reading matter could be used as vocabulary sources. The *Functions* section would direct you to a list of functions and give you information on where to find realizations and practise them. Having practised the visit on your own — on the spot or in your imagination — the simulation could be carried out with me during interview time, recorded and evaluated.

It should not be concluded from the foregoing that the sections on practising reading comprehension, listening comprehension and oral expression contain all the answers to the practical problems you may encounter while learning English on your own. This is far from being the case. Much remains to be done in the way of finding materials and methods. Hopefully, we shall *all*

[1]For reasons of space only one of these three sections is reproduced here. (Editor's note)

learn something in the coming year.

DECIDING HOW CLOSE YOU HAVE GOT TO YOUR OBJECTIVE

As far as possible, *you* should be the person doing this. You will see, when reading the sections on practising reading comprehension and listening comprehension, that a good number of the activities suggested there are such that you can check on your performance yourself and, in general, one has a fair idea of whether one is understanding a foreign language or not. Checking your oral expression is a bit more difficult, but you will see, in class and at interviews, whether you are making yourself comfortably understood — and this is the main thing. You will also get help from me of course. Self assessment should be a regular feature of your work. Every time you carry out an exercise, try and evaluate your performance and make a note of your verdict. This will serve as a guide to future work and (hopefully) as an encouraging sign of progress being made.

WORK RECORD

You should keep a careful record of everything you do, noting in each case: objective, material, method and evaluation of results. This will not just be a record of work done; it will also serve as a source of methodological ideas for the future.

INTERVIEWS

You are supposed to come for an interview of about 20 minutes once every two weeks. The interviews will probably take place in Room 448 during the times when you would normally have been having an English class, i.e. Tuesday 17.00 to 18.30 and Thursday 10.30 to 11.00. Detailed arrangements (i.e. who comes when) will be made later.

The purpose of these interviews is:

to review your progress
to help you with problems in English
to help you with assessment of your performance
to help you plan future work
to give you time to do simulations with a native speaker
to give you a regular chance of speaking English for an extended period

20 minutes isn't really a lot of time, so in order to avoid wasting any of it, please be ready when you come for interview, to:

present your problems rapidly and clearly
show what work you have done (notes, résumés, transcriptions, new vocabulary, recordings of yourself, etc. . .)
show the assessment you have made of your performance
say what you would like to do next
say what material (cassettes, photocopies) you will be needing in the near future.

PROJECTS

You will be expected to undertake a small project which should be completed for the period April '79 to June '79. This need not interfere with working towards objectives, since you can choose or invent a project which coincides with the objectives you have chosen. You are expected to present the results of your project in the classroom. In addition to giving you an opportunity for public speaking in English, this will give the other members of the group practice in asking questions and the results of your project may be of technical, linguistic or general interest or help to them.

A number of possible projects are sketched out below, but these are only suggestions. Your ideas are welcome too.

TENTATIVE LIST OF PROJECTS

1. Collect documents on a technical theme and give a short talk, e.g.
   Stress corrosion
   New energy sources
   Catastrophe theory
   Manganese nodules
   Cassettes and/or literature are available for the above topics.
2. Analysis of cassettes/literature leading to preparation of module for class use on functional aspects of:
   Giving a talk
   Asking questions at conferences
   Discussions
   Scientific/technical articles
3. Preparation of questionnaire and study of interview technique leading to interview with and report on:
   English/American lecteurs in Nancy
   Mormons in Nancy
4. Give a talk on any subject that fires you with enthusiasm.

PRACTISING LISTENING COMPREHENSION ON YOUR OWN

This section will consist of two parts: materials and methods.

Materials

You will probably do most of your listening comprehension practice using our courses and/or authentic material recorded on cassettes since this allows you to stop and listen again to things you don't understand. Don't forget, however, that continuous listening practice is available in the form of BBC radio broadcasts and films in English on the television or at the cinema and that you can make your own authentic English cassettes if you have a radio cassette recorder. You can also watch recorded television programmes in English at the old Sound Library on certain days of the week. The above points will now be discussed in greater detail.

Cassette Players. If you have no cassette player of your own, we can lend you one. But you will have to pay a deposit of 50 F which you can recover when you give the player back again. If you need to, ask about this when you come along to the first interview.

Courses recorded on cassettes. These have advantages and disadvantages. The advantages are that they allow you to work on a specific listening problem without the bother of finding your own material and inventing your own exercises. The disadvantages are that courses may not give any help with your particular problem, may not give you authentic English to listen to and may not present subject matter which interests you.

The courses available on cassette are as follows:

Kernel Lessons Intermediate. Comprehension and Expression. Intermediate level. Non-authentic recordings. No answers to questions supplied but there are transcriptions of the recordings.

CIAO Comprehension and Expression. Intermediate level. Non-authentic recordings. Answers and transcriptions supplied.

PECOS Comprehension only. Advanced level. Authentic recordings. Answers supplied.

CACO Comprehension only. Advanced level. Authentic recordings. Answers to exercises supplied.

Varieties of spoken English. Comprehension and Expression. Advanced level. Authentic recordings. Answers to exercises supplied.

All the Best from Today. Not a course. Consists of radio recordings plus comprehension exercises. Advanced level. Answers supplied.

We have a number of coursebooks for the above, but not enough for everybody. Copies of the courses will be available for consultation in Room 448 most weekday mornings and afternoons and also at the Sound Library, Room 447 (see door for opening times).

Authentic English recorded on Cassette. These cassettes are for the most part recent recordings made in England. There is a choice of 500 or so items (talks, plays, interviews, songs, discussions, sports commentaries, short stories, humour, documentaries, etc. . .) and all are samples of authentic English in the sense that they were not prepared with a view to teaching English but intended for English listeners. Very few of these programmes are completely spontaneous, but at least they are *real* English and not the simplified, artificial 'English' often found on recordings designed for learners of English. Authentic recordings give you the chance of getting to grips with English as it is really spoken and are also the best source of material for enriching your speaking ability. In addition, our growing collection of authentic English on cassette gives you a good chance of finding something interesting to practise listening comprehension on. A list of these cassettes is posted on the door of the Sound Library (Room 447) as well as in the Library itself. A list will also be available for consultation at interview time. If you have interests not catered for by our present cassette stock, let me know and I'll see what I can do. You can obtain further information on the difficulty and contents of any cassette which may interest you when you come for interview. Should a cassette turn out to be unsuitable, it can be changed immediately; there's no need to wait until your next interview comes round. Methods for the exploitation of these cassettes will be discussed further on under Methods.

Making your own authentic English recordings. If you have your own radio cassette recorder there's nothing to stop you making your own authentic English cassettes, since reasonable reception of certain English language programmes can be obtained in Nancy. We can lend you a blank cassette and you could record whatever interests you on it. This method could be particularly interesting for those of you who want to listen to up-to-date news and Pop Music. Whether you make recordings or not, listening regularly to the radio to 'keep your ear in' is not a bad idea. Details of programmes and frequencies can be obtained from me.

British and American TV programmes. Recordings of these are shown regularly at lunchtime in Room 441. Programmes and showing times will be posted on the door.

Dictionary. If you haven't got one or if yours is inadequate, English dictionaries may be consulted (not taken away) in: a) the Library; b) the Sound Library; and c) Room 448.

Exercise Book. It is advisable to write up new words and expressions you meet with in an exercise book and to look them over from time to time to keep them in your head.

Methods

The following suggestions for practising aural comprehension on your own are intended to be applied to cassette recordings of authentic English since the other sources of recorded English mentioned above either give you working instructions (courses) or are only suitable for casual listening (live radio broadcasts, films, TV programmes).

Broadly speaking, there are two sorts of aural comprehension: global and detailed. Global comprehension means understanding just the essential points of what is being said. Detailed comprehension means understanding every single word. When it comes to listening to English in real life, however, the ability to discriminate every single word is quite often not necessary for understanding the message. Unfortunately, many learners of English want to do this and the effects are often catastrophic. Stopping to worry about words you didn't hear or understand can make you miss what follows and in extreme cases leads to a loss of concentration sufficient to make you lose the thread and give up trying altogether. Detailed comprehension practice is a useful way of training your ears and powers of concentration and of acquiring new vocabulary, but it is not advisable to seek perfection in this field. Detailed comprehension is rarely essential to effective communication. Global comprehension, on the other hand, *is* important. So when you work on a cassette, the best thing to do is to try, first of all, to understand the essential points of the item you're listening to and then to choose just a part of it for detailed study. Some ways of practising global and detailed comprehension will now be outlined. These methods will be demonstrated, practised and discussed in class.

GLOBAL COMPREHENSION

Success in global comprehension depends on being able to:

1. guess the meanings of incompletely understood utterances from the words you *did* understand
2. predict what's coming next
3. distinguish essential from non-essential material
4. concentrate

Here are a few suggestions for practising these skills:

1 — GUESSING

(a) For difficult cassettes: take a short extract and list the words you understand in the order they come in. Now try and guess the missing bits. This means using all possible grammatical and contextual clues to the utmost (and lots of imagination too). If you can't make sense of your list, listen again to check that your words are the right ones and possibly to hear some new ones. Keep trying. You can check your hypotheses at the next interview or if you use *PECOS* or *CACO* cassettes (where transcriptions of the recordings are provided) you can check up yourself. With practice you should eventually be able to dispense with: a) the list-making (carry the words in your head); b) the going back and listening again (make your hypotheses as you listen); and c) cutting the recording into short passages.

(b) Another way of practising piecing together a coherent interpretation of disparate pieces of information is to take a short extract from a not too difficult recording and, instead of playing it straight through, play it in random bursts of a few words each, leaving out the intermediate words. Then try and guess what the extract is about. Note your ideas on a piece of paper. Now start from the beginning again and play another selection of random word groups. This time you will probably get a much better idea of what's going on. Make as many selections as you need to, then check up on your impressions by playing the extract all through without interruption.

2 — PREDICTING

Keep interrupting your recording in mid-sentence and try to predict the next word or even the way the sentence will finish.

Then let the cassette run on to see if you were right or not.

3 — DISTINGUISHING ESSENTIAL FROM NON-ESSENTIAL MATERIAL (talks, lectures) To do this you have to be permanently alert to the logical and discursive structure of what you are listening to. This means being aware of the speaker's indications of the structure and weighting of his message (outlining plan, changing subject, emphasizing, digressing, summing up) and also being able to recognize less important material (examples, explanations, detailing, etc . . .).

Ideally, you should be analysing in this way as you listen, but if this is too difficult you could start by getting or making transcriptions of lectures and analysing them instead.

When you get to the stage of being able to distinguish essential from non-essential as you listen, you can start practising note-taking, just recording the main points without stopping the cassette.

4 — CONCENTRATING

To practise concentrating, interrupt the cassette from time to time and then try to remember the content of what you've heard in as much detail as possible. Note it down if you need to. Now wind the cassette back and see how much you *did* remember.

The above are a few ways of training yourself in the skills needed for global comprehension. When it comes to actually *doing* global comprehension you should, of course, listen to the item you have chosen from beginning to end, since this is the way you would listen to English in real life. Then make a note of the main points of what you've heard (or take notes as you listen). After that you'll be able to start again, stopping in the places where you had difficulty the first time, persevering until you feel you have a fair understanding, overall, of the cassette. Note the points which you missed earlier. You can then evaluate your performance during the first listen. How much did you miss of what was essential? Why? What went wrong? What could you do to prevent it happening again?

DETAILED COMPREHENSION

This can be pretty tedious work but it can help you to make progress not only with your comprehension but also with your speaking of English.

Choose a short passage to work on and attempt to make a transcription of everything you hear. Your first transcription will probably have some holes in it. (If it hasn't and you haven't learned anything, get a more difficult cassette, quick!) Now see if you can fill in the holes. Look hard at the context. This entails looking not only at the immediate grammatical context and at the 'sense' of the incomplete sentence, but also at the broader context; the preceding and following sentences. What word(s) could reasonably be put in the hole? If you can think of something in French, but don't know the English for it, look in the dictionary.

Does (do) the missing word(s) sound like that? If this doesn't work, try to write down the sound in the blank. Is there anything like it in the dictionary? If so, does it fit the context?

Working in this way you're going to come across new words and expressions. If you don't want to waste the time you've spent finding them, make a note of them and glance at your accumulated results from time to time.

You can check your work at interview time or on your own if you use cassettes for which transcriptions already exist (*CIAO, Kernel, PECOS, CACO, Varieties of Spoken English, All the best from today*). If your transcriptions are legible they could be used in photocopy form by other students.

The transcriptions you make can also be used as material for analyses which will help you with speaking English. For example:

Functional Analysis (plays, discussions, interviews, lectures). Notice how language functions are realized and how they vary with the communication situation. Realizations you haven't met before and which you think may be useful should be noted.

Logico-discursive Analysis (talks, lectures). Notice how information is organized and presented.

The above methods for practising listening comprehension give indications of how you can evaluate your performance yourself. More detailed techniques can, perhaps, be worked out (in terms of your objectives and the difficulty of the material you work on) during the year when you come for interview. The interviews themselves and classroom sessions will give you additional opportunities to assess your aural comprehension in the more delicate face-to-face-with-a-native-speaker situation, since English will, as far as possible, be the language used.

Excerpt from 'Objectives in English'

LISTENING COMPREHENSION OBJECTIVES

	Rate Yourself 0 to 5	Priority	Progress
Could you understand complex information or unexpected enquiries over the phone?			
Could you understand a visiting engineer talking informally on professional matters? Could you understand a visiting engineer talking informally on non-professional matters?			

Could you grasp the essential points of a technical lecture at a conference/seminar? Could you understand a technical lecture in detail? Could you take notes at the same time?			
At a meeting of a technical nature, could you: grasp the main points? follow arguments in detail? grasp nuances of sense in tone of voice/choice of words? take notes or minutes?			
Could you perform the feats above if the speaker had an accent?			
Could you understand: the news on radio/TV? a play or film? other TV programmes? a conversation between English people? unexpected questions in the street?			

The Questionnaire

The aim of the experiment described above was to obtain information on the effectiveness of the new method relative to traditional teaching methods in force at the *Ecole des Mines* and, with a view to wider application, to see if the former could be handled comfortably by part-time staff with not too much time to devote to preparation. Unfortunately, as far as the first and most vital question is concerned, it was not possible to perform the experiment in such a way as to obtain an objective comparison between the two methods (i.e. using a control group and progress tests). The main source of information available was a questionnaire which the students taking part in the experiment were invited, near the end of the experiment, to fill in anonymously. In this questionnaire the students, who had already sampled traditional *Ecole des Mines* English tuition for one year, were asked to compare their year's work in semi-autonomy with the previous year's work in terms of the progress they felt they had made and any pleasure they might have experienced. They were also asked to compare the classwork and semi-autonomous work carried out during the experiment from the same points of view and to say which features of these two components they had felt to be good and which they had felt to be bad. To the students' impressions of the experiment as revealed by the questionnaire may be added those of the teacher, and it is in this order that the results of the experiment will be presented. It must be emphasized, however, that any conclusions drawn from this experiment will be based on subjective (and hence possibly unreliable) data and that they are, of course, only relevant to the very limited context in which the experiment took place.

Results

The number given after each answer is the number of students out of 13 who answered in that particular way.

General questions on this year's work in English

1. How much progress do you think you made in English this year?
   - More than last year 4
   - Less than last year 2
   - The same as last year 7
2. If you feel you made less progress in English this year, to what do you attribute this?
   - The teaching methods used this year 0
   - A reduction of effort on your part 2
3. On the whole, did you find the work you did in English this year
   - More enjoyable than last year? 8
   - Less enjoyable than last year? 0
   - As enjoyable (boring) as last year? 5
4. Which method was more helpful in improving your spoken English? Why?
   - Last year's 1
   - This year's 11
   - No difference 1
5. Would you like to carry on with semi-autonomous learning next year?
   - Yes 9
   - No 4

About the Thursday morning class

6. Did you find the class more or less useful than the semi-autonomous work you did?
   - Class more useful 1
   - Class less useful 5
   - Class and semi-autonomous work complementary 7

7. Did you find the class more or less enjoyable than semi-autonomous work?
   - Class more enjoyable 8
   - Class less enjoyable 3
   - Both equally enjoyable 2
8. Do you think the class served any useful purpose?
   - Yes 9
   - No 2
   - Don't know 2
9. What was good about the class?
10. What was bad about the class?
11. Suggestions concerning the class?

About the semi-autonomous work

12. Do you think that *Learning English on your own* gave you adequate preparation for semi-autonomous work?
    - Yes 13
    - No 0
13. How often did you use *Learning English on your own*?
    - Often 0
    - Occasionally 7
    - Never 6
14. Did you find the supervision of your semi-autonomous work
    - Too *directif*? 0
    - Not *directif* enough? 0
    - Just right? 13
15. Did you find the interviews
    - Too long? 0
    - Too short? 0
    - Just right? 13
16. What was good about semi-autonomous work?
    - Independence (choice of objectives, materials, time and speed of work) 8
    - I talked more 4
    - You *have* to work 3
    - Interviews useful 2
17. What was bad about semi-autonomous work?
    - Temptation to idleness 7
    - Discouragement when problems arise 3
    - Less stimulating than classwork 3
    - I talked less 2
18. Suggestions concerning semi-autonomous work:
19. Any other comments on the year's work:

Discussion of the results of the questionnaire and teacher's observations

The first question required the students to compare their progress during the year of the self-directed learning experiment with that made under normal teaching during their first year with us. That, of course was the $64,000 question and the answers to it needed to be interpreted with some caution. First of all, the comparison the students were asked to make was not merely between two different teaching methods since they had not been exposed to the same teachers in the first year as in the second year. Thus, the differences in progress noted cannot be ascribed with any certainty to purely methodological factors, as differences in the personalities and competences of the teachers involved may also have played a part. In addition, the students, with the best will in the world, may not necessarily have been very good judges of what progress they had made. What conclusions, then, may be drawn from the answers to this question?

Firstly, it should be noted that the two students who felt they had made less progress during the experiment than in the preceding year appended to their answer the observation that they had not worked so hard during the second year. This may be a reflection on the appropriateness of self-directed learning to less motivated students (in one case it was — the student later identified himself and explained that the partial lack of a rigid timetable had led him into temptations to idleness to which he invariably succumbed) but it also suggests that one need not be too dismayed by these two negative answers. Secondly, the other answers indicate that about one third of the group felt they had made more progress with self-directed learning while about half of them found the new method neither better nor worse than the previous year's. Thus, although no really firm conclusions can be drawn as to the relative merits of the two methods, there does not seem, at least, to be any strong indication that the self-directed learning method used is any worse than the traditional *Ecole des Mines* methods and there is some indication that certain students (30% of our sample) may get along better with it. The answers to Questions 6, 7, 8 and 18 confirm that four of the group preferred self-directed learning to working in class.

Question 3, concerning enjoyment of the experimental year's work, was put to the students because it is often supposed that self-directed learning is necessarily less fun than classroom learning. (Whether having fun necessarily results in better learning is, perhaps, another matter.) It is felt that the answers given to this question are fairly reliable. No great soul-searching or complex quantifying seem to be involved and although the writer, in all his modesty, was somewhat surprised by the absence of *less enjoyable than last year* answers he is tempted to accept even this result since this group seemed to be pretty forthright. They had not hesitated to protest when dissatisfied with a certain aspect of the teaching they had received the year before and did not mince their words when asked in the questionnaire to say what features of the experiment had displeased them. Eight of the students, then, found the self-directed learning experiment more enjoyable than the previous year's work and none of them admitted to enjoying it less. This seems to be a fairly satisfactory state of affairs. But at this point it is advisable to enquire into just *what* was found to be enjoyable. That the self-directed learning component of the experiment did not contribute enormously is shown by the answers given to Question 7. Only three of the students enjoyed self-directed work more than classwork (this does show, nevertheless, that self-directed learning *can* be more fun than classwork for some people); but eight of them enjoyed classwork more, which, while lending weight to the 'self-directed learning is no fun' argument, also suggests, when taken in conjunction with the eight 'more enjoyable than last year', that the efforts made to render the class activities entertaining were fairly successful, and that it is possible to sugar the pill of self-directed learning in this way. It would be pleasant to be able to conclude this paragraph here, but it must also be pointed out that just over half the participants in the experiment felt moved to observe (Question 17) that the self-directed learning part of their work provided dangerous opportunities for letting English slide, and it must be confessed that this fact may not be entirely unconnected with some of the enjoyment experienced.

The overwhelming majority view that the self-directed learning experiment led to more progress in oral expression than had the previous year's work came as something of a pleasant surprise. This group was known to have been quite lively in the classroom during its first year at the *Ecole des Mines* and, consequently, it had been feared that the replacement of one of the twice-weekly classroom sessions by solitary work would produce a considerable sense of slowing down in this skill. The increase in progress was unanimously attributed to the interviews. These led, if not to more talking-time for everybody, at least to a fairer distribution of talking-time than occurred in the classroom. Thus, those students who habitually remained tongue-tied during whole-group class activities could not avoid speaking during a face-to-face with the teacher. As a matter of fact, a good proportion of the students who tended to be quiet in class seemed to compensate for this by a superabundance of talkativeness at the interviews. The interview system was probably particularly appreciated by this kind of student. Not by everybody though: two students reported that they had less chance to speak because of the semi-autonomous work (see the answers to Question 17). However, one of these two students explained on his questionnaire that his answer was due to a particular zest for conversation in a whole-group situation and admitted that he had probably had more than his fair share of talking-time the previous year.

The fact that nine of the group wished to carry on with self-directed learning (Question 5) seems encouraging but the motives underlying this choice are not known. At the most, one half only of these students could have been motivated, wholly or partially, by a sense of more progress made with self-directed learning (see answers to Question 1). As eight students had said that they had enjoyed themselves more during the experiment than during the previous year, it seems likely that a fair proportion of those choosing to carry on with self-directed learning were prompted by hedonistic reasoning. Nothing wrong with that, perhaps, but it did come to the ears of the writer that 'some' of the students had been influenced by the thought that a vote for semi-autonomy would mean a reduction in hours of obligatory presence and surveillance at the college. This raises the question of whether unmotivated students learn significantly more during unwilling class attendance than during minimal self-directed work.

We come now to the questions concerning the classwork component of the experiment (Questions 6–11).

Only one student found the class more useful than semi-autonomous work (the one who enjoyed conversation in a big group). Of the others, seven considered that classwork and semi-autonomous work were complementary and five found classwork less useful than semi-autonomous work. Four students were not even convinced the class was at all useful.

The fact that three of the group actually enjoyed self-directed work more than classwork has already been mentioned in passing but may be re-emphasized here. This finding is in agreement with previous C.R.A.P.E.L. experience; certain learners take up self-directed learning, not through lack of any other alternative, but simply because they like it better.

Some explanation of why five students found self-directed work more useful than classwork was found in the answers to the questions where the students were asked to comment on positive and negative aspects of the class. These showed that, despite the attempts made to liven up the class and provide opportunities for everybody to communicate, there were still complaints of lack of speaking practice and occasional boredom. Examples: 'It's always the same people who do all the talking'; 'The class has got to be interesting for *everybody*'.

On the brighter side, the use made of video* was appreciated by the majority of students. From the teacher's point of view, the technical problem-solving activities in particular had been very successful inasmuch as they had created some enthusiasm among a body of students who usually howled in anguish at the mere mention of Technical English. So the need to ginger up the classroom session brought about by the installation of self-directed learning gave rise to some useful spin-off in the way of new teaching material.

The next part of the questionnaire dealt with the self-directed learning part of the experiment (Questions 12–18).

All the students thought *Learning English on your own* had been an adequate preparation for semi-autonomous work. Nearly half of them only read it once, the rest only occasionally. It would be agreeable to be able to conclude from this that a competent author had been blessed with attentive and enthusiastic readers endowed with good memories. But, in fact, the methodological part of the booklet left very little impression on most of the students, who often needed reminding of its contents during their interviews. It may even be doubted, in the light of previous experience at the *Ecole des Mines*, whether some of them ever *did* read this part of the booklet.

The feeling of all the students that the degree of supervision of their self-directed learning had been just right is encouraging insofar as nobody complained that he had been abandoned by the teacher. Actually, no serious protests of this kind were anticipated since student autonomy plays a great part in the technical teaching policy of the *Ecole des Mines* to which these students had already been exposed for one year at the start of the experiment. But (again) the majority of the students needed a disappointingly large amount of supervision (harassing might be a more appropriate word). Only three out of the thirteen showed any real independence in their choice of objectives and methods or any tenacity in pursuing the former.

*This refers to a series of exercises developed by the writer which aimed at stimulating discussion amongst the students.

Similarly, the seven students who found the length (20–25 minutes) of the interviews just right gave no cause for rejoicing. The length *was* adequate when not much work had been done, but otherwise this time was too short, in some cases, even for dealing adequately with the problems encountered by the student. Thus, training in methodology and self assessment tended to be neglected and planning of future work done hastily and badly when the arrival of the next interviewee signalled that the interview was already at an end.

Over half of the students mentioned their appreciation of the way self-directed learning let them choose their own objectives, materials and methods as well as place, time and frequency of work. Against this favourable reaction must be set the comparable proportion of students who commented on the opportunities for neglect of English which the method afforded to those so inclined, either through lack of interest or through pressure of work in more important subjects. Slacking during self-directed learning is, however, more readily detectable than in the classroom and some of the students were not unimpressed by this. 23% of the group felt self-directed learning actually made them work. There was a fair amount of comment to the effect that self-directed learning was not very stimulating and that sometimes problems met with while working alone could lead to the work being abandoned. One or two students suggested here that these two problems might be overcome to some extent if self-directed learning were carried out in small groups. So much then for the students' impressions of the experiment. Now, what about the teacher's?

Some disappointment from this side of the fence has already been voiced concerning lack of attention paid to the methodological advice given in *Learning English on your own* and the need to harass unmotivated students. To this must be added a fairly general distaste for, and avoidance of, systematic work on necessary grammar and vocabulary and the fact that the time allowance for self-directed learning was, in the majority of cases, by no means fully used. An attempt was made to quantify very crudely the work done during self-directed learning by looking at each student's work-record and guessing how many hours of work had been done. The quotient *hours of work done* over *hours of work which should have been done* turned out, on average, to be 0.4. On the face of it, this figure can hardly be regarded as being indicative of any great conscientiousness on the part of the students. In mitigation, it should be mentioned that a number of students observed, on their questionnaire, that semi-autonomous work required much more effort than classwork and was much more concentrated. One student felt that he achieved more in 15 minutes of semi-autonomous work than in an hour in the classroom. The fact remains, however, that the majority of the students were not pulling their weight.

But to put things into perspective, very few students of English at the *Ecole des Mines* (apart from beginners) show great enthusiasm for the subject. When enthusiasm does manifest itself, it is usually due to some pressing professional need, such as the imminence of a year's study in the USA. This general lack of interest in English is probably due in part to a preoccupation with studies more directly relevant to a future engineer and to the fact that not taking English seriously seems to be, in itself, insufficient grounds for stopping anybody walking out of the place with a diploma under his or her arm. Thus, nothing startling in the way of motivation can reasonably be hoped for.

As far as the group taking part in the experiment is concerned, it can at least be said that the new way of working does not appear to have produced any marked reduction in effort (measured in terms of participation in class and attendance) as compared with that furnished by English groups expected to show comparable motivation (this latter being indirectly proportional to level and length of stay at the college).

But the self-directed learning part of the experiment was not, from the teacher's point of view, entirely a matter of disappointments. The blossoming-out, during the interviews, of the quieter personalities has already been mentioned. In addition, useful feedback on the classroom sessions was obtained in these one-to-one contacts, whereas the students were much less forthcoming *en masse* about their reactions to class activities. Also, the specific needs of each student imposed fairly rapid action in the matter of finding or creating materials and methods to match these needs. This led to the accumulation of a new stock of teaching tools which might otherwise never have been acquired and which proved to be useful elsewhere. Although this preparatory work was very time-consuming in the early stages, there was a considerable slacking off later on, and over the year the preparation involved was no greater than for a conscientiously prepared normal class, where not too much reliance is placed on a ready-made course. It seems possible, than, that supervision of self-directed learning could be undertaken by *enthusiastic* part-time staff once a pool of materials and methods sufficient to meet the majority of individual learner requirements has been built up. Another positive feature of the experiment was that the more personal contact between teacher and student allowed better assessment of each student in terms of his efforts, achievements and personality. Finally, this closer relationship gave considerable satisfaction to the teacher, satisfaction both personal and pedagogical.

Conclusion

The chief aim of this experiment was to get an idea of whether the self-directed learning method employed was likely to give better results than the traditional classroom teaching methods in use at the *Ecole des Mines* in Nancy.

Obviously, the small-scale nature of the experiment and the unsophisticated methods of assessment employed preclude the drawing of any firm conclusions but, nevertheless, indications of positive and negative features have emerged.

On the credit side it would seem, if the judgement of the students involved is to be trusted, that the method is, at the worst, no less effective than the existing methods. For the majority of the students the method was felt to have led to more progress in the speaking of English, and about a third of them considered the method to be both superior to, and more enjoyable than traditional work. Two thirds of the students welcomed the independence the method gave them and a quarter of them felt the method ensured they did more work. Students habitually reluctant to participate verbally in class were given, and usually took, the chance to make up for lost time during the interviews. From the teacher's point of view the method gave much more job satisfaction and, although demanding, was not unduly so. It produced a fair amount of teaching materials spin-off and allowed better assessment of the students.

On the debit side, some students reported that self-directed learning was less stimulating and more productive of discouragement than normal classwork. If the advantages of independence were savoured by two thirds of the students, a comparable proportion of them mentioned the perils of the ease with which English could be dropped in favour of anything more pressing. On average, less than half the time allocated to self-directed learning was used. Only three students out of thirteen took their work anything like seriously. The time allowed for interviews was often too short.

Despite the problems posed by the self-directed learning method investigated, there would nevertheless seem to be enough in the way of positive features to warrant further experimentation along these lines. It seems likely that the method will give good results with students who are motivated and keen on self-directed learning (and who might be identified in the first year and given the chance of working in this way during the subsequent two years) but only a more rigorously conducted, long-term comparison with normal *Ecole des Mines* methods backed up by more detailed questionnaires will give reliable information on the relative merits of the two systems in the case of less motivated students. The idea of self-directed learning in small groups seems interesting. A method combining classwork, individual self-directed learning and small group self-directed learning might well bring about an improvement. This latter activity would increase opportunities for communication in English and should go some way towards eliminating complaints about lack of stimulation and too much discouragement in individual self-directed learning. It might even lead to a bit more work being done. More preparation and practice in self-directed learning techniques also seems to be needed. Future work will be aimed in the directions outlined above.

12 Teaching learning: redefining the teacher's role

M–J. Gremmo and D. Abé

The operations of any teaching and/or learning system involve a number of different tasks and roles which have to be shared out between the different components which make up the system. In systems based on a traditional structure (teacher and group) it is the teacher who performs the majority of the tasks and who takes on most of the roles: he is, therefore, the main component in the teaching/learning situation. However, recent research into applied linguistics, into the psychology of learning and into psycholinguistics has underlined the importance of the *learning* process as such, serving as a useful reminder of the fact that it is really the learner who is the essential component in any pedagogical event. If we accept, therefore, that we should now try a more learner-centred approach, what happens as regards the distribution of the various tasks and roles?

Instead of studying the activities of the teacher and those of the learner as separate realms, we thought it would be more worthwhile to try to investigate in detail just what the tasks are which have to be carried out in a teaching/learning situation and what the roles are which cluster around the two poles of the system: in other words, the nature of the tasks and their importance in the learning situation should help us define the respective roles of teacher and learner. To do this, we will use as examples three types of learning system, all of which are in operation at present at the C.R.A.P.E.L.

The first, and best known, of these systems is the *traditional course*: at the C.R.A.P.E.L. this is often referred to as 'evening classes' simply because they are given to adults who come to study English in the evenings after work. The point being made here is that evening classes take place at regular intervals (e.g. Tuesday and Thursday at 6 p.m.) and involve a group in a classroom with a teacher. It is this organizational structure which is traditional.

The second system we will be talking about is the *self-directed group*.

This is the most recent system to have been set up at the C.R.A.P.E.L.: it has been going for five years now (1982) and was an experiment run as part of the activities of the *Université du Troisième Age et du Temps Disponible de l'Université de Nancy II* (a 'university' within our university, for people who are retired or who simply have some spare time). In this case, the learners are provided with classrooms, equipment and material, but no teacher is present during their working sessions. (See pp. 275–81).

The third system we operate is that of *self-directed learning with support* (pp. 191–205). In this system, the learners do not belong to a group: they mostly work alone or, occasionally, in pairs. The teacher provides them with documents when they have none of their own and discusses their learning programme with them. Because this system tends towards the acquisition of autonomy, we call these learners *autonomes* (independent learners) and, to simplify matters, we will use the term *autonomy* when discussing the tasks and roles in all three of these systems.

In what follows, we are going to try to list the various tasks which have to be performed in any learning programme under three headings: the first section will deal with those tasks which have to be performed during the *planning* or *preparatory* stage of the learning programme. The second section will discuss the operations carried out during the actual learning sessions. Finally, we will touch on the psycholinguistic or psychological aspects of learning.

Preparing to learn

This first section deals with tasks which have to be performed before undertaking any teaching/learning programme. Four such tasks will be discussed here:

Collecting information about the learners' motivations and about those aspects of the external situation which incite them to learn a language;

The analysis of these data, to determine learning objectives and the content of the learning programme;

Information concerning the facilities provided by the institution;

Decisions concerning contents, methodologies and modalities.

1. *Information concerning needs*

One of the first tasks is to obtain information concerning the needs, expectations and linguistic knowledge of future learners. This information has to be reasonably exact, because it will be used as a basis for determining the learner's programme of action. It will concern those factors which incite the participants to learn a language. These needs can be of several types: 'professional' needs, such as looking after a foreign visitor to one's firm; 'personal' needs, such as a journey abroad; 'psychological' needs, such as wishing to get out of a rut; or 'social' needs, such as wanting to meet people or do something.

Before establishing a learning plan, it is also interesting to know the learners' linguistic history: whether they have already studied the foreign language and, if so, in what circumstances; whether they have already learnt a foreign language and, if so, what they thought of that way of learning, etc.

A further type of information to be sought is in clues concerning the learners' image of the language which they are going to learn: do they see it as a stock of words, as a set of grammatical rules, or as a tool for communication in real situations?

2. *Analysing the learners' needs*

Once the learners' needs and their conception of them has been elicited, they have to be analysed, to decide on learning objectives and on the content of the learning programme. It is rare for all members of a group to have the same needs: even if one manages to group together all the people having the same apparent need — travelling abroad, for example — one finds that some are going to England, others to the United States, some will stay in hotels, others with friends, some will go by plane, others by car, etc. We therefore need a set of categories which will allow a more detailed analysis. These are provided by functional criteria, which allow us to break down the long-term objective into a series of intermediate objectives. For example, an analysis of the needs of all the learners we have just spoken about will probably show that they all need to ask for information, to thank, to ask people to repeat what they have said or to speak more slowly when they have trouble understanding them, etc.

Information about the learners' needs, about the facilities made available by the institution and about criteria for bringing the two into line makes it possible to tackle the essential phase in preparing a teaching/learning programme: decision-making. The choices will include short- and long-term objectives; which skills to practise (written/spoken comprehension, written/spoken expression), the type of language to be studied ('specialized' or 'general'); registers and levels of language to be studied; the type of competence aimed at (linguistic and grammatical or communicative competence); methodology (will a particular progression be followed or will activities of different degrees of difficulty be mixed? will just one course be used or several? will there be structural drills or more creative activities? etc.). A choice has also to be made of materials and documents (will they be authentic or not, will they be related to the real-life situations in which the learners are going to find themselves?) and of the types of evaluation to be employed.

3. *Information about the institution*

If the teaching/learning process is seen as an interaction between the two essential elements, teacher and learner, it seems natural to expect an exchange of information between these two elements. It should be possible, therefore for the learner to obtain detailed information about the facilities made available within the teaching institution. Generally, learners who are taking up some course of study want to know how many hours of classes there are per week, what the total length of the course is and when and where it will take place. Only relatively rarely do they ask questions about how their learning programme will be realized: is it going to be a highly structured course, or a miscellany of exercises and activities in 'general' English? Is the course grammatical rather than functional? Are authentic materials used, or have the documents and recordings presented in the course been specially created for language-learning purposes? Does the system provide the possibility of conversations with native speakers, or are all the models non-natives?

4. *Decisions, decisions*

There are a considerable number of decisions which have to be taken before beginning any learning programme. Until recent years, it has to be admitted, it was the teacher who performed this task. This is true of our evening classes, for example, where the decisions are taken *before* the learners arrive. We offer them a course in general English, which is advertised as such. Naturally, at the beginning of each course the teacher discusses their needs, motivations and objectives with the members of the group; but this is done to see if any members of the group are there under a false impression, to make everyone aware that a compromise involving some sort of common core is necessary in such a situation and to describe the C.R.A.P.E.L.'s methodology. The teacher leads the discussion as and where he wants (indeed, the description of the methodology usually comes as quite a surprise for the majority of the participants).

However, our experience with the *Université du Troisième Age* and the independent learners has shown that learners can carry out this investigation themselves if given the chance. In the case of the independent learners, in fact, this is vital, since the system is centred on them. Some independent learners only have to be asked 'Why do you want to learn English?' for them to give a detailed analysis of what we in our jargon call needs, motivation, priorities, level of competence, etc. Of course, not all of them are ready to make all these analyses; their previous experience of learning has conditioned them to the idea that all this is part of the teacher's domain, which is why, as we said earlier, few of them ask questions about the teaching methods to which they are going to be exposed. This is above all because they lack the necessary information; some of them have no criteria for analysis whatsoever. The teacher's role in such a situation is to provide those criteria. This is usually done in the course of interviews with them, though it is perfectly possible to imagine it being done in writing, using informative questionnaires, lists of suggestions, etc. The aim of this operation is to make the learner aware of his own motivations, to help him determine his objectives and thereby to integrate him further into the teaching/learning process.

What, then, are the roles of the teacher during these opening phases? In the traditional approach, exemplified here by our evening classes, his role is one of *producer*. He is the person responsible for carrying out the different steps we have just mentioned, constructing his programme on the basis of the various kinds of information which he obtains. But this information is only one of his sources: he also has his own ideas as to what makes a 'good' course, a 'good' teaching method, a 'good' teacher and as to what type of language to deal with first. All this helps him to accomplish the task of decision-taking that we have looked at: the methodology or methodologies, timetables, programmes etc. He is the one who organizes, who decides.

What happens, though, if these tasks are performed, even if only partially, by the learners, as is the case in the other learning systems available at the C.R.A.P.E.L.? The role of the teacher becomes that of consultant expert. Instead of taking the decisions himself, that is, he gathers as many tools as possible to enable the learners themselves to take these decisions in the most favourable conditions. For example, he will gather questionnaires, checklists etc. to help learners identify their objectives. He thus plays the role of a research officer whose job is to make available the greatest possible variety of methods (in the widest sense) so that the learner can choose. He also makes himself available to the learner so that he can help him make his choice.

The learning sessions

In this section we are going to discuss those tasks which are performed during the sessions when the teaching/learning actually takes place.

1. *Material tasks*

As any teacher knows, an hour's work with a group can be very demanding: we distribute handouts, set up equipment and operate it, write on the blackboard, distribute more handouts, go back to the blackboard, get out the tape recorder — we hardly stop. It is rare for one of the participants to offer to work the tape recorder, for example. In the *Université du Troisième Age*, though, the participants do all these things without the slightest problem: they collect their equipment and their materials and operate the equipment without any help from a teacher, except, perhaps, at the beginning when the teacher may have explained how to use the equipment or have given a few suggestions as to the different ways of using a tape (for example, learners do not always realize that they can rewind several times to help clear up comprehension problems).

In our evening classes, it is not unusual for the teacher to ask one or more members of the group to operate the equipment: he may also stop writing on the blackboard, leaving this to the members who wish or feel the need to do so. This is an admittedly naïve but nonetheless fairly effective way of inviting the learners themselves to take part in the material tasks, so that the teacher goes from being a sort of head technician to being just one operator among others.

2. *Transmission of knowledge or a skill*

Apart from the purely material tasks, a certain amount of knowledge (or a skill) has to be transmitted. As it is usually the teacher who possesses the necessary linguistic and methodological knowledge, he is the one who has the privilege of playing the roles of linguistic informant and methodological expert. In a traditional course the teacher is the one who knows the target language best; he is the one who is supposed to speak it best and he is also the one who knows the tricks of the trade for sharing this knowledge. Not only the teacher, but also the learners see things this way: this is doubtless the reason why learners often regard the teacher as a walking dictionary or grammar, asking him for the equivalents of words in one language or the other and getting him to spell out and explain the rules of syntax of the target language.

There used to be some justification for this attitude. When there were no tape recorders, the only linguistic informants available to learners were the teacher and the textbook. Between them, these two were the only sources of the target language with which learners were ever confronted, and for this reason the learners naturally took the teacher as their model. Nowadays, however, the teacher is not the only one to give out linguistic information: the mass media often publish or broadcast in foreign languages, and exchanges, journeys abroad or contacts with foreigners are frequent, so that learners have a wide variety of sources available to them. Neither is the teacher the only informant available as regards vocabulary: information concerning the workings of the target language can be obtained not only by listening to a teacher's explanations but also by studying authentic materials and using them to locate unknown elements of grammar or vocabulary. The teacher's role changes from knowing everything and explaining everything to showing where the information can be found and how to obtain it: he is no longer the sole linguistic model; he is a *guide* to different types of discourse. In a sense, his role is teaching people how to use a dictionary.

Obviously, the teacher will continue, where necessary, to give out grammatical, lexical or functional information. But he is no longer the only informant, he is one among many. In those learning systems where the teacher is not always present, it is obvious that he is there as a last resort when all the learners' other attempts to solve their problems have failed; but even in these cases, the learner will use a native speaker as his informant where possible.

Another of the teacher's 'traditional' tasks is to arrange for learners to practise using what has been or is to be acquired: he therefore uses all sorts of exercises to encourage his learners to express themselves in the foreign language. His objective is to get his learners to 'communicate', that is, to simulate real life as it exists outside the classroom. But as Riley (1977) has shown, almost all classroom interaction and communication goes via the teacher and even those learners who were supposed to be practising or inventing their own dialogue addressed the teacher, not one another, so that the teacher was even obliged to manage their turn-taking for them. In such circumstances, it can hardly be claimed that the teacher stimulates communication between the members of the group: in fact, his presence alone is enough to short-circuit it, because he is seen as a leader and because the learners keep turning to him.

To free himself from this role, the teacher can either use a large number of authentic materials as 'informants' or he can arrange for the participation of native speakers with whom the learners can practise under more realistic conditions. A third possibility is to form sub-groups, he himself withdrawing from the groups and leaving the members to practise directly with one another. This is how the members of the *Troisième Age* groups and our 'autonomous' learners manage to communicate without the help of a teacher (who simply is not present) but with the aid of documents and native speakers. The teacher's physical presence has been replaced by other factors so that satisfactory communicative exchanges can take place.

The second task which has to be carried out in the construction phase of a teaching/learning programme is to choose a set of working methods. The initial exercise has to be chosen; a choice of materials has to be made; the pace of the exercises has to be decided on. What proportions of the work will be devoted to studying documents and to memorization, or to the use of authentic materials and processed documents? How will the time available be distributed in terms of rest and work periods? Will any time and work be given over to revision, or will it be a matter of ploughing straight on?

Here, again, it is usually the teacher who makes these decisions. But things can be ordered otherwise. For example, the autonomous learners and the *Troisième Age* groups are able to choose their materials and methods themselves. In self-directed group learning, the learners usually study documents provided by the teacher, some of which have been processed, some not, different groups having different preferences in these matters. Some groups bring along their own documents. Work on authentic documents, whether provided by the teacher or not, calls for a choice of working technique, which, in turn, may or may not be copied from the teacher or from teaching materials. Autonomous learners, on the other hand, almost always take these decisions for themselves; if they use materials recommended by the helper, they also use their own. And, of course, they also decide when they are going to work, how long for, how often and the progression which they are going to follow. This choice is made on the basis of two essential criteria: their own personal tastes, and efficiency as regards the achievement of the objective in question.

They usually proceed by trial and error. The teachers' role here involves helping with the identification of analytic criteria, advising on methodology and providing materials.

3. *Evaluation*

Different aspects of the teaching/learning programme have to be evaluated while it is actually under way in order for the necessary steps to be taken for the following part of the programme. It is not enough just to plan a programme, or even to carry it out: there also has to be a continuing process of assessment, to see whether or not objectives are being achieved.

In what ensues, we will be following Holec (pp. 177–8) who argues that the evaluation process includes two different operations: the first is evaluation of the quality of the learner's performance in the foreign language; is it correct or incorrect with respect to the objectives originally chosen? For example, if the objective in question is to be able to ask for information on the phone, the learner needs to be able to assess his performance once it has been realized, using criteria such as 'Was I reasonably fluent? Were my sentences grammatical? Did the person I was speaking to understand what I was asking? Was I polite enough?', etc.

The second kind of operation involved in evaluation is the interpretation of this assessment. Here, criteria such as satisfactory/unsatisfactory come into play: 'Can I improve my performance, or is that my limit for the moment? Do I want to be able to speak like an Englishman, or will that do for me, even if it wasn't perfect?'

If the performance is judged to be satisfactory with respect to the objective in view, the learner can consider that that part of his learning programme is complete and move on to the next point. If not, he has to decide whether to go back and start again. If he does go back, he is then faced with the choice of working method: is he going to work in the same way as before, or choose another? When the teacher is present during the learning sessions, he decides what is and what is not satisfactory; it is the teacher who makes the learner repeat, go back and start again when something does not seem to have been properly learnt — and the learner is quite content to let him do so. Often enough, though, the teacher does it without knowing if the learner is satisfied with his performance or not (and the learner then accepts the teacher's judgement).

Now, clearly, it is the learner and *only* the learner who can decide if *his* objective has been achieved or not. The criteria for evaluation in terms of correct/incorrect can be provided by his interlocutor's behaviour: 'Did he ask me to repeat what I was saying? Did he seem impatient? Did I get an adequate reply? Did he seem to think that I'd got a word or sentence wrong?' By basing his judgements on the reactions of his interlocutor the learner becomes an evaluator. Obviously, self-evaluation means that the learner must have certain points of reference.

The role of the teacher is not to be the one and only point of reference, but to provide the means of comparison. As we have already mentioned, native speakers (who are not teachers) or other members of the group can also help in discussing these matters. Similarly, the teacher can also provide criteria of analysis for the learner's performances: the rhythm, speed, intelligibility, communicability, grammaticality acceptable to the interlocutor as regards expression. For comprehension, the criteria for analysis would probably include: global or detailed comprehension; ability to understand the main words or get the gist; understanding at first hearing or after several attempts; whether a script was needed or not; having recourse to an outside form of evaluation (using the script, for example) or relying on a subjective impression.

To sum up this section, then, we can say that the teacher's contribution is not necessarily limited to participation in the learning activities. His role is to create conditions which are favourable to the learners' being able to take over those different operations which are necessary in any learning programme.

Psychological factors

In this section we will be discussing psychological and psycholinguistic aspects of the learning/teaching programme. In addition to the tasks which have already been discussed, there remain a number which, by their very nature, are more difficult to observe. They include the learning process itself, the stimulation which is necessary if learning is to take place and the encouragement which is given at certain points during the learning programme. Finally, we will be discussing group dynamics.

1. *Psycholinguistic factors*

First let us consider the psycholinguistic factors. The aim of the numerous tasks which have been mentioned above is to create the conditions necessary if the learner is to be able to learn. The ultimate task of any teaching/learning situation must be the acquisition of knowledge. Only the learner can carry out this final operation. Previously, it used to be believed that, provided the teacher gave a good lesson, the learner would learn the information it contained. Research in psycholinguistics has shown, though, that this is anything but the case; in fact, between the moment when the teacher provides the information (input) and the moment when it is assimilated by the learner (intake), a number of cognitive phenomena occur about which we still know very little.

This problem is aggravated by the fact that the only way in which we can measure the intake is by measuring the output, that is, the information which the learner returns. As we have little idea what actually goes on in the human brain, it is difficult to know exactly what information should be given in order to achieve a satisfactory intake and, therefore, a satisfactory output. In any traditional course, obviously, the teacher makes use of an approach which he believes will facilitate this acquisition or intake. If the learner's way of learning does not correspond to the methodology envisaged by the teacher, however, he either learns nothing at all or spends a great deal of time trying to understand and acquire the teacher's techniques. One way in which this problem can be solved is by offering the learner a wider variety of choice. As he proceeds by trial and error, the learner is more likely to come across the method which suits him best. This is how the autonomous learning scheme works: not only is there methodological variety, but there is also a variety of materials and English speakers. Most learners choose to try out a number of different materials and methods of working during the same period.

In self-directed group learning and the evening classes, a wide variety of authentic materials of every kind (tapes, slides, video, etc.) is used. The structure of the class also varies, as do the exercises, and the teacher makes sure that this variety is kept up. We have also noticed that, in the intensive courses we organize, the learners usually enjoy the fact that there is a great diversity of materials, teachers, methods, etc., even though they may be rather wary of this approach to start with.

Here, again, the teacher sees his role changed: if he is a believer in one particular methodology, he has to accept the fact that certain learners are just not going to 'click' with him. On the other hand, if he wants to be able to deal with a wide variety of learners he has to become an adviser on methodology.

2. *Psychological factors*

Other more specifically psychological phenomena are also encountered in a teaching/learning situation; there is the problem of *motivation*, which is known to play an important role in the learning process, and there is the support given when learners are discouraged, which the teacher often considers as one of his most important tasks.

a) MOTIVATION

In traditional courses, one of the teacher's roles was to provide learners with external motivation by doing activities they enjoyed, so as to make learning attractive. Indeed one of the problems of secondary school teachers is that they have to replace this external motivation by internal motivation, which is something many of their pupils no longer have.

The situation is different, though, where adults are concerned: most of the time they are not obliged to follow the course or even to learn anything. Nonetheless, in the evening classes, the teacher continues to try to stimulate his learners: first, simply by offering a regular course at fixed times, but also by being friendly with them, by organizing activities which they enjoy, and so on. In self-directed group learning, the teacher may also stimulate learners' motivation by means of the materials and exercises which he suggests, but motivation comes more from the group itself. In the autonomous learning scheme, the teacher's role in stimulating external motivation is reduced to a minimum, since it is up to the learners to contact their helper when they need him: there is no longer anyone physically present to make them work, so if they are to continue at all they need a high degree of internal motivation. It is here that the teacher can help prepare the learner psychologically, by showing him that a learning programme has to be constructed and that this is an activity in which he, the learner, has a crucial role to play.

A further psychological factor is related to the fact that a teaching/learning situation is one where individuals establish relationships with one another. The effects of these contacts as far as learning is concerned may be either positive or negative. In those structures where a teacher is present, every participant either has or would like to have some sort of privileged relationship with him. If the impression the teacher makes on the learner is not a good one, however, instead of stimulating learning he actually becomes an obstacle to it. If an evening class group does not like its teacher, it will learn less or even nothing at all. In the autonomous learning scheme, on the other hand, if the learner and the helper do not get on particularly well, it does not really matter since clashes of personality have less direct influence on the learning programme: the work and acquisition is done far away from the helper, while in a traditional group the learner is more or less condemned to learn in the teacher's presence.

Similarly, an individual learner's motivation may be either stimulated or inhibited by the other members of the group. Some learners refuse to join the autonomous learning scheme because they like the company of other people. Some like to study without having to follow along with others or to talk with them. To satisfy these different requirements, the institution has to make different learning systems available.

b) SUPPORT

Observation of almost any kind of learning session will show that a good part of the teacher's time is taken up with 'supporting' the learner — congratulating him on his performance or his progress, for example. Learners tend to be rather sensitive at such times for two main reasons: the first is the inequality which exists between the one who knows and the one who doesn't know. The second reason is that the learner is reorganizing his cognitive system and it is known that during such periods the assimilation of new elements can have an upsetting effect on the individual; he even seems to lose part of the knowledge he had previously acquired, and this phenomenon of regression is often accompanied by periods of depression. The other members of the group may increase or decrease the individual's degree of discouragement. The learner may find his own performance inadequate when compared to other members of the group, or he may find that they are not getting along any faster than he is, a discovery which encourages him. In any case, the teacher is continually trying to upgrade learners' opinions of themselves by complimenting them on their performances and so on.

We have not yet been able to identify who provides support in self-directed learning groups.

In the autonomous learning scheme, as our recordings of the interviews between learners and helpers clearly show, this was one of the helpers' most frequent tasks. The helper does not automatically praise the learner's performance, but when the learner's self-assessment is a negative one, he tries to reassure him by stressing the positive aspects. He does this not by saying 'What you are doing is fine', but by getting the learner to compare his present state with what he was like earlier, as well as by helping him find ways of altering his programme so that he feels he is making progress.

c) ORGANIZING A GROUP

Another of the teacher's roles, and a preponderant one, is that he is the leader of the group: he is the one who is responsible for its cohesion, the one who sees to it that everyone is at their ease, who smoothes over the differences between the members, who sees that the course is properly organized and who distributes speaking turns.

The *Troisième Age* groups usually choose a leader, sometimes several, who take it in turn.

In the autonomous learning scheme the task of leader also occurs, but in a slightly different form, during the interviews between learner and helper. Very often, it is the helper who plays the role of leader, organizing the interview by introducing the different topics for discussion and changing from one topic to another. The recordings of these conversations are important to us because they bring out the learner's attitudes to the teacher as well as enabling us to study their respective roles in the conversation. We have observed that these roles vary from interview to interview and even within the same interview. At times the learners seem to take the initiative, and if in fact this is the case it seems reasonable to hypothesize that they can take the initiative in their learning programme.

This leads to the conclusion that the role of leader is not necessarily attached to the teacher, and that any learner can play this role, provided the teacher gives him a chance.

Conclusion

Our purpose in listing the tasks which are necessary in any learning programme was to show that these tasks are not obligatorily and exclusively the province of either the teacher or the learner in their mutual interactions. It can be seen that the tasks which were traditionally carried out by the teacher can just as well be done by the learner. The teacher is no longer the one who does things, but the one who helps other people to do them. (This is why at the C.R.A.P.E.L. we use the term 'helpers' for the people who work with the autonomous learners.)

These two types of responsibility — doing and helping to do — are not mutually exclusive. They are the two poles of a range of possibilities, possibilities which determine a variety of teaching/learning systems. What is important, in our view, is the fact that this analysis allows both teacher and learner to become aware of just what sort of learner and teacher they are and of their pedagogical personality, and to decide just what sort of system suits them best and what roles they are willing to undertake within that system.

13 Aspects of autonomous learning

This section is a synthesis of the following four papers, all of which originally appeared in *Mélanges Pédagogiques*:

'Learning oral expression autonomously', D. Abé, C. Henner–Stanchina and O. Régent.
'Evaluation in an autonomous learning scheme', C. Henner–Stanchina and H. Holec.
'Taking learners' needs into account in self-directed learning', H. Holec.
'An experiment in self-directed group learning', P. Riley and M. Sicre.

Learning oral expression autonomously

As part of our work in setting up an autonomous learning scheme we have tried to develop materials which aim specifically at the acquisition of oral expression and which will allow learners:

1. To learn to communicate satisfactorily in the types of communicative situations in which they are going to find themselves;
2. To learn to learn, that is, to manage their own learning process in such a way as to be able to maintain and improve their level without having perpetual need of a teacher or a course.

To be able to achieve these aims, learners have to learn how to analyse their own communicative needs. This problem will be dealt with in more detail on pp. 263–75. For the moment, we will limit ourselves to a few, basic indications of what 'analysing their own communicative needs' means in functional terms. It means, firstly, being able to identify the situations with which learners will be confronted, such as meeting a visitor at the station, chairing a discussion, taking a colleague round one's laboratory, etc. It also means being able to identify the communicative acts which learners will have to perform in such situations. For example, someone meeting a visitor at the station will have to check their identity, introduce himself, engage in a certain amount of phatic communication, invite the visitor to follow him, etc. Someone who has to chair a meeting, on the other hand, has to be able to hand over the floor, interrupt, etc. Lastly, it means being able to define these communicative acts in terms of relevant parameters. These would include such considerations as the relationships holding between the interactants (hierarchical, affective, etc.), the psychological tenor (friendly, neutral, aggressive, etc.) and the situationally appropriate modalization (one does not apologize for being a quarter of an hour late in the same way as one apologizes for being two hours late). This analysis will enable the learner to determine those verbal and non-verbal elements which he needs to master.

A second important consequence of the two basic objectives is that the learning materials must be constructed in such a way as to provide the learner with a training in methodology. Ideally, the use of the materials should in itself lead to the acquisition of procedures and categories which enable the learner to go beyond the necessarily narrow limits of the materials.

For these reasons, the material should not try to deal with all the possible situations of all potential learners (indeed, this would be going against the whole idea of autonomy); but it should be presented in a way which is accessible and useful to learners, especially as regards the categories of analysis which are used, even if they are not completely satisfactory from the purely linguistic or sociolinguistic points of view.

It is with these considerations in mind that we are developing at the C.R.A.P.E.L. a series of modules for communicative oral expression.

Description of the modules

First, there is a *general introduction*, valid for all the modules, which contains information about their contents and advice on how to use them. The information given concerns the meaning of the symbols +, 0 and – as they are used in the classifications of the various realizations of acts which are listed. They represent an extremely generalized attempt to give the learner some indication of register: + indicates 'formal', 0 indicates 'generally acceptable, neutral' and − indicates 'informal' or 'colloquial' (these points are taken for discussion and detailed exemplification in each module with reference to a specific function).

As regards their use, the learner is told that the modules represent a range of possibilities from which he has to choose and some of the possible activities are described.

The module itself is presented in the following way: first, there is the title, for example 'Comment demander un service à quelqu'un;

comment accepter ou refuser' ('How to make a request; how to agree or refuse'). This is followed by the sequence of all the acts which are characteristic of the situation and in which the act mentioned in the title occurs:

Greeting	Preparation	Request for help	Agreement or refusal and explanation	Thanks

This sequence is followed by a series of examples *in French* which help the learner not only to grasp the meanings of the terms used to label the communicative acts, but also to gauge intuitively the correct values of the symbols +, 0 and – for the acts in question. Next, there are a number of expressions in English exemplifying some of the realizations of the different acts, accompanied by the appropriate symbols.

Finally, there is a series of situationally contextualized examples: these consist either of extracts from authentic recordings or, where this is not possible, from semi-authentic documents (improvised recordings made by native speakers who have been given a description of the situation, but no script).

Here is an example of the written component of a module, that is, the text which accompanies the cassette recording.

Comment demander un service à quelqu'un
Comment accepter/refuser

(interpellation)	(preparation)	demande	acceptation/ refus (explication)	remerciements

1. EXEMPLES EN FRANCAIS

Demande:
+ *Excusez-moi, je ne voudrais pas vous déranger, mais pourriez-vous ouvrir la fenêtre s'il vous plaît?* (1)
+ *Pardon, Monsieur. Est-ce que vous auriez du feu, s'il vous plaît?*
O *Est-ce que je peux vous demander d'ouvrir la fenêtre s'il vous plaît?*
O *Vous n'auriez pas du feu s'il vous plaît?*
– *Tu peux me donner du feu?*
– *Passe-moi du feu s'il te plaît.* (2)

à la demande: *Est-ce que ça t'ennuierait beaucoup de me prêter ta voiture demain soir, car il faut absolument que j'aille . . . (1)*

Réponse:
acceptation: *D'accord. A quelle heure?*
peu enthousiaste: *Attends que je réfléchisse. Demain soir? Apparemment, ça devrait aller. Oui, je ne pense pas en avoir besoin.* (3)
refus: *Ça m'ennuie demain soir, parce que . . . (4)*

1 Les formules utilisées sont de plus en plus longues lorsque l'on veut être de plus en plus poli, ou si la demande est importante, ou si on ne connaît pas la personne, etc . . .
2 Dans les formules familières, les demandes sont pratiquement des ordres (un ami peut refuser d'exécuter un ordre, alors qu'une personne inconnue ne le peut pas).
3 Les acceptations peu enthousiastes sont précédées de périodes de réflexion.
4 Les refus sont très souvent accompagnés d'explications.

II. TABLEAU

	DEMANDE (QUELQUE CHOSE)	ACCEPTATION
–	Oh dear, I haven't got *any matches*.	I have, Here you are.
+	Do you think you could give me *a glass of water*?	Certainly.
–	You haven't got *a light*, have you?	Yes, here you are.
0	Have you got *a light*, please?	Yes, certainly.
		REFUS
–	Oh dear, I haven't got *any matches* on me.	I'm afraid I haven't either.
0	You wouldn't have *a light*, would you?	I'm afraid not.
+	Do you think I could possibly have *a glass of water*?	I'm sorry. *I don't think it's possible at the moment.*
–	You haven't got *a light*, have you?	Sorry, I'm afraid I haven't.
O	Have you got *a light*, please?	No, I don't think I have actually.
	DEMANDE (SERVICE)	ACCEPTATION
O	Can you *open the window* please?	Oh, certainly.

O	Do you think you could *open the window* please?	Sure.
+	Would it be possible for you to *open the window*?	Er . . . Yes certainly.
+	Would you be so kind as to *open the window* for me please?	I suppose I could.
O	Do you think you could *lend me your car*?	Erm . . . I suppose so.
+	I wonder if you could possibly *lend me your car*?	If you like.
O	Do you think I could *borrow your car to-morrow*?	Erm . . . I suppose so.
		REFUS
O	Can you *open the window*, please?	Er . . . I'd rather not. *It's . . . it's a little chilly.*
O	Could you *open the window*, please?	I'm not sure, you see . . . *it's a bit er . . . blocked at the moment.*
+	Would you be so kind as to *open the window*?	Well . . . I'd like to but *I don't think I can actually.*
O	Do you think you could *lend me your car*?	Awfully sorry, *using it.*
+	I wonder if you could possibly *lend me your car.*	Oh, sorry, I can't, you see . . . *It's not insured for another driver besides me.*
+	I wonder if you could possibly *lend me your car.*	Well . . . *it doesn't actually belong to me.*
O	Do you think I could *borrow your car*?	Sorry, erm . . . *I don't really like lending it.*

REMARQUES:

1. Pour qu'une demande de service ne paraisse pas trop abrupte à l'interlocuteur, on la fait souvent précéder d'une hésitation: *er . . . erm . . .* Vous trouverez de nombreux exemples de cela dans les exemples en situation.
2. Une demande pourra aussi être précédée d'une interpellation ou d'une excuse: *Excuse me, sorry to bother you, but . . .* On pourra 'préparer' l'interlocuteur à l'aide de:
   – Could you do me a favour?
   0 I've got a bit of a problem . . .

III. EXEMPLES EN SITUATION

1. Dans le train, 2 personnes qui ne se connaissent pas.
   HE: Excuse me, have you got a light?
   SHE: Oh yes, hang on a minute — I'll look in my handbag.

There we are.
HE: Thanks.

2. Deux amis sont en train de bavarder.
HE: Have you heard about this play that's on tomorrow night?
SHE: Oh no, what is it?
HE: It's, er, *'Le Misanthrope'* by Molière. It's, er, going to be very interesting. It's, er, the Académie Françaíse Theatre Company that's going to do it.
SHE: Oh really — that seems very interesting. I studied that play at school.
HE: Yeah, I'm just off to get some tickets now, so I can't really stay to talk to you, but, er . . .
SHE: Oh, do you think you could get me one too?
HE: Yes, certainly, er . . .
SHE: We could go together, could we?
HE: Yes, er . . .
SHE: That would be marvellous.
HE: I'll pick you up about 7 o'clock, O.K.?
SHE: Oh, thank you very much, fine.
HE: Bye!

3. On frappe à la porte d'une maison en pleine campagne.
HE: Hallo.
SHE: Um, I'm terribly sorry to interrupt you — er, I mean, you know, we're in the countryside and, erm, could I possibly use your toilet?
HE: Er, oh, erm . . .
SHE: You see, because we're out here on a picnic, and, I mean we're miles from anywhere and I — please could I use your toilet?
HE: Oh, well, I suppose if it's that desperate yes, certainly you can.
SHE: Yes it is actually — where is it?
HE: It's down the garden at the end, you'll see a little brick hut. If you go in there that's the toilet.
SHE: Oh yes, er, thank you very much.
HE: O.K. Bye.
SHE: Bye.

4. Chez le cordonnier.
SHE: Do you think it'll be possible to have these mended? I'm afraid they are rather worn down.
HE: Er yes, erm I could repair the heel for you. I shouldn't think that would be any problem. Would next Tuesday be all right?
SHE: Erm, could you possibly make it by Monday, do you think? You see I'm going away on Wednesday and to come in Tuesday might be a bit difficult.
HE: Yeah, everybody's going away on holiday — yeah O.K. I'll say Monday, I'll get them ready for Monday morning for

you.

SHE: Oh, thank you very much. Oh, could you give me any idea of the price?

HE: I should think probably about two pounds fifty.

SHE: Two pounds fifty?

HE: Well, yes, because they have got a lot of work to be done on them.

SHE: Yes I see. Is that heeling or heeling and and soling?

HE: That's heeling and soling.

SHE: Oh. Oh, that's all right then, yes, that's fine.

5. Quelqu'un entre dans un compartiment de chemin de fer.

M: Oh, excuse me, is this seat free?

A: Yes, it is — look Joe, do you think you could give that lady a hand with her luggage?

J: Yes, would you, would you like a hand? It's no bother.

M: That's very kind of you. Thank you very much.

J: It's a pleasure.

Discussion

It is perhaps worthwhile emphasizing some of the characteristics of these modules.

1. The communicative acts are not dealt with separately, but as elements in a sequence, the minimum sequence being the 'exchange' (or 'return'; see p. 51).

2. Since the modules are based on the analysis of authentic interactions, the sequences of communicative acts they contain are not based on the authors' intuition but on sequences which have actually been observed in the corpus.

3. To avoid the problem of the learner's artificially separating the realization of an act from its communicative environment, the realizations are always contextualized.

4. The module calls on the learner's knowledge of the world and of communication in his mother tongue. In fact, it is by observing linguistic behaviour in the mother tongue that he learns to define the acts and the sequences of acts which form his learning objectives. However, it should be noted that in those cases where the target language differs from the mother tongue, the differences are mentioned explicitly. For example, in English, the act of 'complimenting' is usually followed by the act of 'thanking', which is not the normal sequence in French. Again, in English, the act of 'greeting' is not usually accompanied by a handshake, whereas in France it is.

5a. The modules should not be thought of as together forming a textbook, nor should the separate modules be regarded as its chapters

or units. Each learner, once he has defined his needs, chooses those modules or parts of modules which correspond to his objectives and to his needs at a given point in his learning programme. So, for example, he chooses not only the communicative acts, but also the particular realizations of those acts which correspond to his needs.
5b. It is left up to the learner to define and choose the actual learning methods and techniques which suit him best. Suggestions as to how this can be done are included in the general Introduction and the helper is available to advise him and to help him discover, use and evaluate his different techniques.
5c. The evaluation of the learning programme takes the form of self-assessment (see pp. 257–8) and it is therefore the learner himself who carries it out, by comparing his performance with the recordings, in discussions with the helper and in real situations with native speakers who are not teachers.

Conclusion

It is perhaps worth mentioning that these modules are not the only materials for oral expression available to our autonomous learners. There are also more traditional materials, such as textbooks and courses of different kinds, and all the authentic documents they could want.

Finally, it may well seem that there is a contradiction between the functional approach, implying as it does interpersonal communication, and autonomous learning, which is usually done alone. But it is essential to distinguish between learning to communicate and real communication. The modules obviously do not place the learner in real communication situations, but they do provide him with the tools to prepare himself for the day when he will need to speak English in such situations. They form part of the learning process, along with other materials and other activities. For the moment they are experimental in nature and only time and experience will allow us to judge whether or not they really are suitable instruments for learning.

Evaluation in an autonomous learning scheme

Our discussion of evaluation within the autonomous learning scheme will focus on the following three questions:

What are the functions of evaluation in the autonomous learning scheme?
What is the nature of evaluation in this scheme?
How is evaluation achieved in the autonomous learning scheme?

1. *Functions of evaluation in the autonomous learning scheme*

In the autonomous learning scheme, evaluation constitutes an integral part of the learning process, on a par with the definition of objectives, of content, etc. This means that it is not a final, extra feature of the scheme, external to the learning process, whose only purpose is to provide quantitative assessment of the learning that has been done, for the benefit of the teaching institution or any other body in the broader social environment where learning takes place. It is, on the contrary, part of the learning process without which no learning can be achieved.

If learning is analysed as a series of successive learning acts, and these in turn are broken down into the five steps below which were defined by Diezeide (1971), then it is clear that evaluation is indeed one of the constituent steps of the learning act:

1. information: the seeking and gathering of data to be learned;
2. exploitation: the organization and elaboration of gathered data;
3. assimilation;
4. transfer: the application of the knowledge acquired;
5. control.

The function of evaluation is, within each act, to provide feedback information (on assimilation and transfer) necessary for the satisfactory completion of the act; at the end of each act, to provide input information for steps 1 and 2 (information and exploitation) of the following act.

More specifically, from the learner's standpoint, evaluation serves the double purpose of assessing performance as a language learner (assessment of learning competence) and assessing performance as a language user (assessment of communicative competence).

As a language learner one needs feedback and input information on learning strategies, learning techniques, etc.; in other words, on the suitability and effectiveness of learning in relation to personal learning criteria and personal goals. This information will increase the learner's awareness of how he learns and help him make decisions about the continuation or modification of his learning activities.

As a language user, one needs feedback and input information on what is being learned, not only in terms of the nature of the acquisition (vocabulary, grammar, communicative functions, cultural dimension, etc.) but also in terms of the adequacy of this acquisition in relation to personal communicative and cultural needs.

This analytical and essential distinction between assessment of performance as a language learner and as a language user does not imply that there is no relationship between the two. In fact, evaluation of communicative competence will always be a basis for evaluation of learning effectiveness, in that learning, as a means to an end, cannot be evaluated independently from that desired end.

2. *The nature of evaluation in the autonomous learning scheme*

As an integral part of the learning process, evaluation in the autonomous learning scheme is not of a comparative nature. It is not norm-referenced, or based on a comparison between personal achievement and externally defined norms, whether these norms are defined in terms of the subject-matter, or with reference to a syllabus. Neither is it other-referenced, or based on a comparison between personal achievement and other learners' levels of achievement. It is, rather, a form of self-assessment in which the learners simultaneously create and undergo the evaluation procedure, judging their achievement in relation to themselves, against their own personal criteria, in accordance with their own objectives and learning expectations. This type of evaluation is consequently characterized by variations in aspects such as content, threshold, form and timing, all of which must be redefined for and by each learner.

Evaluation in the autonomous learning scheme is of a different nature depending on whether it applies to performance as a language learner or as a language user.

As has already been mentioned, evaluation of language-learner performance is evaluation by the learners of the suitability and effectiveness of the learning strategies and techniques they have developed. In a teaching-centred approach there is to some extent evaluation of the suitability of strategies and techniques, but this is done by the teacher on the basis of majority rule within a group of learners (in the best cases) and on the sole basis of the teacher's specifications (in the worst). The criteria for judging these strategies and techniques are highly personal (as personal as the definitions of the notions of 'suitability' and 'effectiveness' themselves), so that a particular learner may choose to take any one of the following criteria (and this list is by no means exhaustive) into account when judging the suitability of learning strategies and techniques.

1. *Compatibility between learning strategies and techniques and personal constraints*, such as time and space available (certain strategies and techniques might be too time-consuming or impose a study

schedule incompatible with professional obligations); material possibilities (relation between technical facilities available and technical facilities required, cost-effectiveness of strategies chosen); intellectual capacities (relation between personal memory capacity and demands made on memory by a particular technique, for example); or physical capacities, etc.

2. *Correspondence between learning strategies and techniques and personal expectations*, such as the reward derived from learning activities (in terms of pleasure, ego-satisfaction, status, etc.)
3. *Correspondence between learning strategies and techniques and personal optimal rate of learning*
4. *Correspondence between learning strategies and techniques and work load tolerance*
5. *Relation between learning strategies and techniques and optimal degree of difficulty tolerated* (some learners will prefer the challenging tasks set by some techniques, others will not, etc.).

In the case, for example, of a learner who has chosen transcribing as a technique geared to improve his listening comprehension skill that learner will determine the suitability of this technique by deciding:

1. whether transcribing slows him down too much, taking up too much of the limited time he can devote to learning, and making for a frustratingly slow rate of learning;
2. to what extent transcribing is compatible with the physical setting in which he does his learning: if, for professional reasons, he spends a great deal of time driving, and this is the only possible time he can set aside for learning, then obviously transcribing is neither realistic nor suitable as a solution;
3. whether the work involved in transcribing (stopping, rewinding, replaying, etc.) is pleasant, acceptable or unbearable to him;
4. whether it involves him in a task too difficult for his level of learning.

As for evaluation of learning effectiveness, this, as previously stated, is based on an assessment of the nature and adequacy of what is being learned, or on performance as a language user. Here again, the evaluation criteria will be individually determined and will correspond to a personal definition of successful performance, both in terms of the elements constituting successful performance and the achievement level aspired to. Some elements of performance that might be considered essential by a particular learner (thereby having a direct impact on the learning process) are:

1. (traditional) phonetic, grammatical correctness;

2. lexical richness and/or precision;
3. stylistic variability (allowing for adaptation of performance to momentary mood, temper, degree of formality, etc.);
4. fluency;
5. intelligibility;
6. communicative efficacy of combined verbal and non-verbal behaviours;
7. individuality of performance in relation to learners' personality traits (getting humour across, etc.);
8. existence and operation of compensation strategies (how to compensate verbally and non-verbally for the fact that one is not a native user of the language, etc.)

One or any combination of these and other aspects will be selected by a learner as important components of performance (a different aspect, or aspects, may be retained at different stages of the learning process. The criterion 'being oneself while communicating' can obviously only be applied after a certain amount of learning has taken place). Having selected from among these elements, a learner will then apply his personal criteria of satisfactory achievement level, the scale ranging from simply getting along in the language to perfection. For example, a learner might value being himself when communicating in the foreign language, thus relegating phonetic/grammatical correctness to a lower position, while stressing the importance of individuality and stylistic variability in his performance. His subjective satisfactory level of achievement would then be defined in terms of sufficient/insufficient individuality and variability. Subjectivity plays an important role in this type of evaluation. Although ways may be found of 'guiding' or 'enlightening' this subjectivity, it will never lend itself to any degree of measured control. This is subjectively regarded as perfectly legitimate in a learning-centred approach!

Evaluation in the autonomous learning scheme is, then, entirely different from traditional external evaluation. As the description provided here reveals, it does not lend itself to any form of standardization. No formal test could possibly take all the criteria described into account (if only because any attempt to define them precisely would itself pose insuperable problems) or allow for the variable achievement levels involved. This raises a number of questions (some of them will be dealt with in the conclusion of this paper), among which the most immediately relevant to the preoccupations of any language teacher ('helper' in the autonomous learning scheme) is: 'how can such evaluation be achieved?'

3. *The realization of evaluation in the autonomous learning scheme*

As a preliminary consideration, attention must be drawn to the fact that learning how to learn is a gradual process and not a prerequisite for participation in an autonomous learning scheme. The learners engaged in this scheme are, thus, still in the process of learning how to learn, so that they are in fact confronted simultaneously with the task of learning how to carry out evaluation of their performance as language learners and language users, and the task of actually evaluating this performance. These two tasks are very closely associated in the learning process. Since the nature of evaluation in the autonomous learning scheme is such that learners are encouraged to assess their performance with their own personal tools (personal criteria and personal expectations as to desired level of achievement), it follows that learners must be aware of their personal categories. Another aspect, then, of the self-assessment task is to discover and define those categories one will want to use in evaluating performance. This will usually conflict with the learners' previous experience with evaluation which instilled the notion of externally-referenced norms, and consequently, may be a relatively slow process. Once the categories are defined, however, learners are in a much better position to define their intermediate and final learning objectives.

Basically, evaluation requires that there should be performances to assess. Moreover, and this cannot be overemphasized, these performances should be as authentic as possible, to ensure that what will be assessed will be genuine learning and communicative behaviour, reflecting genuine learner competence (one of the major drawbacks of external evaluation based on standardized tests is that for various reasons — test design constraints among them — the performance generally elicited from the learner is artificial and its validity in relation to the learners' competence cannot be easily ascertained). These performances are then analysed *by the learners* in terms of their individually defined categories.

In the autonomous learning scheme, these two operations are carried out as follows:

1. For the assessment of language learning, no special performance need be elicited from the learners, for it is simply their day-by-day behaviour that will constitute the performance to be analysed. Learners may assess the suitability of the learning strategies and techniques they developed whenever they feel the need to do so; at variable intervals, alone, or during a helper–learner session, with the

helper assisting as listener (making it easier for learners to objectify their situations) and as counsellor (passing on information gathered from other learners or from experience with language learning). Learners may also request peer-matching sessions, during which they can discuss their learning problems with other learners. This assessment — along with that of learning effectiveness, which can be inferred from the evaluation of what has been learned (if communicative competence has been acquired, then the strategies and techniques are deemed effective) — serves as a basis for further decisions regarding the continuing learning procedure.

2. In order to evaluate the actual results of learning, that is, the acquisition of communicative competence, learners will need to be placed in authentic communicative situations in which their competence at that particular time will be revealed. This can be done through:

(a) *direct contact with authentic materials*: video or sound recordings, if the learners want to check their listening comprehension; samples of the written texts they have to use in real life, for checking reading comprehension.

(b) *direct contact with native speakers*, which learners initiate and organize as to time, location, type of exchange, depending on the aspects of performance they wish to test. These contacts might range, for example, from a short session with a native speaker acting as listener merely to test the intelligibility of the learner's reading aloud of a paper to be presented at a conference, to a longer session of informal conversation over dinner, etc.

(c) *simulations*: reproducing as closely as possible the real life communication situation for which learners are preparing; for example, a spontaneous oral commentary on a technical slide presentation before a non-French-speaking audience.

Learners analyse these performances using recordings, if any have been made, or from memory, in terms of the categories they have selected for each particular performance (they are advised not to check too many categories at a time), and may write out statements about the quality of the results obtained.These statements would be of a descriptive type, very much like those contained in Mats Oskarsson's forms for self-assessment of language functions and exponents (Oskarsson 1980).

It must be emphasized again that no evaluation of this type can be undertaken by the learners until they have defined the analytic tools. Obviously, some of the criteria we have described (such as grammatical correctness or the correspondence between learning strategies and techniques and personal constraints) will be discovered immediately. Other criteria, though, (such as adequate stylistic variability or satisfactory use of compensation strategies) will take more time for the learner to internalize and put into operation. They entail a certain amount of reflection on communication in the mother tongue, as they are not part of the individual's learning experience.

Conclusions

Having provided a description of the internal type of evaluation that is characteristic of our autonomous learning scheme, we hope that it will in turn shed light on the very nature of the strategy itself and on the fundamental differences between our approach to learning and the various approaches to teaching being developed elsewhere. Any scheme in which evaluation remains externally referenced (whether it be in the form of self-administered normal tests or other forms which, in any case, are not in the hands of the learners) cannot claim to be a true learning scheme.

The internal type of evaluation proposed here raises a number of problems that still have not been stated clearly, let alone resolved. These range from simply spreading information about this alternative to traditional testing to potential learners, teachers, employers, and all other parties concerned with language learning, to actually implementing this type of evaluation in different contexts.

On the pedagogical scene, the more progressive circles of educational planning are presently focusing their attention on the possible choice between external and internal evaluation, and on the relationship that could eventually hold between these two types of evaluation. Oskarsson, 1980, contains a very good description of their work and a clear statement of the arguments involved. Proponents of external evaluation through formal testing argue that this type of assessment is indispensable, as it is the only way to satisfy the societal need for certification. To this, proponents of internal evaluation reply that, as far as adult education is concerned, this need for certification has been grossly over-estimated, since 'many if not most adults who participate in courses do so because they want to satisfy their desire to learn something, not because they need, or attach great value to, a certain formal attestation of their performance' (Oskarsson 1980, p. 3).

An additional argument in favour of internal evaluation might also be that professional selection, among others, is still very largely conditioned by the status quo in the field; if sufficient information were given to selection bodies on progress made in communication analysis, needs analysis and evaluation techniques, they might very well discover that the information obtained from formal tests is insufficient, if not altogether irrelevant for their purposes. They would, for instance, discover that among the criteria used for judging the competence of, say, a would-be public relations executive, the non-standardizable criterion of 'being oneself in communication' occupies a prominent place linked to the importance of contact qualities in the specification of such a job. All this militates strongly in favour of further research into job-communication specification.

On the other hand, if both types of evaluation are maintained, the problem of possible contradictions will have to be examined: what, for instance, would the psychological reaction of a learner be if his own evaluation turned out to be radically different from the formal external evaluation? Further experimental research is certainly necessary here. Would a reasonable temporary decision be to restrict external evaluation to those cases where certification is necessary?

In the autonomous learning scheme, internal evaluation is one of the fundamental pedagogical requisites. Further research is presently under way, aiming at a better knowledge of the different criteria used intuitively by learners to describe their performance (this will also reveal some of the learners' representations of learning/knowing a language) and at the discovery of more varied performance-elicitation techniques.

Taking learners' needs into account in self-directed learning

Since the beginning of the 1960s, there has been a considerable increase in the variety of pedagogical approaches being practised, partly due to the greater numbers and types of learners involved and partly to the progress which has been made in such areas as the description of the functions of language, the psychology of learning and teaching methodology. Within the general pattern of diversification, three main tendencies can be discerned.

Firstly, there are those approaches which try to increase the efficiency of the learning process by *improving teaching methods*. This usually means updating objectives and syllabuses in the light of the latest views on how language 'really' works: the oral skills are given greater importance, ideas concerning lexical and grammatical frequencies are taken into account, different registers and levels of language are distinguished and more recently there has been the shift in aim towards the acquisition of communicative competence. We can also include under this heading the introduction of teaching/learning techniques regarded as being more suited to these objectives: structural drills, the use of visual materials, communicative activities such as role-playing and so on.

In the second kind of approach, an attempt is made *to adapt the teaching to the type of learning public.* In this case, the increase in efficiency is no longer seen as depending on some quality inherent in the teaching, but rather as resulting from the degree to which the learners' characteristics are taken into account. The emphasis is no longer placed on the knowledge to be acquired as such, nor on the specific techniques by which it is to be acquired, but on the relationships between knowledge, techniques and learner. This results in a wide range of objectives and syllabuses (Languages for Special Purposes, for example) and in the adoption of teaching strategies, such as distance teaching, which free the learner from certain practical constraints.

The third type of approach — much more recent and, consequently, much less widespread — is an attempt to improve learning both qualitatively and quantitatively by suitably *training the learner* to learn. This type of approach calls into question the usual didactic methods which are based on the idea that there is a direct causal relationship between teaching and learning, and on the realization of just how complex pedagogical situations can be in terms of different and changing needs, different learning conditions and different learning processes. This approach concentrates on 'improving' the learner, whose importance in the learning process serves to underline the very obvious fact that we only do well what we know how to do. To teach the learner to learn, that is to enable him to carry out the various steps which make up the learning process, is considered as the best way of ensuring that learning takes place. This 'autonomy' of the learner enables appropriate solutions to be found to the problems of differences in the needs, conditions and processes referred to above, in that, once he has acquired a satisfactory competence in learning, the learner, individually *or as a member of a group* (autonomy is not synonymous with solitude), can construct his own programme by intervening directly at the various stages, thus narrowing considerably or even closing completely the gap between what he wants to learn and what he does in fact learn.

It is this third approach we have been trying out experimentally at the C.R.A.P.E.L. since 1973 (though fortunately we are no longer the only ones to be doing so) and in this article we will be considering 'meeting the students' needs' from the point of view of 'autonomous' or self-directed learning.

Taking needs into account is crucial when objectives are being defined and when evaluation is being carried out and we will look at how this is done in self-directed learning before going on to consider the wider question of the training a learner needs to be able to perform these operations. Certain parts of the discussion which follows are taken from a report prepared by the author for the Council of Europe (Holec 1980).

Defining learning objectives

In any approach to teaching, whether it is content-based or learner-centred, the definition of objectives is based on the following principles:

1. There is a core of knowledge which is essential for all learners, which has been identified beforehand by linguistic analysis and which is different from the specific knowledge of the language which a given group of learners might wish to acquire. This central core may be regarded as just the barest fundamentals of the language or as the complete range of oral and written competence which is possessed by the average (and usually 'educated') native speaker.
2. The minimal level of competence is defined on the basis of criteria which are independent of the learner, usually taking the native speaker as a model. The teaching does not need to take into account whether the learner himself is a perfectionist or whether he is easy-going.
3. The whole point of defining needs is to set up a teaching system and to develop teaching materials which are efficient or cost-effective: for this reason, the definition covers as wide a range of learners as is possible, since it is based on those needs which are common to all learners or which are shared by the greatest numbers. Again, the frequency with which the needs are re-assessed also depends on this idea of overall efficiency. In other words, instead of defining the fluctuating needs of an individual learner, the needs of a stable, idealized learner are described, the knowledge to be acquired forming a monolithic and compulsory chunk and the time required for it being fixed from the very beginning.

In self-directed learning, none of these principles applies. Instead:

1. The knowledge to be acquired is defined by the learner (or group of learners) on the basis of his (or their) communicative aims alone, without reference to the complete range of competence of a native speaker or to the needs of other learners. These aims consist of the communicative behaviours which the learner believes he will need to master in order to perform successfully in the situations in which he will find himself; by describing them in terms of interactive and illocutionary acts, topics and verbal and non-verbal realizations, the learner is able to distinguish between those items which are essential to him and those which are of no use. It is no longer a matter of 'common core', nor of specialized areas of knowledge; all that remains, at most, is a hierarchy based on urgency, or frequency, or interest, or learning conditions. Moreover, this hierarchy will vary from one learner to another and for the same learner at different times.

   To take a concrete example: to be able to ask your way — that is, to be able to construct and use utterances such as:

   Excuse me/Sorry but . .
   Which way is it to the station, please?
   Could you tell me how to get to the station?
   Thank you.
   Thanks a lot, I'm sure I'll find it now.

   will not be an aim common to all learners: those who want to read specialized articles in their field, to listen to the news on the radio, to attend congresses in their native country — to take just a few examples — will not include this kind of request for information among their objectives.

2. In the same way, in self-directed learning it is the learner himself who decides what level of competence he wishes to reach. One of the criteria which everyone will apply is that of 'communicability'; (coined by analogy with 'intelligibility', which unfortunately usually only refers to the phonetic quality of verbal messages). This level will depend closely on who is communicating with whom, what type of communication is involved (face-to-face, letter, telephone) and the purpose of the communication. The learner does not define his needs *a priori*, but works them out empirically as he goes along, and once he has reached the minimal level of 'communicability' he is free to decide what other criteria to take into account (*cf.* the section on evaluation below) and the performance of the native speaker will not necessarily be one of them.

3. As was mentioned above, it is difficult to integrate anything but the

most generalized set of objectives into a teaching system, with its structures (classes with teachers, timetables, rooms, syllabuses, etc.) and its teaching materials (identical textbooks for all learners). But this problem is considerably reduced if each learner (or group) is free to pursue his (or its) own objectives independently without committing other learners or groups to the same objectives. And the wide variety of objectives will result in a corresponding flexibility in terms of times, places, syllabuses, methodologies and learning techniques, simply because self-directed learning allows a multiplicity of approaches which is prevented by the very nature of other pedagogical strategies. In the same way, every learner can base his objectives on his own needs, without having to worry about whether they are the same or not as those of other learners; moreover, he can reassess them whenever he likes during the learning process, since any change of objective will only effect his own learning and not that of the other learners. Obviously, this flexibility is reduced in the case of a group, but the effect will only be slight if the group-work is combined with individual work or work in sub-groups.

We can say, then, that in self-directed learning the definition of objectives can be made to correspond very closely to the learner's needs (both linguistic and in terms of the learning process itself) in that the learner's personal characteristics can be taken into account at any time. The ways in which the defining is done allow the learner a number of possibilities:

1. He can, for example, acquire the knowledge and skills which he chooses (which means that he can take into account not only his needs, but also some of the practical limitations, as regards time and materials, which oblige him to give priority to certain aspects of his work). In this way it is possible for him to construct an idiolect (or rather its communicative equivalent) which satisfies his needs at the linguistic level as well as at the level of the psychosocial relationships he may wish to establish with other people (amusing/serious, warm/stand-offish, dominating/shy, etc.) according to his personality and those of his interlocutors.
2. The learner can vary his learning programme at any time (not just at the start) to take into account changes in his needs. Such changes are almost inevitable after a certain time, either because the situation which originally motivated the learner changes (a learner whose motivation is professional may be promoted or moved to a different department, for example, and similarly a change in his social circle may bring a learner whose motivation

is social to revise his needs) or because in the course of his learning the learner realizes that certain objectives are not in fact attainable at a particular level, or that knowledge already acquired reveals the necessity of other or different objectives. Faced with such changes, the learner can modify the course of his learning as soon as he considers it necessary and practicable. As an example, take the case of Mme X, whose original need was to acquire the skills necessary for reading and writing business letters in English: six weeks later, the firm which had promised her a job changed its conditions and required her to be capable of answering telephone calls instead, as the letters could be dealt with by someone who had been taken on in the meantime. Immediately, Mme X changed to the acquisition of English for the telephone and succeeded in the four months which were left in qualifying for the job she was after.

Evaluation

Evaluation (here taken to mean *internal* evaluation, which is to be distinguished from *external* evaluation or *certification* — see Holec 1980) is at least as important as defining objectives in meeting needs.

1. Firstly, evaluation is the operation which determines how far the result *aimed at* corresponds with the result *achieved* and which therefore checks that the objective has been reached.
2. Secondly, evaluation is the operation which determines how far the result *achieved* corresponds with the result which is *necessary* in the circumstances, and which therefore makes it possible to check whether what has been learnt does in fact meet the needs which motivated the learning, that the objective has been correctly defined, and also that the need has been correctly analysed.

For the learner, these two checks are by no means of equal importance; unlike some teachers, the learner never forgets that he is not learning simply for the sake of learning; in the majority of cases, it is the second of these checks which is both the outset and the result of the process of evaluation, the first check being used simply as a tool to carry out the second.

Evaluation implies that there are performances to be judged, critical criteria and levels of reference. How are these to be defined in self-directed learning?

PERFORMANCE

The learner produces performances which are 'relevant' or susceptible to the *first kind of check* in all the different activities in which he participates, whether they involve work on expression or comprehension or even formal grammar. These performances go from drills, including each separate item, to interactions with native speakers or work on authentic documents.

To produce performances which are susceptible to the *second kind of check*, on the other hand, the learner has to take part in real acts of communication, since this is the only way in which the match between results achieved and results aimed at can be confirmed. Examples of the sort of occasion where this is possible include:

1. interaction with native speakers;
2. listening comprehension with authentic recordings;
3. reading documents produced for 'real' readers; for example, letters which will really be posted, abstracts or articles which will be published, and so on.

Tests do not elicit performances which are valid enough (in terms of their authenticity) to be used in this second type of check.

One of the most valuable characteristics of self-directed learning is that it leaves the learner free to judge the importance or relevance of any particular performance for himself. He may, for example, decide not to regard a particular performance as really revealing on the grounds that on that day he was not on his best form, or because he was handicapped by some outside factor, or simply because he did not get on with the person he was speaking to and so did not try as hard as he might otherwise have done.

This freedom to up- or down-grade particular performances, as well as making the evaluation more just, also helps the learner to become aware of aspects of communication which he might otherwise have neglected.

CRITICAL CRITERIA

The most important single characteristic of auto-evaluation (that is, internal evaluation within a self-directed learning programme) is the way in which it integrates the personal dimension. The learner is free to choose, on the basis of his own ideas, what a successful performance will be like and which of all the theoretically possible criteria he will in fact apply on a given occasion; in this particular situation, these are the aspects of his performance which he regards as important. This has two main consequences:

1. Every evaluation of a performance is carried out on the basis of specific criteria or specific combinations of criteria; the same criteria may be used over and over again (but this is not necessarily

the case) and flexibility of evaluation allows the learner to adapt his evaluation to the nature of the communicative task in question and to his own level of achievement. (This also applies to the levels themselves; see below.)

2. Not all learners necessarily use the same criteria, or the same combinations of criteria, nor do they regard the same criteria as equally important, even when evaluating identical performances. For example, when evaluating his performance in reading, one learner may regard speed as the most important criterion, whilst another may put full and detailed comprehension above everything else; this will of course be a reflection of the type of readers they are and of the sort of reading they want to have of this particular document.

The criteria chosen are related firstly to the objectives (this is one of the reasons why it is so important that the learner should carry out both operations; how many times, in traditional teaching, do we come across learners who are completely unable to judge the value of what they have learnt since they do not know what they are aiming at in the first place!). There is no need to labour the point, but it is worth remembering that the learner's personal characteristics are given considerable importance here.

Secondly, the criteria chosen are related to personal judgements concerning a performance which was not included among the objectives, either because it was simply forgotten — *errare humanum est!* — or because there are aspects of the performance in question which it is just impossible to express in terms of learning objectives; an example would be the positive or negative affective tone which a learner might like to be able to give to his participation in an interaction, as is the case when a man wants to let a lady know — without explicitly saying so — that he thinks she is pretty and that he enjoys her company.

Examples of other criteria which might be chosen include:

At the lexical level, the traditional criterion of a rich and accurate vocabulary; but also repair strategies — what to do in case of a gap in vocabulary for example, how to get round the problem or paraphrase it, how to ask for help. Perhaps the 'stylistic' effects brought about by a careful choice of words should also be included here; have I found the right words to say what I mean in an original (funny, precise, etc.) way?

At the phonetic level, the traditional criterion of correctness, tempered with intelligibility.

Overall fluency; stylistic flexibility (the ability to adapt to the prevailing humour, atmosphere, etc.).

LEVELS

The important point to note here is that learners generally operate in terms of satisfactory/unsatisfactory and that the finely graduated scales of traditional teaching are of little interest to them. For the learner, the main thing is to determine whether his performance is psychologically satisfactory or not. This has the following results:

1. The levels of achievement which are chosen vary according to what aspect of performance is being evaluated and are directly related to the relative degree of importance accorded to the aspect in question;
2. These levels vary from one learner to another;
3. These levels vary with time for the same individual; early on, the level of 'phonetic correctness' may be fixed lower than at a later stage because the learner may be less demanding in this respect to start with.

These levels, which take into account the personal characteristics of the learner (such as the development of his knowledge in the domain or the extent to which he is or is not a perfectionist) are not established by chance. In particular, experience shows that learners never accept levels of achievement which are universally unsatisfactory, that is, which are situated below the level of 'communicability'. Obviously this is only true if the real motivation is the acquisition of some form of communicative competence; if the learner has taken up language learning to take his mind off his problems, for example, anything can happen. Moreover, learners' judgements of the various aspects of their performance tend to reflect the judgement of their overall performance, so that if they think that, overall, they are intelligible they tend to judge each separate aspect more favourably.

In a self-directed programme, then, evaluation is carried out in a way which offers the learner the greatest number of possibilities for personalizing his learning programme. At this level of the learning process there is no reason why every single personal characteristic, above all the learner's needs, should not be taken into account. In self-directed learning, therefore, there is every chance that the learner will learn what he needs to learn. There is one obvious condition, however: he needs to be able to learn, that is, he has to be capable of managing his learning programme.

But before tackling the problem of how the learner is to be prepared for self-directed learning, I would like to give an example — unlikely, but completely true — of what self-evaluation of attainment can mean in real life:

M. R, a learner of English at intermediate level, had chosen as his main, indeed almost his only criterion, the ability to amuse people; he wanted to be able to make people laugh in English. He soon realized that if he made mistakes, it often made people laugh. So he absolutely refused to correct his errors, even going as far as deliberately making certain errors (e.g. Gallicisms) which he found to be especially effective from this point of view. This done, he decided that he now knew enough English for his purposes. And who could say he was wrong? (It is true that the wife of the gentleman in question spoke good English and went everywhere with him, dealing with the many other things which he was quite incapable of handling; indeed he had gone to great lengths to encourage her to persist with her own lessons until she reached an advanced level!)

Learner training

The description which has been given above of the ways in which objectives are defined and evaluated in self-directed learning is at one and the same time a description of the *learning needs* which people involved in such a programme are likely to have, since, for the vast majority, undertaking these tasks is no simple matter.

AIMS OF THE TRAINING

The training which learners should receive (and which does not necessarily take the form of teaching) should prepare them to direct the course of their own learning, that is, it should take them from their states of varying degrees of dependence to the state of the greatest degree of independence or autonomy which is possible in a given set of circumstances. If this is to occur, experience shows that there has to be at the very least a change of psychological attitude towards what learning is, as well as the acquisition of a number of relevant learning techniques.

At the psychological level, the aim of the training is mainly a gradual deconditioning of the learner. This is because the adult who begins a learning programme of some kind brings all his previous experience with him: he is never a pure beginner. He has very clear ideas of what a language is, of what learning a language means, of the respective roles of teacher and learner, of the materials which are necessary, and so on. These ideas are based on his previous educational experience and also on what he might have seen or learnt elsewhere — from colleagues who have gone to evening classes, advertisements for schools of languages, children at secondary school, etc.

To adapt to the new approach with which he is faced, the learner needs to modify these ideas in various ways and degrees. This adaptation can only take place:

1. if he manages to re-examine all his prejudices and preconceptions about language learning and his role in it; these include notions such as the existence of an 'ideal' method, the belief that you can only learn a language in the presence of an expert teacher, that you must never make use of the mother tongue, that learning objectives cannot be defined by someone who does not know the language, etc.
2. if he is sufficiently well-informed concerning the new approach so that he can see for himself its advantages and disadvantages; but, above all, so that he will have a clearer idea of what his place and role in it will be, as well as of what is to be expected of the other components of the system.

These, then, should be the two main aims of the training at the psychological level.

At the technical level, the aim of the training is the acquisition of the knowledge and techniques necessary if the learner is to fulfill his role. He should learn to define his objectives on the basis of his needs, which presupposes the acquisition of adequate descriptive categories. (In practice, this can usually be done by taking the mother tongue as target language for, say, defining needs); he should learn to make use of the various tools available which might be a help (dictionaries, grammars, extracts from commercially published courses, etc.). He should learn to collect and use his own corpus of materials, to make his own glossary and reference cards, to develop ways of evaluating his progress and so on.

TRAINING METHODS AND TECHNIQUES

As was said earlier, training of this kind does not necessarily imply a teacher. In fact, the less you try to teach learners to learn, the better it probably is.

The basic methodology for learner training should be that of *discovery*; the learner should discover, with or without the help of other learners or teachers, the knowledge and the techniques which he needs as he tries to find the answers to the problems with which he is faced. By proceeding largely by trial and error he trains himself progressively.

As for psychological training, this is carried out gradually in conversations with the helper or counsellor or with self-directed learners of longer standing. This should help the learner understand the approach, but deconditioning can only be carried out by personally observing and thinking about his own learning.

EVALUATING THE TRAINING

This is done by the learner either alone or together with the helper on the basis of the various learning activities as they are tried out (I am speaking here of the learning process as such and not of the results of the learning). By estimating the efficiency of his work, the learner is able to gauge the degree to which he has mastered the necessary knowledge and techniques.

TRAINING STRATEGY

For both theoretical and practical reasons, learner training should begin at the same time as the language learning itself. It would be simply unrealistic to try to do it beforehand and absurd to leave it until after the required competence has already been acquired. In addition, it seems well-nigh impossible to learn to learn in the abstract, that is, without learning to learn something. This being the case, it is only reasonable to introduce the actual language learning right from the beginning.

FINAL REMARK

It is at the level of learner training, that is, preparation for autonomy, that the learner has the greatest need of outside help. Without this help, he would have to start by learning how to train himself, and the problem would be shifted to a further level of complexity.

Conclusions

This learner training, which can be seen in general terms as a way of improving language learning and in more specific terms as a way of meeting learners' needs, entails a necessary change in teacher training; the roles of teacher and learner are mutually defining, and the vast majority of teachers are unprepared for the new tasks which their new roles imply, and for much the same reasons as the learners. They, too, need to be prepared at the psychological and methodological levels.

Establishing self-directed learning schemes reveals just how urgent it is to do research into language *learning*; after all these years of research into language *teaching*, it is high time to look at what *learning* is. Only in this way will teachers and teaching be efficient in helping the learner to learn.

An experiment in self-directed group learning

Background

The first *Université du Troisième Age* was founded in Toulouse in 1973. It aimed at making it possible for older people, whatever their educational or professional backgrounds, to continue to develop intellectually and culturally even after their retirement. At least fourteen such 'Universities' now exist, including one in Nancy. All are attached to traditional Universities and make use of their existing infrastructure as regards accommodation, teachers, etc., but the various courses and activities they offer are organized specifically for their membership.

Given the pattern of demographic development in France, with the increase in life expectancy and the lowering of the retirement age, this public is one of increasing size and importance. However, it is not always easy for retired people to find suitable ways of participating in social life. The *Université du Troisième Age* is one possible solution.

In 1976, a certain number of the members of the *Université du Troisième Age de Nancy* asked for language courses to be organized on their behalf. The C.R.A.P.E.L. was approached and this paper describes the experimental learning system that was established (and which was still going strong in 1982), the rationale behind it and our first observations.

Preparation of the experiment

THE QUESTIONNAIRE

In order to have as clear an idea as possible of the characteristics of the public in question and of their expectations, a questionnaire was distributed to all members of the *Université* in Nancy who were interested in a language course of some kind. 69 replies were received, 61 of which concerned the study of English (there were, as it turned out, almost as many people again who did not answer the questionnaire but who were interested in studying English).

The questionnaire revealed the following information: the average age of the respondents was 59; they were nearly all former business executives, teachers, doctors, army officers, etc. with only a very few shopkeepers or workers. They had mostly reached the *Baccalauréat* and a certain number had higher qualifications. As regards their previous learning experience, more than half had learnt English at school, which means that in many cases they had done no English for about 35 years. Their main objectives were to speak and understand spoken English for practical purposes, with reading and writing coming in second place.

SELF-DIRECTED GROUP LEARNING

As reported elsewhere in this book (pp. 191–205) the C.R.A.P.E.L. established an autonomous learning scheme in 1974 for adults who, for various reasons, could not or did not want to follow a traditional course; the centre also runs various courses, evening classes, etc. At the institutional and pedagogical levels, however, we were faced with a rather knotty problem: for purely practical reasons, such as the number of teaching hours that would have been required and the lack of accommodation in the Faculty of Letters, we could not provide the *Université du Troisième Age* with any adequate courses (solutions such as four groups of 40 people for one and a half hours per week being regarded as definitely inadequate). On the other hand, the autonomous learning scheme as it then operated was almost entirely a matter of private study, yet it was quite clear that one of the main motivations of the people concerned was social, to meet one another. We therefore sought a compromise: what was eventually decided on was an adaptation of the principles of autonomy to the particular situation in question — *self-directed group learning.*

In this kind of learning system, the programme is managed not by the individual, as is the case in autonomous learning, but by the group. It is the group which takes responsibility for making all the relevant decisions including the definition of learning objectives and contents, the choice of working techniques, methods and materials, organization and development of the programme and evaluation.

The self-directed learning scheme

In the members of the *Université du Troisième Age* we were faced with a group of learners which was both large and unfamiliar to us. When we were asked to make some sort of provision for English for them we could neither simply impose a pre-determined structure, nor go before them empty-handed. What we did, therefore, was to propose a scheme based on the considerations mentioned above, which remained flexible enough for unforeseen problems and objections to be taken into account. This is why there are a certain number of differences between the scheme as we originally suggested it and as it was in fact applied.

The original plan

The original strategy was for a self-directed learning system where the participants would organize themselves into groups of about ten members according to their learning objectives and their level of English. Each group would name a 'manager' — temporary or permanent — and would define its learning objectives and pace as it went along, as well as carrying out periodic self-assessment. However, an *exception was to be made for absolute beginners*, who would have classes for the first year (three hours per week, fifteen members per group).

The project would start with a *one-week session on methodology*, during which members would work with the C.R.A.P.E.L. teachers on points such as the definition of learning objectives and on various work techniques and methods. There would also be a test, the groups would be formed and so on.

In general, the C.R.A.P.E.L. would be responsible for handling material problems, such as booking classrooms and providing equipment and materials. Advice on pedagogical problems would also be available on request, though visits by members of the C.R.A.P.E.L. to the groups would have to be limited to one per month.

The *contents* of the programme were to be defined in terms of written/spoken language and comprehension/expression skills, according to the learner's level at the beginning of the year. It should be noted that, according to the information we had gleaned from the questionnaire, the vast majority of people interested in studying English wished to follow a practical and not a literary course. From our point of view, this was just as well as we are not particularly competent to teach literature, which is more the domain of the English department in the Faculty of Letters.

The various means to be made available to learners were to include visits by native speakers of English, who were not teachers, and membership of the Sound Library, which contains a wide range of sound and video recordings, both authentic and didactic (see pp. 286–98). We expected a certain number of problems to crop up. These would include, we imagined, problems arising from the personal relationships between individual members and problems related to the nature of group work for people whose sole previous experience was traditional teaching. There would also be problems concerning the 'new' study techniques, problems resulting from irregular attendance and, finally, problems linked to the upper-class background of most of the learners.

The plan as actually applied

THE TRAINING COURSE IN METHODOLOGY

This consisted of five half-day sessions which took place in early October. About 100 members of the *Université du Troisième Age* were present and six members of the C.R.A.P.E.L. The meeting began with an outline description of our propositions, as described immediately above. The reaction of our audience was lively and even hostile: about a quarter of those present either walked out or remained only to express their vociferous opposition. This loss was made up by new members arriving during the following few weeks.

At the beginning of the training course, we announced that for pure beginners, by which we meant people who had *never* studied English, there would be two classes of one and a half hours per week. We suggested this not because we thought self-directed learning impossible at the beginner level, but because our earlier experiences in this domain had shown us that the lack of suitable materials did make it very difficult. However, the immediate result was that well over half those involved now claimed to be pure beginners and it required a considerable amount of tact and patience to bring the numbers down to a realistic 25 or so.

In order to help with the definition of their *learning objectives*, the learners were asked to fill in a form saying why they wanted to improve their English and what aspects of the language they thought would need most attention. This was largely to get them thinking about the problem themselves. A sample of 50 learners was interviewed for this purpose and *all* of them wished to improve oral comprehension and expression, written comprehension and written expression. They *all* gave their aims as:

'To be able to follow and join in a conversation.'
'For tourism.'
'To be able to listen to the radio or watch TV in English.'
'To read English newspapers.'
'To write letters in English.'

They all declared that they wanted to do everything, and so refused to break down their needs in terms of more precise objectives. It was clearly impossible to form groups on the basis of their different objectives, as these learners all had the same objectives.

The idea of using a *test* to establish the different groups was also dropped, not because of any opposition to tests as such — indeed the members were strongly in favour of them — but because they cheerfully admitted that individuals would ignore the results, choosing the group where their husband, childhood friend, colleague or fellow-soldier happened to be. Rather than introduce an 'exterior' factor in forming the groups, we decided to rely on the more advanced learners in each group helping the weaker members. The groups were set up, then, by the members themselves, on the basis of personal friendships and acquaintances (all members were already known to one another if only because they had been following other courses together for some weeks) and taking into account the limits imposed by their individual timetables. Five groups of between ten and twelve people were established, later growing to eight.

Each group was asked to choose its 'manager', someone who would be responsible for dealing with any practical problems which might arise and who would act as go-between with the C.R.A.P.E.L. teachers and the administration. Choosing group managers did not involve any problems. It was pointed out to the groups that they could choose the same person for the year, or that all the members could take it in turn to be manager. It was left to the groups to decide how often and for how long they would meet. On average they agreed to meet twice a week for one and a half hours.

In the final part of the preparatory session, each of the groups worked with one of the C.R.A.P.E.L. teachers, trying out various self-directed learning techniques and familiarizing themselves with the use of the tape recorder. They were shown, for example, how to use the recorder for overall and detailed listening comprehension. They were also shown different ways of using a transcription: all members or only one having a copy; using it before or after listening; making partial transcriptions themselves, etc. Once a technique had been demonstrated, it was practised by the group without the teacher intervening. Similarly, with oral expression, the teacher would suggest and demonstrate various activities — drills and exercises, games, role plays and simulations — which the group would then try out on their own.

OBSERVATION OF THE SELF-DIRECTED GROUPS AT WORK

Observation of a self-directed group is by no means easy, since there is the danger of observer-effect, the very presence of an outsider tending to distort the behaviour he is there to observe. This was felt particularly strongly in the early phases of the programme in question, since the learners had a marked tendency to turn to the observer and to try to turn him into a teacher. For these reasons, we will not try to draw any very generalized conclusions from our observations.

As far as personal relationships between members of the groups are concerned, there do not seem to have been any particular problems except in one group. In that group, the person chosen as manager proved to have a very forceful personality and his attitude towards other members soon caused trouble. He saw his role as that of teacher and took it on himself to choose, prepare and give various grammar lessons and translation exercises. Neither his attitude nor his choice of materials and techniques satisfied all members of the group. Five of them protested strongly and then withdrew to form an extra group along with several newcomers. At no time did the C.R.A.P.E.L. intervene in this affair: it was left to the group to find its own solution to the problem, which we believe it did in a very satisfactory manner.

Two other groups found that, with thirteen members in each, they had become rather unwieldy, so that not all members benefited from the work to the same extent. Nonetheless, one group decided that pleasant company was more important than efficiency and they continued to work as a single group for the rest of the year. The second group decided to split into two sub-groups, which continued nonetheless to work in the same rooms at the same times, thus preserving the overall unity of the group. Despite these figures, in response to the questionnaire issued at the end of the year, most participants replied that they thought the ideal size was eight or nine members.

80% of all the working sessions of all the groups took place without any outsider being present at all. In the other cases, a member of the C.R.A.P.E.L. was present either as an observer or to give advice. Some groups quickly developed a structure for their meetings (for example, three equal parts for listening comprehension, grammar exercises and conversation or games) which they stuck to for the whole year; others varied from one week to another, or devoted the whole session to one particular type of work.

Problems did, of course, arise: one group, for example, complained that they had the impression that they were making no progress at all in listening comprehension. Their technique involved listening to the tape once and then translating the text sentence by sentence into French. They then listened to the tape again to make sure they had understood. Here the C.R.A.P.E.L. representative was able to remind them of the other types of technique which had been demonstrated to them during the preparatory session. They decided to change techniques and soon reported that they were much more satisfied with the progress they were making. Nearly all groups kept a 'diary' which was available for reference.

Some groups used English only, even refusing to speak to the C.R.A.P.E.L. representative in French. Others had 'conversation' phases at the beginning and end of each session. Some groups did language laboratory drills together, or studied grammar, others played games, wrote dialogues, sang songs, listened to recordings, discussed current events, gave talks — and so on. Finally it is worth noting that, as the year went by, the requests for 'visitors' (native speakers of English who were not teachers) increased considerably. These visits were limited, for financial reasons, to two hours per month per group, but they could be 'saved up' if the group so wished.

The members of the *Université du Troisième Age* made very little individual use indeed of the Sound and Video Library, which tends to confirm the analysis of their motivations given above (p. 278). Nonetheless, some 75% of these learners claimed (in response to a questionnaire issued at the end of the year) to spend time working on their English at home. Indeed, one thing that struck everyone involved in this experiment — observers and learners alike — was the *quantity* of work which the learners got through. Again and again they commented on it in their diaries, during discussions with members of the C.R.A.P.E.L. and in answer to the questionnaire. It was almost unthinkable for a member of these groups to come to a working session without having revised the last week's work or having prepared something new: 'It's excellent. It really makes us work and it's stimulating.' For the idea of group work in general there was even wider approval, with adjectives like 'interesting', 'stimulating', 'useful', 'enjoyable' and 'efficient' occurring in 90% of the questionnaires. Ironically, having expressed surprise at how hard they have worked, how much they seem to have learned and how much they have enjoyed it, they often then went on to deplore the absence of a teacher!

It is interesting to compare the *attendance rate* of these self-directed groups with that in our own 'traditional' evening classes. The overall 'drop-out' rate for self-directed groups was 15%; in evening classes it was over 30%. This is at least partly due to the unusual degree of homogeneity in these groups, not of level, but of age, interests, background and personal relationships.

Editor's note: A great deal of time was taken up during this first year trying to persuade these learners to 'have a go' at self-directed learning. As has already been said, their initial reaction was by no means always positive; even those who did not actually walk out needed a considerable amount of convincing that the scheme was a feasible one. To some extent, too, their suspicions were a reflection of their image of us: young (well, relatively!), university ('impractical', 'abstract') teachers — who refused to teach. In subsequent years, we found that we were able to get round this problem by simply asking the previous years' managers to describe the activities and progress of their group. From the mouths of their peers, in concrete terms, the project sounded far less radical and has now been running successfully for a number of years.

The exploitation of authentic materials

> . . . le professeur doit être essentiellement celui qui oriente. Ce savoir qu'il est son rôle d'impartir, il n'en est pas le seul dépositaire. La multiplication du livre, la constante spécialisation des divers domaines lui font de l'humilité devant le savoir un devoir impérieux. Il doit être celui qui guide vers ces autres enseignants que sont les ouvrages scientifiques, les revues, et pourquoi pas les machines. Il est donc éminemment orienteur, dans le sens où sa tâche doit être une tâche de 'dispatching' vers les sources actuelles du savoir dans sa spécialité.
>
> *Yves Châlon*

It is easy to make fun of the sort of language one finds in language teaching materials. Every teacher, and a good many learners, can quote examples illustrating just how inane, bizarre or funny textbooks and phrasebooks can be; even people who have never opened one since they left school can tell you about postilions being struck by lightning. Personally, I cherish the memory of an East German textbook of English which had all the passengers boarding a London double-decker bus and saying to the conductor 'Hello, Clippy!'. Moreover, work in discourse analysis and in the study of Languages for Specific Purposes has shown that this is not just a matter of momentary anecdotal aberration but that didactic language is drastically and consistently distorted. It would be silly, of course, to claim that there is no place for didactic texts in language learning, particularly in the acquisition of morpho-syntax. The problem is that most learners and teachers remain convinced that didactic materials, especially textbooks, are the only possible sort which can be used by anyone who has not already learnt the language perfectly. 'Real' materials are obviously far too difficult and have to be left till the end of the course or, indeed, till after the course. At this general level we find the idea of a progression from simple to complex on which the separate units and volumes of published didactic materials are also based.

On examination, however, the ideas of 'simple' and 'complex' prove to be slippery ones. They are usually taken in a purely linguistic sense — 'simple vocabulary', 'complex grammar' and so on — but in fact, in purely linguistic terms, such an ordering of elements is largely arbitrary: a description of a language can start anywhere. In practice, though, these elements are mostly used with reference to learning — 'simple to learn', and so on. Here the assumption is that there is a natural order in which the constituent elements of a language should be learnt — and that this is it. A further assumption is that if the elements are taught in a particular order they will be learnt in that order. Work on the learning process (such as the paper by Collin and Holec, pp. 135–53) makes these assumptions questionable.

We need to ask 'simple for whom?', 'complex for whom?'. We need, that is, to take the learner into account and above all to look at his needs and knowledge.

As soon as we do this we realize that 'simple' and 'complex' are terms which only have sense in relation to a particular learner. A welder just beginning English knows precious little about the language, but an awful lot about welding, and it is this which enables him to understand technical documents which, for the teacher who is not a welder and who applies purely linguistic criteria, are 'difficult'.

An obvious practical implication here is that authentic documents have to be available to the learner. That is often the case, especially with written documents which our learners often provide themselves. However, this is not always possible, especially where recorded and video materials are concerned; in this case, the institution responsible for the learners tries to acquire as wide a collection as possible and put them at the learner's disposal. Chapter 14 is a description of just such a collection — a Sound Library. It is a straightforward account of the layout and organization of the library and does not discuss how learners can be helped to use it efficiently (but see the paper by Moulden, pp. 206–32).

In their paper (Chapter 15), Abé, Duda and Henner–Stanchina discuss the relationship of the teacher to authentic materials and to 'expert' knowledge in general: should the teacher be a specialist in the same field as the learners? Their answer is no, and they justify this on pedagogical grounds, drawing on three different ESP courses for exemplification. However, one point that they do not make, and which I feel is important for purely practical reasons, is that while it is feasible for a language teacher to become a specialist in, say, medicine if he has generation after generation of doctors passing through his hands, this would not be a practical proposition for dealing with a one-off course. Now in the last few years, the C.R.A.P.E.L. has been called on to provide specialized language courses to a wide range of groups, including compositors, doctors, welders, business executives, secretaries, telephone operators, workers in a bottle-making factory, forestry research workers, lighting specialists and so on. Clearly it is impossible to arrange for a teacher with the relevant specialized knowledge each time such a course takes place. But is it necessary or even desirable?

All the different groups mentioned above worked on authentic materials, and it is on such experience, gathered over a period of about ten years, that the authors of Chapter 16 have based their explanation of the rationale for the use of authentic materials.

The final paper in this section, Chapter 17, tries to fill a gap by looking at the specific contribution which authentic video-materials can make to the teaching and learning of oral comprehension. Readers interested in following developments in this field are referred to a subsequent and excellent report entitled *Video in language teaching* (Candlin, Charles and Willis 1982). At the C.R.A.P.E.L. we are continuing this work by examining the role of deictic reference of all kinds in the structure and negotiation of meaning (see pp. 8–10).

14 The Sound and Video Library

P. Riley and C. Zoppis

Background and layout

When the *Diplôme d'Etudes Universitaires Générales* (DEUG) was first announced by the French Ministry of Education in 1973, it appeared that some students whose curriculum had not previously included languages would be required to study one modern language. English was sure to be a favourite, and the Ministry was prepared to pay for two language laboratories of eighteen booths each which, they thought, would help provide an adequate answer to the teaching problem posed by this new public.

Our experience of language laboratories, which we think have a useful but limited part to play in the learning of a foreign language (see Bouillon 1971; Holec 1971; Holec and Kuhn 1971; Riley 1974; Harding and Legras 1974.) together with our deeply-felt desire to launch an experiment aimed at developing the student's capacity to teach himself, led a team from the C.R.A.P.E.L. to design and put forward a project for a Sound and Video Library. This, we thought, would not only cater for the new needs created by the DEUG but would also give all students of English an easy contact with the spoken word which they are otherwise denied. Among the possible users of the Sound and Video Library we included students who took English as their main subject, others who took it as a subsidiary subject, and extra-mural students; in fact we estimated the number of potential users at about 4,000, in the event of 80% of the total DEUG students (4,922) opting for English. By opening the projected Sound and Video Library 50 hours a week, it would be possible to accommodate each student for one and a half hours a week, with an average attendance of 60 students per hour, which was much more than could have been done with the two language laboratories initially proposed.

If one of our initial aims was to make sure that the Sound and Video Library would actually be able to take in all its potential users for as long as possible each week, we also wanted it to be a place where we would apply some of the pedagogical principles and strategies we firmly believe in. Foremost among these was the principle of *autonomous learning* for advanced and fairly advanced students. In our view, students who have reached a certain level in English can improve their listening comprehension, their oral expression or their written comprehension by regularly working in semi-autonomy with adequately prepared teaching material or in complete autonomy using 'raw' *authentic material* (see Duda *et al.* 1972, 1973 and this volume pp. 321–31). For instance, frequent exposure to authentic documents over a fairly long period seems to us to be indispensable for any progress in listening comprehension, just as a frequent use of the linguistic code is absolutely necessary if one wants to make some headway in speaking a language. This type of autonomous learning presupposes the setting up of new pedagogical strategies which complement the more traditional types.

For one thing, students must be able to find the *right kind of materials whenever they are free and ready to use them* — hence the necessity for having an abundant and varied supply of adequate materials in stock, a practical filing system and convenient opening times (ideally the Sound and Video Library should never close). But it is also necessary to persuade students that they can be their own tutors and that the presence of a teacher 'in the flesh' is not always indispensable.

Bearing in mind these pedagogical aims and the practical estimates concerning future users, we then proceeded to examine what kind of hardware would serve our purpose best, within the limits imposed by a fixed budget and by a room which we had not chosen and which had not been built with that particular use in view; its being on the fourth floor, for instance, is hardly an incentive for the average student unused to any strenuous exercise.

For both the sound and the video sections of the library, we selected cassette recorders made by a European firm which, in 1973, had the greatest experience of this then fairly new type of equipment. The room was divided into four main sections (see over Figure 1):

1. The entrance lobby.
2. The sound section.
3. The video section.
4. The technician's section.

The entrance lobby is equipped with a notice board and a filing-cabinet which is the focus of the whole library.

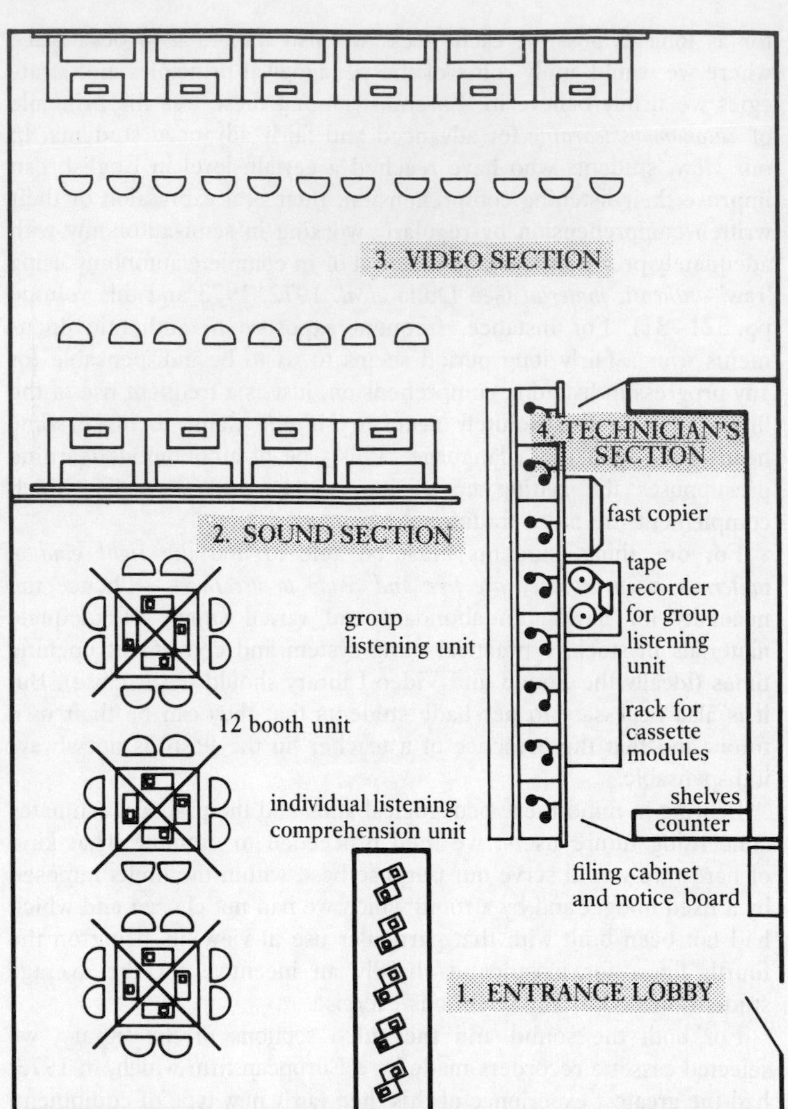

FIGURE 1

The sound section comprises three different types of equipment. It contains twelve booths, with audio-active-comparative cassette recorders, which are meant for those materials that include oral expression exercises. Each booth can accommodate two students. There is no monitor desk. As will be seen from Figure 1, these booths are arranged in groups of four. Booths are separated from each other by sound-absorbent partitions, arranged diagonally as indicated. This has the advantage of creating enough elbow-room for two students at a time to use a booth, whilst avoiding the strictly classroom discipline of the usual linear layout.

The sound section also contains twenty cassette players, making up a listening comprehension unit. Half of these players are fixed on to a table, the other ten constitute a reserve only used when the library is very busy.

Finally, the sound section has a group listening unit, consisting of a tape recorder and eight earphones fixed to the wall at intervals above a long bench. The tape recorder plays a non-stop programme meant for those students who are only free for a short period of time.

The video section is made up of ten video-cassette recorders, each linked to a black and white TV screen. Two students can watch the same screen simultaneously and hear the sound-track through earphones.

The *technician's area* contains twelve cassette modules, corresponding to the twelve sound booths described above. For security reasons, we thought it a better idea to have the technician feed the cassettes into the machines — which are set in a rack — than to let the students do it themselves.

There are also shelves for the master tapes and for at least one cassette copy of most of the documents in stock, and a fast copier, used for preparing cassettes from the master tapes, either in advance or at short notice; three copies can be made simultaneously at eight times the original speed. In other words, a forty-minute recording can be reproduced in five minutes.

Functioning

In this section, we are going to describe and discuss the procedure which a student follows when he makes a visit to the Sound Library, that is, how he goes about selecting, requesting and using a document ('document' is used throughout this paper to include all types of material, whether written, tape-recorded or video-recorded). All interested students are taken in groups on a detailed 'guided tour' of the Sound Library to familiarize them with the layout and facilities; this is a preliminary to the methodological training which most need if they are to make the most of their work there.

Selecting a document

On arrival in the Sound Library, the student proceeds first to the catalogue, a series of drawers containing filling cards. The *cataloguing system* has been developed to meet three main criteria: it had to be practical, informative and cheap.

IT IS PRACTICAL

The cataloguing system can be understood and used by the student himself without any specialist help; indeed, the cataloguing process itself can be carried out by an intelligent non-librarian. This was an essential characteristic, as funds were not available for even a part-time librarian. The system itself is based on key-words, that is, commonly used notional categories such as 'Humour', 'Conversation' or 'Law', which are coded in a way which is immediately meaningful to the user (HUM, CONV, LAW and so on) followed by a number which simply records the order of arrival of that particular item. HUM 15, then, was the fifteenth recording to be acquisitioned by the library.

In this system, instead of starting out with a complete, encyclopedic list of categories into which documents are sorted on arrival, we create categories in an *ad hoc* fashion as documents actually arrive. Obviously, such a system is considerably less detailed and refined — less systematic, in fact — than the professional librarian's taxonomies; nor does it handle the special problems of recorded materials with any particular subtlety, leaving decisions as to who is the author of an interview, or when an interview is a discussion, to the discretion or intuition of the cataloguer rather than basing them on any objective criteria. Experience has shown that it is efficient enough for our purposes. A generous amount of cross-referencing reduces the risk of a student's missing an item completely, and the full list of key-words is always displayed prominently above the catalogue.

Below is an extract from the list of key-words. It is important to remember that key-words are only created when needed, and that a conceptual blank is not an omission: it simply means that no document on that particular topic has as yet been received by the library.

JRN	JOURNALISM	NTH	NATURAL HISTORY
LANG	LANGUAGES	NR	NATURAL RESOURCES
	— etymology		— coal
LAW	LAW		— mining
LIT	LITERATURE		— oil
	— book review		

	— drama
	— essays
	— novel
	— poetry
	— Sherlock Holmes
	— short story
	— Wordsworth
MED	MEDICINE
MON	MONOLOGUE
MUS	MUSIC
	— business
	— freelance musicians
	— opera
	— quiz
NEWS	NEWS
PNT	PAINTING
POL	POLITICS
	— France
	— local
	— nationalism
	— race relations
	— terrorism
PLT	POLLUTION
POP	POPULATION
PUB	PUBLIC SPEAKING
RAD	RADIO
	— children's programmes
	— comedy
	— discussion
	— drama
	— interview
	— magazine
	— series

Although the key-words cataloguing system can be applied to any collection of documents, this particular list applies exclusively to the contents of the Nancy Sound Library.

IT IS INFORMATIVE

In order to help the student in his choice and to reduce the number of unnecessary, inaccurate, or unsatisfactory requests, the maximum possible amount of information is included on each filing card entered in the catalogue. This information falls under three broad headings: information helping in the *retrieval* of the item (coding, title, etc.); information concerning the *content* of the recording (synopsis, cross-references); linguistic information (spontaneity, accents, speed). This information is presented to the student as in Figure 2 (see over).

A: *Author or interviewer*. This heading has often to be interpreted extremely loosely ('person responsible for a recording', 'leading figure or personality involved', etc.) or even to be left blank; at other times, of course, it is of major importance.

B: *Source*. Where did the recording come from? Was it published commercially, was it made privately, was it a gift from the British Council, Voice of America or another University?

A: Author, interviewer		B: Source	C: Code
D: Title Series			E: Written document
F: Synopsis			
G: Key words — cross-references			
H: Spontaneous Non spontaneous	J: Accents	K: Speed	L: Length of recording
I: Archive N°			M: Date of recording

FIGURE 2

C: *Code*. The key-word entry appears here.

D: *Title and Series*. It is often both necessary and convenient to invent a title for a recording which does not have one. The 'Series' title acts as a useful further cross-reference.

E: *Written document*. If there is a written document of any kind to accompany the tape — a textbook, a transcription, a newspaper article or a script — it is marked here. The student has to request it separately.

F: *Synopsis*. What is the recording *about*? This should help the student decide whether or not it will be of interest to him, and it may also help him follow certain aspects of the recording when he listens to it.

G: *Key-words*. This section contains cross-references to related items and headings in the catalogue which may also be of interest to the student.

H: *Spontaneous/non-spontaneous*. Is the recording 'spoken prose' (someone reading aloud) or is it unrehearsed speech?

I: *Archive Number*. Of no interest to the student.

J: *Accents*. One of the main problems facing the foreign learner is the variety of British and American accents. By indicating what accents are present in any given recording, the card enables the student to choose or reject it according to his level of attainment and interests.

K: *Speed.* A rather impressionistic attempt is made here to indicate to the learner the speeds at which participants in the recording talk. Each participant is marked on a scale from 1 (very slow) to 5 (very fast) by native speakers.

L: *Length of recording.* This might be useful to a learner in planning his or her own work.

M: *Date of recording.* This can sometimes help the learner by providing a reminder of the context in which the recording was made.

Taken together, H, J and K should give the learner a reasonably clear impression of the level of linguistic difficulty presented by a particular recording. If the quality of a recording is poor, a comment to that effect is usually included under F (synopsis).

Figure 3 is an example of an entry under 'CRIME'.

Bill Monroe Frank McGee		Voice of America	CR 10
Federal regulations to combat air hijacking Series: Crosstalk			Transcript
A discussion concerning new security measures and laws on air piracy			
CRIME : Hijacking : Travel : Air : US Law			
Spontaneous	U.S.	BM : 5 FMcG : 3	10'
299			12/1/72

FIGURE 3

IT IS CHEAP

In the cataloguing system described above, no special supports, materials, or machines are required. A filing cabinet, filing cards and a typewriter are all that is necessary.

The considerable amount of work involved in listening to new tapes, summarizing and describing their contents and (sometimes) transcribing the recordings is carried out by one of the young English or American *lecteurs* who work at the University each year and who each have an hour or two of this kind of work included in their duties. In addition, the library employs a secretary for a few hours each week whose main task is classifying and typing out new entries in the catalogue.

Requesting a document

Having selected an item from the file, the student fills in a request slip, which he hands to the technician or library assistant at the desk. The request slips provide the data for statistics as shown, in translation, in Figure 4.

BORROWER	PLACE		CODE
SURNAME			Letters
FIRST NAME			Numbers
English Major	First year Second year Postgraduate	Teacher	Date
DEUG 5%	Law Economics Psychology/ Sociology	Evening class student Other	Time borrowed Time returned
Remarks			Transcription Borrowed Returned

FIGURE 4

If the request is for a course tape requiring student-recording facilities, the student is directed to one of the audio-active-comparative booths. The technician places the cassette in the corresponding slot in the console, but the student retains complete control through the switches in his booth, even though he is physically separated from it.

If the request is for a video-tape, the technician himself sets the cassette in place and operates the video-tape player. Students are requested never to touch this equipment: they are less familiar with this type of machine and it is more delicate and expensive. This means that students wishing to work intensively on the language of a video-tape cannot keep stopping and starting the tape. Instead, a recording of the sound-track is also made available; having watched the document, the student moves to one of the individual listening posts where he is able to work on the recording as he wishes.

If the request is for any other document the technician will probably have to make a cassette copy on the fast copier while the student waits. The student takes the cassette from the technician and goes to one of the listening posts where he himself inserts it into the cassette player and operates the machine.

Using documents

The type of work which can be done with sound and video recordings varies greatly. Indeed, one of the main advantages of the Sound Library is that it allows users to discover their own learning techniques. Whereas in the traditional language laboratory full audio-active-comparative facilities are provided in every booth, whether the student working there needs them or not, in the Sound Library different types of equipment are provided for different types of work. For example, a student working on listening comprehension does not need recording facilities, so a simple cassette player is enough: there are sound financial as well as pedagogical reasons for making this kind of distinction, since *one* language laboratory booth costs the equivalent of *thirty* cassette players.

The various types of work can be grouped under three main headings: listening comprehension; oral expression; viewing comprehension.

LISTENING COMPREHENSION

A wide range of documents is available to the learner wishing to practise listening comprehension. By choosing between didactic and authentic materials and between recordings for which there are or are not written texts, the learner is able to vary the level and approach. In many cases, he is also able to select documents which satisfy his specialized requirements; if, for example, he is preparing to attend a learned congress he will find recordings of academic seminars; if he wants to be able to follow the news, he will find recordings of news broadcasts. By working as far as possible on authentic documents relevant to his specific needs, the learner makes more economic use of his time and reduces the gap between the learning situation and the real-life situation for which he is preparing. Where possible, learners are shown various techniques by teachers of other courses they may be following — some kind of methodological preparation is usually necessary. In general, all types of comprehension exercise which can be done in a class with a teacher can also be done by the learner working alone. There are also specialized courses available, written by members of the C.R.A.P.E.L. (H. Holec, *Cours de compréhension orale*; F. Roussel, *Cours avancé de compréhension orale*, 1972, C.R.A.P.E.L.).

ORAL EXPRESSION

The library possesses a range of courses in oral expression, either commercially published, or produced by the C.R.A.P.E.L. itself. Learners work in the laboratory-type booths, recording, repeating, listening and answering. Materials are available on specific aspects of English: phonetics, phonology, morphology, syntax and communicative functions. Students are guided in their choice either by their teachers in class or by the *moniteurs* who are present in the library during certain periods each week. For users not following other courses a grid classifying materials in terms of skills and levels is displayed on the notice-board.

VIEWING COMPREHENSION

Little close study has yet been made of viewing comprehension (though we intend to investigate this skill during coming years). At present it is little more than an act of faith that 'watching TV is good for you'. Again, the emphasis is on authentic recordings.

Apart from the three linguistic activities mentioned above, it is worth noting that an increasing number of students are attending the library not so much to improve their English, as to find information. Students of law, economics, and other disciplines find up-to-date discussions of immediate relevance to their field of study, or lectures by well-known experts. Nor should we exclude from serious consideration those students who attend simply because they enjoy it, finding in *Hancock's Half Hour*, or *American Folk Music*, or *Hamlet* a source of civilized entertainment.

Future developments

The most immediate and obvious problem facing the Sound Library is the acquisition of further materials. Although the present collection is already fairly large (approximately 1,000 items, consisting of 40 TV recordings, 20 courses, and some 950 authentic documents), it is still not varied enough to meet many of the specialized needs of some of the users. Ideally, a cardiologist due to chair a conference or a travel agent needing to speak and understand English on the phone would find relevant authentic recordings in the library to work on. At present, our policy is to accept almost any recording we are offered, at the same time trying to obtain recordings to meet particular needs as they arise. The major institutional sources of recordings have already been tapped and to a large extent we are now dependent on exchange arrangements with individuals: we can afford only a small number of commercially published materials. TV and sound recordings are also regularly produced here, but it is quite impossible to get the necessary variety to satisfy all interests and needs.

A major development being considered is the establishment of a home-loan system for sound cassettes. Since large numbers of people now possess cassette recorders or players, and since the same cassette can be re-used a number of times, such a system would be quite feasible as far as the users are concerned. But it is doubtful whether the library's present copying facilities would be able to meet both internal and external demands, and it is certain that the library's present secretarial and administrative personnel would have to be increased: the one part-timer at present employed could not possibly cope.

As a first, tentative step, a home-loan system has been operated exclusively for a group of 100 extra-mural students (although only about half this number actually availed themselves of it). Although the results were in general encouraging and the system operated smoothly, our experience is too limited to allow further generalization.

The Sound Library described in this paper is an attempt to develop in a concrete way the pedagogical and technological experience gained in language laboratories and classrooms during the last decade. It is itself still at the experimental stage. Consequently, it is necessary to keep all aspects of the functioning of the library under close observation; hence the details required on the request slips, for example.

The request slips which students fill in are kept and at regular intervals sorted out and classified so as to obtain:

1. The figures concerning the number of requests overall and for each of the three main types of documents available (courses, authentic documents, TV programmes);
2. Attendance figures according to the day of the week and the time of day;
3. Information about what departments the students come from.

We need to know how learners work under these conditions, what techniques and strategies they adopt, and what problems crop up. On the basis of the information thus acquired, it should be possible to improve the presentation of all types of documents. We also hope to establish a repertoire of working procedures which could be investigated, extended and taught to other users: such research is essential if autonomous learning schemes are to be anything more than a mixture of guesswork and do-it-yourself.

Editor's note

The library described above has now been open for eight years. Requests during the last four years or so have been running at the rate of almost 14,000 per academic year; since use of the library is still on a purely voluntary basis, it is clear that learners find it useful.

No major changes in the system have been introduced, although the statistical records are now computerized; we are also experimenting with ways of putting the catalogue itself on computer. A cassette-to-cassette fast copier has been installed and has made the service easier and smoother. New additions to the archives are now often on cassettes.

The lack of standardization in video equipment has been a considerable nuisance, since it has meant the introduction of different types of video recorder to correspond with the different kinds of cassette we receive, usually on an exchange basis, from language teaching institutions in other countries.

The library now contains approximately 3,000 items. Visitors tend to exclaim at our 'luck' in possessing such a collection, or to wonder 'how we can afford it'. In fact, only a small proportion of the tapes are purchased; the rest are provided by the people who use the library, teachers and learners. The day the library opened there were less than twenty items on the shelves. The present collection is the accumulation of eight years' work and is perfectly within the reach of any small, organized group of teachers.

15 A specialist? What specialist?

D. Abé, R. Duda and C. Henner–Stanchina

Introduction

This paper consists of three reports describing courses organized by the C.R.A.P.E.L. for groups of highly specialized learners. Evidence is provided to support the contention that a 'non-specialist' language teacher can help highly specialized learners to develop specific language skills and functions closely related to their professional communicative needs.

That this approach to the teaching and learning of English for Special Purposes is by no means universal can be seen from the following passage, taken from the ALSED, a bulletin published by the UNESCO, in which an opposite and more orthodox opinion is advanced:

> The methods used to teach a language for professional purposes do not differ from those which are generally used in language teaching to adults: however, the form and content of such courses should correspond to the professional context and the teachers should have an expert knowledge both of the subject and of the language specific to it. (ALSED 1976)

This study, which is based on three courses organized by the C.R.A.P.E.L. during the academic year 1975–6, shows that it is possible to help forestry research workers, information scientists or doctors to communicate in English without the teacher's necessarily being a specialist in the subject in question: it then goes on to discuss the factors which determine the roles of teacher and learner in the learning situation.

English or forestry research?

Between November 1975 and April 1976, the C.R.A.P.E.L. was responsible for organizing an English language programme at the *Centre National de Recherches Forestières de Nancy–Amance*. There were two main components in this programme: first, practice in written comprehension; second, practice in oral expression and comprehension. In this paper, we will be referring only to this second component.

In the 'oral' group — which was quite separate from the 'written comprehension' group — there were twelve participants; nine of them were researchers and three were members of the administrative staff. Although the group was homogeneous as regarded *language learning objectives*, in the sense that all the members needed to improve their skills in oral expression and comprehension, it was certainly not so as regarded *communicative needs*. As it happened, it was the research workers who were best able to define their needs, which were therefore taken as a basis for the work (though it has to be admitted that this was slightly to the disadvantage of the other learners). The group included one or two members whose *linguistic* competence in oral comprehension needed some preliminary brushing up to enable them to benefit from the training in *communicative* competence.

This group was, therefore, heterogeneous from the points of view of both needs and of linguistic levels. One of the ways we tried to deal with these problems was by establishing a Sound Library at the Research Centre itself, where the learners could work, either alone or together, at any time. The contents of the library are described on pp. 301–5.

The main communicative needs of this group fell into two categories:

1. Meeting and looking after foreign visitors to the Centre's laboratories;
2. Participating, either actively or simply as a member of the audience, in congresses or seminars where the working language was English.

It was this second need which was, in the opinion of the learners themselves, by far the most important and the most difficult.

Working together, teachers and learners produced the following brief analysis of the principal communicative activities and functions involved in attending seminars and congresses:

ACTIVITIES:

1. Listening to and understanding talks and lectures (it is worth noting here that these learners found they had little trouble understanding written English).
2. Reading aloud papers in English which they themselves had written.

FUNCTIONS:

1. How to chair a working group or a lecture, which includes procedures such as: introducing the speaker; thanking him; throwing the discussion open to the floor; interrupting over-lengthy contributors; repeating questions by reformulating them, etc.
2. How to play for time when in trouble (because the speaker has forgotten what he was going to say, or can't find the right words); asking for a question to be repeated; dodging questions, etc.

Could the teacher, who had absolutely no specialized knowledge of forestry research, help to meet these needs by arranging adequate training activities? It seems to us that the answer is 'yes': indeed we would argue that the fact that a non-specialist can nonetheless give valuable help of this kind is one of the major advantages to be derived from describing needs in communicative terms, since such descriptions do not necessitate a detailed knowledge of the content of the communicative activities in question.

The teacher's role in this programme, therefore, was to establish a Sound Library and to organize, observe and comment on the simulated seminars which formed the greater part of the training in oral expression which was given.

The Sound Library

The Sound Library contained:

1. A single course in spoken English for intermediate students (*Kernel Lessons Intermediate*). This was to help the weakest learners catch up with those who were more advanced. Obviously, this presumed that they would do extra work in the Sound Library, alone or with the help of a more advanced colleague.
2. Recordings of technical documents for oral comprehension and for practice in reading aloud. Unfortunately, authentic recordings made at seminars and congresses were not available and we had to make do by recording written texts. This was only a temporary measure, though, and we were later able to supplement these specially-made recordings with a small number of authentic texts. This may seem to be a mere detail, but in fact texts which have been written to be read in silence differ considerably from those which have been written to be read aloud, both syntactically and in terms of their overall organization. This inevitably has repercussions (for the reader or listener) on the processes of perception, decoding and interpretation.

The materials for listening comprehension consisted of three components: the recording itself, a partial transcription and a key. The recordings were made by British and Canadian readers. An extract from one of these documents (Bengtson 1972) follows.

DOCUMENTS D'ENTRAINEMENT A LA COMPREHENSION ORALE

I. Instructions

Ecoutez l'enregistrement que vous avez choisi, une première fois sans arrêter la bande et en prenant des notes (en français ou en anglais indifféremment). Ne consultez pas le script d'accompagnement.

Ecoutez à nouveau l'enregistrement, en l'arrêtant si nécessaire, pour compléter ou étoffer vos notes.

Prenez enfin le script, et, en vous servant de l'enregistrement, transcrivez *sur une feuille à part*, les parties laissées en blanc. Le cas échéant, vous pouvez transcrire en français ce qui vous semble être la *signification* du segment en anglais, si vous n'êtes pas en mesure d'identifier la *forme* de celui-ci.

Consultez enfin le corrigé qui vous est fourni.

II. Corrigé

Texte 1

Fertilizers and forest insect-disease relationships

(1) and when the cankers are located on the tree stem
(2) made worse by fertilizers
(3) for increased rust infection in fertilized trees?
(4) where fusiform rust hazard is high
(5) of two different populations of slash and loblolly pine
(6) neither early growth initiation nor tree height
(7) their susceptible counterparts
(8) Nitrogen increased rust in six
(9) and decreased rust in one experiment
(10) a change in rust incidence in response to fertilization
(11) will not necessarily increase rust
(12) local climatic and ecological conditions
(13) since P fertilizers also
(14) was due to earlier growth flushing
(15) in this disease problem
(16) on which the rust fungus can be grown
(17) rust resistant populations performed similarly well
(18) the genetic resistance mechanism is effective
(19) bred expressly for rust resistance

Texte n°1

Fertilizers and Forest Insect-Disease Relationships

When the nutrition of plants is significantly altered, as in a fertilized forest, it is inevitable that mechanisms whereby the trees resist or escape attack by insects and diseases will be modified.

The results may be either favorable or unfavorable and generalizations are somewhat risky. In his excellent review of this subject, Foster (1968) made several which have stood up rather well. Weetman and Hill (1972) have expanded on these in a review which will be of interest to the serious student of fertilizers and biological concerns. But it is beyond the scope of this paper to discuss the myriad of possibilities, so let's take just two for which new data are available and use them to illustrate the nature of progress and problems in this area.

In the South, an important disease of slash and loblolly pines in many areas is fusiform rust. Cancerous growths caused by this fungus arise most often on young trees
(1) can cause serious deformation and early mortality. Some plantations have been rendered completely useless by this disease. There is little disagreement with Foster's (1968) generalization that fusiform rust is (or more accurately can be)
(2) But in attempting to deal with the problem and to live with it, one might raise several questions. Do all fertilizer treatments which stimulate growth increase incidence of the disease? What factors account
(3) Where are losses most severe? What is the ratio of probable gain in growth from fertilization versus that of loss from rust? Can breeding for rust resistance reduce rust losses?

Two recent studies have made a start toward answering some of these. Working in south Mississippi,
(4) Dinus and Schmidtling (1971) found that cultivation and NPK fertilization
(5) increased height growth of both species but increased incidence of rust only in slash pine (the authors acknowledge earlier work which indicated that loblolly susceptibility was increased by cultivation and fertilizers). Their observations indicated that
(6) was responsible for increased rust in slash pine. Regardless of treatment, the more resistant populations within each species remained consistently less infected than
(7), etc . . .

It will be noticed that the blanks in the script correspond generally to specialized words or groups of words. As is often the case for research scientists, the recognition and comprehension of technical terms in writing is far less of a problem than in the spoken form, which is one reason why the learners in question were interested in this type of work.

The materials for reading aloud were recorded by a British reader. The learners had scripts which indicated how the text had been 'exploded' for recording purposes. This type of reading allows the learner to repeat what he hears read aloud on the tape. An audio-comparative booth in the Sound Library also allowed learners to assess their own performances. An example follows: the diagonal lines indicate where the pauses occur in the recording.

NUTRIENT CYCLES AND NUTRIENT BUDGETS

Forests are generally recognized / as highly efficient ecosystems, / capable of efficient use of solar energy / on a minimum of nutrient capital / (Bormann and Likens, 1967). / Students of nutrient cycles and nutrient budgets in forests / have provided a background of concepts and information / which should be required reading for every decision-maker / in the area of forest fertilization. / For not only do they provide / a highly useful rationale for appropriate timing / and rates of fertilization / to sustain high rates of growth in commercial forests / (Switzer, Nelson and Smith, 1968; Curlin, 1970) / but they also suggest the kinds of practical problems / which may be introduced / by injudicious use of fertilizers / in relatively stable forest ecosystems / (Ovington, 1968; Lugo, 1970; Weetman and Hill, 1972; Hornbeck and Pierce, 1972). / But unfortunately for development of a balanced view on this subject, / there seems to be in some quarters / a preoccupation with maintenance of the nutritional status quo in forest ecosystems. / It is almost as though it has been decided / that all 'natural' systems are perfect in their nutritional status / and that any disturbance of forest ecosystems by 'unnatural' inputs / or by man-caused removals or 'leaks' / represent irreparable harm. / Certainly all foresters must respect the need for maintenance of the integrity of nutrient cycles in certain watersheds / and in unique forest ecosystems / prized for aesthetic, ecological, or natural values. / But by the same token, we must ask for recognition / that nature and man have left the land designated for timber production / pitifully low in nutrient capital / and that we have the means to correct these deficiencies. / Some 'leakage' from such systems / following fertilization / if the downstream effects are not serious / may be tolerable / if in the process of intensive silvicultural practice, / including fertilizer application, / we are able to raise the capacity of the ecosystem / to make more effective use of the solar energy it receives (Weetman and Hill, 1972). / Fertilizers also offer a means of replacing nutrient capital removed in harvests / and lost, as are N and S, in wildfires. / Such losses, if not replaced, / constitute 'leaks' in nutrient cycles / and can lead to undesired ecological trends / just as serious as any which might be caused by injudicious fertilization. / Adamant rejection of intelligent fertilizer use in such situations / is to be condemned equally with the shotgun approach (Leonard, Leaf and Berglund, 1970) / to forest fertilization. /

Research in nutrient cycles and nutrient budgets / should be an integral part of any comprehensive program in forest fertilization research. / These areas, unfortunately, / have been assigned a back seat to production-oriented research / in most of the cooperative research programs mentioned earlier. / This is unfortunate, for it is in the area of fertilized versus unfertilized ecosystems / that the least work on nutrient budgets and cycles has been done. / Hopefully, this situation will be corrected / as initial priorities are satisfied / and as outlooks broaden.

Simulations

Given that we do not yet have any functional descriptions of seminars, both teachers and learners had to rely on their personal experiences and intuitions when deciding what functions to take for study and practice (in response to this need, a C.R.A.P.E.L. research team has carried out a study of seminar English on behalf of the *Centre National de la Recherche Scientifique*: see Heddesheimer *et al.* (1982)). The teacher would simply discuss and list stereotyped realizations of the functions which he and the learners had identified, and then the learners would try to use them during the simulations which followed (on topics such as 'The influence of Concorde on higher atmospheric levels', 'Procedures for the refertilization of forests', etc.) During the simulations, the teacher only intervened when requested to do so by the learners. At the end of the simulation, though, he would make comments on points of grammar, pronunciation and communication.

As can be seen, then, it is possible for a teacher, with his linguistic expertise, to collaborate usefully with learners who have highly specialized needs. This depends, however, on the introduction of a communicative dimension to language learning; if the teacher continues to concentrate on lexis and grammar, he will never help the learner to achieve communicative competence.

English or information science?

The second programme in English for Specialised Purposes was undertaken by the C.R.A.P.E.L. on behalf of Pont-à-Mousson S.A. The aim of the programme was to enable computer technicians to understand IBM brochures in English and thereby improve the efficiency and productivity of the firm's computer department.

The group of learners in question consisted of thirteen people who were having problems reading technical documents which were necessary to them in their work. These brochures were published in English: translating them was out of the question, as they would have been out of date by the time the translation was complete. Only one of the participants had received any previous instruction in reading computer-related texts in English, having followed a year's evening classes. Three of the participants had never studied English before: of the others, some had done between one and three years of English at school some considerable time earlier, while others had learnt English on their own, following the various commercial courses available, most of which are audio-visual.

The homogeneity of the group was partly due to their level of specialized knowledge, partly the result of their high degree of motivation which was in turn the result of psychological and socio-professional factors. In particular, their inability to read texts in English meant that they either had to guess at the meaning or to consult colleagues, procedures which are timewasting and which can even lead to mistakes being made. However, not all the technicians did the same kind of work and there was a certain amount of variety in the texts which they needed to understand.

The objective of the programme was to help the learners understand their texts independently, and to do so as rapidly as possible. To do this, they also had gradually to take over the management of their learning programme themselves, so that they would be able to evaluate their progress, analyse their difficulties and solve their problems once the actual teaching part of the programme had come to an end.

The programme was divided into two separate phases: first, a period of systematic teaching consisting of two hours per week for 20 weeks, during which the necessary linguistic foundations would be laid, followed by ten 'mobile' hours, which would be fixed at times requested by the learners once they had started dealing with the texts in their work situation.

The learners and their texts

The technicians already knew most of the concepts mentioned in the texts, as well as the ways in which they could be combined in their field of specialization: this state of affairs is represented by the shaded part of Figure 1.

The 'transparency' of a number of technical terms meant that they were able to construct hypotheses about the contents, but they were not able to go back to the text to check these hypotheses or to resolve any ambiguities that might arise from relationships between the concepts in combination. For example, it is not much use being able to recognize and understand the words 'study', 'treasury' and 'publish' occurring in a text in that order if one is still uncertain as

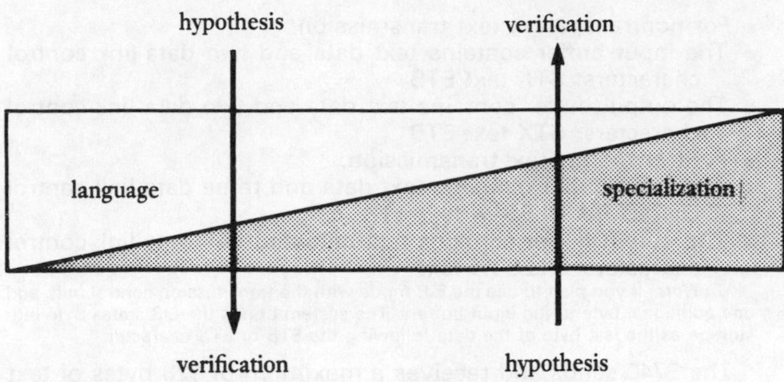

FIGURE 1

to whether someone is going to publish a study on the treasury or whether the treasury is going to publish a study or, indeed, has already published it. Obviously the degree of transparency of the context will be crucial here, but if it is anything less than absolutely explicit the problem can only be aggravated.

At the functional level, the learners were quite capable of finding a description, instructions for use, or a warning by comparing the text with computer texts in French which they may have read. But they still could not understand the contents of this particular instruction or warning.

The teacher and the specialized texts

The teacher was not a specialist in computer science, so for him the technical terms were completely opaque — just as they would have been in his mother tongue, in fact. He could only grasp the fact that certain words were related to one another, or that one term was subordinated to another, in the way that such relationships occur within a nominal group, for example. In this way, the teacher was rather like a mathematician establishing the relationships between two unknowns without knowing their values or the precise nature of the relationships holding between them. The reader can judge this by reading a typical text.

> **BTAM BUFFER REQUIREMENTS**
> Buffering techniques are explained in the appropriate manuals for your system. However, you must understand what is contained in the data buffer. This is generally the same as what appears on the communication line; that is, text data and data-link control characters

- For nontransparent text transmission:
- The input buffer contains text data and two data-link control characters: STX text ETB
- The output buffer contains text data and two data-link control characters: STX text ETB
- For transparent text transmission:
- The input buffer contains text data and three data-link control characters: DLESTX text ETB
- The output buffer contains text data and two data-link control characters: DLESTX text

Note: If you plan to use the EIB mode with the transmission control unit, add one additional byte to the input buffers. The system brings the EIB status byte into storage as the last byte of the data following the ETB or ETX character.

The 3740 sends and receives a maximum of 128 bytes of text data in the above formats.

With the Expanded Communications feature, the 3741 can transmit and receive blocked records. The maximum record length is still 128, but a block may be 512 bytes (not including BSC framing characters). If the 3741 is transmitting, include in the count the IRS (interrecord separator) character placed at the end of each record by the 3741. Also, the 3741 puts only an integer number of records in each block. For example, only three 128-byte records would be sent per block. If the 3741 is receiving, exclude the IRS character from the byte count. Thus the 3741 can receive 512 bytes of data. In receive mode, the 3741 can also receive spanned records; that is, a record may start in one block and end in the next. Because of this spanning capability, the blocks sent to the 3741 may be any length through 512 bytes.

The 3747 Blocking/Reformatting feature allows up to 8050 bytes of text data. However, you should limit transmission blocks to 512 bytes because of host system or multiplexer buffer sizes, line quality, and effects on total system throughput. The content of the text data in the transmission block depends upon the blocking/reformatting program at the 3747. See the *3747 Data Converter Reference Manual and Operator's Guide*, referenced in the Preface, for details.

At paragraph level, the teacher was generally able to recognize functions such as identification, definition or classification, but it was impossible for him to distinguish between major and minor information or to judge what aspects of the new information were redundant.

The roles of the teachers and learners

The systematic phase of the learning programme was based on the *Cours de Compréhension Ecrite pour Débutants*, published by the C.R.A.P.E.L., at the rate of one unit per week, approximately. The learners practised recognizing grammatical morphemes and analysing their functions in authentic (and therefore complex) sentences, so that they could rapidly identify sentence structures. Each unit was then applied to computer-related texts, but — during this first phase — this was strictly for the purpose of identifying sentence structure, not sentence meaning.

The teacher also gave some technical instruction during this period: the participants learnt how to use their glossaries or dictionnaries more efficiently. Again, from the methodological point of view, they were introduced to individual study-methods, since most of the work involved on the *Cours de Compréhension Ecrite pour Débutants* is meant to be done outside the classroom. The classroom periods themselves are devoted to clearing up any difficult points which may remain and to the study of the point of grammar dealt with in the next unit. However, the degree of learner-autonomy is limited, since the teacher's presence is felt in the conception and choice of the exercises and texts.

As they began tackling the contents of their specialized texts, the learners took over a number of tasks which are more usually performed by a teacher; they themselves chose the texts to be studied, basing the choice on their own sense of priorities, on the frequency with which particular texts had to be used and on comprehension problems which they had already met. Significantly, the learners gradually took over responsibility for having texts copied for classroom work.

Even more noteworthy, however, is the fact that only the learners were able to decide on the meaning of their texts and on how well they understood them: this evaluation was carried out by pooling the different members' interpretations: starting out from linguistic hypotheses they would verify the meaning in terms of computer science. In the same way, hypotheses based on the contents were tested according to the rules of discourse and syntax; at first this was done by the teacher, but as the learners built up their own stock of rules they were able to do it themselves. Working with a non-specialist teacher does not seem to have bothered the learners; rather, they were obliged to make a useful distinction between the problems which had linguistic causes and those which were the result of gaps in their specialized knowledge about computers. They also seemed very satisfied to have a major role to play in the learning programme, even if their comprehension of their texts was not always one hundred percent in computer science (not linguistic) terms: in such cases, they did have to call on outside help.

English or medical science?

This section describes an experimental medical English course that was organized by 'non-specialists' (non-doctors, in other words) at the Medical Faculty in Nancy. The writer's ulterior motive is, admittedly, to provide at least an initial riposte to all those who would contend that none but the specialists themselves (in this case doctors whose native language is English) are capable of teaching, or ensuring the acquisition of specialized English.

The group

The group of learners was composed of university teachers, surgeons, researchers and interns, and a 'working knowledge of English' was stipulated as the prerequisite for registration. In order to verify that entry levels were indeed sufficient, a modified version of the C.R.A.P.E.L. placement test was given: the usual, general aural comprehension test plus an additional exercise based on a BBC radio discussion of cancer; a test in written comprehension; and a writing exercise calling for a brief account of each individual's work or research. The test allowed us to set up a group that was more or less homogeneous from a linguistic point of view, although not so from a medical point of view, for the seven members represented five different fields of specialization.

NEEDS

Despite the diversity in professional situations, the group members all expressed the same needs:

1. to understand a native speaker of English;
2. to be comfortable enough in English to be able to give a paper at a conference, intervene, or simply engage in informal discussion with the conference participants;
3. to increase speed in reading medical journals, etc.;
4. to be able to write an abstract in English, or to translate their own abstracts (or articles) into 'acceptable' English.

The very notion of 'acceptable' English raises the controversial question of whether or not the French medical profession should in fact be obliged — in order to gain international recognition — to publish in English. The consequences of the alternative are twofold: since it has been shown that even medical articles submitted to 'Anglo-Saxon' journals in French fall short of the so-called 'acceptable' standard (Veylon 1975), it follows that the problem is not merely one of writing satisfactorily in English, but also of adopting certain reasoning processes and formal constraints which are fundamental to English language scientific publication norms (cf. pp. 105–20).

OBJECTIVES

It was obviously not up to the C.R.A.P.E.L. to resolve the matter of what is to be published, where and how, nor to change the choice of the international language used at medical conferences. Assuming, first, that the content of a given article or paper is of interest to the medical population, and second, that the authors choose to publish or read their papers in English, our only concern was to meet their needs; in other words, to help them improve their aural comprehension, oral expression and interactive skills, on the one hand, and their rapid reading and written expression skills (applying the criteria on pp. 313–18) on the other.

The time allotted for the course was two hours a week over a period of approximately ten weeks.

THE 'HELPER'

As the 'teacher' of this course was not a student of medicine, a content-oriented approach to highly specialized medical problems had to be ruled out. The helper, therefore, relied on the fact that the learners were sufficiently versed in medicine and in their respective specializations that, among themselves, they could resolve any problems stemming from medicine itself.

The following report on the type of activities engaged in aims at shedding light on the functions of the 'helper' and the possibilities available to him as a non-specialist.

Aural comprehension

A number of tapes (such as 'Medi-kassets' produced for British doctors, Telelingua tapes, recordings of U.S. radio discussions dealing with such problems as drug addiction and the American Food and Drug Administration's role in the crisis called 'drug lag', and British recordings such as 'Cancer, an incurable disease?') were used extensively; complete transcriptions were available for all of these tapes. Although the tapes were perhaps not geared specifically to a medical audience, neither were they geared uniquely to a lay audience. This intermediate style made it possible to exploit the tapes with our audience of specialists. Though no tapes of medical conferences were available to us at that time, there were tapes of conferences in other fields at our disposal. These were used to glean certain of the speech acts common to conference interaction: floor taking, interrupting, asking questions, disagreeing. One tape having nothing to do with medicine was introduced as a brief study of hesitation phenomena, at the request of the group. Similarly, a tape contrasting British and American accents was also analysed.

In addition, the World Health Organisation in Geneva was very cooperative in furnishing video cassettes which we copied for later use. The interviews of different specialists around the world on particular problems of worldwide interest provided the group with the opportunity to assess their comprehension of a variety of accents, whether the people were native speakers of English or not. This seemed to be a very worthwhile preparation for the international conference scene.

Oral expression

Some of the tapes made at conferences or acquired from the World Health Organisation served not only as an exercise in aural comprehension but also as a springboard for discussion. For instance, a talk on an experimental strategy for teaching medicine in a Canadian university was recorded by a C.R.A.P.E.L. member at a conference on Educational Technology and used as a basis for a discussion on the teaching of medicine in France. Having heard the talk and since he has had contact with the French medical school system, the helper was able to participate in the discussion.

Silent video cartoons humorously evoking serious problems such as alcoholism, drugs, tobacco, heart conditions, the level of general health education in France and the French health system, were also used to elicit discussions in which the helper could participate by asking questions or making comparisons with these problems as they are experienced in the United States and elsewhere. This type of exercise is appreciated as a preparation for the more informal type of conversation that also goes on at conferences.

In order to prepare group members more specifically for their tasks as conference participants, several simulations of the conference situation were carried out. One member of the group would prepare a short paper in his or her field of specialization and would present it to the rest of the group (reading or delivering more spontaneously, depending upon his personal style) who would then ask questions and make comments. In view of the high degree of specialization of these papers (titles included: Neuromuscular Hyper-excitability; PKU babies and brain damage; Lupus Erythematosus) it is obvious that the helper could not play an active role in the discussion, which the group members carried on alone. In this case, the helper's role was to record the simulated conference (sound-track only, as it was impossible in the circumstances to video-tape the simulation) and replay it for the group, allowing them to hear and evaluate their own productions. Emphasis being placed on successful communication, we sought to improve the pronunciation of technical terms like 'phenylketonuria', and more common terms like 'hypothesis', and to develop an awareness of how to modulate a message (a sincere question can be transformed into a sarcastic comment).

Although time did not allow these to be tried, information transfer exercises could constitute a third type of activity, using a chart, diagram or graph as a pretext for an oral presentation.

Rapid reading

Very little time was devoted to rapid reading. The only exercise done required the group to scan two lengthy articles on the environmental causes of cancer (Cairns 1975; Davis 1975) within a given period of time. The learners, taking the word 'environment' and expanding it to include such markers as 'environmental factors', 'toxic substances in man's environment' 'exposure to cancer-producing (carcinogenic) substances', were able quickly to pick out the environmental factors responsible for rising cancer rates.

Written expression

TRANSLATION

Translation was undertaken here not as a means of 'discovering latent grammatical errors' (Pugh 1975) but rather as a means of helping members of the group to improve their skills in translating their own abstracts from French. Two different approaches were adopted.

In the first approach, photocopies of a summary taken from a well-known French medical journal, *La Revue du Praticien*, were distributed (note that this summary is already a translation, appearing next to the French résumé in the journal) and the group was asked to identify anything that they felt smacked of the French. In the second stage, students were asked to rewrite those parts. An example of this kind of summary can be seen below:

SUMMARY

Clinical aspects and treatment of non cirrhotic alcoholic hepatitis

Alcoholic liver cirrhosis is always preceded by the lesions described under the name of alcoholic hepatitis. These lesions are reversible in most cases. It is useful to detect them as thus liver cirrhosis can be prevented, which is an irreversible pathological condition always entailing a reserved prognosis.

The clinical aspects of non cirrhotic alcoholic hepatitis are chronic alcoholic hepatitis, acute alcoholic hepatitis and rare forms such as steatotic alcoholic hepatitis with severe cholestasis.

In the usual chronic form, treatment is essentially withdrawal. In the acute form hospitalisation is necessary for a purely symptomatic treatment. No medication has so far proved effective in acute alcoholic hepatitis, the mortality rate of which is not negligible.

La Revue du Praticien, November 11th 1976

The third stage consisted of comparing their suggested versions and checking the original French résumé, an example of which is given here, to make sure there were no misinterpretations.

RESUME

La cirrhose alcoolique du foie est précédée par des lésions décrites sous le nom d'hépatite alcoolique. Ces lésions sont réversibles dans la majorité des cas. L'intérêt de leur détection est de réaliser une prévention de l'installation d'une cirrhose hépatique, qui est un état anatomique irréversible de pronostic toujours réservé.

Les aspects cliniques de l'hépatite alcoolique non cirrhotique sont l'hépatite alcoolique chronique, l'hépatite alcoolique aiguë et des formes rares comme l'hépatite alcoolique stéatosique avec cholestase intense.

Le traitement est dominé par le sevrage alcoolique dans la forme chronique habituelle. Dans la forme aiguë, l'hospitalisation est nécessaire pour un traitement purement symptomatique. Aucun médicament n'a fait la preuve de son efficacité dans l'hépatite alcoolique aiguë, dont la mortalité n'est pas négligeable.

In the second approach, most of the flaws had been erased from the text by the helper. Members of the group received a set of texts with blank spaces, along with the original French résumé, and were asked to fill in the blanks. They then compared their own solutions to the translations appearing in the journal, the latter proving to be much less 'acceptable' than their own! An example of this exercise is given below.

Fill in the blanks:

are very
frequent in the three first years
and several origins. One
may understand them

three
stages: asleep, sleeping
and awakening. of these
stages may be disturbed.
stud-
ies
a cyclic organiz-
ation of each cycle
a peaceful phase and
a restless one with rapid
movements of the eyes. The
length of sleep varies
and specific factors linked
to intellectual and
development.
in the first three
months are frequent and

or to

From 3 to 9 months sleep
troubles are rarer and often
caused by dental eruption.
Sometimes
as in lack of
motor and affective stimulation of the child by an
exhausted mother.

It is between 9 months and
3 years old that
are the most
frequent. They
to motor
to
of the opposition
type. Sometimes anxiety
dominates the picture

or primary
linked to the mother's
Feeding troubles and
phobic elements
More rarely, sleep
impairments are observed in
the field of a psychosis.
The treatment
which are
sometimes
in
order to reestablish a cycle of
artificial sleep
are some-
times necessary. When the
mother–child relationship is
concerned,

La Revue du Praticien,
November 21st 1971

RESUME

Les troubles du sommeil, très fréquents dans les trois premières années, relèvent de causes diverses. On ne peut bien les comprendre qu'en se rappelant la physiologie du sommeil. Le sommeil comprend trois temps: l'endormissement, le sommeil et le réveil; chacune de ces phases pouvant être perturbée. L'étude électro-encéphalographique a montré l'existence d'une organisation cyclique du sommeil, chaque cycle comprenant une phase de sommeil calme et une phase de sommeil agité avec mouvements oculaires rapides. La durée du sommeil varie en fonction de l'âge du sujet et en fonction de facteurs individuels liés au développement moteur, intellectuel et affectif.

Les troubles du premier trimestre sont fréquents et relèvent souvent d'erreur alimentaire, ou d'une perturbation de la personnalité de la mère dominée par l'anxiété.

De trois à neuf mois, les troubles du sommeil sont plus rares et souvent imputés à l'éruption dentaire. Parfois, il s'agit d'une origine plus complexe, tel le manque de stimulation motrice et affective de l'enfant par une mère épuisée.

C'est entre neuf mois et trois ans que les troubles du sommeil sont les plus fréquents. Ils peuvent être liés à une hyperactivité motrice avec retard du langage, à des troubles du caractère à type d'opposition. Parfois, l'anxiété domine le tableau soit qu'elle succède à un traumatisme affectif, soit qu'elle soit primaire, liée aux perturbations de la mère. Il s'y associe, fréquemment des troubles alimentaires et des éléments phobiques. Plus rarement, les troubles du sommeil s'observent dans le cadre d'une psychose.

Le traitement comporte avant tout des conseils éducatifs parfois suffisants. Les sédatifs seront prescrits pour rétablir un cycle de sommeil artificiel pendant quelque temps, les anxiolytiques sont parfois nécessaires. Lorsque c'est l'ensemble des relations mère–enfant qui est en cause, une psychothérapie de la mère sera conseillée.

The translated text appearing in the journal read as follows:

Sleep impairment in infants

Sleep impairments are very frequent in the three first years and have several origins. One may understand them only by reminding the physiology of the sleep. The sleep has three stages: falling asleep, sleeping and awakening. Each of these stages may be disturbed. Electro-encephalographic studies demonstrated the existence of a cyclic organization of the sleep, each cycle contains a peaceful phase and a restless one with rapid movements of the eyes. The length of sleep varies with the age and specific factors linked to the motor, intellectual and affective development.

Troubles in the first three months are frequent and correspond to feeding mistakes or to impairment of the mother's personality particularly to their anxiety.

From 3 to 9 months sleep troubles are rarer and often caused by dental eruption. Sometimes the origin is more complicated as in lack of motor and affective stimulation of the child by an exhausted mother.

It is between 9 months and 3 years old that the sleep impairments are the most frequent. They may be linked to motor hyperactivity with speech delay, to personality affections of the opposition type. Sometimes anxiety dominates the picture whether accompanying an affective traumatism or primary and linked to the mother's abnormalities. Feeding troubles and phobic elements are frequently associated. More rarely, sleep impairments are observed in the field of a psychosis.

The treatment consists first in educative advices which are sometimes efficient enough.

Sedatives are present in order to reestablish a cycle of artificial sleep in the first phase. Anxiolytics are sometimes necessary. When the mother-child relationship is concerned, mother's psychotherapy is available.

La Revue du Practicien,
November 21st 1871

ABSTRACT WRITING

As a preparation for abstract writing, several abstracts from American medical journals were provided by the group and were studied in an attempt to define the structure of the abstract. This preliminary step seemed necessary, for if the group members had already written abstracts, they admitted to having no explicit description of what information should be included or how it should be presented. One exercise that seemed promising — though it was not repeated enough to be conclusive — was taking an abstract, mixing up the sentence order and asking for a reconstruction of the abstract in its original form. The sentences seemed to correspond to the stereotyped stages of full-length scientific articles, that is, hypothesis, methods, results, conclusion and/or discussion, although in some cases the hypothesis appeared at the end of the text.

The fact that further work has to be done at this level (both analytical and practical), as well as at the syntactic level, was borne out by the abstracts written by members of the group and presented to the others for study throughout the course.

Another use of the abstract in preparation for the actual writing was as a source of what might be called commonly occurring semantic combinations: 'detailed analysis of the results . . .' 'similarity to findings in other studies . . .' 'failure occurred . . .' 'findings sug-

gest . . .' 'undergo operation . . .' 'long-term side effects . . .' 'administration of drugs . . .'
Such combinations are extremely useful tools to have available when writing. The group was introduced to the idea of culling them from texts they read regularly and devising ways of filing them for further reference.

One last effort was made to reduce their chances of making 'mistakes': a list of spelling differences between English and American was distributed.

The results of this experiment were obtained both through discussion at the close of the course and through a questionnaire distributed to all members of the group, which attempted to define their attitudes towards having a non-specialist *animateur*, their preferences and their expectations for the course if it were to be continued the following year. Discussion revealed that all the participants were satisfied and felt the course had helped them. As for the questionnaire, all seven participants replied 'yes' to the question 'Do you think that a course in medical English can be useful even if the teachers themselves are not specialists in medicine?'. Only one answered 'yes' to 'Would you have preferred the teachers to be both native speakers and qualified doctors?' All expressed the wish to continue taking the course, under the same conditions, the following year.

We hope this paper has shown that there are indeed numerous possibilities (many of which have not been explored here) for a non-specialist helper in a group of specialists. We were able to accomplish the activities related here because the following conditions were satisfied:
1. The helper was a native speaker of English.
2. The learners possessed a thorough knowledge of their specialization.
3. The field of specialization was not totally obscure for the lay helper, which made the practice of several language skills possible.

Conclusion

The three experiments described show that the roles of learners vary along the following parameters:
1. Level of specialized knowledge.
2. Level of competence in the target language.
3. Skills to be developed.

For the teacher, the parameters are:
1. Mother tongue and level of bilingualism.
2. Skills to be developed.

3. Degree to which the specialization can be understood by a layman.
4. Level of knowledge about the structures of the two languages.

The situation of a learner who wishes to acquire a specialized communicative competence in a foreign language can be schematized as in Figure 2.

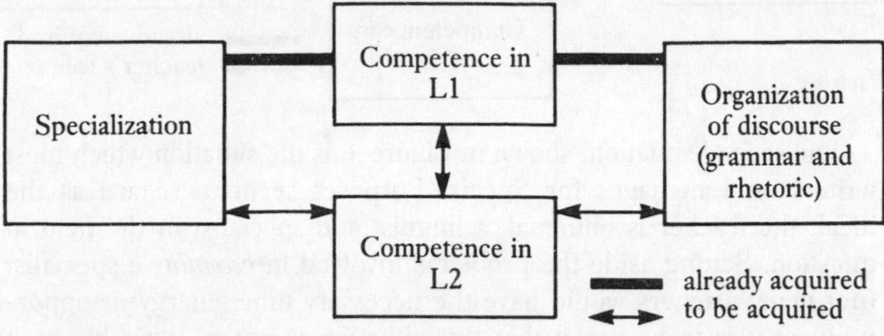

FIGURE 2

Figures 3–5 show the ways in which the role of the learner varies according to the characteristics of the teacher.

In Figure 3, the teacher is bilingual and a specialist but not a linguist (see Duda and Luceri 1975).

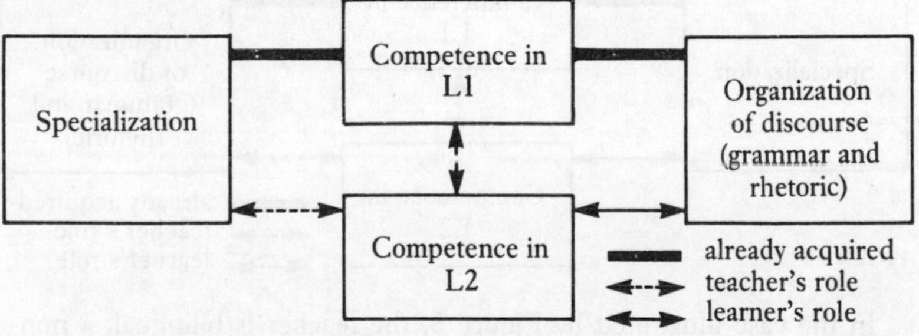

FIGURE 3

In such a situation, the teacher sets up the correspondences between the L2 and the specialization on the one hand and between the L1 and the L2 on the other, but only superficially. This may seem to be quicker and more convenient for the learner, but only in the short term. If the learner ever hopes to do without a teacher (and a teacher with this profile is often very difficult to find) then he himself will have to become a linguist and discover the rules which govern the functioning of the L2. Neither his specialized knowledge nor his previous study of English is likely to be of much help to him here.

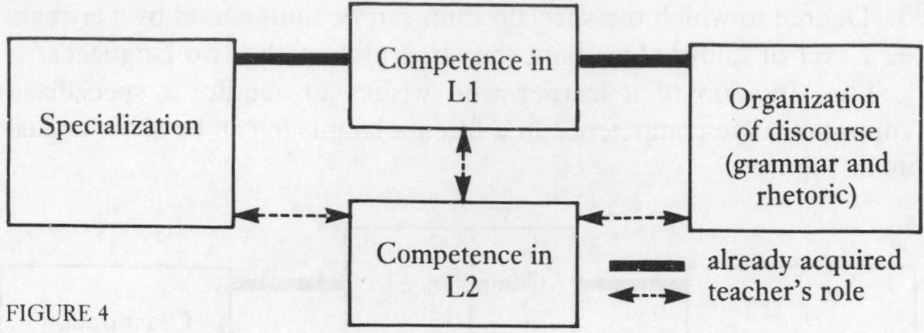

FIGURE 4

The second situation, shown in Figure 4, is the situation which most writers on Languages for Special Purposes seem to regard as the ideal: the teacher is bilingual, a linguist and specialist in the field in question. Setting aside the problems involved in *becoming* a specialist (not many teachers would have the necessary time, energy or opportunities) it is to be noted that this situation is not as desirable as it might at first glance seem. The fact that it is the teacher who knows and controls everything may be very reassuring for both him and his learners, but will also militate against the learners ever achieving any degree of autonomy in the matter.

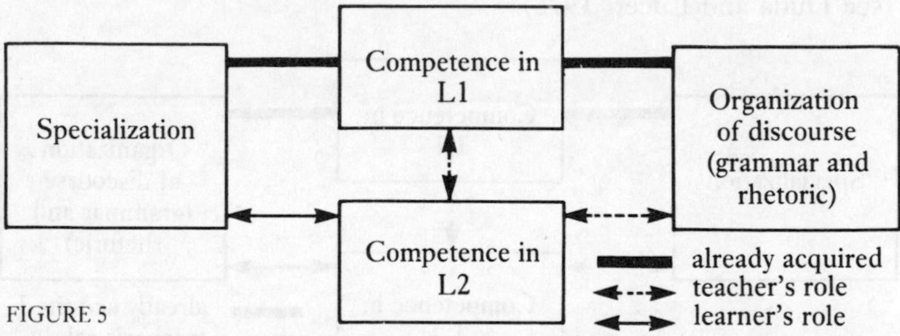

FIGURE 5

In the case illustrated by Figure 5, the teacher is bilingual, a non-specialist and a linguist. Here the teacher can establish the relationships between the L1 and L2, not just superficially but in a deep and systematic way which will enable him to explain the rules of grammar and discourse involved. The learners will be able to use their mother-tongue knowledge of their field of specialization to set up links between the L2 and the specialization. This situation has numerous advantages: the non-specialist teacher is easier to find; the learners make an essential contribution to their learning programme in the shape of their specialized knowledge; and the work they need to do is more closely related to their skills than carrying out linguistic analyses and descriptions would be.

16 Using authentic documents for pedagogical purposes

D. Abé, F. Carton, M. Cembalo and O. Régent

The present rapid increase in techniques for reproducing documents of all kinds makes available to language teachers and learners alike materials which illustrate real language use in a wide variety of communicative situations. It is possible nowadays to video-record a debate or a lecture, to use a TV broadcast or to copy an article — none of these possibilities existed until recently. This introduces a new dimension to the crucial problem of choosing materials. Is it possible to imagine a language-learning programme based on authentic materials which does not make use of texts created by language-learning specialists but which still follows a systematic progression?

What we would like to do in this paper is to summarize briefly the main conclusions of some ten years' methodological theorizing and experimentation (Kuhn 1970). First, we will give our view of the meaning and extent of the idea of authenticity; then we will discuss the rationale behind the choice of authentic materials; finally we will go on to discuss aspects of their use. Obviously there can be no question of our giving a single set of instructions: authentic materials always have to be collected and used in response to the specific needs of individuals or of particular groups. The vast number of different types of written documents and of oral communication, along with the immense variety of their contents, means that they can be selected and exploited in ways which suit the learners' needs exactly. Any article on the topic is bound to be theoretical, to avoid giving the impression that a particular application is a model to be followed. For this reason, our concluding section will simply be the description of one particular training course with its own specific material and institutional context.

What is an authentic document?

A first, negative, definition of an authentic document is that it is *one which has not been produced for language-teaching or language-learning purposes*; in other words, it is not a didactic document. A more positive approach is to say that it is one which has been produced (as a message) in a real communication situation. This means that written or spoken texts which have been produced or modified for language-teaching purposes are not authentic. Neither are the discourse of language teachers (or even of native speakers if they are trying to teach) nor the foreign language productions of learners — though they may still be very helpful or even necessary in the learning process. Such types of discourse are invariably 'marked' by their pedagogical aims. To construct a text for language-teaching purposes, to modify it or even to speak with the aim of teaching or learning a language in mind is a very particular kind of linguistic behaviour. Whereas in authentic materials the discourse attempts to communicate a message by means of the language, in teaching materials this process is reversed. In such materials we find the language (a grammatical structure, for instance) being communicated by messages (which exemplify that structure). No longer is it the message which is crucial, but the way it is expressed.

It is, therefore, in terms of its *communicative aims* that we can judge the authenticity or otherwise of a document. Even if it is sometimes impossible to know just what the aims of a particular document or utterance are, or if it is difficult to describe them, we never have any trouble recognizing the very special situation which is second language learning.

A further problem concerning the nature of authenticity involves the decoding process: can we extract texts from their original context and divert them away from their communicative aims for language teaching purposes? Is it possible to talk of 'authentic materials' even when the conditions of reception and decoding are no longer the original ones?

We question the notion of authenticity of reception: in a given linguistic community a text can be decoded in any number of ways. Who is to say that a specialized medical article is read in a more authentic way by the doctors it is addressed to than by a linguist studying word frequency, a compositor setting up the article in print or a chemist who is interested in medicine? Each of these readers has a different aim, so that their separate readings cannot be contrasted qualitatively, even if quantitatively the writer himself may hope that his article will mostly be read by fellow-doctors.

Since any document can be received by readers or listeners other than those for whom it was originally destined, it seems legitimate to make language learners into language observers. However it is decoded, an authentic text still remains a real object in a particular linguistic code: once the message has been produced the encoding characteristics and those of the message remain unchanged, and it is still the result of a genuine communicative act. Nothing in the text changes even if the addressee changes.

An authentic document is like a photograph of a given discourse at a particular moment in time and, once taken, has its own existence. It is not in itself 'reality' but is an adequate representation of it and, together with other photographs, helps us to build up an overall picture of what that reality is like. 'Authentic' should not be confused, though, with other parameters of discourse such as 'oral'/'written' or 'spontaneous'/'prepared'. These terms refer to aspects of the encoding process which, although they have extremely important effects on the resultant type of discourse, are independent of the communicative aim. A TV commercial, the BBC News, a pop song, recordings of lectures, conversations and poetry readings are all authentic, as they were not produced for language-teaching purposes.

Why use authentic materials?

There are two main reasons for using authentic documents in language learning: firstly, they represent a fraction or the whole of a real piece of communication produced in a given situation, or an accurate copy of it — they expose learners to examples of language *use*; secondly, if the documents are carefully chosen to correspond to the learner's needs, they will, by definition and because of their richness and variety, form an accurate and exhaustive syllabus.

The communicative reality of authentic materials

We have long been aware of the disadvantages of written or spoken texts which have been completely made up for language-teaching purposes: by simplifying the richness and complexity of authentic instances of language use, they delay any contact with real language, where they do not actually prevent it. They omit many essential factors in communication: the role of illocution (the values of different speech-acts); socio-cultural constraints; the relationships between speakers and all their discursive corollaries such as gesture, facial expression and prosodic markers; situational features such as implicature. Léon (1979) has shown how the degree of grammaticality tends to diminish as the role of implications increases in oral communication, with a corresponding increase in prosodic markers. In addition, there are all the hesitations, repetitions, false starts, slips and so on which occur in spontaneous oral discourse. Although all these elements seem to be present in every language, their realizations vary. They should, therefore, be taken into account in the learning process; since it is completely impossible to reduce all these features to the written form, it becomes all the more necessary to use authentic materials which exemplify the separate characteristics of these two codes.

The objective of language learning is not simply to be able to produce or understand a large number of grammatically correct sentences, but also to acquire the skills necessary if they are to be appropriately used; this means being able to adjust what is to be said or understood to the way it is said in a particular situation. Examples of these skills include knowing how to use a telephone or to ask for information, being able to take the floor in a group discussion or to formulate a hypothesis in writing.

Each of these speech acts can be realized by a very great number of different utterances which bring into play various combinations of the features we have been discussing, in codes which are specific to the language in question. The interrelationships between these codes form the language's 'communicative grammar'. The learner discovers these codes for himself in a succession of cognitive steps and states which are the result of observations, hypotheses and tests (Corder 1976). This is why it is important to put the learner in contact with real utterances in communicative situations, in other words, with materials which allow him to formulate correct hypotheses. It is only by working with authentic materials representing real communicative acts that the learner will be able to carry out this operation. Moreover, since each document is the product of a unique situation, it is perceived as something having a relative status, rather than as the only way to realize an act in a given situation, as is the case with didactic texts.

Pedagogic consequences

INDIVIDUAL LEARNING STRATEGIES

Given a homogeneous group of learners, having the same language needs and the same interests and one or more common objectives, it is perfectly possible to establish a teaching programme which aims to attain those objectives. Despite this group-teaching strategy, however, each learner will go his own way as far as his individual learning process (observations, hypotheses and tests) is concerned. The richness of authentic materials, and the fact that they do not in themselves impose any particular approach or technique, leaves the individual free to carry out that process on any aspect of the language he may choose.

MEETING LEARNERS' NEEDS

The use of authentic materials makes it possible to meet learners' needs accurately and economically: by choosing documents of the type he encounters or will encounter in his area of interest, the learner is able to concentrate on their lexical, grammatical, functional and discursive characteristics without wasting time on what are, for him, irrelevant problems. The technician who needs to be able to read the operating instructions for new equipment, or the research worker who wishes to attend a congress and follow lectures on his specialization are both able to focus on doing just that.

Clearly, the use of documents which appeal to the learner's interests will help reinforce his motivation. In those cases where there is a clash between the learner's needs and his interests (for example, the computer operator who is temporarily sick of computing texts) there is no problem if the learner himself does the choosing. The use of materials which are easily available (newspapers, magazines, books, radio broadcasts, records, TV, etc.) makes self-directed learning easier. Nonetheless, most learners need to be trained in the choice and use of such documents.

Using authentic materials

Authentic materials and language skills

Authentic materials are so numerous that the teacher or learner is always obliged to make a selection of some kind. To facilitate this choice, it is convenient to classify the materials according to whether or not they have been processed, whether they are written, audio or video and according to the quality of the print or recording, to their length, vocabulary and so on. The relevance of these categories to the choice of documents depends on the learning objective in question. For example, the wish to acquire communicative competence in a particular language skill results in a narrowing down of the field of choice: a learner who wants to improve his oral comprehension has to work with authentic sound or video recordings. In this case, the document can be used 'raw', since the learner does not intervene directly in the interaction; he is an observer, and his presence has no effect on the document itself. He tries to play the role of a member of some foreign speech-community. Of course, his aim is not to become a native speaker (or, rather, 'native listener' in our example) but to reach the level of competence which he has set himself (Holec 1979).

On the other hand, it is no good the learner trying to improve his oral expression by simply repeating word for word everything that one of the participants has said in the interaction recorded on a tape. He would produce a 'discourse' in which he had no kind of choice and yet which he himself would not have encoded in the same way. He would be an actor in an interaction which he could not influence at all. This absence of choice completely distorts the nature of oral expression, one of the major characteristics of that activity being that it is in fact made up of a series of successive choices. To do away with these choices would alter the conditions of production to such an extent that the resultant learning exercise could not be regarded as oral expression. Because every authentic document is unique, it cannot be used as a model for imitation or repetition; it has to be used indirectly, as it were, as material for study and observation which will prepare the learner for expression. The learner then tries to imitate the speaker, while leaving out those features of the discourse which are not stable, in other words, those which are determined by the characteristics of the particular situation, such as relationships between the participants, presuppositions, place and time and so on. At the same time the learner must try to take into account his own experience, character and social position.

As regards written expression, it is perfectly possible for learners to do straightforward imitations of their authentic documents. The different types of written communication are both less numerous and more highly structured than the spoken mode, there being clearer lines of demarcation between the genres (letters, articles, reports, telex) and the relationships between reader and writer being more strictly codified. Moreover, the absence of any direct interaction limits the range of possible choice and since it is not necessary to keep adapting to an interlocutor, the learner can imitate the set phrases to be found in business letters, reports, telexes and so on.

Authentic materials can, therefore, be used for expression to different degrees, direct imitation being much easier with written documents than with sound recordings.

Authentic materials at different levels

Just what *is* a document in simple language, easy for a beginner to understand? Didactic materials have the advantage that they can be easily manipulated as regards morphology and grammar, so that a progression from simple to complex can easily be established; but it is still by no means certain that a progression from simple to complex actually facilitates the learning of syntax. In any case, there are many other factors in communication such as situational and socio-cultural features, interactive strategies and discursive organization, etc. These factors cannot just be ignored, because to do so is to risk producing a situation where a message which is syntactically simple is completely incomprehensible to the learner because of other factors which are unknown to him. For example, 'Clunk, click, every trip' would be meaningless in a society where cars are rare and seat-belts rarer. It is difficult to imagine a single progression which could take all these factors into account simultaneously — and anyway it is very doubtful if the problem of simplicity should be posed in terms of progression. Simplicity is more a matter of the differences between mother tongue and target language, and of the contents of the document and the ways in which they are presented. Simplicity can only be defined with reference to the particular learning situation of a particular learner. Anyone, even a complete beginner, can form hypotheses about an authentic document.

Numerous experiments have shown that it is perfectly possible for beginners to retrieve information from authentic materials related to their field of specialization (for experiments involving French, see Beacco *et al.* 1978; for English, see Duda 1976). The use of such materials activates learners' discursive competence, calls on their extra-linguistic knowledge and allows them to use similarities in vocabulary, morphology or syntax: this is why people usually find it easier to grasp the meaning of documents drawn from some area of specialized knowledge, scientific or otherwise. In other words, the more familiar the topic, the easier it is for the learner to understand the document in question. Every type of discourse, 'specialized' or not, has its own characteristics, so that even the beginner may find himself dealing with linguistic, stylistic and discursive features, with contents and with specifically scientific modes of conceptual organization which he knows already. All these familiar elements increase the learner's ability to predict elements which he could not otherwise have understood. Because part of the contents at least is 'transparent', other lexical, syntactic and discursive elements become clear. On the other hand, if the document concerns a subject about which the learner knows nothing it will seem far more difficult to him, even if its level of lexical and syntactic difficulty is 'objectively' lower. There is nothing to prove that knowledge of the foreign language, as such, is necessary for the comprehension of the strictly specialized aspects of a 'specialized' discourse. In any case, if any kind of progression is to be established, it cannot be done once and for all; it will not be based on strictly linguistic criteria, but rather on types of skill (Duda 1979).

The presentation of authentic materials

Since an authentic document is an example of a particular type of discourse, it is essential that it should be dealt with by the learner in its original form. It is pointless trying to master the spoken language by studying transcriptions of conversations, however detailed; and it would be unsuitable, or even positively harmful, to give such learners recorded versions of newspaper articles which have been read aloud. The encoding rules for writing and speaking are not the same, and the specific characteristics of each mode disappear as a text is translated from one to the other. The learner who comes across these characteristics for the first time in real life will be completely baffled. Moreover, types of competence which have been acquired in the mother tongue are completely ignored: for example, it is impossible to 'scan' an article which has been read aloud, and even if the learner studies an infinite number of transcriptions he will still be incapable of understanding a spoken text.

Obviously, it will sometimes be necessary to process documents in order to prepare them for certain learning activities, but the aim of this task will always be for the learner to be able to grasp the document in its original form.

Choice of materials by learners

If materials are to be as suitable as possible, the choice has to take into account the learners' needs, objectives and interests and it is the learners themselves who are best fitted to make this choice, especially as regards their specialized texts. It is also often easier for them to get hold of specialized texts in the foreign language. Two approaches are possible: the learners can be asked to provide a series of documents which teacher and learners then choose from according to the techniques or strategies which they intend to adopt; or a quantity of materials can be made available to the learners from which they then choose. In either case, the teacher's role and image are profoundly altered.

Authentic materials in use: an example

To conclude, we are going to describe a training programme which was developed for a heavy engineering firm, Metlor. This firm was a market leader in the construction of oil rigs, which meant that the staff had to deal in English with customers from all sorts of backgrounds and in a number of different situations: face-to-face, when customers visited the firm, or when items were delivered; on the telephone; in technical documents and drawings; and in correspondence by telex both with the customers and with other factories in the same group. The employees who were directly involved in the use of English were members of the administrative staff (in particular, secretaries and telephone operators), certain members of the research department, draughtsmen and production managers.

The training programme was organized around the learners' different objectives and consisted of the following four courses:

1. The telephone: comprehension and expression for operators.
2. Written comprehension.
3. Telex writing.
4. Spoken English: comprehension and expression.

The materials were collected directly from and by the learners themselves. For the written comprehension materials, the course organizers visited those departments which used English, collecting the different documents in use and discussing in detail their problems with the people concerned. During these visits, a certain number of completely unexpected learning materials came to light. Several of the departments had technical works of various kinds, some of which contained multilingual glossaries: but most useful of all was the handbook of welding standards, since this included a section where the explanations were all illustrated, which made it possible to understand the greater part of the technical terminology. Among the other documents made available to the course organizers there were drawings and plans, schedules, orders, amendments and all sorts of other documents relating to Metlor's most recent products. The selection was carried out by the learners themselves, on the basis of their own personal or professional criteria.

Similarly, photocopies of recent telexes were also made available to the course designers.

The problem of collecting telephone materials was far more difficult. For technical reasons, it was not easy to make recordings directly at the Metlor switchboard and, as luck would have it, the number of phone calls in English during this period happened to be very low. For these reasons, we were obliged to find our own authentic materials. This we did by recording phone calls from the C.R.A.P.E.L. to England. Only those calls which were between two native speakers were used and, of those, only calls which went via an operator.

Materials for oral comprehension were collected by recording situations which occurred in the Metlor workshops. One of the course designers would be present at the various transactions and recorded them as discreetly as possible. The recordings which were made included the handing over of a number of items, a discussion on the welding techniques to be used in the manufacture of a particular product and the reception and visit of a Norwegian engineer.

The materials which were thus collected were used in one of two ways, depending on whether they were aimed at expression or comprehension. The written documents were used directly as comprehension material. The learners' task was to try to solve in a systematic fashion the problems which they came across in the document. The teacher's job was to collect and categorize all these problems and to prepare exercises for each type. Of course, the exercises themselves were also based directly on the documents. The methodology was that which had been developed for C.R.A.P.E.L. courses in general written English (Cembalo, Esch and Hildenbrand 1971; Abé and Duda 1974), but applied to the specific problems of the documents in question. There was one major difference, however, namely that the progression for this course was based on an analysis of learners' problems as observed during the first few hours' work on the documents. As a result of this, for example, special attention was given to problems of number and quantity, and the auxiliary verbs were dealt with at the very outset.

The telexes were dealt with slightly differently, since they were used both for comprehension and as a corpus for written expression. For comprehension purposes, they were used in the same way as the other written materials, but their role in expression work was very different. There they were used as the raw material for different types of exercise based on pastiche. Learners were asked to produce telexes similar to the ones they themselves had received but with slightly different meanings brought about by variance in vocabulary, modalization, etc. The learners themselves established a 'functional index' in which were listed the different realizations of particular functions (giving a reference, confirming, ordering, etc.), so that they could easily be looked up.

The use made of the recorded telephone calls also depended on whether they were being studied for comprehension purposes or for expression (it is important to remember that the learners in question were complete beginners). The comprehension work consisted of two stages: first, sensitization to the structure of interaction on the telephone and, second, detailed comprehension exercises on each of the different elements which make up that structure. The first stage involved listening to the recording and identifying what point in the conversation had been reached; in other words, the function of the utterance in question had to be recognized. Was it a request for an extension number, thanks, an explanation, the speaker introducing himself? This work was carried out before any lexical or grammatical explanations were given which might have helped with the comprehension of the strictly verbal aspects of these utterances. The learners were soon able to identify functions in this way after working on three recorded conversations.

The second stage consisted of elucidating the contents of each speech act. Once the act had been identified in other words, it was taken for detailed listening comprehension with special regard to its linguistic forms and their meanings. This was followed by systematic exercises, where different realizations of the same act were found in the corpus, and by the study of artificial examples which were provided to fill certain gaps in the corpus such as numbers and the names of all the departments.

In expression work, the recorded conversations were used as raw material for observation and re-use. In the first phase, observation, the learners were familiarized with the forms to be used by a process of discrimination and then repetition of relevant passages. This was followed by systematic exercises which used as stimuli passages taken from the authentic materials and then by exercises which used stimuli which had been specially made up for that purpose. Most of this work was done outside teaching hours, which were devoted to dealing with problems which had cropped up at work.

In addition, phone calls in English were made from the C.R.A.P.E.L. by native speakers to the learners, who were thus obliged to put into practice the skills in which they had been trained.

17 Viewing comprehension: l'oeil écoute

P. Riley

Introduction

The basic question considered in this paper is a very simple one — at least as far as the formulation is concerned. It is this: how can we use video equipment for the teaching of comprehension? For practical reasons — here we are referring to things as crude as the relative cost of the equipment — this question is taken as meaning 'What is specific to video?' or 'What can we do with video that we can't do with sound-only recordings?'. In other words, 'Is video worth it?'

Any serious attempt to answer these questions will involve an examination of the role of the visual channel of communication in interaction and so the first part of this paper is devoted to a relatively theoretical consideration of that problem. However, it should not be thought that this is merely an exercise in armchair linguistics: the discussion is based on the experience of a number of teachers who have been using video in the classroom for the past five years, as well as on the observation of learners using the video section of the Sound Library (pp. 286–98). To start with, the work was based on an act of faith: 'Watching TV is good for your English'. This paper is an attempt to describe why this might be so, by providing the teacher/learner using video with an analytic grid which should help him make better use of an extremely rich medium.

Aspects of communication in face-to-face interaction

A long time ago, in the days when face-to-face interaction was something adolescents did on park benches in the Spring, applied linguists worked on the comforting, ennobling, assumption that their job was to apply Linguistics. No one knew quite *how* you applied it, that was what all the research, argument and experimentation was about, but the actual aim was clear enough: Applied Linguistics was Linguistics applied. That is, a linguistic description of a given language had to be transferred to the learners: once they had all the necessary bits and pieces — the phonemes, morphemes and syntagmemes — they would know the language. One is reminded of Virginia Wolfe's Mrs Dalloway, looking for someone who 'would just slip Greek into her head'.

Whether we talk in Virginia Wolfe's terms of 'slipping it in' or in Noam Chomsky's terms of 'systematic ambiguity', the belief that linguistic descriptions have psychological reality (that they are what goes on in people's heads and that they therefore form a summary of what has to be taught, being at once the aim and the syllabus) is still around. On the one hand, it allows purely theoretical linguists to pontificate about how languages should be taught (though Chomsky himself has been very careful to state that he doubts if his work has any practical application), and on the other it provides applied linguists and language teachers with a rationale for their work which is both scientific and accessible.

There is however, a major objection to this approach: it doesn't work.

Partly, of course, this is because when one starts 'applying Linguistics' one does so in real life, with real people who have real problems, on particular days in actual classrooms, in certain groups — so that a whole range of extraneous, non-linguistic factors, from the weather to company policy, will determine what a particular individual will or will not learn, and how and when. Of all the variables in the language-learning situation, only a few are 'linguistic'.

But there is a second reason, and it is one which is related not so much to the applications as to the linguistics, to the descriptions themselves. The whole of the movement towards a functional or communicative approach, which we have been witnessing for the past seven years or so, is a reaction against the inadequacy of purely linguistic descriptions. The nature of that inadequacy is by now so well discussed that I feel I need do no more than summarize it by saying that 'grammar is not enough', that formal rules for the construction of sentences do not provide the ability to *use* the language which learners need to communicate. We have learnt the hard way that we can develop a model or description of great sophistication, going from phonetic and phonological contrasts, through morphological and lexical and syntactic forms and structures, in great detail, from the base of the pyramid to the top, and if we are lucky our learners will acquire that detail; yet they are still unable to produce or interpret utterances in context.

It is generally agreed that this is because the learner does not know the rules of use, the discourse rules of the language and/or because he does not possess the necessary situational or pragmalinguistic information. This is by no means a new observation — how many seminars have there been on topics like 'Teaching communicative competence' during the last few years? However, for the moment let us concentrate on an observation which is just as obvious — and a good deal older, by some thousands of years. It is this: just as it is possible to possess all the rules in the pyramid, from perfect phonetic variation to doubly-embedded clauses, and still be incapable of using them, so it is also possible to possess none of them and still be able to communicate and understand. If I am travelling by train across Poland, say, and someone leans over and offers me a cigarette and I accept it and smile my thanks, then communication has taken place.

These are not, by the way, rare cases, even if they are extreme ones: we have all met people who are linguistically perfectly competent, but who, in a particular situation, are unable to communicate, just as we have all met people who can't speak a word of the language but who, in a particular situation, manage to communicate adequately. What is important for us as teachers, of course, is that there is an infinite number of combinations along the cline which joins these two extremes.

The point being made here, then, is that in face-to-face interaction there is a large number of non-verbal, extra-linguistic sources of information and meaning. And they are not to be despised; true, they lack the semantic or referential precision of the verbal component, but in pragmatic and relational terms they are generally far more important. We will return to the nature of their contribution to the meaning of messages later; for the moment, let us just emphasize the point that such factors as proxemics, kinesics and deictics are all part of the message. They are not just a sort of gloss on the verbal component.

We need to get out of our heads completely what we might call the 'audio-visual course' notion of the role of non-verbal features. There, the gestures or pictures are used as a gloss, as a parallel code to reiterate and explain the message being transmitted orally (Holec 1975); a customer ordering fish in a restaurant has a little bubble containing a picture of a fish coming out of his head. This semiotic relationship — parallel coding of the same message — is totally different from the integrated and cumulative role played by non-verbal features in face-to-face interaction, where they converge to contribute to a final meaning or message of which they are an intrinsic part.

Clearly, the conceptual and descriptive problems involved in this overall approach to interaction in what we might call 'non-autonomous linguistics' are immense, since human communication is a multi-channel phenomenon: we can communicate along any of the sensory channels by patterning any available substance which is capable of conventional coding and short term manipulation. Weird and wonderful examples abound, of course, from smoke, sign and whistle languages, through Braille and perfumed notepaper, to prisoners tapping on pipes.

But of course, two of the sensory channels are especially privileged from this point of view, by which I mean that, given the physical nature of man and of the world he lives in, they are able to carry greater loads of information, in more varied ways and they have more rapid fading. These are the visual and acoustic channels.

Relatively speaking, the acoustic channel is by far the better studied, although until the advent of modern phonetics it was the patterning carried by the channel — words and sentences — which was studied, rather than realizations. It is highly instructive to look at those aspects of oral messages which are absent from the written form: tone, tonicity, key, voice qualities, tempo and rhythm, for example. These vocal non-verbal features, which are highly systemic, highly linguistic, realize meanings which are discoursal, relational, interactional and pragmatic, but only very rarely semantic.

All this is even more true of the various visual components of meaning, and our ignorance of how they operate, or even what they are, is far greater. It is no coincidence that the gap between the invention of apparatus for recording sound and that for recording vision is about the same as the gap which separates phonetics and phonology from . . . from what? Optetics and Optemics? But the ability to record the data, however vital, is only the first step; what we also need is a series of categories which will help us describe the contribution of various visual messages to the overall meaning which is created in face-to-face interaction. What, that is, are the communicative functions of visual, non-verbal features?

The communicative functions of the visually perceived aspects of interaction

How does what we see relate to what we hear during an interaction and how is this information integrated into meaning? To the best of our knowledge, very little work has been done on the ways in which messages perceived visually are articulated with messages transmitted along other channels: if we turn to the field of semiotics, for example, we find studies which are of great interest to the theoretical linguist, but which are far too abstract and generalized for more detailed descriptive purposes (although the integrative approach to the nature of meaning being followed here clearly owes much to modern semiotic theory). If we turn to those linguists whose interests include the non-semantic functions of language — Jakobson and Halliday come most readily to mind — we find little or no discussion of non-verbal realizations. Most disappointing of all is the work being carried out under the banner of 'Pragmatics' or 'Speech Act Theory' which, on examination, proves to be concerned with the semantic cover of artificial sentences in isolation, being completely devoid of any social or interactional dimension. Indeed, we would argue that the refusal by speech act theorists and generative semanticists to consider non-verbal communication vitiates their work, since it obliges them to attribute to the verbal element communicative functions which are largely carried non-verbally in interaction.

More rewarding by far is the work of the ethnolinguists such as Sacks, Labov and Hymes, whose approach is ably represented in France by the group working with Bourdieu at Paris XIII (Bachman 1980; some valuable insights are also to be found in a recent article by Roulet, 1980). Even so, none of these investigations has tried to put forward a repertoire of categories specifically for the visual component of meaning.

What follows, then, is a first tentative step in that direction. It is both eclectic and based on the findings of a C.R.A.P.E.L. research team working on the analysis of face-to-face interaction. We will try to indicate some of the most important pedagogical implications of the analysis which is outlined here, but since the area is such a vast one it will not be possible to enter into any great detail. This does not preclude practical, albeit tentative, suggestions. For the sake of clarity of exposition, the pedagogical aspects are discussed as each function is presented, but this is obviously an artificial procedure, since in reality it is often impossible to isolate and identify functions and their realizations in this way. A particular behaviour can realize several functions; for example, a gesture of 'surrender' in an argument ('OK, have it your own way!') may realize indexical, modal and interactional functions simultaneously.

THE DEICTIC FUNCTION

The importance of deictic reference for the verbal component is already widely recognized and studied, and the term is here used in the generally accepted sense of 'pointing at' objects which are physically present in the communicative situation. We refer to them without naming them, as when we use pronouns, for example: 'he', 'this thingummy', 'the man over there' or 'you' only have an effective referential value when used in a situation. But what has seldom been discussed is the way in which the reference of such elements is specified or made unambiguous. In face-to-face interaction this is almost always done visually. The actual realization may vary, of course, from a gesture ('Look at this', holding out the object in question) to gaze ('you' is very often the person one is making eye-contact with) to the simple acknowledged presence of the referent within the sight of the participants. An excellent way of appreciating the importance of this function in the construction of meaning is to take a sound-only recording of some goal-directed activity (*not* a discussion or debate). Without some source of information as to who the participants were, what the activity was and where it took place, such recordings can be almost totally incomprehensible:

A: Give me a couple more (noises) of . . .
B: I can't . . .
A: Try the next one . . . behind . . .
B: These?
A: The bigger ones. Put them down with the others.

We are not saying that this type of meaning (or any of the other types we will be discussing) cannot be transmitted some other way, of course: radio plays and telephone calls would be impossible if this were the case. But this is how most deictic reference is communicated in face-to-face interaction. Indeed, the extent to which deictic reference is shifted to the acoustic channel gives us the basis for a very interesting typology of discourse. The 'sound effects' of BBC radio dramas are not just limited to background noises — the crunch of boots on the gravel in the drive, the merry whistle, the chime of the front-door bell: 'Ah, that will be the postman!'. In the nature of things, the verbal component here carries a higher load, the message becomes more 'explicit' — but only in purely verbal terms.

There is a very important implication for language teaching here, since almost all constructed didactic materials belong to this second, verbally explicit type of discourse and therefore do little to prepare the learner for the highly allusive deictic discourse usual in face-to-face interaction. This can only be done by exposing the learner to discourse which shows rather than tells. Recordings of such TV programmes as do-it-yourself lessons or group activities for children can be highly suitable, as well as almost any recording of people participating in a goal-directed physical activity such as cooking or burglary. By asking questions such as 'What has X just seen?', 'What is Y indicating?', 'Where does Z want it put?', 'What person or object is he referring to?', 'Where exactly is "here" or "higher" or their non-verbal equivalent?', the teacher can bring to the learners' notice aspects of the interaction which would otherwise frequently escape their attention. There is no doubt about the fact that realizations of deictic reference vary from culture to culture; was it not Sapir who reported on an Indian who 'pointed' with his lips? There are also very strong grounds for believing that different cultures actually select different aspects of the situation for deictic reference. Together, these form a cogent argument for the explicit teaching/learning of this aspect of comprehension.

THE INTERACTIONAL FUNCTION

One of the most important characteristics of discourse in face-to-face interaction is its *reciprocity*: it is the collaborative construct of two or more participants whose contributions or *turns* combine to form interactive structure in terms of who speaks when and to whom. This structure and these behaviours are almost exclusively regulated by visually perceived non-verbal communication, by gaze above all, but also by posture, orientation and gestures. These features realize the *address* system of the language, which we have shown to be of fundamental importance to discourse (see pp. 14–15).

Address, then, is a discourse term which refers to the imposition of rights and duties (to take the floor, for example, or to reply) on participants in an interaction. Here, too, it is *possible* for address to be realized verbally (e.g. by nomination: 'How about you, John?'). Again, though, the extent to which this occurs will influence the discourse type. A clear example is the telephone call, where all the non-verbal attention signals (nods, gaze, facial expression, etc.) have to be replaced by verbal signals ('yes', 'uh-huh', etc.).

Now for many linguists and teachers this point is so obvious as to be trivial and it is interesting to consider why this should be so. One of the basic concepts of linguistics (*the* basic concept according to some observers) is the *interchangeability* of speaker and hearer. From Saussure to Chomsky this parallelism has been axiomatic. The 'ideal speaker–hearer' is a simplification without which modern linguistics simply would not exist; but it is a simplification that is made at a price, since it leaves no room for variation, personal or social. Comprehension is just expression in reverse. As long as we stick to mere coding and decoding this approach is insightful. But as soon as we start to look at interaction we realize that it is painfully inadequate: it is simply not true that all participants have equal rights to the floor in all interactions — children do not have the same rights as their parents, backbenchers do not have the same rights as ministers, employees do not have the same rights as employers. Understanding these rights and the dynamic discourse roles which manifest them (that is, understanding who is communicating with whom) is comprehension in the most profound sense.

In the foreign language classroom, where the teacher is a native speaker of the target language, a number of seemingly disparate difficulties related to such matters as participation, comprehension and attitude appear to be due to a cross-cultural failure to identify and understand address behaviours by both teachers and learners. We are only just beginning to appreciate the size of this problem: at a recent workshop in Lyons, examples were drawn from a very wide range of situations — French for North Africans, Turks and South Americans, English for Vietnamese, Finnish and French learners, Russian and German for French learners.

The manifestations of these differences vary enormously, as is only to be expected: we are dealing here with the most fundamental aspect of interaction, the way in which contributions from different sources are fused into a single discourse. For example, there are cultures where it is impolite to meet the gaze of a teacher, or where it is regarded as extremely presumptuous to answer a superior's question, or where general address (in which the teacher throws open the floor to all the students present) is always interpreted as a rhetorical question. It is also extremely common to find address behaviours which have opposite meanings in different cultures; for example, an attention signal can be taken as a bid for the floor. For the moment, of course, most of this evidence is anecdotal but it is now quite clear that any description of the language of the classroom must take address behaviours into account. It is pointless to expect, say, a better linguistic performance from Ali when Ali has trouble even recognizing when a question has been asked or when he is expected to speak.

Obviously, much of this holds true outside the classroom, usually with more serious results. A Frenchman participating in an international meeting or group discussion will sometimes give the impression that he is over-categorical, aggressive and continually interrupting, largely due to his turn-taking and turn-keeping procedures: for example, the French signals for 'I'm just finishing' are invariably interpreted by British participants as a blunt 'Keep quiet and don't interrupt!', fertile ground for misunderstanding and friction which, for a businessman or a trade unionist wishing to negotiate agreements with his British opposite number, could well prove disastrous.

Sound-only recordings usually misrepresent address behaviours simply because they are limited to nomination or purely verbal address. One finds, for example, people who are supposedly in sight of one another consistently using proper names, a relatively rare occurrence (in British English, at least: there seem to be considerable differences in the standard American system of address).

For teaching comprehension, TV recordings of group discussions can be very useful, although professionally produced materials can be too 'polished', the cameraman and producer using their own intuitive knowledge of address behaviours to switch the picture from person to person in synchrony with their speaking turns, thereby often neatly editing out the very behaviours we would like our learners to see.

Teachers who doubt that their learners have any problems of this kind sometimes receive a nasty shock when they find that they are quite unable to answer questions such as: 'Is A interrupting B here, or was it his turn to speak?'. Other useful questions for focusing the learners' attention include: 'Who is A speaking to?', 'When does he show that he is ready to hand over the floor?', 'How does he show that he wants B to have the next turn?', 'How do C and D show that they do or do not also want to say something?', 'Who can speak next?', 'How does B know that it is his turn to speak next?' and 'Does A expect a reply?'.

THE MODAL FUNCTION

Modalization is notoriously difficult to define and we do not propose to try to do so now, although we believe that many of the difficulties involved are pseudo-problems resulting from the failure to recognize the importance and role of non-verbal behaviour. For the moment, it is taken as covering all the different ways which are available to an actor to signal the extent to which he is committed to the literal meaning, the propositional content, of his utterance: is he serious, joking, enthusiastic? Since it is largely through modalization that actors try to regulate their psycho-social and affective relationships, this is obviously a crucial factor in face-to-face meaning. An 'understanding' smile, a 'dismissive' gesture or an 'aggressive' posture are all important contributions to the final meaning created in a communicative act, so important that they can actually override the surface linguistic meaning, as is the case with irony or sarcasm, for example.

Like the other functions listed here, modalization has already been recognized as far as the verbal component is concerned, though attention has been concentrated on the semantics of the modal verbs (but see Roulet 1980; Roussel 1974). However, as I have already said, the realizations of these functions are not exclusive to one channel or another; modalization often occurs simultaneously at the vocal non-verbal level (facial expression above all, in Western society, but also gesture and posture) as well as at the verbal level.

The enormous complexity of this phenomenon at the theoretical and descriptive levels should not, however, deter the language teacher or learner from trying to tackle the problem. By asking questions such as 'Is A teasing B?' or 'Is A being sarcastic?', the teacher goes directly to the heart of the matter. There is little point in waiting until we have, say, an integrated theory of the meaning of facial expression before asking ourselves why A smiles at a given moment. Again, it may be objected that to do so is trivial and unnecessary, since the learners will understand naturally. Such an argument can be refuted on a number of points: firstly, it is based on an unacceptably naïve view of the nature of language and communicative behaviour; secondly, the balance needs to be redressed — conditioned by their previous experience, learners tend to concentrate on the verbal component at the expense of all other aspects of communication; and thirdly, experience shows that in fact learners do often make wrong judgements on the key of an act or interaction. This last point has long been familiar to teachers of literature who groan inwardly as a frothy, amusing short story is taken literally and understood as a sombre sociological statement of fact; such misjudgements seem to be at least as common in interaction, even between people from related cultures.

THE INDEXICAL FUNCTION

If modalization, then, is generally *other-related*, if it refers to the ways in which an actor tries to influence others, then it is to be distinguished from the indexical function, which is *actor-related*, which provides information, in other words, about the actor's self (Laver and Hutcheson 1972).

Anatomy, size, skin, muscle and hair type and condition, cosmetics and grooming, clothing, status symbols, adaptors and tools, facial expression, gesture, posture, breathing and blinking rates — these are only some of the visual signals which can transmit indexical information. This information includes such socially vital markers as nationality, sex, age, state of health, class, profession and emotional state; it tells us, that is, about the identity of an actor and about the probable nature of his participation and role in a given interaction. These matters are so important that often the 'business' of an interaction does not begin until participants have had a chance to size one another up; 'photic communion' or 'small talk' plays a fundamental role in social intercourse by providing a vehicle for the exchange of indexical information.

Much of what has been said about modalization also holds good for the indexical function. Indeed it is often difficult to distinguish between them; when we say that someone is 'enthusiastic', for example, we are usually referring both to his attitude towards his interlocutor and to his own emotional state. But descriptive problems of this kind need not bother us in the classroom; in fact, indexical information can be tackled with complete beginners — 'Is A angry?', 'What sort of a job do you think A does?', 'What is A's attitude to B?', 'What is the relationship between A and B — have they just met?', 'Why do you think A is dressed like that?', 'Is A a conservative type or is he rather trendy?'.

Such an approach can prove a healthy antidote to the 'phlegmatic Englishman, inscrutable Chinese' sort of stereotype by providing the learner with the categories necessary for more refined judgements. How many English students of French, for example, really understand what it means when a Frenchman of a certain age wears a beret? Or when he has a small rosette in his buttonhole? And how many French students of English really understand the social implications of a bowler hat or certain kind of tie? And if this seems to belong to the realms of folklore, then consider the absolutely basic fact that the French and English misread each other's behaviour so much that they are often incapable of telling whether the other is angry: the Englishman thinks the Frenchman is angry when he is not and the Frenchman thinks the Englishman is not angry when in fact he is absolutely furious.

THE LINGUISTIC FUNCTION

For many people linguistic non-verbal communication is a contradiction in terms, and it has to be conceded that it is not a particularly happy phrase. Yet it can be shown that some non-verbal behaviours at least can be highly conventional, systemic and semantically precise. It is convenient to distinguish four categories of these behaviours, generically known as gestures, on the basis of their communicative function (this is discussed at greater length in Riley 1976):

1. Emblems: these normally function as verbal surrogates and

include gestures such as 'thumbs up' or 'V-sign' (Scheflen 1973).

2. Illustrators: gestures which are related to the propositional content of the message ('It was this sort of shape . . .').
3. Enactions: gestures related to the illocutionary force of the communicative act (beckoning to command 'Come here', for example).
4. Batons: those behaviours which are related to the prosodic characteristics of the message such as rhythm and tempo (this does not imply that they are subsidiary to the vocal or verbal realizations).

Until recently, almost all work on non-verbal communication was in fact restricted to the first of the categories listed above, gestures which are conventional, replicable, conscious and easily expressed in words. A number of gesture-repertoires have been collected for different cultures which have confirmed the conventional nature of gestures: they have to be learnt and the 'same' gesture varies in meaning from culture to culture. The use of these lists is limited but real and it seems only reasonable to use video to teach them for comprehension purposes. This is a relatively straightforward task, rather like teaching a few new items of vocabulary, but one which always fascinates learners since it is often their first introduction to a further dimension of communication.

At a more sophisticated level, it has been shown that video-recordings of native speakers can be an excellent means of sensitizing students to problems of stress, rhythm, tempo and intonation, since these prosodies are often synchronized with batons (Heddesheimer and Roussel 1977).

THE SITUATIONAL FUNCTION

'Situation' could, of course, be regarded as a macro-category subsuming everything which has been discussed so far. It is used here in the sense of the spatio-temporal setting perceived as a scene for a specific type of communicative event, in so far as it impinges on or is relevant to communicative behaviour. The identification of the significant features here will probably have to be left to anthropological semiotics (Douglas 1970) with off-shoots such as architecture and proxemics (Hall 1962) and, most recent of all, chronemics, which studies the significant use and perception of time (Bruneau 1979).

Much interesting work is being done here, but the area is a vast one. The problems are detailed and concrete, not just airy-fairy academic abstractions. It can be amazingly difficult for, say, a new arrival in New York to see a telephone kiosk or letter-box or underground station — he just doesn't know what to look for. Banks, churches and examination halls are all places where an Englishman's behaviour becomes formal, reverential and hushed: but when one looks at, say, banks in the Middle East, churches in Italy or examination halls in France, it soon becomes obvious that this is not an immutable law of nature, merely a cultural choice.

This is not to say that language teachers should be experts in semiotics or anthropology but, by definition, they are involved with cross-cultural communication and should therefore, be aware that perception of setting and situation varies from culture to culture. A shop in the Middle East is a setting for situations involving negotiation and bargaining: this is not the case in most European cultures. North Africans in France, for example, either risk annoying the shopkeepers by trying to beat them down or accept the price as displayed and go away feeling sure they have been cheated. When Italian tennis fans recently took their 'rowdy' behaviour to Wimbledon — they cheered, shouted encouragement, stamped and so on — it was regarded by the English as absolutely shocking, a mixture of cheating and bad manners. Even a game of tennis is not the same situation in two different cultures.

This awareness of social norms is not easy to acquire, since it implies close familiarity with the foreign country in question, but the observation and discussion of authentic video material does seem to be a valuable preparation for the countless situations, from pubs and cricket matches to family reunions and business meetings, in which a learner may one day find himself.

The functional approach to the acquisition of spoken language

The papers in this section, indeed almost all the papers in this book, illustrate practical aspects of a continuing search for a communicative methodology or, rather, methodologies. Holec, in Chapter 18, describes a beginners' course in spoken English in which communicative considerations are given priority, while at the same time taking into account the differences between expression and comprehension and the specific characteristics of the group of learners in question. One of the main problems tackled in this course, the integration of the communicative and linguistic components, is still absolutely central to all discussion of communicative methodology. Obviously this is not meant to imply that we believe that this problem has been 'solved' (apart from anything else, the question will have to be posed anew for each fresh group of learners). But it does show that *a* solution was possible in those particular circumstances, and this is what we ask of an effective applied linguistics.

Chapter 19 is made up of reports on two different projects which involved very similar groups of learners, but whose circumstances could hardly have been more different. The first group was attending a French course in France, while the second was receiving distance-teaching in South America. This change in the parameters of the learning situation highlights the severe limitations which can be placed on theory by practical circumstances. It provides a simple but clear example of methodology as a systematic attempt to relate ends to means.

18 A beginners' course in spoken English based on the functional approach

H. Holec

Introductory note

The beginners' course in oral English which is described here was designed and developed by the author in collaboration with M. Cembalo and P. Riley. It was first run in the academic year 1974–5 and has been given each year since, though with certain modifications.

It is important to note that this course was designed for *adults* and that it therefore forms part of an overall pedagogic strategy designed for that type of learner (Cembalo and Holec 1973). It is part of the systematic phase in the learning programme; in other words, there is a teacher with a group, and all members of the group follow the same syllabus. It is an *option*, 'oral English' having been chosen in preference to 'written English' by the learners as their main objective. The overall objective, then, is the acquisition of a minimal competence in oral comprehension and expression.

When it was first given, this course was original from a number of points of view: it was based on a new functional analysis of language and, consequently, on a new definition of what it is we need to learn when we learn a foreign language; it was based, too, on a psycho-pedagogical analysis of the type of learner we were dealing with, which in turn determined the methodology; and, finally, it was based on a number of pedagogical choices and decisions which in turn justified the teaching/learning techniques which were used.

However, many of these topics have since been further studied and are discussed in greater detail in other papers in this book, so there seems little point in reproducing earlier reflections here. (For the pedagogical implications of macro-linguistic analysis, see pp. 124–32. For the psycho-pedagogical analysis, see pp. 174–79.) In the original paper, the discussion of pedagogical choices was largely devoted to an early attempt to justify and exemplify the use of authentic materials (pp. 321–31).

What remains in this abridged version is, therefore, the bare bones of the course, but it is still worth including because, it seems to us, it distils some of the crucial problems and decisions which all communicative courses have to face, problems such as the relationship between the 'linguistic' and 'communicative' progressions which are still the centre of very lively debate, and because it represents a very early attempt to teach communicative competence in a serious and systematic way.

Micro-linguistics v. macro-linguistics

For some years, research carried out both by the C.R.A.P.E.L. and by other centres of applied linguistics has shown the inadequacy of linguistic analyses which are limited to the internal functioning of the verbal code, to the exclusion of the circumstances (speakers, situation, etc.) in which the code is used. The micro-linguistic approach simply does not correspond to the needs of language learners who are not interested in becoming linguists, but in communicating in a foreign language. Instead, a new line of development, drawing its support from a number of socio-linguistic and ethno-linguistic studies, has extended the field of research to include both the internal functioning (morphosyntax, lexis, phonology), and the external functioning (relationships between text and situation, text and speaker, etc.) of the verbal code.

In other words, descriptions carried out according to this new approach are based not just on the sentence, but on the verbal exchange in its entirety. This sort of analysis aims at bringing to light both the rules of construction and the rules of use for utterances produced in verbal exchanges. It is no longer regarded as sufficient to describe a sentence such as 'John has gone' as, say, a 'positive declarative sentence consisting of a subject and a predicate' (with the terminology varying according to the type of description chosen). Instead, the new analysis must also define the function of the utterance in the verbal exchange in which it was produced, by relating it to the other factors relevant to that exchange, such as context, situation, speakers and non-verbal signals in order to determine whether it is a reply to a request for information, an excuse, a reproach and so on.

This analysis has very important implications for language teaching; instead of seeing the language as nothing more than a verbal code, it is now regarded as a 'tool of communication'. Consequently, learning a language is not just a matter of acquiring a code whose rules permit us to construct utterances, but also involves acquiring communicative competence, the ability to construct utterances *and to use them* to carry out the communicative acts which our verbal exchanges consist of.

> . . . there is less talk of 'grammar' and 'structure': the key words are '*communication*' and '*discursive function*'. It is no longer a matter of knowing how to build *forms* called 'sentences', but of knowing how to use them to good effect for the purpose of expressing certain functions.

The macro-linguistic analysis should make clear what are the realizations of various functions in the different dialects, registers and styles which have been established. For instance, the phrases 'You are annoying me' and 'You really get up my nose' (together with all their prosodic and paralinguistic characteristics) can be realizations of the same function operating at different levels and registers (the pedagogical implications of these distinctions are discussed below).

Although the concept of communicative competence is equally applicable to all language skills and media, for clarity the notes which follow only refer to an oral course for beginners.

Since we are largely ignorant of all the discursive and communicative functions and of the behaviours which realize them, we are obliged to use authentic materials (there are also a number of good pedagogical reasons for doing so; pp. 323–5). In a course for beginners, this desire to use only authentic texts as far as is possible gives rise to quite a few problems (particularly at the level of the teaching of oral expression). Our solution is as follows:

1. In the sections dealing with oral comprehension, all texts are authentic.
2. In the sections dealing with oral expression, many of the texts (which are in general rather short phrases) are either texts which have been culled from the corpus but re-recorded, or texts which have had to be constructed because of gaps in the corpus. Texts are re-recorded either to obtain a better acoustic quality or to avoid using as models (for repetition, for example) utterances containing idiolectal features of performance. It would be worthless, probably even dangerous, to have learners reproducing all the hesitations, repetitions and errors which the speakers produced in the original text. This breach of our fundamental rule is less serious than it might seem: 'expression' is never studied independently of 'comprehension' and, taken together, the two sections include far more authentic texts than constructed texts, if only because of the greater length of the texts used for comprehension work.

Objectives

The overall objective of our beginners' course in spoken English is the acquisition of a minimum adequate communicative competence in oral English which will allow our students to begin on 'non-systematic' studies, as defined in our overall strategy. This subsumes two specific objectives:

1. Acquisition of a minimum adequate competence in oral comprehension;
2. Acquisition of a minimum adequate competence in oral expression.

If we take these in turn for more detailed discussion, we can see that objective 1 aims at enabling the learner to understand communicative functions and their meanings (understanding, for example, that an utterance is an order and that in this particular case it is an order to go and move a badly parked car). These communicative functions are encountered in a variety of verbal exchanges, such as everyday conversation, telephone calls, news broadcasts, television commercials and so on. The competence thus acquired is not limited to the comprehension of oral discourse alone, and the range of dialects, levels, registers and styles is as wide as is practicably possible: British and American accents; cultivated and uncultivated levels; formal, informal and familiar registers, and so on.

The minimum level aimed at is well above that which is aimed at in expression, which reflects both the fact that progress in comprehension always advances much more quickly than progress in expression, and their relative importance.

Objective 2 aims at enabling the learner to express verbally as many as possible of the communicative functions which are met in everyday speech and in the 'vital' verbal exchanges in the foreign country.

The competence thus acquired is limited to the production of spoken text in British English, at a cultivated level in both the formal and informal registers and in an unmarked style (one which is not peculiar to journalism, science or literature, or any specific area).

Progression

The fundamental problem concerning the grammatical progression of the course concerned the relationship between the acquisition of the morphosyntax and the acquisition of the communicative functions. There is no one-to-one relationship between the functions and the morphosyntax: a given function can be realized by several different utterances, and the same utterance can realize a variety of different functions. For example, the 'interrogative form' can be used to realize a request for information, an order or a threat; take, for example, the utterance 'Will you be finished soon?'. In the same way an order can be realized by an utterance which is interrogative or imperative or negative — for example:

'Give me a drink.'
'How many times do I have to tell you that I want a drink?'
'A nice cool beer wouldn't do me any harm.'
'Please, I'm thirsty.'

Theoretically, then, there are four possibilities to choose from:

1. To base the progression on the functions, fitting in the morphosyntax afterwards;
2. To base the progression on the morphosyntax, fitting in the functions afterwards;
3. To provide a common progression for both the functions and the morphosyntax;
4. To dissociate the functions and the morphosyntax, providing separate progressions for each.

The first three possibilities are excluded on pedagogical and/or linguistic grounds: 1 and 2 would result in a disproportionate overloading of the first units of the course, because the introduction of even one function would necessitate the introduction of a large part of the morphosyntax. If, for example, you were dealing with 'Requests for Information', you would have to deal with all the tenses, since the realization of that function is not limited to a given tense. Conversely, the introduction of a single element of morphosyntax would necessitate the introduction of a large number of functions.

The third possibility is excluded on linguistic grounds, since there is no one-to-one relationship between functions and the morphosyntax.

Only the fourth possibility remains, and so it is the one that we have chosen. In our beginners' course, the functions and the morphosyntax are learnt at the same time, but separately. They also differ according to whether they are being taught for comprehension or expression.

For comprehension, there is no progression whatsoever of either the functions or the morphosyntax: the necessary systematization is carried out by means of regular revision exercises.

For expression, there are two separate progressions:

1. Morphosyntax: 'traditional' progression;
2. Functions: a progression from 'set phrases' such as 'How are you?', 'Very well, thank you' — where the utterance is to be produced as a

whole in the appropriate situations—to 'set phrases' of the type 'I am sorry but I . . .'—where part of the utterance has to be constructed at the moment when it is produced in an appropriate situation.

General plan of the course

The course is divided into two parts of unequal length. The first part (which took four sessions of four hours each) consists of a general introduction, including:

1. An introduction to the concept of a 'language function', based on the examination of verbal exchanges in the mother tongue (French);
2. An introduction to English intonation, based on the description given by Halliday (1970), followed by discrimination exercises on the tones and the place of tonic;
3. An introduction to the rhythm of English, based on Abercrombie (1966);
4. An introduction to the *Initial Teaching Alphabet*, followed by exercises;
5. An introduction to the basic morphosyntax of English, followed by exercises in the recognition of forms and constructions.

The second part (21 sessions of four hours each) consists of a series of comprehension units and expression units, constructed in keeping with the progression and objectives described above. The form of the units depends on their contents. Briefly, the units are used as follows:

Oral comprehension: in the presence of a teacher;
Oral expression:

1. Morphosyntax: successively
   with the teacher (introduction, first phase of acquisition);
   in semi-autonomy (acquisition);
   with the teacher (re-use);
   in semi-autonomy (revision).
2. Functions: successively
   with the teacher (introduction, acquisition, re-use);
   in semi-autonomy (revision).

It is to be noted that each unit includes a cassette recording of the texts used in class, followed by exercises and additional texts.

19 Two experiments in communicative teaching

M–J. Gremmo and F. Carton

Editor's note:

This section consists of two papers, in slightly abridged versions, describing different aspects of our work with the Latin American postgraduate students who have come to the C.R.A.P.E.L. each summer for the past four years. These papers deal with problems involved in helping them acquire 'survival French' in the short-term and 'academic French' in the longer term. Not the least of these problems is the cultural shock they undergo and the related psychological shock resulting from a drop in status from qualified engineers in their home countries to student/migrant workers in France. Being able to get along in French at the earliest possible moment is not just a matter of practical necessity for these learners, it is also a question of face and is profoundly related to their sense of personal identity. Both the objective and the psychological urgency of their need to acquire an adequate level of communicative competence led the C.R.A.P.E.L. team in question to concentrate in a relatively narrow way on meeting their immediate needs.

The first paper describes in some detail the course which was developed, as well as some of the modifications which had to be made in the light of experience. The second deals with an attempt to respond to their request that future students should receive some sort of help with their French before their arrival, the journey across France having proved traumatic in certain cases. It is fair to say that the situation was a difficult one: the distance and time involved, the level of the learners (there were many absolute beginners), their solitude and working conditions ('stuck down a mine halfway up a mountain' as one reported) and their conviction by and large that the only possible solution — distance-teaching — was a very poor one indeed, all united to make the options available extremely limited. That the resulting materials were modest in their overall aims and effects goes without saying. Nonetheless, if taken on their own terms with the constraints of this particular learning situation in mind, they were reasonably successful.

These two papers, then, provide an interesting example of pedagogic research as a process of to-ing and fro-ing between practical constraints and general principles.

1. Learning to communicate: an experiment in teaching French (M-J. Gremmo)

Although most teachers nowadays are said to be convinced of the importance of communicative competence and of the functional approach, these concepts cannot be said to have had very much influence on actual teaching practice. Two typical teachers' reactions are to say 'Well, that's what we have always done!' or 'All well and fine, but you can't do it in the classroom!'. This paper describes in some detail the methods and strategies used at the C.R.A.P.E.L. for teaching and learning oral expression in one particular course which we hope will exemplify our approach to these matters as it has developed over the last few years.

Methodological principles

NEEDS ANALYSIS

If a learning programme is to be effective, it must be based on an analysis of the learners' linguistic needs. This analysis should provide precise information about the communicative tasks which these particular learners will need to be able to perform. Teachers and learners together can then rank these tasks in an order of priority reflecting their frequency and importance. This enables them to define their syllabus in linguistic terms.

SEPARATION OF THE LANGUAGE SKILLS

Since the four language skills involve different types of psychomotor activities, they require different learning techniques. Moreover, if the skills are separated each can be learnt at a different speed, whereas if they are all linked they will all be learnt at the same speed, which is the speed of the skill which is most difficult to acquire, oral expression. This puts a brake on the acquisition of comprehension, which can be learnt far more quickly, and consequently restricts the learner's ability to cope with a real communication situation. If oral comprehension and oral expression are separated, though, the learner can progress in each at the rate required for that skill.

The same argument holds for distinguishing between the spoken and written skills: different linguistic codes need to be learnt differently and this should be clearly reflected at the pedagogical level. Similarly, there are differences of communicative activity according to the skill in question: you can only interrupt someone orally. Again, other communicative acts are only performed by certain people. In real life we very often find ourselves in situations where we need to understand far more types of language functions than we will ever need to express. So functional learning should also vary according to the skill involved.

COGNITIVE APPROACH

Since all our learners are adults, not children, with their own ideas about what learning a language means, and since they always want to know what they are doing and why, we adopt a cognitive approach, one in which an explanation of each element in the learning programme is available to the learner and, ideally, where the learner himself is able to describe and explain what it is that he is doing (in terms such as acquisition or revision, grammar, oral comprehension, and so on). This means that the teacher should always define clearly the activities he suggests, and particularly that he should allot part of the classroom time to an explanation of why a given strategy is being followed.

PREPARATION FOR AUTONOMY

No three-month course can prepare the learners for all the linguistic problems they are going to meet during their stay in France. The course should, therefore, prepare the learners to deal with these problems themselves. This preparation cannot be carried out overnight, as it requires the learners to make a radical change in their views of the teacher's role. The teacher has to help the learners take over certain aspects of that role by gradually turning over to them various pedagogical decisions such as the choice of materials.

The course

THE LEARNERS

With the exceptions of one student from the Philippines and one from Japan (both of whom spoke English) all the participants were from

Latin America. They came from Mexico, Venezuela, Colombia, Bolivia, Peru and Brazil to do at least one year's scientific training in France (some stayed as long as three years to do a French Ph. D.). They were all engineers, specializing in mining, the food industries, agriculture and electronics. Certain differences between the various national groups were noted: the Mexicans, Venezuelans and Colombians, or about 60% of the participants, were mostly recent graduates. The others were elder people doing some form of refresher course.

There were also considerable differences between their financial situations. The Brazilians, for example, could actually afford to bring their families with them, while others had to scrape along on a modest student grant.

Those who came from the Andes had considerable difficulty adapting to lower altitudes. They were often tired and had trouble concentrating.

On arrival, the students' knowledge of French varied considerably: the Andeans were almost all beginners, the Mexicans had already had a course in French before leaving home and the Brazilians had only been selected if they already spoke good French.

Finally, a major difference of 'mentality' is to be noted, with the Mexicans and Venezuelans being highly 'Americanized' while the other participants from countries where communications were still very difficult, were far less westernized.

They also had a number of common characteristics. The status of an engineer in Latin America is higher than in France and, in such rigidly hierarchical societies, is a major factor influencing social relationships. Most of the participants were members of the newly-emerging middle classes in their countries, a fact of which they were both very conscious and very proud. However, their situation on the French social scale was a very different one indeed, since they were now students again and treated as such. Indeed, they were often looked on as immigrant workers, with all that that implies. This loss of status was a considerable psychological shock. Moreover, it implied a change in both their social and linguistic attitudes — a change which they found very difficult to accept, but of which they were very much aware.

All had an enormous respect for knowledge and for teachers. For them, a teacher is someone who knows everything and who shows he knows it by imposing it on his pupils. The pupil has to adapt to the teacher's demands and bow to his decisions and to his will. This made it difficult for them to understand the concept of autonomy and even more difficult for them to accept it in practice.

THE TIMETABLE

Classes were held from Monday morning to Friday noon, leaving a long weekend for the students to put what they had learnt to good use, by going sightseeing, for example.

The students were divided into five groups: two groups of beginners (25 hours per week) and one elementary, one intermediate and one advanced group (20 hours per week each).

In the afternoons, the students could use the open-access language laboratory and the TV room for independent study. Cassettes and cassette players were available on loan.

The teaching of oral expression

It is perhaps worth noting that all the decisions concerning the organization and contents of this course were taken by the teachers themselves working together as a group. Moreover, the materials which will be described below were designed and produced by the teachers working in sub-groups.

It is also important to remember that this paper only refers to those parts of the course which were relevant to oral expression.

NEEDS

The analysis of the linguistic needs of the students showed that there were two main areas to be covered. They were going to have to participate in scholastic situations — what one might call their 'professional' needs — and in a variety of everyday situations, such as going shopping, dealing with the authorities, getting to know French people such as their neighbours and so on.

Their professional needs fell into the following categories: questions after classes and lectures; technical discussions with their research supervisors; classroom talks on some aspect of their specialization; technical discussions with other students.

These needs were, therefore, highly specialized and in certain cases specific to their situation: they would never need to give talks in any other circumstances, for example. But although their main reasons for coming to France had been and remained professional, it was in everyday circumstances that they were first called on to use their French, so the specialized training was left till towards the end of the course.

Given their needs, the students would have to be able to communicate in two rather different registers: firstly, what we might call the student register for their contacts with other students. This register is colloquial and is marked by a characteristic slang. Secondly, they would need a more neutral, formal register for use in their professional situation and outside student circles (in shops, for example). The experience of some of our teachers the previous summer with a similar group of Latin American students (though on a course which had not been organized by the C.R.A.P.E.L.) made us very wary indeed of trying to introduce the 'student' register into our course, since it goes completely against the image which these learners have of the French language, which they see as an instrument of culture, hyper-correct and completely without slang. We decided, therefore, to stick mostly to the formal register as far as expression was concerned, dealing with the student register as a comprehension problem. This decision was taken largely to avoid an outright rejection of the materials by these learners for psychological reasons, but it can also be justified on the grounds that a foreigner can perfectly well use the formal register with his fellow students where a native French student could not.

A further aspect of their needs which had to be taken into account was that, like any other foreigners arriving in France, they would have to go through a certain number of administrative procedures — applying for a residence permit, opening a bank account, passing a medical check-up and so on. All of them, even the absolute beginners, would have to do these things. They therefore needed — immediately — enough French to cope with these problems.

COMPREHENSION/EXPRESSION

The timetable for the course was based on the principle of the separation of the language skills which was mentioned above.

During the first month, the emphasis was placed on oral comprehension work, so that the learners could rapidly reach a level of performance at which they felt at ease. For the beginners, 60% of the time devoted to oral work was spent on comprehension: this proportion was gradually reduced as the course progressed, with expression work being correspondingly increased.

TIMETABLE

The learners were given timetables at the beginning of each week which indicated oral expression activities under three headings: phonetics (pronunciation); the grammar of spoken French; and functional oral expression. The first two of these headings can be regarded as tools for the acquisition of the third.

PHONETICS

This part of the course was based on a classic contrastive analysis, but the selection of items to be dealt with was based on communicative criteria.

SPOKEN GRAMMAR

The importance we ascribe to the functional and communicative aspects of language should never be allowed to blind us to the crucial role of morphosyntax, especially as we do not really know what the role of grammar is in language learning. Grammatical structures were dealt with in a systematic way for both comprehension and expression.

FUNCTIONAL ORAL EXPRESSION

This course component dealt with the most important aspect of oral expression: learning to use the language as a tool for communication. The first step was to sensitize the learners to the concepts being used. This was carried out with the aid of a self-assessment questionnaire in Spanish which helped them analyse and evaluate their performances in relevant terms. Whereas the greater part of the materials produced was 'functional', the very first part of the course was strictly 'situational'. This was the *survival kit*, consisting of the six modules corresponding to the most urgent needs of these learners: 'At the police station', 'At the bank' and 'At the hospital' (for the administrative procedures), and 'At the supermarket', 'At the café' and 'Asking your way in the street' (for 'settling in'). Since modules of this type were later used as the basis for the distance-teaching materials described on pp. 367–72, I will not go into further detail here, except to observe that *all* participants worked on these materials during the first week of the course.

A second set of modules — functionally-based, this time — was also developed. These were constructed on the lines of the self-study materials in spoken English which have been described on pp. 248–55.

Once a number of language needs had been identified, it was possible to draw up a corresponding list of functions to which priority should be given and then to base a programme on them. Two main criteria were taken into account when deciding on the order in which the functions would be dealt with: the urgency of the need; and the difficulty of the formal realizations. So the beginners, for example, were first introduced to those functions which are adequately represented by a few set expressions.

Each language function was then taken as the topic for a separate module. In fact, the modules often covered the whole exchange in which the communicative act occurred, not just the act alone: it is obviously both difficult and pointless learning to invite someone without taking into account their possible reactions (accepting, refusing) to the invitation. Indeed, it was found preferable to take some aspects of communication at a more complex level of interaction as what might be called 'macro-functions'. The module on 'Greetings' includes some of the stereo-typed exchanges which occur when two people have to spend a short time together, in an elevator, for example. In any case, each function taken for special consideration was first studied in its communicative context, that is, as one of a series of linked functions, occurring in the same interaction. 'Asking your way', for example, included information on 'going up to a stranger' and 'thanking'.

The handouts given to the learners (in other words, the written parts of the modules) always gave as many different realizations as possible for each function while simultaneously providing the learners with information about those realizations which would help them choose the most suitable one in terms of the situation, their own personalities and so on. This was largely done by the use of a simplified system for the notation of register (see p. 249).

Ideally, all these different realizations would have been culled from authentic materials, as was indeed the case for the distance-teaching materials. However, at the time we are talking of, very little authentic material was available. To avoid the danger of idiosyncracy, therefore, the lists of realizations were collected by all the teachers working as a group.

Obviously, the modules were not the only learning resources available to the learners. Since they were used as classroom materials, the teacher was also there as an informant and could, where necessary, use examples of the learners' mother tongue to sensitize them to the problem, as well as organizing activities in which the functions in question could be practised (the teachers responsible for producing each module also appended a list of suggestions for such activities).

Generally speaking, the study programme was organized in three stages:

1. *Formal acquisition*, where the learners familiarized themselves with the different realizations.
2. *Systematic use*. Under the teacher's guidance, the learners did exercises which varied the parameters of the exchange (relative status of the participants, how well they knew one another, place and time, the importance of the matter in hand, personality, etc.).

The learners also practised finding expressions for shades of meaning in their mother tongue which were parallel but not word-for-word translations.

3. *Situational practice.* Here the teacher would describe a situation and then withdraw control so that the learners could react freely. Similarly, *simulations* were organized in which outsiders came to carry out some task with the students and where students and visitors kept to their own identities, that is, they both played their own roles. Finally, to make up for the lack of contact with the local population, a number of French people (non-teachers) were invited in to meet the students over a drink.

SPECIALIZED ORAL EXPRESSION

Training in specialized oral expression (as defined above) was carried out during the last two weeks of the course, immediately before the students' technical studies were due to start. This training mainly took the form of simulations, the approach adopted being far more empirical, though, than the Presentation/Exercises/Simulation structure used for the functional materials.

The starting point was always the learner's own performance. Each student gave a talk or lecture to the members of his group on a topic of his own choosing. This was followed by a discussion. Lecture and discussion were recorded and sometimes filmed, the recording being taken for further discussion and criticism. The participants themselves tended to concentrate almost exclusively on linguistic details, whereas the teacher commented on the overall structure of the talk and on the communicative behaviour of all the participants. Similarly, a series of lectures in mathematics was simulated by a teacher who was due later to give them a course in that subject.

Conclusion

At first, the learners were very put out by the C.R.A.P.E.L.'s approach in this course to teaching of oral expression. They were all used to structuralist language teaching and many of them refused to accept that there was a distinction between the written and spoken languages, even in their mother tongue. Similarly, since 'correct' speech is highly prized in their own social circles, they were convinced that grammatical correctness is all-important. Their main complaint during the course was that there was not enough grammar: indeed, some of them sincerely claimed that no real grammar had been done at all. Despite all the teachers' efforts to explain and justify their approach, this criticism persisted right to the end of the course. Because of their attitude to how grammar should be learnt, they preferred lectures on grammatical theory to exercises and drills, believing that if they understood the explanation they had mastered the mechanisms of performance. This was exacerbated by the fact that they received their grammar instruction orally, in class, the only written materials being stencilled handouts: they wanted proper grammar books to study alone. This difference of opinion over the importance of grammar in language learning was, in a few cases, the source of considerable psychological resistance to many of the learning activities, which, to these learners at least, seemed pointless.

Another criticism concerned the fact that the specialized oral expression was only dealt with at the very end of the course. Psychologically, it would certainly have been better to have included this training from the very beginning. These criticisms show that there were serious gaps in the 'cognitive' part of our approach and that in future more time and attention should be devoted to discussing methodology with the learners. However, in defence of the team of teachers, it should be added that this was the first time they had been responsible for a course of this kind: in addition, they also had only one week's notice of it and were therefore kept extremely busy with materials preparation during the course itself, so that they lacked time for talking things over with the students.

A major problem for the students was actually finding the chance to use their brand-new French. When the course was planned, it had been assumed that the simple fact that it was to take place in France would mean that the participants would be able to practise their French, and so plenty of free time had been set aside for this purpose. However, Nancy is a university town and is very quiet indeed in summer, with almost no cultural activities of any kind. Moreover, the people who are in Nancy during the summer are not students and it is difficult, above all for a foreigner, to get to know them. In future, contacts will have to be organized, probably on the basis of projects which the students would carry out investigating various aspects of life in Lorraine.

The results of the training in pronunciation were not satisfactory. Although the learners became aware of their problems, there was little noticeable improvement in their articulation. Moreover, they quickly mastered the classroom exercises but there was almost no transfer at all to their spontaneous speech. The approach to this problem therefore needs to be reconsidered.

An especially important criticism results from our analysis of the results of the communicative approach as applied here. In fact, the functional work had very little influence on the learners' performances. They would study their modules very carefully but, then, in the real-life situation, would use expressions translated direct from their mother tongue. This is almost certainly due to the methodology rather than to the contents, so a change of pedagogical techniques is called for. The problem seems to be that the functional approach described here is too fragmentary: we need some way of moving up to a higher level, where learners would practise the strategic linking of communicative acts into longer, discursive units. We had thought that the simulations would provide for this, but it proved not to be the case.

Despite these criticisms, the course proved to be of value to the participants. They found that they were soon able to react in the various situations in which they found themselves — even if it was only to explain that they were foreign and couldn't understand! The beginners in particular appreciated this approach, since they were soon able to move around on their own, without always having to depend on a more advanced fellow-student. Moreover, talking things over with students who had arrived the previous year, they became aware that they had much less trouble in communicating than their predecessors. This difference in level was also confirmed by their lecturers when they started their technical courses.

2. Distance-teaching a functional course (F. Carton)

The experiment described in this paper was an attempt to apply to a distance-teaching situation the pedagogic strategy developed by Jupp *et al.* (1978) which is usually called a functional course. The pedagogical choices which make up this strategy are summarized in Figure 1 (also based on Jupp *et al.* 1978, p. 166). A functional course is grounded

> on the analysis of the public, of their socio-cultural environment, of the situations in which they participate as interactants and, therefore, on the social roles they are called upon to play, on the linguistic functions they should be able to perform and on the notions or concepts they need to master. (Jupp *et al.* 1978, p. 4).

Background to the experiment

The *Centre d'Etudes Supérieures des Techniques Minières* (CESTEMIN), which receives a number of South American post-graduate scholar-

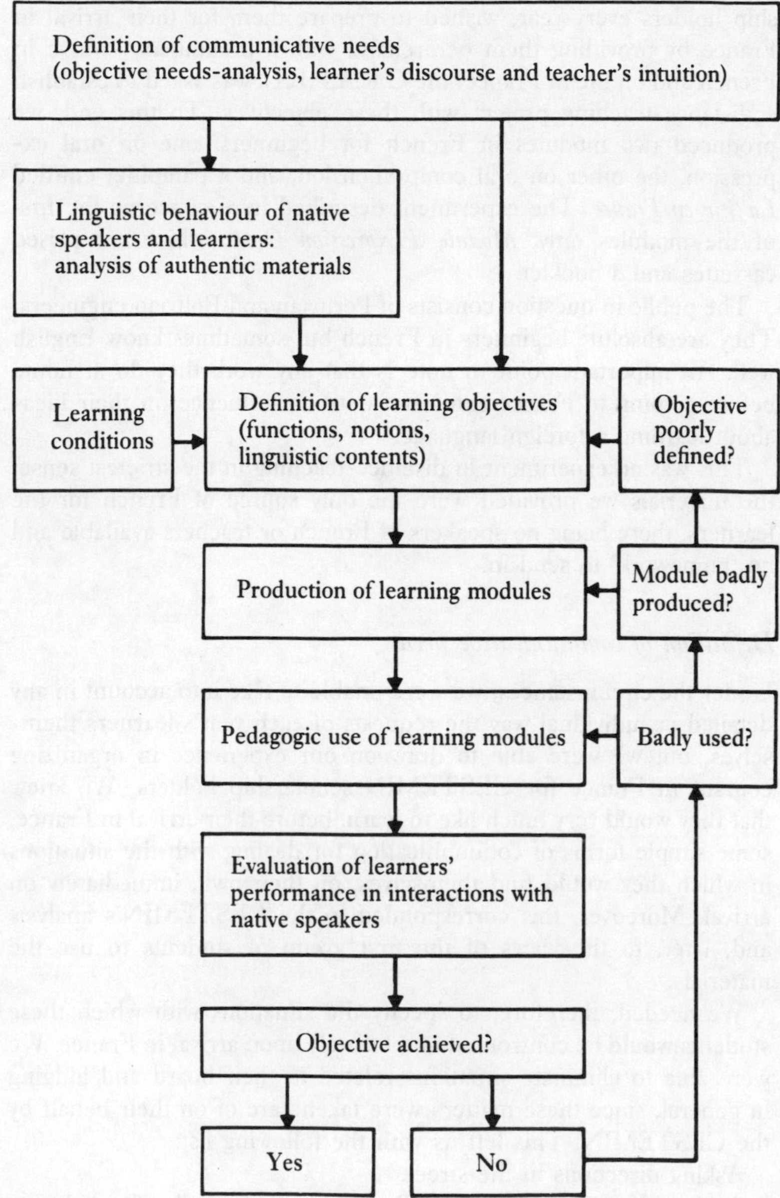
Definition of communicative needs
(objective needs-analysis, learner's discourse and teacher's intuition)
Linguistic behaviour of native
speakers and learners:
analysis of authentic materials
Learning
conditions
Definition of learning objectives
(functions, notions,
linguistic contents)
Objective
poorly
defined?
Production of learning modules
Module badly
produced?
Pedagogic use of learning modules
Badly used?
Evaluation of learners'
performance in interactions with
native speakers
Objective achieved?
Yes
No

FIGURE 1

ship holders every year, wished to prepare them for their arrival in France by providing them beforehand with a preliminary course in French and on life in France: the C.R.A.P.E.L. was asked to establish a distance-teaching project with these objectives. To this end, we produced two modules in French for beginners, one on oral expression, the other on oral comprehension, and a pamphlet entitled *La Vie en France*. The experiment described here concerns the first of the modules only, *Module d'Expression Orale*, which comprised cassettes and a booklet.

The public in question consists of Peruvian and Bolivian engineers; They are absolute beginners in French but sometimes know English well. An important point to note is that any work they do at home before coming to France can have a strong influence on their ideas about learning a foreign language.

This was an experiment in distance-teaching in the strictest sense: the materials we provided were the only source of French for the learners, there being no speakers of French or teachers available and no 'homework' to send in.

Definition of communicative needs

Under the circumstances, we were unable to take into account in any detailed or individual way the requests of each year's learners themselves, but we were able to draw on our experience in organizing courses in France for CESTEMIN scholarship holders. We knew that they would very much like to learn, before their arrival in France, some simple forms of communication for dealing with the situations in which they would find themselves, on their own, immediately on arrival. Moreover, this corresponded to the CESTEMIN's analysis and, later, to the views of the first group of students to use the materials.

We needed, therefore, to specify the situations with which these students would be confronted immediately upon arrival in France. We were able to eliminate situations related to their board and lodging in general, since these matters were taken care of on their behalf by the CESTEMIN. This left us with the following list:

Asking directions in the street.
Asking directions in a building (university, hall of residence, hospital, Social Security office, etc.).
Changing money at the bank.
Buying a train ticket.

The objective of the materials is the acquisition of a competence which is adequate to obtain the information required, or to carry out the transaction satisfactorily. The materials try to give the learners the minimal and most economic means for solving their problems, since a project like this naturally cannot be exhaustive. For example, to obtain the information necessary to catch a train, we simply showed them how to ask for one of the timetables which are available for each line in France, so that they could then do the choosing themselves without needing any more advanced competence in oral comprehension in what is a rather complex area (instructions for reading one of these timetables were included in the booklet *La Vie en France*).

In any communication situation, the learner needs to acquire three types of rules:

1. Those governing the linguistic tasks to be carried out and the discursive strategies related to them;
2. The socio-cultural rules which govern the situation;
3. The rules of morphosyntax, lexis and phonology.

Given the objective we had chosen (the minimum degree of competence necessary to participate successfully in the interactions in question) we decided that it was hardly worthwhile asking our learners to make a great effort to learn the rules of grammar and morphology. The resulting materials for expression look rather like a phrase-book, but it should be remembered that this is only the very beginning of the learning programme.

As regards the socio-cultural rules which have to be learnt, the situations chosen have the advantage of having a number of features in common: in a commercial transaction, or when asking a stranger for information, the roles and status of the speakers are predictable and so the learners are unlikely to meet with any surprises, once they have learnt how to go about accosting someone in the target culture. In situations such as these, then, the learning load is probably lighter than in situations which are more complex from the socio-cultural point of view.

We hypothesized that, for beginners, the most important ingredient for success in an interaction is the mastery of discursive structures, that is, those functions which have to be mastered if discourse is to be constructed syntagmatically.

The analysis of authentic materials and the definition of objectives

The analysis of a corpus of recordings enabled us to establish the structure for 'requesting information in the street' which is summarized in Figure 2 (see over). The communicative event, which is the

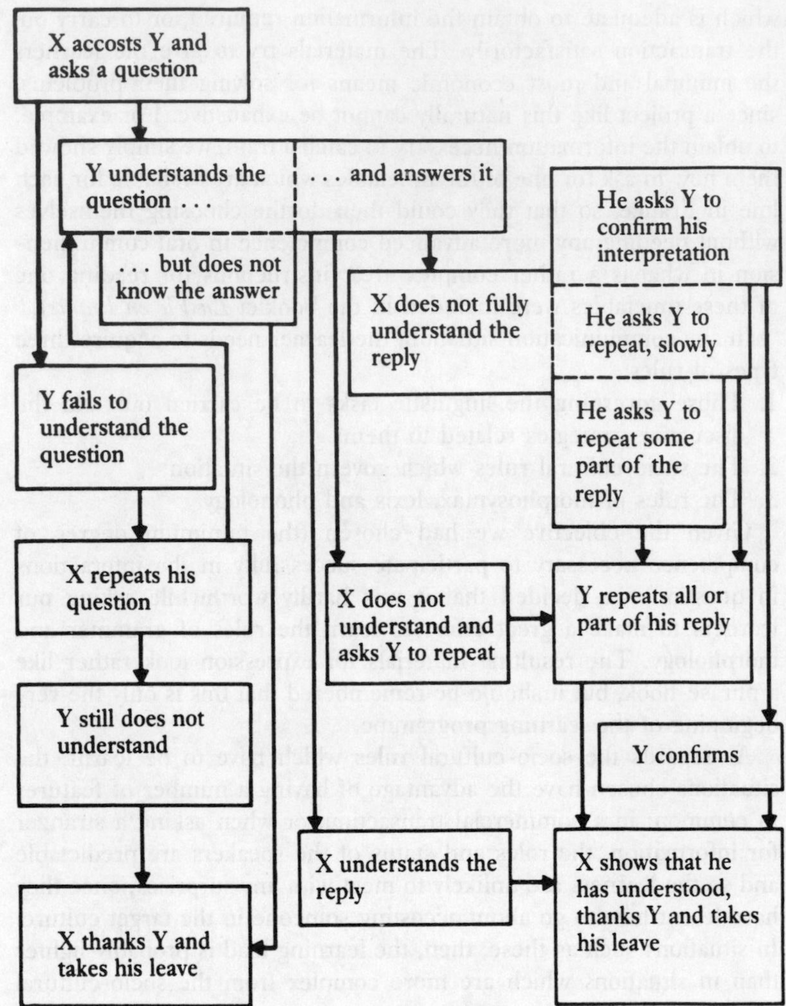

FIGURE 2

maximal unit, is seen as being made up of speech acts, which correspond to learning objectives which have the same hierarchical organization as the speech acts. On the contribution of discourse analysis to modern language teaching see Jupp *et al.* (1978) and Abbou (1980).

This analysis shows clearly that there is one series of functions which is unlike any others: getting someone to repeat what they have said, or to speak more slowly, asking for confirmation or for an explanation, giving further explanations when the person you are speaking to shows that he has not understood, these and similar acts are not specific to one particular type of communication situation. They are repair mechanisms, and one of their main characteristics is that they are transferable from one situation to another, even if their linguistic exponents may vary. (In a theoretical model, these acts would probably be represented as units having almost universal freedom of occurrence in interactive discourse and which serve the meta-discursive function of making a speaker repeat his preceding sequence or, for example, making him articulate any subsequent sequence more slowly.) For this reason, the realizations we give our learners to memorize are the most neutral in our corpus as regards register.

It is obviously also very important that the learners should appreciate the transferable nature of these functions and, above all, that they should learn to transfer them. This is why, in the module, these functions are shown in operation in not one but four different situations. Enabling learners to master these repair strategies (helping them, that is, to deal with the problems and difficulties which may occur at any time in the communication situations with which they are going to be confronted) should be a high-priority objective in any oral functional course for beginners. Jupp *et al.* (1978, p. 149) place great stress on the importance of teaching repair strategies, regarding them as just one example of learning objectives which remain valid even when the purpose for which they were learnt has been fulfilled and the problem eliminated. In much the same way, we introduced ordinal and cardinal numbers and the letters of the alphabet into the module 'Asking directions in a building'. They are used for designating buildings, offices, rooms, staircases, and so on, but it is obvious that their usefulness is wider than that (especially for engineers about to start on a postgraduate course in France!).

Preparation of the learning modules

Our course is, therefore, divided into four units, each corresponding to one of the situations which has been selected, and each of which is presented as a communicative event. Each unit is made up of a series of objectives which have to be achieved one after the other and which correspond to the functions which have to be acquired if the learner is to master the speech event as a whole. Here, as an example, is a summary of the contents of the first recorded module:

ANNEXE

Description sommaire de l'unité un du Module.
Aborder quelqu'un dans la rue et demander son chemin.

OBJECTIF 1:

Repérer les éléments de l'échange (sensibilisation à la situation et à la fonction).

Repérer les éléments de l'échange (aborder quelqu'un [ouverture], poser la question, comprendre la réponse, montrer qu'on a compris et remercier [clôture]), dans des vignettes de bandes dessinées faisant apparaître cette situation, et reproduites sur le fascicule d'accompagnement. Ecouter d'abord avec, puis sans le texte écrit.

OBJECTIF 2:

1 Apprendre à dire cinq formules servant à aborder quelqu'un et à demander son chemin.
2 Mémorisation et réemploi de ces formules.

OBJECTIF 3:

Comprendre les réponses possibles indiquant des itinéraires.

1 Liste de vocabulaire (en fait il s'agit de formules complètes), à comprendre oralement en français (d'abord avec, puis sans leur équivalent en espagnol). Elles sont données sous forme écrite en français seulement.
2 Comprendre des réponses complètes (enregistrements authentiques).

La consigne est de suivre ces itinéraires sur un plan de la ville reproduit sur le fascicule, et de vérifier ensuite la compréhension d'après la « solution » donnée à la fin du livret.

OBJECTIF 4:

Montrer qu'on a compris et remercier.

1 apprendre des formules servant à montrer qu'on comprend.
2 apprendre des formules servant à remercier.
3 apprendre à combiner 1) et 2) pour clôturer l'échange.

OBJECTIF 5:

Fonctionner dans un échange complet (pour le moment l'echange a la structure la plus simple: ouverture + question — réponse — clôture).

1 comprendre un dialogue authentique complet présentant cette structure.
2 dialogue complet avec le magnétophone.

OBJECTIF 6:

Répéter la demande si la personne abordée n'a pas compris.

1 comprendre un dialogue authentique complet faisant apparaître cette possibilité.
2 comprendre les formules correspondantes.
3 dialogue complet avec le magnétophone.

OBJECTIF 7:

Faire répéter la réponse si on ne l'a pas comprise (réponse courte).

1 comprendre un dialogue complet faisant apparaître cette fonction.
2 apprendre et mémoriser quelques formules utiles.
3 dialogue complet avec le magnétophone.

OBJECTIF 8:

Interrompre pour faire répéter un élément de réponse.

OBJECTIF 9:

Demander confirmation.

OBJECTIF 10:

Faire parler plus lentement.

OBJECTIF 11:

La personne interrogée ne connaît pas la réponse.
(L'acquisition des points 8, 9, 10 et 11 suit la même démarche que précédement).

OBJECTIF 12:

S'adapter aux réponses de l'interlocuteur.

1 dialogue avec le magnétophone, intégrant, sans que cela soit annoncé, la possibilité suivante: la personne interrogée ne comprend pas la question.
2 dialogue avec le magnétophone: la personne interrogée ne connaît pas la réponse à la question.

By breaking down the event into a series of separate objectives, it is also possible to make a clear distinction between those acts which the learner will have to learn to produce and those for which his comprehension skills will need to be developed. For the purposes of expression, only a few phrases are necessary at the beginning, but in comprehension, where it is the interlocutor who chooses the phrases used, the learner obviously needs to be able to understand as many phrases as possible. For example, in these particular materials it would have been pointless teaching how to give directions, since they only need to be able to *understand* directions, but this training includes all the different formulae we found in our corpus. This is why a fairly large proportion of the module is devoted to comprehension exercises.

As regards the speech acts which the learner needs to acquire for expression, he has to be shown that there is never one single way of realizing them. Whenever possible, therefore, we try to provide him with several different realizations. For example, in the case of asking your way in the street, five possibilities were given. A note was added to the effect that it was not necessary to learn all five by heart (although there is nothing to stop the learner doing so, either) but that it was preferable to learn more than one, so that the learner could reformulate his request if his first attempt failed. This was done every time an act or notion was included for expression purposes: the 'transferable' functions such as accosting a stranger in the street, framing requests for information, asking for a repetition or for further explanations are, therefore, dealt with independently, even though they are presented as part of a situation. It is not difficult for the learner to see that these strategies can be used in other situations, especially as the other three modules, in addition to their specific contents, also aim at activating these transferable functions.

However, the learner still has to learn to use these units as part of an actual exchange, in real time, taking into account the reactions of his interlocutor: if he does not, there is a risk that communication for him will remain a matter of a series of isolated speech acts rather than a dynamic and complex structure. To try to put this over, we use the following means:

1. Figure 2 is distributed to the learners, along with the necessary explanations and comments. The teaching point here is to sensitize the learners to what can happen during an exchange of this kind, while at the same time emphasizing its overall unity. This diagram is unlikely to satisfy the linguist or the sociologist, but its categories of analysis have to be accessible to the learners — and to be useful to them. We do not claim for one minute that learners can assimilate structures like this and use them in real communication, consciously or otherwise, although this point needs looking into. One could argue that the learner who has a clear idea of what might happen is better equipped for the interaction. Nonetheless, there is a clear analogy (though perhaps a false one) between the learning of the rules of morphosyntax and the rules of discourse: if studying explicit rules of grammar does not facilitate the acquisition of linguistic competence, how on earth can we claim that studying explicit rules of discourse will help with the acquisition of communicative competence? The underlying question is the same for both domains (Kahn 1977); by making cognitive mechanisms explicit and conscious, do we *de facto* facilitate their acquisition?

   Our aim is to draw the learner's attention to the interactive aspects of communication. This diagram also has the advantage of helping the learners understand our choice of methodology; and this is particularly important when you are distance-teaching — and distance-teaching adults, at that. It is important for them to know, at any given moment, what they are doing and why, otherwise they may simply reject the whole package. This is because the methodology in question comes as something of a surprise and could easily put them off, largely because it does not fit in with their preconceived ideas about language learning. This is why a considerable amount of space in the course is given to discussion of its objectives, its contents and the methodology.

2. For every objective, there are exercises involving observation and comprehension which are based on a recording of a complete authentic transaction containing the discursive structure or the function being studied. The idea is not for the learner to understand every phoneme or word, but to grasp what is happening in interactive terms: who is talking? what is he trying to do? In this way the learner is brought into contact with a variety of real pronunciations and speeds of delivery, giving him a truer picture of the type of interaction and thereby narrowing the gap between the language as it is taught and the language as it is spoken by native speakers. As to the problems of comprehension which beginners may obviously have using such recordings, we rely partly on the specific training in that skill provided in the second module, partly on the relative similarities between French and Spanish in this respect.
3. For each new function, there is a dialogue exercise involving the learner and his tape recorder. The exchange containing the new function or structure is first described both on the tape and in the booklet, so that the learner always knows where he is, and he is then asked to try to produce the appropriate utterances at the right times.

In 'Objective 11: requesting confirmation', for example, the learner is given the following instructions:

Go up to someone in the street and ask the way to Place Stanislas.
Listen to his reply.
Ask him to confirm the last part of what he said.
Listen again.
Show that you have understood and thank him.

This last instruction is given so that the learner always works on a complete communicative event. In the final exercise on the tape, the learner is given no advance warning about the material he is going to hear, to which he has to choose an appropriate response. We are well aware that having a conversation with a tape recorder is rather a lame solution to the problem; but what can easily be done in a group in a classroom is well-nigh impossible on a tape, since the recorded replies can never be modified to take into account the learners' reactions. Exercises of this type are included in the three other units: they aim at teaching the learner how to cope successfully with complete communicative events where one or other of the participants dominates the situation.

Use of the modules by the learners

In the terminology used at the C.R.A.P.E.L. distance-teaching is not at all the same thing as autonomous learning: in this particular case, for example, the learners had no say in the definition of objectives, contents or progression, nor in the selection of study methods and techniques (Holec 1980). On the other hand, the learners are able to control the way their learning programme develops as well as being partly responsible for evaluation. Their only source for evaluation purposes is in the models and documents included in the course. To check on their pronunciation, for instance, we suggest that they record their own voices on a second tape recorder so that they can compare their own attempts with the examples they have been given. Again, it is up to them and them alone to choose the pace and rhythm of their learning programme by deciding whether they have learnt a particular point well enough to go on to the next. As regards the various expression exercises, in particular the dialogues, we could not provide any form of correction: there are simply too many different ways of realizing any given function. This was clearly pointed out to the learners. The only way available to them of evaluating their own productions is by comparing them with the various documents provided, but these are not models for imitation anyway. It is reasonable to believe that the importance of their role in this learning scheme will be of use to the learners during the course they follow on arrival in France, which lays considerable stress on preparing the participants for autonomous learning.

Evaluation of the distance-teaching project

Evaluation of a project such as this should be limited strictly to the objectives which had been selected: were the students, when they arrived in France, able to cope with the four types of situation dealt with in the course? For the moment, it is far too early to answer this question in any but the most general terms: it seems that the methodology and objectives selected do correspond to the needs and practical constraints of these learners. Moreover, this type of work does seem to be a useful preparation for autonomous learning. All these points, though, need further investigation during similar projects in the future.

Conclusion

Neither the objectives nor the methodology on which this course were based could be used unmodified for distance-teaching any group other than South American engineers coming to France for a long period. Above all, the very closeness of the two languages allowed us to reduce to a minimum the amount of work devoted to lexical and grammatical problems. This would obviously not be true with, say, Japanese or North African learners.

Again, the methodology which was applied, which leaves a considerable amount of responsibility to the learners, is probably only suitable for adults.

Finally, certain exercises were developed with the fact in mind that the learners were engineers and the contents were defined on the basis of specific needs. In no sense, therefore, is this description of one application of the functional approach to be taken as some kind of model, since the essential characteristic of a functional course is its specificity to a particular group of learners working under a particular set of conditions.

Epilogue

> Ce dont nous avons le plus besoin, ce n'est pas de formation pédagogique, mais de réflexion et de recherches sur la relation d'enseignement et sur l'évolution du savoir . . . Définir une stratégie pédagogique, c'est nécessairement faire un pari sur l'avenir. Les enfants qui entrent aujourd'hui à l'école, accéderont aux responsabilités en l'an 2000. C'est en gardant le regard fixé sur l'horizon 2000 que nous avons le moins de chances de nous fourvoyer. Former aujourd'hui des professeurs pour l'école d'hier, c'est être en retard de deux guerres; c'est aussi un crime contre le seul maître que le pédagogue puisse se donner raisonablement, l'imagination.
>
> *Yves Châlon*

Bibliography

Abbou, A 1980 La didactique de la IIIe génération: des hypothèses aux projets. *Etudes de Linguistique Appliquée* 37. Didier, Paris

Abé, D and Duda, R 1974 *Cours de compréhension écrite pour débutants* (*Anglais*) C.R.A.P.E.L., Nancy

Abé, D, Billant, J, Duda, R, Gremmo, M–J, Moulden, H and Régent, O 1975 Vers une redéfinition de la cómpréhension écrite en langue étrangère. *Mélanges Pédagogiques* (*1975*): 33–44. C.R.A.P.E.L., Nancy

Abé, D, Henner–Stanchina, C and Smith P 1975 New approaches to autonomy; two experiments in self-directed learning. *Mélanges Pédagogiques* (*1975*): 57–80. C.R.A.P.E.L., Nancy

Abercrombie, D 1966 *Elements of general phonetics* Edinburgh University Press.

Allen, D and Guy, R 1974 *Conversational analysis: the sociology of talk* Mouton, The Hague

Allwright, R 1975 *Working papers: language teaching classroom research* University of Essex, Department of Language and Linguistics.

Allwright, R 1977 Turns, topics and tasks: patterns of participation in language learning and teaching. Paper presented at the TESOL National Convention

Alsed 1976 (Anthropology and Language Sciences in Educational Development) UNESCO, Paris

Apel, K O (ed.) 1976 *Sprachpragmatik und Philosophie* Suhrkamp, Frankfurt

Austin, J L 1962 *How to do things with words* Clarendon Press

Ausubel, D P 1968 *Educational psychology: a cognitive view* Holt, Rinehart and Winston, New York

Bachelard, G 1934 *Le nouvel esprit scientifique* Presses Universitaires de France, Paris

Bachman, C 1980 Le social pèse lourd sur le discours. *Applied Linguistics* 1 (3): 217–23

Bannister, D and Fransella, F 1977 *A manual for repertory grid technique* Academic Press, New York

Banton, M 1965 *Roles* Tavistock Press

Bates, E 1976 *Language and context* Academic Press, New York

Beacco, J C, Darot, M and Malandain, J L 1978 Approches fonctionnelles de l'enseignement du français langue étrangère. *Etudes françaises dans le monde*. AUPELF, October 1978: 5–8

Bengtson, G W 1972 Forest fertilisation: promises and problems. *Proceedings of the 1972 National Convention of the Society of American Foresters*: 231–61

Berne, E 1964 *Games people play* Penguin

Berrendonner, A (ed.) 1977 *Stratégies discursives* Presses Universitaires de Lyon, Lyons

Bialystok, E 1978 A theoretical model of second language learning. *Language Learning* **28**: 69–83

Blum–Kulka, S 1981 A cross-cultural study of interactional styles and the acquisition of communicative competence in a second language. *Proceedings of the Congress of the Association Internationale de Linguistique Appliquée* **1**: 441–2. AILA, Lund

Bouillon, C 1971 Du laboratoire de langues à la bibliothèque sonore: l'individualisation de l'apprentissage en langues vivantes. *Mélanges Pédagogiques* (*1971*), C.R.A.P.E.L., Nancy

Brazil, D, Coulthard, M and Johns, C 1980 *Discourse intonation and language teaching* Longman

Breen, M P and Candlin, C 1980 The essentials of a communicative curriculum in language teaching. *Applied Linguistics* **1**, **2**: 89–112

Brumfit, C and Johnson, K 1979 *The communicative approach to language teaching* Oxford University Press

Bruneau, T 1979 The time dimension in intercultural communication. In Nimmo, D. (ed.) *Communication Yearbook 3* Transaction Books, New Brunswick

Bruner, J S 1973 *Beyond the information given* Allen and Unwin

Bruner, J S Olver, R and Greenfield, P 1966 *Studies in cognitive growth* Wiley, New York

Burton, D. 1980 *Dialogue and discourse: a sociolinguistic approach to modern drama dialogue and naturally-occurring conversation* Routledge and Kegan Paul

Cairns, J 1975 The cancer problem. *Scientific American* November 1975

Candlin, C 1973 The status of pedagogical grammars. In Corder and Roulet (eds.) 1973

Candlin, C 1976 Communicative language teaching and the debt to pragmatics. In Rameh, C (ed.) *Semantics: theory and practice* Georgetown University Press

Candlin, C and Breen, M P (eds.) (forthcoming) *Acts of the 1981 Lancaster Seminar on Interpretive Strategies*

Candlin, C, Leather, J H and Bruton, C 1976 Doctors in casualty: applying communicative competence to components of specialist course design. *Intérnational Review of Applied Linguistics* XIV(3): 245–73

Candlin, J, Charles, D and Willis, J 1982 *Video in language teaching: report from the Research Group on video in language teaching* University of Aston

Cazden, C B, John V P and Hymes, D 1972 *Functions of language in the classroom* Teachers College, New York

Cembalo, M, Esch, E and Hildenbrand, D 1971 *Cours d'entraînement à la compréhension écrite* (*anglais*) C.R.A.P.E.L., Nancy

Cembalo, M and Holec, H 1973 Les langues aux adultes: pour une pédagogie de l'autonomie. *Mélanges Pédagogiques* (*1973*) C.R.A.P.E.L., Nancy

Châlon, Y 1970 Pour une pédagogie sauvage. *Mélanges Pédagogiques (1970)* C.R.A.P.E.L., Nancy

Chesterman, A 1977 Contrastive generative grammar and the psycholinguistic fallacy. *Papers and Studies in Contrastive Linguistics XI*, from the XIVth International Congress on Contrastive Linguistics, Poznan: 17–24

Chomsky, N 1965 *Aspects of the theory of syntax* M.I.T. Press, Cambridge, Massachusetts

Cicourel, A 1973 *Cognitive sociology* Penguin

Clark, E V and Clark, H H 1977 *Psychology and language: an introduction to psycholinguistics* Harcourt–Brace, Jovanovich

Clark, E V and Clark, H H 1979 When nouns surface as verbs. *Language* **55** (4): 767–96

Clark, H H and Carlson, T B 1981 Context for comprehension. In Long, J. and Baddeley, A. (eds.) *Attention and performance IX* Lawrence Erlbaum Associates, Hillsdale

Cole, P and Morgan, T (eds.) 1975 *Syntax and semantics, Vol. 3: Speech Acts* Academic Press, New York

Corder, S P 1967 The significance of learners' error. *International Review of Applied Linguistics* **5**: 161–70

Corder, S P 1971 Describing the learner's language. *CILT Reports* **6**: 57–64

Corder, S P 1976 The study of interlanguage *Proceedings of the Fourth International Congress of Applied Linguistics*. Hochschul Verlag, Stuttgart

Corder, S P 1980 *Second language acquisition. Study commissioned by the Council for Cultural Cooperation, Strasbourg* Council of Europe, Strasbourg

Corder, S P 1982 *Error analysis and interlanguage* Oxford University Press

Corder, S P and Roulet, E (eds.) 1973 *Theoretical linguistic models in applied linguistics* Didier, Paris

Corder, S P and Roulet, E (eds.) 1977 *The notions of simplification, interlanguages and pidgin and their relation to second language pedagogy* Droz, Geneva

Coste, D 1979 Analyse de discours et pragmatique de la parole dans quelques usages d'une didactique des langues. *Applied Linguistics* **1** (3): 244–52

Coste, D, Courtillon, J, Ferenczi, V, Martins-Baltar, M and Papo, E 1976 *Un niveau-seuil* Council for Cultural Cooperation, Council of Europe, Strasbourg

Coulson, 1972 Role: a redundant concept in sociology? In Jackson, J A (ed.) *Sociological studies 4: Role* Cambridge University Press

Coulthard, M 1977 *An introduction to discourse analysis* Longman

Coulthard, M, Brazil, D and Johns, T 1980 *Discourse intonation and language teaching* Longman

C.R.A.P.E.L. 1972 *Cours intensif d'anglais oral* C.R.A.P.E.L., Nancy

Davis W 1975 Unmasking the agents. *World Health* November 1975

de Mey, M 1982 *The cognitive paradigm* Reidel, Dordrecht

Di Pippo, A E 1971 *Rhetoric* Glencoe Press, New York

Douglas, M 1970 *Natural symbols* Barrie and Rockliff

Dubin, F and Olshtain, E 1980 The interface of reading and writing. *TESOL Quarterly* **14** (3): 353–63

Duda, R 1976 Compréhension écrite et compétence de communication. *Bulletin CILA*, **24**: 163–76. Commission Interuniversitaire Suisse de Linguistique Appliquée, Neuchâtel

Duda, R 1978 L'apprentissage autonome et semi-autonome de l'anglais à l'Ecole des Mines de Nancy. *Recherches et Echanges* **3** (2) Union des Professeurs de Langues Etrangères de Grands Etablissements Supérieurs

Duda, R 1979 Are language skills irrelevant? *Mélanges Pédagogigues* (*1979*): 17–28. C.R.A.P.E.L., Nancy

Duda, R, Luceri, R 1975 A Course in Advanced Medical English. *Mélanges Pédagogiques* (*1975*): 81–104. C.R.A.P.E.L., Nancy

Duda, R, Esch, E and Laurens, J–P 1972 Documents non-didactiques et formation en langues. *Mélanges Pédagogiques* (*1972*) C.R.A.P.E.L., Nancy

Duda, R, Laurens, J–P and Remy, S 1973 L'exploitation didactique de documents authentiques. *Mélanges Pédagogiques* (*1973*) C.R.A.P.E.L., Nancy

Duncan, S 1972 Some signals and rules for taking speaking turns in conversation. *Journal of Personality and Social Psychology* 23: 283–92

Edmondson, W 1981 *Spoken discourse: a model for analysis* Longman

Faerch, C and Kasper, G 1983 *Strategies in interlanguage communication* Longman

Fillmore, C 1971 Verbs of judging: an exercise in semantic description. In Fillmore, C and Langendoen, T D (eds.) *Studies in Linguistic Semantics* Holt, Rinehart and Winston, New York

Fishman, J A (ed.) 1971 *Advances in the sociology of language, Vol. 1* Mouton, The Hague

Fisiak, J 1981 *Contrastive linguistics and the language teacher* Pergamon Press

Fransella, F 1978 *Personal construct psychology 1977* Academic Press, New York

Frege, G 1892 Uber Sinn und Bedeutung; translated as 'On sense and reference'. In Geach, P and Black, M *Translations from the philosophical writings of Gottlob Frege* Oxford University Press

Freire, P 1972 *Pedagogy of the oppressed* Penguin

Friedan, B 1979 Feminism takes a new turn. In *New York Sunday Times Magazine* 18 November 1979

Garfinkel, H 1968 *Studies in ethnomethodology* Prentice-Hall, Englewood Cliffs

Giorgi, A 1977 Problems encountered in developing a phenomenological approach to research in psychology. In Fransella 1977

Goffman, E 1959 *The presentation of self in everyday life* Penguin

Goffman, E 1971 *Relations in public* Penguin

Goode, J G 1960 Norm commitment and conformity to role-status obligations. *American Journal of Sociology* **66**: cited in Cicourel 1973

Goodey, B 1976 Assessing the perceived environment. In Wheeler, K and Waites, D (eds.) *Handbook in environmental geography* Granada Publications

Goodman, K S 1973 Psycholinguistic universals in the reading process. In Smith 1973

Gordon, D and Lakoff, G 1971 Conversational postulates. In Adams, D, Campbell, M A, Cohen, V, Lovins, J, Maxwell, E, Neigren, C and Reighard, J (eds.) *Papers from the seventh regional meeting, Chicago Linguistic Society* 1971: 63–84. Also in Cole and Morgan (eds.) 1975

Gorosch, M 1982 Review of *E.S.P.: the present position* by Pauline Robinson. *System* **10** (2): 201–2

Gould, P and White, R 1974 *Mental Maps* Penguin

Green, J F 1967 Preparing an advanced composition course. *English Language Teaching* **21**

Gremmo, M–J 1977 Reading as communication. *Mélanges Pédagogiques*

(1977): 17–40. C.R.A.P.E.L., Nancy

Gremmo, M–J, Holec, H and Riley, P 1977 Interactional structure: the role of role. *Mélanges Pédagogiques 1977*: 41–57. C.R.A.P.E.L., Nancy. (Also in this volume)

Gremmo, M–J, Holec, H and Riley, P 1978 Taking the initiative: some pedagogical applications of discourse analysis. *Mélanges Pêdagogiques* (*1978*): 53–68. C.R.A.P.E.L., Nancy

Grice, H P 1975 Logic and conversation. In Cole and Morgan (eds.) 1975

Grossberg, S 1982 *Studies of mind and brain* Reidel, Boston

Gumperz, J J and Hymes, D (eds.) 1972 *Directions in sociolinguistics: the ethnography of communication* Holt, Rinehart and Winston, New York

Hall, E 1962 *The hidden dimension* Doubleday, New York

Halliday, M A K 1970 *A course in spoken English: intonation* Oxford University Press

Halliday, M A K 1973 *Explorations in the functions of language* Edward Arnold

Halliday, M A K and Hassan, R 1976 *Cohesion in English* Longman

Harding, E 1980 *Repair Strategies. A study commissioned by the Council for Cultural Cooperation of the Council of Europe* Council of Europe, Strasbourg Also in *Occasional Papers of the Centre for Language and Communication Studies* Trinity College, Dublin

Harding, E and Legras, M 1974 La bibliothèque sonore et ses implications pédagogiques. *Mélanges Pédagogiques* (1974): 89–104. C.R.A.P.E.L., Nancy

Harri–Augstein, E S 1977 Reflecting on structures of meaning: a process of learning-to-learn. In Fransella 1978

Harri–Augstein, S and Thomas, L 1980 Comment devenir un apprenant: apprendre à apprendre par l'interaction. *Etudes de Linguistique Appliquée* **41**: 86–101

Harris, Z 1952 Discourse analysis. *Language* **28**: 1–30

Hatch, E 1979 Input studies. Paper read at the First Nordic Inter-language Symposium.

Heddesheimer, C 1971 Les dictionnaires, ces inconnus familiers. *Mélanges Pèdagogiques (1971)* C.R.A.P.E.L., Nancy

Heddesheimer, C and Roussel, F 1977 Apprentissage des valeurs communicatives de l'intonation anglaise. *Mélanges Pédagogiques (1982)*: 57–72. C.R.A.P.E.L., Nancy

Heddesheimer, C, Roussel, F, Zoppis, C, Gremmo, M–J, Holec, H and Riley, P 1982 *Eléments verbaux et non-verbaux dans l'analyse discursive du seminaire*. Action Thématique programmée agrée par le Centre National de la Recherche Scientifique. Université de Nancy II, Nancy

Hockett, C F 1960 Logical considerations in the study of animal communication. In Lanyon, W E and Tavolga, W N (eds.) 1960 *Animal sounds and communication* The American Institute of Biological Science, Washington D.C.

Holec, H 1971 Laboratoire et efficacité. *Mélanges Pédagogiques (1971)* C.R.A.P.E.L., Nancy

Holec, H 1973 L'illocution: problématique et méthodologie. *Mélanges Pédagogiques (1973)* C.R.A.P.E.L., Nancy

Holec, H 1975 L'approche macro-linguistique du fonctionnement des langues et ses implications pédagogiques: rôle du visuel. *Mélanges Pédagogiques (1975)* C.R.A.P.E.L., Nancy

Holec, H 1978 *Auto-evaluation de l'apprentissage et apprentissage de l'auto-évaluation. Actes du séminaire sur l'Evaluation, Grenoble* C.R.A.P.E.L., Nancy

Holec, H 1980 *Autonomy and foreign language learning* Pergamon Press

Holec, H, Gremmo, M–J and Riley, P 1980 Prolégomènes à une description de la structure des échanges communicatifs directs. In Nickel, G and Hehls, D (eds.) *Models of grammar, descriptive linguistics and pedagogical grammar*. Heidelberg. Julius Groos. pp. 92–107.

Holec, H and Kuhn, M 1971 Le laboratoire de langues: pour quoi faire? *Mélanges Pédagogiques (1971)* C.R.A.P.E.L., Nancy

Householder, F W V (ed.) 1972 *Syntactic theory I* Penguin

Hughes, P and Brecht, P 1975 *Vicious circles and infinity: an anthology of paradoxes* Penguin

Hutchinson, T 1978 An analysis of the effect on discourse structure of a visual display. In *Practical Papers in English Language Education* University of Lancaster

Hymes, D 1964 On communicative competence. In Pride and Holmes (1972)

Illich, Y 1970 *Deschooling Society* Harper and Row, New York

Illich, Y *et al.* 1973 *After Deschooling, What?* Harper and Row, New York

Jacobs, R A and Rosenbaum, P S (eds.) 1970 *Readings in English transformational grammar* Ginn, Waltham

Javal, L E 1905 *Physiologie de la lecture et de l'écriture* Alcan, Paris

Johnson, K 1982 *Communicative syllabus design and methodology* Pergamon Press

Jupp, T C, Hodlin, S, Heddesheimer, C and Lagarde, J–P 1978 *Apprentissage linguistique et communication. Methodologie d'un cours fonctionnel pour travailleurs immigrés* CLE International, Paris

Kahn, G 1977 Pédagogie des langues étrangères et théories linguistiques. Quelques réflexions. *Etudes de Linguistique Appliquée* **25**: 54–66. Didier, Paris

Kaplan, R B 1972 *The anatomy of rhetoric* Center for Curriculum Development, Philadelphia

Katz, J and Postal, P 1964 *An integrated theory of linguistic descriptions* M.I.T. Press, Cambridge, Massachusetts

Kelly, G 1969 See Maher, B A (ed.) *Clinical psychology and personality: the selected papers of G. Kelly* Wiley, New York

Kendon, A 1967 Some functions of gaze direction in social interaction. *Acta Psychologica* **24**: 22–63

Kramsch, C J 1981 *Discourse analysis and second language teaching: theory and practice* Center for Applied Linguistics, Washington

Krashen, S 1981 *Language learning and language acquisition* Pergamon Press

Krebs, W M 1975 Dissolved oxygen measurements in brewery systems, *MBAA Technical Quarterly*, Vol. 12, No. 3, 1975

Kuhn, M 1970 Pour une nouvelle approche de l'entraînement à la compréhension de l'anglais écrit. *Mélanges Pédagogiques (1970)* C.R.A.P.E.L., Nancy

Kuhn, T S 1962 *The structure of scientific revolutions* Chicago University Press, Chicago

Labov, W 1970 The study of language in its social context. In *Studium Generale* 23: 30–87. Also in Fishman 1971

Labov, W 1972 *Language in the inner city: studies in the black English vernacular*

University of Pennsylvania Press, Philadelphia

Larsen–Freeman, D (ed.) 1980 *Discourse analysis in second language research* Newbury House, Rowley

Latham, X (ed.) 1975 *The road to effective learning* Ward Lock

Laver, J and Hutcheson, S 1972 *Communication in face-to-face interaction* Penguin

Lavorel, P M 1982 Le syndrome de dyslexie: connais pas: schéma pour une classification des troubles de la lecture. In Sprenger–Charolles 1982b

Lee, E, Whitburn, M and Winter, F 1982 Culture and semantic opacity in foreign language learning. In Nivette J (ed.) Cultural Aspects of Foreign Language Teaching. *ABLA Papers* 6: 135–66. Association Belge de Linguistique Appliquée, Brussels

Lehtonen, J and Sajavaara, K 1980 Phonology and speech processing in cross-language communication. In Eliason, S (ed.) *Theoretical issues in contrastive phonology* Julius Groos, Heidelberg

Leon, M 1979 Culture didactique et discours oral. *Le Français dans le Monde* **145**. Larousse–Hachette, Paris

McNeil, E B and Rubin Z 1977 *The psychology of being human* Canfield Press, New York

Maingenau, D 1976 *Initiation aux méthodes de l'analyse du discours* Hachette, Paris

Mitchell, K 1980 lllocutionary acts in a pedagogical description — the grammar of requests and offers. In Richterich and Widdowson 1981

Moirand, S 1982 *Enseigner à communiquer en langue étrangère* Hachette, Paris

Morris, S 1980 The self-image of the language learner. Paper presented to the annual conference of the British Association for Applied Linguistics

Murphy, D and Candlin, C 1976 *Engineering discourse and listening comprehension. K.A.A.U. project in listening comprehension: first annual report* University of Lancaster

Neisser, U 1976 *Cognition and reality* W.H. Freeman, San Francisco

Oskarsson, M 1980 *Approaches to self-assessment in foreign language learning* Pergamon Press

Palmer, J D 1980 Discourse, register and the teaching of writing. *The Canadian Modern Language Review* **36** (4): 683–92.

Piaget, J 1953 *The origins of intelligence in the child* Routledge and Kegan Paul

Piaget, J 1969 *The psychology of the child* Routledge and Kegan Paul

Pirsig, R L 1976 *Zen and the art of motor-cycle maintenance* Corgi

Pocock, D C D 1979 The contribution of mental maps in perception studies. *Geography* **64** (4): 279–87

Porcher, L 1981 Les chemins de la liberté. *Etudes de Linguistique Appliquée* **41**: 127–35

Pride, J B and Holmes, J (eds.) 1972 *Sociolinguistics* Penguin

Pugh, A K 1975 Approaches to developing effective adult reading, paper presented at the Fourth International Congress of Applied Linguistics, Stuttgart

Quillian, M–R 1974 A propos de concepts: théorie et stimulation des capacités sémantiques de base. In Melher, J and Noizet, G (eds.) 1974 *Textes pour une psycholinguistique* Mouton, The Hague

Richards, J (ed.) 1974 *Error analysis: perspectives on second language acquisition, applied linguistics and language study* Longman

Richards, J C 1971 A non-contrastive approach to error analysis. *English Language Teaching* **25**: 204–19

Richaudeau, F, Gauquelin, F and Gauquelin, M 1969 *Méthode de lecture rapide* Marabout Service, Paris

Richterich, R and Widdowson, H (eds.) 1981 *The pedagogical description and presentation of language* Didier, Paris

Riley, P 1974 The language laboratory: implications of the functional approach. *Mélanges Pédagogiques (1974)*:53–64. C.R.A.P.E.L., Nancy. Also in *ETIC Documents* **75** (1) British Council, London

Riley, P 1976 Discursive and communicative functions of non-verbal communication. *Mélanges Pédagogiques (1976)*: 1–20. C.R.A.P.E.L., Nancy

Riley, P 1977 Discourse networks in classroom interaction: some problems in communicative methodology. *Mélanges Pédagogiques (1977)*: 109–20. C.R.A.P.E.L., Nancy

Riley, P 1979 Towards a contrastive pragmalinguistics. *Papers and studies in contrastive linguistics* **X**. Also in Fisiak 1981

Riley, P 1980 *Directions in the descriptions of discourse structure* Council of Europe, Strasbourg

Riley, P 1982 Topics in communicative methodology, including a preliminary and selective bibliography on the communicative approach. *Mélanges Pédagogiques (1982)*: 93–122. C.R.A.P.E.L., Nancy

Rogers, C 1961 *On becoming a person* Houghton Mifflin, Boston

Rogers, C 1972 *Liberté pour apprendre?* Dunod, Paris

Ross, J R 1970 On declarative sentences. In Jacobs and Rosenbaum 1970

Ross, J R 1975 Where to do things with words. In Cole and Morgan 1975

Roulet, E 1980 Interactional markers in discourse. *Applied Linguistics* **1** (3): 224–33

Roussel, F 1974 The modulation of discourse functions. *Mélanges Pédagogiques (1974)*: 41–52, C.R.A.P.E.L., Nancy

Russell, B 1940 *An inquiry into meaning and truth* Oxford University Press

Sacks, H 1972 On the analyzability of stories by children. In Gumperz and Hymes 1972

Sacks, H 1971 *Aspects of the sequential organisation of conversation* (draft m/s)

Sacks, H, Schegloff, E and Jefferson, G 1974 A simplest systematics for the organisation of turn-taking for conversation. *Language* **50** (4): 696–735

Sadock, J M 1970 Whimperatives. In Sadock, J M and Vanek A, (eds.) *Studies presented to Robert B. Lees* Linguistic Research Inc., Edmonton, Illinois

Sadock, J M 1975 *Towards a linguistic theory of speech acts* Academic Press, New York

Sajavaara, K 1981 Psycholinguistic models, second-language acquisition and contrastive analysis. In Fisiak 1981

Schank, R C 1975 The structure of episodes in memory. In Bobrow, S A and Collins, A M (eds.) 1975 *Representation and understanding in cognitive science* Academic Press, New York

Scheflen, A E 1973 *How behaviour means* Gordon and Breach, New York

Schegloff, E A 1968 Sequencing in conversational openings. *American Anthropologist* **70**(6): 1075–95

Schegloff, E A 1972 Notes on conversational practice: formulating place. In Sudnow 1972

Schmidt, R W and Richards, J C 1980 Speech acts and second language learning. *Applied Linguistics* **1**(2): 129–57

Schumann, J H 1978 The acculturation model for second language acquisition. In Gingras, R C (ed.) 1978 *Second language acquisition and foreign language teaching* Center for Applied Linguistics, Arlington

Schumann, J H 1979 Three theoretical perspectives on second language acquisition. Paper presented at First Nordic Symposium on Interlanguage.

Searle, J R 1969 *Speech acts: an essay in the philosophy of language* Cambridge University Press

Searle, J R 1975 Indirect speech acts. In Cole and Morgan 1975

Seliger, H W 1977 Does practice make perfect? A study of interaction patterns and L2 competence. *Language Learning* **27**: 263–78

Selinker, L F 1969 Language transfer. *General Linguistics* **9**: 67–92

Selinker, L F 1972 Interlanguage. *International Review of Applied Linguistics* **10**: 209–31

Selinker, L F and Lamendella, J 1978 Two perspectives on fossilization in interlanguage learning. *Interlanguage Studies Bulletin* **3**: 143–91

Sinclair, J McH 1980 Some implications of discourse analysis for ESP methodology. *Applied Linguistics* **1**(3): 253–61

Sinclair, J McH and Coulthard, R M 1975 *Towards an analysis of discourse. The English used by teachers and pupils* Oxford University Press

Singleton, D M 1981 *Age as a factor in second language acquisition* Centre for Language and Communication Studies, Dublin

Skutnab–Kangas, T and Toukomaa, P 1976 *Teaching immigrant children's mother-tongue and learning the language of the host country in the context of the socio-cultural situation of the immigrant family* UNESCO, Paris

Smith, F 1971 *Understanding reading — a psycholinguistic analysis of reading and learning to read.* Holt, Rinehart and Winston, New York

Smith, F 1973 *Psycholinguistics and reading* Holt, Rinehart and Winston, New York

Spencer, C and Darvizeh, Z 1981 Young children's descriptions of their local environment: a comparison of information elicited by recall, recognition and performance techniques of investigation. *Environmental Education and Information* **1** (4): 275–84

Spencer, C and Weetman, M 1981 The microgenesis of cognitive maps: a longitudinal study of new residents of an urban area. *Transactions of the Institute of British Geographers.* **6**: 375–84

Sprenger–Charolles, L 1982a Quand lire c'est comprendre. Approche linguistique et psycholinguistique. *Pratiques* **35**: 7–26

Sprenger–Charolles, L (ed.) 1982b *La lecture. Pratiques* **35**

Sridhar, S N 1981 *Contrastive analysis, error analysis and interlanguage* In Fisiak 1981

Stevens, P 1974 *Patterns in nature* Peregrine

Strawson, P F 1952 *Logico-linguistic papers* Methuen

Strawson, P F 1964 Intention and convention in speech acts *Philosophical Review* **73**: 439–60

Stubbs, M 1976 *Language, schools and classrooms* Methuen.

Sudnow, D (ed.) 1972 *Studies in social interaction* Free Press, New York

Tarone, E 1974 Speech perception in second language acquisition: a suggested model. *Language Learning* **24**: 223–33

Tarone, E 1980 Communication strategies, foreigner talk and repair in interlanguage. *Language Learning* 30: 417–31

Thomas, J 1983 Cross-cultural pragmatic failure. *Applied Linguistics* 4 (2): 91–112

Thomas, L and Harri–Augstein, E S 1979 *The self-organised learner and the printed word* Brunel University

Tinker, M A 1965 *Bases for effective reading* University of Minnesota Press, Minneapolis

Toffler, A 1970 *Future shock* Bantam Books

Tulving, E 1976 Rôle de la mémoire sémantique dans le stoquage et la récupération de l'information épisodique. *Bulletin de Psychologie* N° spécial annuel 1976: 19–25

Veylon, R 1975 in *La nouvelle presse médicale* 4 (6): 435–6

Whorf, B L 1956 See Carroll, J B (ed.) *Language, thought and reality: selected writings of B L Whorf* M.I.T. Press, Cambridge, Massachusetts

Widdowson, H 1975 EST in theory and practice. In *English for academic purposes* British Council

Widdowson, H 1977 Approaches to discourse. In Gutknecht, C *Grundbegriffe und Hauptströmungen der Linguistik* Hoffmann und Campe, Hamburg

Widdowson, H 1978 *Teaching language as communication* Oxford University Press

Widdowson, H 1980 *Strategies for discourse processing* Council of Europe, Strasbourg

Wunderlich, D (ed.) 1975 *Linguistische Pragmatic* Athenäum, Wiesbaden.

Wunderlich, D 1976 *Studien zur Sprechakttheorie* Suhrkamp, Frankfurt

Index

acquisition, *see* learning
address, 6, 13–16, 42, 46, 50, 57, 338
authentic materials, 176, 192, 216–219, 283–344, 346–347, 348
reading 78–80, 92–93, 94, 193, 196
written expression 98–104
see also sound and video library
autonomous learning scheme, 160, 191–205
see also self-directed learning
'autonomization', *see* learner-training
autonomy, xxi, 170–172, 173–190

background knowledge, 4–5, 68–69, 70–71, 83, 123, 124, 254, 255

cognitive approach, 72
C.R.A.P.E.L., xix–xxii, 171
communicative acts, 3, 4, 17, 93–95, 97, 98–99
see also illocution, speech act theory
communicative approach, *see* functional approach
contrastive rhetoric, 91–92, 105–119
Council of Europe, 125, 171
see also functional approach, Threshold Level
cross-cultural communication, xiii, xvi, 66, 74–75, 90, 91, 105–108, 119–120, 339–344, 352–355

discourse, 1–2, 16–19, 41–45, 48, 51, 126–127
coherence in, 32, 64–66
comparative approach to, 108–119, 168
interactive/non-interactive, 26–34, 49–50
see also interaction
interruption, 62–63
poral/written, 23, 26
processing, 6, 7, 11, 121, 69–71
realization, 16–17, 63–64
teaching/learning specialized, 299–320
see also address, negotiation of meaning
distance-teaching, 362–373

evaluation, 241, 255–263
see also self-assessment

functional approach, 1, 12–13, 41, 124–132, 345, 346–351, 352–362, 367–373
to reading, 67–119

grid technique, 161–165

illocution, 4, 17, 32, 43–44, 48, 59–63, 64, 116–119
  see also communicative acts, speech act theory
interaction, 6, 12–20, 32, 35–46, 48, 59–63

language of the classroom, xvi, 42–46, 54–59, 61, 126, 167, 168–169, 238–240, 283–284, 300–301, 305, 318–320, 339
languages for special purposes, 72–73, 83, 193–198, 299–320
learner-training, 161–165, 180–188, 192, 211–221, 233–247, 248–249, 261, 272–275, 278–282
learning, 121, 169, 242–246
  development of, 150–152, 135–152
  'Learning English on your own', 211–221
  learners' views on, 81–82
  models of, 121–122, 156, 160, 170–171
  self-directed, 174–180, 180–188, 206–210, 225–232, 234, 240
  case studies, 193–201
  group learning, 233, 237, 238, 240, 245–246, 275–282
  strategies, 123, 131, 257–258
  variability in, 135

linguistic knowledge, 4, 68, 123–124
linguistic descriptions, 154–157

memory, 69
  see also background knowledge
mental maps, 11
methodology, 125
  research xxi, 159–160
mother tongue, 122–123
  see also sensitization

needs analysis, 235–236, 263–275
negation, 136–139
  acquisition of, 135–153
negotiation of meaning, xv–xvi, 2–10, 67–71, 131
non-verbal communication, 15–16, 57
  see also address, viewing comprehension

objectives, 80, 125, 175–176, 222, 265–268
oral comprehension, 216–221, 222, 295–296, 302–305
oral expression, 296
  learning oral expression autonomously, 196–201, 248–255

performance, 52–53
personal construct theory, 11, 154–169
positing sentence, 91, 111
predicting, 84–85

role, 13, 36–42
  in interaction, 42–46, 54–59, 61–62
  of teacher, 233–247
  in the acquisition of autonomy, 184–186, 202–203
  see also learner-training in
  LSP, 299, 305, 307–311, 318–320
reading, 67–73, 74–90, 91–104
  specialized written discourse, 105–120, 193–196, 305–310
  surface organization in, 108–111

self-assessment, 177–179, 182–184, 255–263, 268–272
semantic (cultural) opacity, 84, 165–169
sensitization, 165–168
separation of language skills, 86–87, 353–354
speech act theory, 7, 54, 126, 127–129
  see also communicative acts, illocution
strategy, xiv, xv, 6, 10, 11, 74, 76, 84, 123–124, 130–131, 169
sound and video library, 192, 286–298, 301
  see also authentic materials

Threshold Level, 125, 127–131

utterance linking, 6–7, 68–69
  see also discourse processing

viewing comprehension, 296, 332–344
  see also non-verbal communication

written expression, 98–104, 313–317